RESTRICTIVE COVENANTS OVER FREEHOLD LAND: A PRACTITIONER'S GUIDE

AUSTRALIA
LBC Information Services
Sydney

CANADA and USA
Carswell
Toronto

NEW ZEALAND
Brooker's
Auckland

SINGAPORE and MALAYSIA
Thomson Information (S.E. Asia)
Singapore

RESTRICTIVE COVENANTS OVER FREEHOLD LAND: A PRACTITIONER'S GUIDE

BY

ANDREW J. FRANCIS M.A. (OXON.)

OF LINCOLN'S INN, BARRISTER

LONDON
SWEET & MAXWELL
1999

Published in 1999 by Sweet & Maxwell Limited
100 Avenue Road, Swiss Cottage
London NW3 3PF
(http://www.smlawpub.co.uk)

Phototypeset by Selwood Systems
Printed in Great Britain by Butler & Tanner Ltd

No natural forests were destroyed to make this product,
only farmed timber was used and re-planted.

A C.I.P. catalogue record for this book is available from the British Library

FOREWORD

The author of this book deserves to be commended for bravely tackling what he describes as "a dry and difficult topic". I can agree with him that the topic may be difficult, but I challenge his use of the word "dry". Some of the most interesting, even absorbing, cases heard in the Lands Tribunal concern that jurisdiction exercised under section 84 of the Law of Property Act 1925 to discharge or modify restrictive covenants. Some are applications to determine who (if anyone) is to be admitted to the proceedings as an objector. The question whether a person "appears to be entitled to the benefit" of the relevant restrictions frequently involves a fascinating examination of the conveyancing (and social) history of an area of land. Some are substantive opposed applications for discharge or modification, which may well take on the atmosphere, if not the function, of a local planning inquiry, replete with maps, plans, expert witnesses and lengthy site inspections; the last, incidentally, usually take place on a wet day in November, when little can be seen.

Mr Francis readily and rightly acknowledges that there are major scholarly works on the subject of restrictive covenants, and he refers to them where appropriate. His own work is sub-titled "a practitioner's guide" which may suggest something akin to the *Nutshells*, which are used by law students for last-minute revision. In my view there is no need for modesty. This is a work of scholarship and the depth of research and understanding it displays is impressive. The author has, however, marshalled his material in a practical and methodical way, to provide a step-by-step guide for the busy practitioner to the intricacies of this obscure, though esoteric, corner of the law of real property. If that busy practitioner follows faithfully step by step, he or she is unlikely to stumble.

Bernard Marder
Richmond, March 1999

(His Honour Bernard Marder Q.C. Hon. FSVA, former President of the Lands Tribunal, President of the Land Institute)

PREFACE

"I am not determining a point of law; I am restoring tranquillity"
(Edmund Burke)

As its title says, this is a practitioner's guide. It has been written with the aim of restoring tranquility (and understanding) to the minds of those seeking guidance in the field of restrictive covenants which affect freehold land.

But, in writing such a guide, on a dry and difficult topic, it is hard to know where to begin both in the literary and the geographical sense.

It is common for authors to visit the places associated with the work they are attempting to pen. This may be done in order to understand the character of the subject of a biography, or an attempt to waken the Muse in something more romantic, or it may even be compulsory, as in the study of battlefields. Where should you start when writing a book on restrictive covenants? This is a difficult question.

Is it logical to start in some well-maintained suburb where the covenants remain intact to preserve the ideas of the aesthetically-minded original owner? Or should it be the Old Hall in Lincoln's Inn, where so much of the equity on which the rules which follow are based has its origin? By design I have settled on Leicester Square, if for no other reason than everyone who has ever touched on this subject will recall the authority of *Tulk v. Moxhay*. Although the somewhat worn appearance of the Square is hardly a testament to a strict control of land use (and its preservation owes more to the mid-Victorian efforts of a flamboyant Kidderminster M.P., Albert Grant, than the victory of Mr Tulk), it was a good starting point for one other reason. In the Square there are two statues; one of William Shakespeare and the other of Charlie Chaplin. Each of them has been an example to me; the former as a master of written English and the other in achieving mass appeal. So, with their example in mind, I have tried to write a book which is clear and which will tempt those seeking a practical guide to the subject. I hope it meets those aims.

I decided to write it because of a demand which I perceived existed for a simple explanation of a tricky area of land law. The major works on the subject are detailed and contain much learning. I express my indebtedness by references to them in the footnotes in this book. But I feel the busy practitioner is stranded by the absence of a simple explanation of many of the rules and practice in the field of restrictive covenants. I have, therefore, attempted to write such an explanation. It is intended to be used as a first resort, and potentially as a last resort, when clear advice on restrictive covenants is required; these days invariably required urgently and by "return of fax". There is a danger in over-simplification and I hope I have not fallen prey to that danger. Those seeking more detail can consult other works on the subject and where necessary I refer to them—gratefully. I have tried to explain matters in a way which will give those advising clients the ability to find the answer to the problem before them with the minimum of difficulty.

I have to thank Julie Abbott of Royal Sun Alliance for her contribution in the form of Chapter 18 which deals with insurance against the risks posed by restrictive covenants. Her practical knowledge and experience is, I believe clearly demonstrated by her chapter, which I know I could not have written. She wishes to acknowledge the help given to her by Joan Hornsby also of Royal Sun Alliance.

I gratefully acknowledge the help which I have received from my colleagues in Chambers, friends in Lincoln's Inn, the many practising solicitors who have given me great insight into many of the day-to-day problems which arise in this field of property law and the publishers.

I am particularly indebted to His Honour Judge Marder Q.C., who, until the end of July 1998 was the President of the Lands Tribunal, for his invaluable help and for taking the time and trouble to read the draft chapters and for writing the foreword.

Last, but certainly not least, I express my debt of gratitude to my wife and children for the forbearance which they have displayed for more than a year while this book was in the process of gestation.

Despite this assistance I have been given, all errors are my own.

I have endeavoured to state the law at March 1, 1999, although account has been taken so far as possible of new Civil Procedure Rules coming into effect on April 26, 1999.

A.J. Francis
Lincoln's Inn
Lady Day 1999

CONTENTS

TABLE OF CASES

TABLE OF STATUTES

TABLE OF STATUTORY INSTRUMENTS

GENERAL INTRODUCTION

"Many thousands of words of restrictive covenants clutter the titles of house property and bedevil modern conveyancing. In many cases these covenants are difficult to construe and there is doubt as to whether they are enforceable or whether anyone has power to release them."[1]

1. Setting the Scene

The words extracted above summarise the difficulties in one paragraph. Restrictive covenants come in many shapes and forms, both as to their terms and the problems they pose. Here are just a few of them.

A familiar story?

Restrictive covenants have always been the bane of the law student's life, placed in the same untidy corner as perpetuities and the rule against double portions. The law of covenants was never reformed to any great extent in 1925; hence the complexity. The most we recall at college is that the rules which relate to them owe something to a decision in 1848 about Leicester Square. It is at this point that our grasp slackens, until we enter practice.

From thereon, if we are conveyancers, we see great tracts of them daily, copied, or sewn in to Land certificates, or occupying acres of abstracts and eating up pages of epitomes. Unless we are litigators we never really see them work. We try to explain them to clients, but the copperplate references to motor houses, fellmongers, catgut spinners, and beaters of flax, bring blank (or black) looks. The odd client may raise a question about the neighbour's garage or washing line. We look at the deeds and they seem to be silent on the topic of new garages, or washing lines blocking out the light. Developer clients may hurry into a development without much more than a passing word of caution from us about them. We cross our fingers. We mutter something about the Lands Tribunal and having found that whatever magic wand this body may wave can take two years, and cost as much as a full trial, we move on, usually none the wiser. We may trouble to insure against them.

But then, one day, thump, and a really large restrictive covenant problem emerges. The client's neighbour is threatening to put up the carbuncle of all time. We look for yellowing land charge searches and blackening photocopies reminiscent of Mr Fox Talbot's "sun pictures" at Lacock Abbey, and we look at the land certificate and we find that what is called "the benefit" is not on our client's title. We are dismayed to say that we do not really know whether

[1] Royal Commission on Legal Services, Annex 21, para. 3. (1979) Cmnd 7648.

the client can sue, or whether he can get any damages, and if he can, how much. If we act for a Really Big Developer we are uncertain whether it will be injunctions at dawn or worse. It is at this moment that we look at the text books and wish we had paid attention in 1975 or 1985 or 1995 in a lecture theatre with the sun coming through the windows—just as it sometimes shines in Leicester Square.

It is at this moment that we recall *Tulk v. Moxhay*, but little else.

Grim reality?

You are faced with a client who is a developer and who is considering acquiring land for that purpose. The title shows that it is affected by restrictive covenants, potentially preventing the planned development. You do not know how to find out whether anyone could prevent the development. Once you have discovered that there is a risk of prevention, what do you do next? Is insurance an option?

A client has just been served with a writ seeking an order that stables (which have been in use for some years—albeit in breach of covenant) be knocked down and that a projected extension is restrained. How far should the client defend the claim?

Another client has an inner-city site where covenants will fetter development. Can these restrictive covenants be removed, and if so how, and how long will it take? Can the threat of an injunction be avoided by a declaration that those with the benefit of the covenants are not entitled to enforce?

Finally, a client in a leafy suburb has the benefit of a covenant restricting the use of the neighbouring property to occupation by one family. The local health authority plans to use the property as a home for elderly folk. What remedies are available to your client? What if the land next door was compulsorily acquired; what would the remedy be for breach of covenant?

Relief is at hand?

This book is designed to meet the need of the busy practitioner who requires easy access to a topic which often seems difficult to understand and where existing publications may not serve that need. To that end the emphasis is on practical answers rather than academic scholarship. The aim is to give answers to the questions which restrictive covenants raise in practice. The scene set above shows the sorts of problems which can arise. If it does nothing else, the book should give the answers to those, and other, problems.

2. The Scheme of the Work

In keeping with the aim expressed above, this book is divided into Chapters which deal with the following topics:.

Part 1: Explaining the **words used** in the field of restrictive covenants, and the meaning of "restrictive covenant" (Chapters 1, 2 and 3).

Part 2: Identifying how the **existence** of covenants can be found, and whether they are **valid** (Chapter 4).

Part 3: How covenants can be made to **work**, both in terms of enforcement by the person entitled to the benefit of them and against the person bound by them (Chapters 5, 6 8 and 9).

Part 4: What do certain covenants **mean** and how do we construe them? (Chapter 14).

Part 5: Can covenants be **extinguished or modified**? (Chapter 16).

Part 6: If there is a breach of covenant (following the rules of construction in Chapter 14) and assuming they are valid and in existence as covenants which can be enforced, how can they be enforced and what **remedies** exist for that purpose? (Chapter 15).

Part 7: Is it possible to **insure** against the risk of restrictive covenants being enforced, and in what way can this be done? (Chapter 18).

Part 8: What special rules apply where restrictive covenants are encountered in the context of **public and other authorities** where statute defines their powers? (Chapters 10, 11 and 12).

Part 9: Are there any **drafting rules** to be followed? (Chapter 17). There are **precedents** at Appendix 7.

Part 10: The statutory and other material for reference at Appendices 1–3.

3. How to Use this Book

Trying to make it simple

The best place to start is the flowchart at pages 6 and 7.

With the aid of the flowchart, the checklists at the end of the chapters where they appear can assist in identifying the matters which need attention if a problem is to be solved.

In addition, here are some simple rules to follow when looking at restrictive covenant problems in practice.

Rule 1

Whenever you have a problem which requires looking at restrictive covenants ask yourself, what does the covenant mean? Always start here.

Is my client (or the other side) doing anything which falls within it?

If the answer is no—end of problem.

(Under this rule we look at problems of construction particularly in the light of *Mannai Investments* [1997] A.C. 748, and also at the problems posed by covenants requiring the consent of a party to the covenant.)

Rule 2
If what is proposed to be done, or is being done, falls within the covenant, is it restrictive? This means that for the covenant to be restrictive it must be negative in effect.
(Under this rule we look at what is a "restrictive covenant" as opposed to a positive one.)

Rule 3
If the covenant was created after December 31, 1925 and if the person against whom it is to be enforced is not the original party who gave the covenant, that person is not going to be bound *unless* the covenant is registered. If it is not, you cannot be sued on the covenant; so end of story. (There may be an exception in rare cases where H.M. Land Registry have failed to register covenants and the register is rectified against you). Under this rule we look at the manner in which successors in title to the original covenantor can be bound; in the case of pre-1926 covenants the doctrine of notice still applies; for those covenants created after that date we look at either the D(ii) entry or the entry on the register according to whether the title is registered or not.

Rule 4
If you are not the original person in whose favour the covenant runs you will have to show that you have the benefit of the covenant. This is often the difficult bit, as not only are the rules tricky, H.M. Land Registry do not help as their policy is not to enter the benefit of the covenants on the register of title to the land which can (arguably) claim such benefit. If you don't have the benefit, you cannot sue; so end of story again.

(Under this rule we look at the effect of section 78 of the Law of Property Act 1925 on post-1925 covenants and, in cases to which that section does not apply, at express annexation, express assignment of the benefit and at building schemes.)

Rule 5
If you are unable to show who has the benefit, you *may* be able to convince an insurance company to kindly take on the risk (at a price) of someone eventually proving you wrong.

(Under this rule we look at the factors which apply to those cases where indemnity policies may be available.)

Rule 6
If you can show that you have the *benefit* and that the neighbour is subject to the *burden* you may be able to sue to prevent the threatened eyesore from ever happening—or at least to get damages for it. But what does it take to get an injunction, and what sums of damages are we talking about?

(Under this rule we look at the vexed question of injunctions, particularly the David and Goliath problems posed by interim applications. We also look at damages and the "ransom" principle.)

Rule 7
There are special rules which apply to local and public authorities which allow them:

(a) to enforce certain types of covenant even though they own no land in the vicinity;

(b) to do things in breach of a covenant—or even to override it—on payment of compensation only.

These need to be examined carefully.

Rule 8
It is possible to remove or vary restrictive covenants by application to the Lands tribunal under section 84(1) of the Law of Property Act 1925. In addition the High Court can declare what covenants mean and who may enforce them under section 84(2) of that Act.

4. What is Not Covered in This Book

As the title suggests, positive covenants are not dealt with in detail, but to assist the reader in view of the fact that positive and restrictive covenants may sometimes be intertwined, at Chapter 1 below there is a summary of the rules which affect the enforceability of such covenants.

I have also not dealt with rent charges, covenants for title, and again as the title indicates, covenants in leases.

I have not dealt with reform proposals. The reason for not doing so is because The Law Commission's Report on the Law of Positive and Restrictive Covenants (Law Com. No. 127) (1984) has been formally abandoned, although the Law Commission has been asked by H.M. Government to consider how future developments in property law might affect the recommendations in that report.[2] The same fate appears to have befallen the Law Commission's Report on Obsolete Covenants (Law Com. No. 201) (1991).

The present Government's plans for tenure reform may or may not include the reform of covenants, and if some form of "commonhold" is introduced, such reform will be inevitable in the context of that form of tenure, if not elsewhere. But that reform appears at present to be a few years off. For the present and (at the time of writing) the forseeable future, any practical guide to the law of restrictive covenants will have to deal with the present "ungodly jumble".

5. Further Reference

As this is a practical guide, I have attempted to draw a course through the

[2] See House of Lords' *Written Answers, Hansard* Vol. 587, cols 213/4 (March 19, 1998).

rocks and shoals of the subject with as much clarity as possible. As in the case of a map or chart, that does not always give the fullest picture, and where necessary, I refer in the footnotes to the other works on the subject where greater depth of treatment is available.

I have included in the appendices much statutory material. Some of it is crucially important such as the extracts from the Law of Property Act 1925; other extracts are less important but may be difficult to find (without a full set of statutes or other volumes of Government material) and may be useful when agreements or deeds are seen which refer to the statutory provisions in question, and when drafting where such material has to be considered.

CHAPTER 1

INTRODUCTION

This chapter examines:

- the words used in the context of restrictive covenants and their meanings;
- the reason why the law of restrictive covenants is difficult;
- the different rules which apply to positive covenants.

1. THE MEANING OF WORDS

1–01 The law in respect of restrictive covenants which affect freehold land can be difficult and confusing. Much of the difficulty arises from the words used. The starting point is with the two key words, "restrictive" and "covenant".

"Restrictive" means that the obligation is negative in substance; even though the language may be in positive terms. Chapter 3 deals with this aspect of the law in detail.

"Covenant" means a promise contained in a deed or a contract. There are two points of importance here.

(a) The law of restrictive covenants falls within two areas; that of contract and that of land law. As to the contractual element, a covenant is no more than a contract made by deed. As we will see further on, the difficult part comes when we look at the land law element.
(b) Section 1 of the Law of Property (Miscellaneous Provisions) Act 1989 governs the formalities which attend the making of a deed. We are not concerned with them here, but to be enforceable as a covenant, it requires consideration being given for it; either by virtue of the execution of the deed, or by virtue of the terms of the contract. A deed is not always required.

"Freehold Land" denotes the estate to which the restrictive covenant relates. Covenants in leases are outside the scope of this book.

1–02 The right to enforce the covenant is "the benefit". The obligation to observe is "the burden". In terms of the parties it is "the covenantee" who has the right to enforce and it is "the covenantor" who is under the obligation to observe.

Those terms will be used in that sense in this book.

Where the word "covenant" is not used, there can be doubt as to whether a covenant (in the strict sense of the word) is being given. The parties may agree to a set of **stipulations**, *e.g.* "to hold unto the purchaser subject to the stipulations [or conditions] set out in the schedule hereto". In such a case there may be doubt as to whether the parties did intend to create an equitable burden on the land so as to bind successors. In such cases the stipulations may bind the original parties only. It is the policy of H.M. Land Registry to enter stipulations in such a way as to make it clear that no words of covenant have been given.[1] In practice you should avoid using words which are ambiguous in this sense; unless you want to create stipulations only.

2. Why are Restrictive Covenants Difficult?

1–03 The operation of restrictive covenants affecting freehold land is governed by the special rules which allow these covenants to be enforced not only by and against the original parties, but also by and against successors to those parties who are the owners of freehold land to which the covenant relates.

If the law of restrictive covenants was simply governed by the law of **contract**, the rules of privity would not allow enforcement between those who were not parties to the contract. Unless the parties were the personal representatives of the original parties, or unless there was evidence of the assignment of the benefit of the contract (but not the burden), the covenant would not be enforceable by or against non-parties. Because of this contractual liability, the original covenantor remains liable on the covenants into which he has entered, in theory, until the covenants are released or in some other way brought to an end. The original covenantee may also sue even after he has parted with the land for which the covenant was taken, but would only get nominal damages. In practice, the liability of the original covenantor will be limited by words in the instrument creating the covenants which terminate such liability once he ceases to have any interest in the property burdened by the covenants. In addition he (and his successors) will obtain a covenant of indemnity from the transferee of the land against any liability which may attach under the covenants for future breaches.[2]

It is to overcome this limitation that special rules have been developed which allow restrictive covenants to be enforced by and against successors to the original covenanting parties. These rules have developed for two reasons.

1–04 First, because of the limits on enforceability which the common law imposed

[1] See, *Re Rutherford's Conveyance* [1938] Ch. 396; *Kingsbury v. Anderson* (1979) 40 P.&C.R. 136. The absence of the verb "to covenant" was not a bar to the Lands tribunal treating the application before it as one involving covenants, within the jurisdiction under s. 84 of the Law of Property Act 1925, see *Re Crest Homes' Application* (1983) 48 P.&C.R. 309. See Chap. 16 below for the extent of this jurisdiction.

[2] See *Emmet on Title*, paras 19.016–19.019.

on such covenants. The Courts of Equity devised rules in the first half of the nineteenth century to overcome those limitations, but it is those rules which are themselves complex. Since 1875 when law and equity were fused we should not really need to worry about the historic difference, but there are some circumstances when we need to remember the distinction, such as in the context of damages, dealt with in Chapter 15. As this is a practical guide the emphasis will be more on the rules which have to be satisfied rather than their origin, but an understanding of the background shows why the rules are complex.

Secondly, if restrictive covenant are to be effective and to satisfy the needs of the landowner who retained land and who wanted protection, it is essential that the covenants are fully enforceable both by and against the parties' successors. The first half of the nineteenth century was a period of economic expansion and without any other means of control over building and development, the restrictive covenant had to be effective in securing control.

This is where rules which have more to do with **land law** come in, and which lead to the result that a restrictive covenant is, as to its burden **an equitable interest** in land (if fully enforceable) and as to its benefit, **a right** which is enforceable by successors who can show that the benefit is vested in them. It is the rules which deal with the manner in which the burden and the benefit run which cause the difficulty. As will be seen below the running of the burden is often easier to prove than the running of the benefit. That is one reason why the former will be taken first.

3. Positive Covenants

1–05 Although this is a book about restrictive covenants, some understanding of the law of positive covenants is required. The appreciation of this distinction is required in view of the different rules which apply to the enforcement of positive covenants as between successors in title to the original parties.

The principal and most important rule regarding the enforcements of positive covenants against successors to the original covenantor is that the burden does not run against such successors. Thus, a covenant to pay a sum of money on a defined event (*e.g.* to pay the uplift in value of land on the grant of planning permission) will not be enforceable against a successor of the original covenantor, even if he has notice of the covenant. As will be seen below the rule regarding the running of the burden of a restrictive covenant is different—and in most cases the covenant is enforceable against a successor.

1–06 There is only one exception to the rule which prevents enforcement of positive covenants against successors, but it is limited and requires the person seeking to enforce the positive burden to show that for the successor in title to the covenantor to enjoy certain benefits which are conditional on the performance of certain burdens, he must discharge the latter. It is also necessary to show that the benefit and the burden must be relevant to each other and it is not enough simply to attach a right (*e.g.* to use services) to a condition for payment to make the positive condition enforceable against a successor.[3]

In order to circumvent the strict limitation on enforcement of the burden of positive covenants devices such as the use of legal or equitable charges to secure payment obligations, estate rent charges, rights of re-entry, ransom strips and restrictions on the register of title. Chapter 17 and the precedents at Appendix 7 below deal with this subject further.

[3] See *Rhone v. Stephens* [1994] 2 A.C. 310, affirmed in *Thamesmead Town Ltd v. Allotey* (1998) (76) P.&C.R. D20.

Chapter 2

THE FLOWCHART

2–01

In this Chapter a flowchart shows how it is possible to answer the question "Is a restrictive covenant enforceable?"

The questions are asked which a practitioner might ask when acting for either a potential plaintiff (seeking to enforce a covenant) or a potential defendant (seeking to resist enforcement).

The flowchart identifies the areas as they are covered in the following chapters.

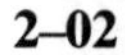
2–02

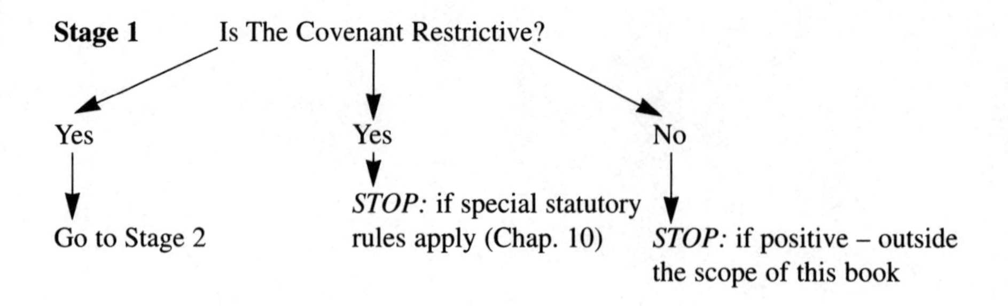
Stage 1
Is The Covenant Restrictive?
Yes
Go to Stage 2
Yes
STOP: if special statutory rules apply (Chap. 10)
No
STOP: if positive – outside the scope of this book

Stage 2 *What does the covenant mean?*
(*STOP:* unenforceable on grounds of public policy or by E.C. Treaty, Art. 85) (Chap. 14)

Stage 3 *Has there been or will there be a breach?*

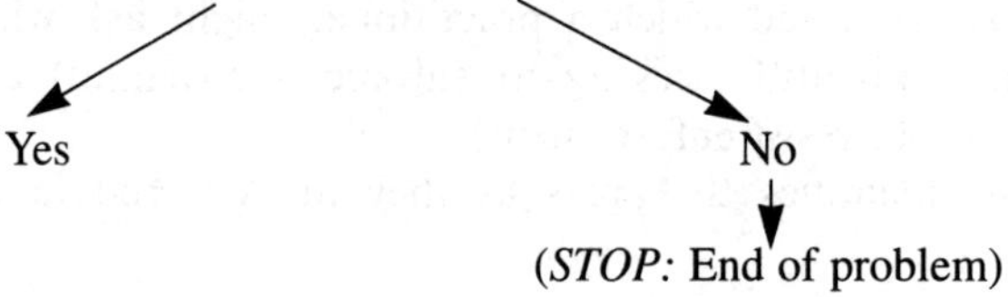
Yes
No
(*STOP:* End of problem)

Stage 4 *If there is a potential or actual breach:*

— Who is in breach?

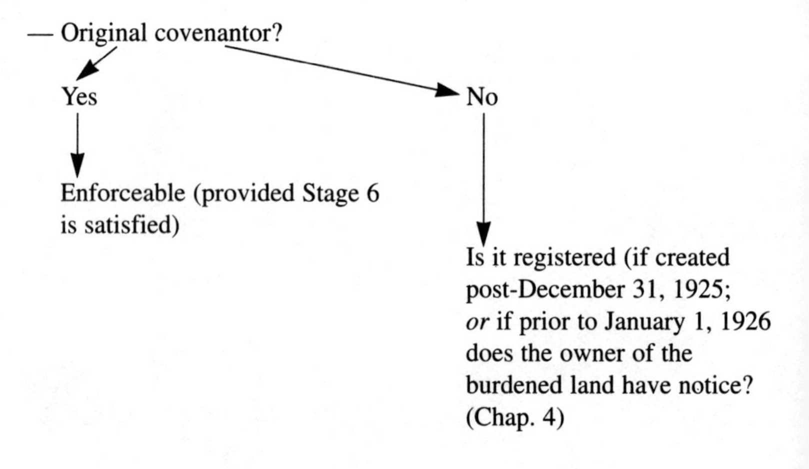
— Original covenantor?
Yes
Enforceable (provided Stage 6 is satisfied)
No
Is it registered (if created post-December 31, 1925; *or* if prior to January 1, 1926 does the owner of the burdened land have notice? (Chap. 4)

Stage 5 *Only if the registration or notice test is satisfied can the covenant be enforced against the successor to the original covenantor.*

If the answer is yes, go to Stage 6. If no, the covenant cannot be enforced.

Stage 6 *Who is seeking to enforce?*

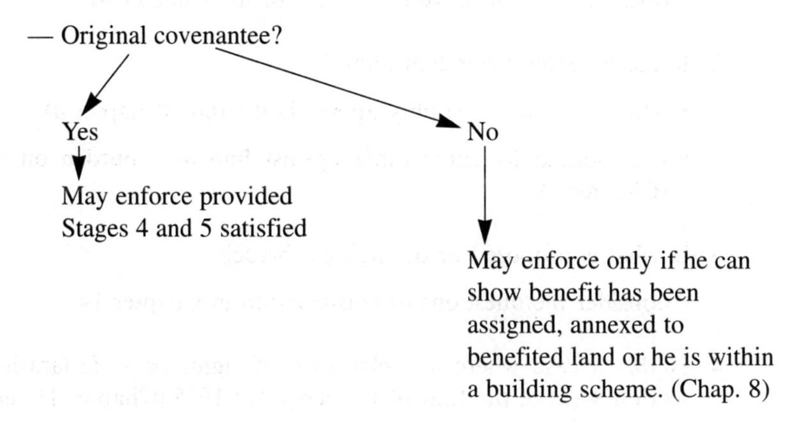
— Original covenantee?
Yes
No
May enforce provided
Stages 4 and 5 satisfied
May enforce only if he can
show benefit has been
assigned, annexed to
benefited land or he is within
a building scheme. (Chap. 8)

Stage 7 *Consider if in doubt:*

— Do you need to insure? (Chap. 18)

— Do you need an order for discharge or modification or a declaration as to enforceability? (Chap. 16)

Stage 8 *If proceeding to enforce, what is the remedy?*

— Declaration as to enforceability?

— Injunction?

— Damages (Chap. 15)

Checklist of Questions

When acting for the potential plaintiff

2–03

1. What covenant is the plaintiff seeking to enforce
   - is it restrictive? (Chapter 3)
   - does the plaintiff have the benefit of it? (Chapter 8)
2. Is the potential defendant liable?
   - which rules as to validity apply? Is it valid? (Chapter 4)
   - is it potentially enforceable against him as a burden on his land? (Chapter 5)
3. Is what is proposed or occurring a breach?
   - consider the questions of construction in Chapter 14

2–04

4. Is this a case where a declaration of right, or a declaration under section 84(2) of the Law of Property Act 1925 (Chapter 16) necessary, or desirable?
5. Is this a case where an application under section 84(1) of the Law of Property Act 1925 to discharge or modify the covenant has ever been made, and with what result? Is the defendant likely to make such an application in this case? (Chapter 16)
6. What is the remedy for any breach? (Chapter 15)
   - will the defendant want to negotiate a release and what will the plaintiff's price be? (Chapter 15)
   - is this case where an injunction will be granted, or is this a case where damages will be the appropriate remedy?

2. When acting for the potential defendant

2–05

1. What covenant is the plaintiff seeking to enforce?
   - is it restrictive? (Chapter 3)
   - which rules as to validity apply, is it valid? (Chapter 4)
   - does the plaintiff have the benefit of it? (Chapter 8)
   - is the covenant a burden on the defendant's land? (Chapter 5)
2. Is what is proposed incurring a breach?
   - consider the questions of construction in Chapter 14
   - consider negotiating a release; what will the price be? (Chapter 15)

3. What is the plaintiff's remedy and what defences does the defendant have? (Chapter 15)

4. Should the defendant apply to discharge or modify the covenant under section 84(1) of the Law of Property Act 1925?

5. Should the defendant consider making an application for a declaration of right, or a declaration under section 84(2) of the Law of Property Act 1925 (Chapter 16), or insuring (Chapter 18)?

3. *Special situations*

2–06

(a) When acting for a client where the covenants were imposed or granted under statutory authority, consider the effect of the statute on the ability of any party to benefit or be bound by the covenant (Chapters 10, 11 and 12)

(b) If a breach of covenant is threatened or committed under stautory authority, consider the limits on the remedies for breach. If acting for the authority seeking to act in breach, consider the ways in which covenants can be overridden. (Chapter 12)

CHAPTER 3

IDENTIFICATION OF COVENANTS WHICH ARE TRULY RESTRICTIVE

3–01 This Chapter considers how a covenant can be defined as truly "restrictive."

As every law student knows, the leading case on the identification of whether a covenant is restrictive or not is *Tulk v. Moxhay*,[1] concerning the obligation to keep what is now Leicester Square open. The text of the covenant runs as follows:

> "that [the covenantor] his heirs and assignees should, and would from time to time, and at all times thereafter at his and their own costs and charges, keep and maintain the said piece of ground and square garden, and the iron railing round the same in its then form, and in sufficient and proper repair as a square garden and pleasure ground, in an open state, uncovered with any buildings, in neat and ornamental order."

3–02 What is interesting in the text of the covenant is that it is expressed in positive terms, but amounts in substance to a negative obligation, *i.e.* not to build. The textbook writers differ in terms of how they define the test,[2] but in practical terms and the purposes of the practitioner, the test is relatively easy to perform.

You ask yourself this question:

Does this covenant require the expenditure of money for its performance and does it restrict the use and enjoyment of the land affected?

If it does not require such expenditure and if it affects the use and enjoyment of land in a restrictive sense, it is negative in substance.[3]

[1] (1848) 2 Ph. 774; 41 E.R. 1143. This was not the first case which defined the circumstances in which the burden of a restrictive covenant would run in equity, but is the one which is regarded as decisive.

[2] *Preston & Newsom*, para. 3–07; *Megarry & Wade*, p. 774; *Scammell*, p. 11; *Halsbury's Laws*, Vol. 16, para. 788.

[3] For a modern example of a *Tulk v. Moxhay* type of restrictive covenant see *Abbey Homesteads Developments Ltd v. Northamptonshire County Council* (1986) 53 P.&C.R. 1. In addition, the recent authority of *McAully v. Chiswick Quay Freeholds* [1998] E.G.C.S. 163, provides a modern definition of what is a restrictive covenant in the context of s. 10 of the Leasehold Reform Act 1967, in which the Court rejected any distinction between covenants against user of land and covenants against development of land or buildings on it.

Positive covenants (*e.g.* to repair) are, therefore, excluded from this definition.

3–03 In practice there are certain "hybrid" forms of covenant which may be less easy to identify. These may be classified as:

(a) Those which appear to be positive covenants but are in reality negative. The commonest example is the covenant not to build without first submitting plans.[4] The payment of the fee for approval does not alter this conclusion, for compliance with the covenant against building requires no action or payment.

(b) Those which appear to be restrictive but which are in reality positive. One example is an obligation not to sell without offering the land to a specified person first.[5]

3–04 (c) Those where positive and restrictive obligations are mixed up. *Tulk v. Moxhay* was an example of this, in that the obligation encompassed the maintenance of the Square. The Court's approach here will be to separate (so far as possible) the positive from the negative. If that is not possible it may be that the covenant will not satisfy the test of negativity.[6]

(d) Certain covenants are imposed under statutory authority. They may contain both positive and negative elements, but because of the special rules which apply to them, they do not fall within the general classification of "restrictive covenants".[7]

[4] See *Ridley v. Taylor* [1965] 1 W.L.R. 611.

[5] *Manchester Ship Canal Co. v. Manchester Racecourse Co.* [1901] 2 Ch. 37.

[6] See *Shepherd Homes Ltd v. Sandham (No. 2)* [1971] 1 W.L.R. 1062. Much obviously depends on the style of drafting. Using a modern form where covenants are listed *seriatim* in a schedule the Court ought to be able to sever the positive from the negative. See Chapter 17 *et seq.* on drafting covenants and precedents at Appendix 7.

[7] See Chap. 10 *et seq.* for the manner in which such covenants arise.

CHAPTER 4

IDENTIFYING THE EXISTENCE OF RESTRICTIVE COVENANTS WHICH ARE VALID AND BINDING

4–01 This Chapter looks at two questions.

First, how does the *existence* of restrictive covenants manifest itself.

Until you can establish whether covenants exist to operate as a potential burden or as a potential benefit over your clients' land, everything else which follows is academic.

Secondly, what rules apply to determine the *validity* of restrictive covenants against persons *other than* the original covenantor. The word "validity" is used in the sense that the covenant has in some way to bind such persons, as opposed to the use of that word denoting the legality, or illegality of the covenant and its enforceability as a matter of law or public policy. In the latter sense of the word such an inability to sue or be sued on the covenant will affect not just successors but also original parties. Covenants which are an unreasonable restraint of trade are an example of the latter.

The answer to the two questions posed above is not always easy and a summary of the answers is placed at the beginning of the chapter.

1. SUMMARY

Existence

4–02 The *existence* of covenants will be determined by the type of title to which the burdened and the benefited land belongs.

(a) *Finding the burden*

Finding whether the land is burdened by covenants should be easy. There are two historic divisions. Covenants created after December 31, 1925 have to be registered to be valid against successors who have acquired the burdened land for value, and, therefore, their existence must be disclosed by evidence of registration. In the case of covenants created on or before December 31, 1925, their validity will depend on notice which must be apparent from the title disclosed.

(b) *Finding the Benefit*

Finding whether land has the benefit of a covenant is more difficult, particularly where the title is registered. The reasons for this are set out below and there may be no substitute for detective work amongst a number of neighbouring titles—and not just your client's.

Validity

4–03 The rules governing the *validity* of covenants in order to bind a successor in title to the original covenantor are as follows:

(a) Covenants created on or before December 31, 1925—the equitable doctrine of notice applies;
(b) Covenants created after December 31, 1925:

- unregistered titles: void against a purchaser for money or money's worth of the legal estate unless registered against the name of the estate owner of the burdened land when created as a D(ii) Land Charge.
- registered titles: void against a purchaser of the burdened land if not entered on the Charges Register to that title, or protected by caution.

Problems can arise as a result of errors in registered entries and searches. The key is to ensure accuracy both in the original registration and in subsequent searches.

2. Validity distinguished from enforceability

4–04 Putting the question of the existence of covenants to one side for the present, and turning to the question of validity, it is vital at this stage to appreciate the distinction between the *validity* of a restrictive covenant and its *enforceability*.

The word "validity" is used in this chapter to mean the manner in which a covenant is protected by notice or registration so as to bind a successor in title of the original covenantor. The use of that word in the sense of "illegality" (such as covenants which infringe legislation, or which may be unenforceable on the grounds of public policy) is a separate subject and it is assumed that the covenants referred to in this chapter are valid and enforceable in that sense.[1]

Validity is a question which arises when a covenant is to be enforced against a person other than the original covenantor (or his personal representative). It requires an answer to the question whether (in the case of covenants created prior to January 1, 1926) the potential defendant is or is not a bona fide purchaser of the burdened land with notice, and in the case of covenants

[1] See chap. 14 below where certain types of covenant (*e.g.* those to protect certain trades) pose problems in the context of restraint of trade and infringment of Art. 85 of the E.C. Treaty).

created on or after that date, whether the registration requirements have been met. In essence the enquiry is whether, for the covenant to *bind* that successor, it is protected by complying with those rules. (See the flowchart at pages 6 and 7 above).

It is only *after* the question of validity of the covenant has been determined that it becomes necessary to consider *enforceability*. The answer to the latter depends upon an application of the rules of law and equity which specify how the burden and benefit of a (valid) covenant can run.

It is, therefore, premature to consider enforceability prior to validity.

If the answer on enquiry is that the covenant is not valid (*e.g.* because it has not been registered) that is an end to the matter if enforcement is sought against a successor in title of the covenantor. Look at the flowchart to see at what point the question as to validity cuts in (at pages 6 and 7 above).

3. Discovering the existence of a covenant: registered and unregistered titles

4–05 Discovery of the existence of a covenant, particularly the benefit of one, is not always so simple.

The existence of any restrictive covenants will be revealed by:

(a) the documents of title themselves;

(b) abstracts or epitomes of title;

(c) Land Charges Registry searches;

(d) Office copies of registered titles.

Classes (a), (b) and (c) are relevant in unregistered land only. In cases of such land it is assumed that any practitioner will have investigated title for the statutory period of at least 15 years.[2] As regards undisclosed land charges not disclosed by such investigation, compensation for them is provided for them under the Law of Property Act 1969, s. 25.[3]

(Note that contracting purchasers of unregistered land are not deemed to have notice under section 198 of the Law of Property Act 1925 of registered land charges at the time of entry into the contract, unless they or their agents have actual notice of them.[4] This protects purchasers of such land and requires disclosure from the vendor. The position is the same as regards purchasers of registered land).

4–06 What follows is the detail of how the existence of restrictive covenants will reveal themselves and what will govern validity by registration.

The first question to ask is whether the freehold title(s) under consideration is or are registered at H.M. Land Registry, and if so, with which class of title. The question usually needs to be asked twice because the answer will require

[2] Law of Property Act 1969, s. 23.
[3] See *Emmet on Title*, para. 5–144 for the provision.
[4] Law of Property Act 1969, s. 24(1) and see *Emmet on Title*, para 1–06, above.

knowledge of the status of both the burdened and the benefited land.

4–07 There are four permutations:

(a) *A restrictive covenant is taken for the benefit of plot A over plot B. Both titles are freehold. Neither title is registered at H.M. Land Registry.*

In this case the rules relating to the protection of the validity by notice or registration of covenants in unregistered land will apply. In terms of discovery of the existence of the covenants it will be the documents of title which will give the answer, coupled with any Land Charges Registry certificates.

(b) *As in (a) save that plot A is registered with title absolute at H.M. Land Registry and plot B is not.*

In this case, for the reasons given below at paragraph 4–19 the existence of the benefit of the covenant will not appear from A's title at H.M. Land Registry. To be valid, the covenant which burdens plot B must satisfy the rules relating to the protection of the validity of covenants in unregistered land; as in example (a) above. Discovery of the benefit may, therefore, be a problem, but discovery of the burden will not be if the covenant is to be valid and bind a successor of the original covenantor.

(c) *As in (a) save that plot A is not registered at H.M. Land Registry but plot B is, with absolute title.*

In this case the existence of the benefit should appear from plot A's title deeds. To be valid and bind a successor of the original covenantor the burden must be entered on the charges register of B's title at H.M. Land Registry and if so, will appear there. Discovery of both benefit and burden should be relatively easy.

(d) *As in (a) save that both plots are registered at H.M. Land Registry with title absolute.*[5]

In this case the benefit will not appear on A's title. The burden, for the covenant to be valid and bind a successor of the original covenantor, must appear on the charges register to be B's title; as in (c) above. In this case (which represents an increasing number of situations concerning two titles) the discovery of the benefit of the covenant will be difficult, but the burden easy.

What if the registered title is possessory only?

4–08 (a) In such a case the task may be more difficult, although the covenant may still be valid against the owner of the burdened land for the reasons which appear below.

(b) If the class of title registered is possessory (as opposed to absolute) the *burden* of the covenant will not appear on the register for the simple

[5] In the event that the titles are registered with a class of title less than absolute (qualified or possessory) see *Ruoff & Roper*, paras 5–06–5–08 and below.

reason that no deeds will have been produced on first registration. In such a case, the covenant will still be valid and binding on the first registered proprietor and his successors provided the covenant was valid at the time of first registration and, if so, takes effect as an overriding interest. In other words, the rules which determine the validity in unregistered land (against successors in title of the original covenantor) of pre-and post-1925 covenants set out at paragraph 4–11, below must be satisfied. This means that while there may be nothing on the register of the burdened land, there may be a valid covenant binding it, and the pre-registration deeds and Land Charges Registry searches will reveal the existence of a covenant and (according to the rules set out below) its validity. That is the danger in possessory titles, and to which they are subject.

(c) In so far as the *benefited land* is registered with possessory title, there will, for the same reason, be nothing on the register and the same searches will have to be made to see if the benefit of any covenant can be claimed.

(d) In some cases the Registry will put an entry on the register of the burdened land to the effect that the title is subject to such covenants as may have been imposed thereon prior to first registration so far as they are legally enforceable. This is because the squatter (with the possessory title) cannot defeat the right of the covenantee and his successors to enforce any valid covenants against the former.[6]

What if the registered title is qualified?

4–09 (a) Such titles are rarely encountered. They are usually granted where, for example, title is defective up to a certain date. There will usually be a provision in the register excepting from the effect of registration any interest arising before a certain date or under a document described in the register. Thus the title is, in effect, absolute, but is qualified in a certain way.

(b) Discovery of the existence of covenants in such titles may, therefore, be complicated by the fact that there are two periods to be looked at. The first is the period covered by the exception where the title is defective and is not shown. The second is that period where the title is shown fully on the register.

(c) Any covenant which falls within the terms of the exception (the first period) will be valid (as to the *burden*) according to the same principles as are set out in paragraph 4–08, above for possessory titles. The existence of covenants burdening the land within the title will have to be found in the same way from pre-registration deeds and Land Charges Act searches. Discovery of covenants created during that period which *benefit* the land with a qualified title can only be found

[6] See *Ruoff & Roper*, para. 5–06 and ss. 6 and 70(1)(h) of the Land Registration Act 1925.

in the deeds and searches lying off the register, as in possessory titles; see paragraph 4–08(c) above.

(d) Covenants which fall within the second period where the title is shown and which burden the land within the title must conform with the requirements of registration on the title to the burdened land in absolute titles. The discovery of the existence of the burden will also be as in unqualified absolute titles. The treatment of the benefit of covenants created within the second period will also follow the same rules as in unqualified absolute title; for which see paragraph 4–19 below.[7] In practice the benefit will not appear and may be hard to find; see situation (b) and (d) at paragraph 4–08 above.

Having been able to discover the existence of the restrictive covenant the next stage is to look in detail at whether the covenant is valid in accordance with the meaning of the word at paragraph 4–04 above in order to discover whether successors in title to the original covenantor will be bound.

4. The Rules as to the Validity of Restrictive Covenants

4–10 It is these rules which indicate whether, having discovered the existence of a restrictive covenant which appears to affect and bind land, such a covenant is valid and binding against successors in title of the original covenantor.

4–11 The validity of restrictive covenants against *non-parties* is governed by the following principles:

(a) *Restrictive covenants created before January 1, 1926* and disclosed in the documents of title will only affect and be enforceable against a *bona fide* purchaser for value of the legal estate with notice, or against a person holding an interest less than a legal estate, such as lessees, squatters, licensees and occupiers at will.[8] "Notice" in practice means disclosure in the documents of title referred to at paragraph 4–05 above. Because the minimum period for examination of title has, since 1970, been 15 years and because of the increasing passage of time since 1926, and with the growth in registered titles, cases where the purchaser for value is without notice may nowadays seldom be relevant.[9]

(b) *Restrictive covenants created on or after January 1, 1926* require:

(i) In unregistered land, registration as a Class D(ii) Land Charge,

[7] See *Ruoff & Roper*, para. 5–08.
[8] See *Preston*, paras 1–17, 3–21, 8–02.
[9] On first registration the policy of H.M. Land Registry in such cases is as set out in *Ruoff & Roper*, para. 12–20.

against the name of the estate owner of the land burdened by the covenant.[10]

(ii) In registered land, entry of the burden of the covenant on the Charges Register as a minor interest.[11]

NB: Two points to remember in practice—

- Registration of the burden of such a covenant which relates to a *registered* title at the Land Charges Registry is of *no effect*; Land Charges Act 1972, s. 14(1). (The Land Charges Registry is not obliged to see whether the covenant affects a registered title; *ibid.* section 14(2)). So, a Land Charges Registry search showing the entry of a covenant against the owner of a registered title is (literally) not worth the paper it is written on. (There is a warning on the back of the standard search certificate!)
- You can protect the burden of the covenant by means of a caution *but* a caution is not recommended save as a last resort.[12]

5. The Effect of a Failure to Observe the Rules

4–12 In unregistered titles, if the covenants are not registered as a Class D(ii) Land Charge, they will not bind and are void against a purchaser of a legal estate for money or money's worth unless registered before the completion of the purchase.[13]

In registered titles, if the covenants are not entered on the Charges Register of the title of the burdened land to which they relate, a purchaser of that land is not concerned with them.[14]

[10] Land Charges Act 1972, ss. 2(5)(ii) and 3(i). If so registered, that constitutes notice to all the world under Law of Property Act 1925, s. 199(1).

[11] Land Registration Act 1925, ss. 2 and 50. *Ruoff & Roper*, para. 35–21/2. The benefit of restrictive covenants is rarely entered and then only in qualified terms; *ibid.* para. 35–23. See para. 4–19, below.

[12] See, *Clark v. Chief Land Registrar* [1994] Ch. 370, for the limited protection a caution may give. Although questions of priority may not arise between those entitled to the benefit of restrictive covenants (*cf.* chargees), it is still felt that only if there is a complete failure by the owner of the burdened land to lodge his land certificate for an entry to be made, should the caution be used as a means of protection. (See *Ruoff & Roper*, para. 35–22).

[13] Land Charges Act 1972, s. 4(6). Note the use of the priority notice under s. 11 and see *Emmet on Title*, paras 10–28, 10–42. It may be possible to defeat the unregistered covenant by selling on before any one wakes up to the fact of non-registration. It may be negligent for a solicitor acting for a client who has an interest in avoiding the covenant not to do that and it would be negligent of him to make the position worse (for his client) by drawing the other party's attention to a failure to register; see *Hartle v. Laceys* [1998] C.L. 3839, CA.

[14] Land Registration Act 1925, s. 59(6). The matters excepted in that subsection would not appear to arise (other than rarely) in the context of restrictive covenants not on the register. "Purchaser" is defined by s. 3(xxi) of that Act as a purchaser in good faith for valuable consideration; somewhat different from the purchaser for money or money's worth in the Land Charges Act.

6. Problems which can emerge in practice

4–13 A number of problems present themselves in practice when applying these rules. These problems are partly caused by the manner in which the registration system works and partly by the policy of H.M. Land Registry of not entering the benefit of restrictive covenants on registered titles.

The principal problems which emerge are:

(a) Defective entries and searches at the Land Charges Registry;

(b) Covenants which have been overlooked on first registration, or which appear erroneously on the register of title;

(c) The general policy of H.M. Land Registry of not entering the benefit of covenants on the title of the benefited land;

(d) The effect of "general" references to covenants on the register where no deeds were supplied on registration.

(e) How to deal with modification of covenants.

(a) Defective entries and searches at the Land Charges Registry.

4–14 There are two reasons why defective entries and searches at the Land Charges Registry occur. First, where the original registration was incorrect in some vital particular, such as the name of the estate owner, or of the land burdened by the covenant registered. Secondly, where the search itself is incorrectly framed. To some extent the problem is less acute under the computerised system which has been in operation since 1974. Prior to that date the old manual system operated by the Land Charges Registry at Kidbrooke relied, to some extent, on the "lateral thinking" of the searchers thereby allowing entries to be found even where the search was not 100 per cent correct. Equally that system was known to produce clear searches where the computer would now give an entry. In many cases the old system produced a clear search against the same (correctly named) estate owner because the manner of description of the land affected differed between the registration particulars and those on the application to search. A computerised search may well reveal the entry if the estate owner's name and the county accords with the registration particulars even though some other details may be at variance. In particular, parish and place names can be notoriously difficult to get right.

The following principles appear to be applicable:

4–15 (i) To ensure that the burden of the covenant runs and the covenant does not lose the advantage of enforceability against successors to the covenantor, it is clear that care must be taken to identify and describe correctly the name of the estate owner, the land

and county when registration is effected.[15] In cases where local government reorganisation has led to county changes (both as to names and changes of boundaries) the county identity requires special care, both at registration and when searching. Notorious areas of change are the West Midlands and the Dorset/Hampshire boundary changes in 1973.

(ii) The same degree of care must be exercised when searching.[16]

4–16 The reason why these principles are important is because of the effect of the following statutory provisions:

(i) Land Charges Act 1972, s. 10(4) which provides:
"In favour of a purchaser or an intending purchaser, as against persons interested under or in respect of matters or document entries of which are required or allowed as aforesaid, the certificate (sc. of search) according to its tenor, shall be conclusive, affirmatively or negatively, as the case may be".

(ii) Law of Property Act 1925, s. 198(1) which provides:
"The registration of any instrument or matter in any register kept under the Land Charges Act 1972 or any local land charges register shall be deemed to constitute actual notice of such instrument or matter, and of the fact of such registration, to all persons and for all purposes connected with the land affected, as from the date or registration or other prescribed date and so long as the registration continues in force."

4–17 When taken together these two provisions mean the registration of a covenant as a Class D(ii) Land charge operates as actual notice to all the world (section 198(1), *but* that is subject to the effect of section 10(4).

Thus, where a search is made the result as stated on the certificate is conclusive of the state of the register. If the result is clear, the purchaser takes without notice, and section 10(4) prevails over section 198(1).[17]

[15] The name of the estate owner should be that given in the conveyancing documents; what other name would a purchaser (or a vendor in the case of purchaser's covenants) know? In respect of estate owners who have died after July 1, 1995, registration against that person's name and not his personal representative will suffice; Law of Property (Miscellaneous Provisions) Act 1994, s. 15. It is usually thought that registration will be too late after the estate owner subject to the covenant has disposed of his legal estate—unless registration is coupled with the use of a priority notice under Land Charges Act 1972, s. 11. For authority on the problems posed by names on registration see *Standard Property Investment Plc v. British Plastics Federation* (1985) 53 P.&C.R. 25; *Diligent Finance v. Alleyne* (1972) 23 P.&C.R. 346. For problems posed by place names, see *Horrill v. Cooper* [1998] E.G.C.S. '51.

[16] References to searching in this respect means making an official search; the same protection is not given by personal searches or by the result of a telephone search alone, unsupported by the certificate which follows.

[17] See *Ministry of Housing v. Sharp* [1970] 2 Q.B. 223, where the Court of Appeal held that the clear certificate was conclusive, albeit in error, overruling Fisher J. on this point, thereby allowing the purchasers of the land affected to take free from a claim for repayment of compensation for lost development value under Town & Country Planning Act 1947 and related legislation.

But what if the *search* is carried out in error? If the search is one which gives reasonable scope for misunderstanding the result will not be conclusive under section 10(4).[18] In such a case section 198(1) will operate so as to treat the person whose search is made in error as having notice and he will be bound by the covenant, assuming of course the benefit is enforceable under the general principles relating to enforceability.[19]

For the practitioner the following *key points* should be borne in mind when dealing with the registration of covenants and the searches for them in unregistered titles:

(i) If you wish to ensure that a covenant binds third parties it must be registered as a Class D(ii) Land Charge with the care referred to above. Registration is not retrospective. Plans rather than a description may be preferable in some cases.

(ii) A clear search may not mean what it says. It may be that the person claiming the benefit of a covenant will, by checking old search certificates, copies of applications for registration and even descriptions in abstracted documents, show why a clear search has been given in error and thereby be able to show that the burden of the covenant is, prima facie, enforceable.

(b) Problems with covenants and registered titles

4–18 Problems can arise in practice when covenants fail to get noted on first registration, or where covenants (which are plainly unenforceable) are erroneously noted on the register.

The first problem (failing to note the covenant) is usually fatal to any prospect of enforcing the covenant against a successor to the original covenantor who is the registered proprietor, and a purchaser under Land Registration Act 1925, s.3(xxi), for he will take free from any covenant not entered on the register.[20] Even if it is a case where it is possible to rectify the register of title to the land burdened by the covenant, under Land Registration Act 1925, s. 82, such rectification will not be retrospective so as to adversely affect the interest of a person who has taken free.[21] There remains the open question of whether the covenantee would be entitled to an indemnity under section 83 of that Act for any loss suffered during the period prior to rectification. The terms of section 83 and *Freer v. Unwins* suggest there may not be an indemnity. Even if an indemnity is payable in a case where the register is not rectified, the value of the claim will be limited to the loss suffered at the time of the error, which could have occurred years ago. Indeed that may be a reason for

[18] *Du Sautoy v. Symes* [1967] Ch. 1146 (description of land faulty); *Oak Co-Operative Building Society v. Blackburn* [1968] Ch. 730 (description of estate owner's name faulty). *Horrill v. Cooper* [1998] E.G.C.S. 151 (problems of place names).

[19] Chap. 8, below.

[20] Land Registration Act 1925, s. 59(6).

[21] *Freer v. Unwins* [1976] Ch. 288. It is hard to see how the right to rectify in such a case could be an overriding interest within Land Registration Act 1925, s. 70(1)(g) and thereby binding on a successor as in *Blacklocks v. J.B. Developments (Godalming) Ltd* [1982] Ch. 183.

arguing that there should be rectification, and that against a proprietor in possession it would be unjust not to rectify against him. Where it is clear that the owner of the burdened land has bought with notice of a registered covenant (even though it has not been revealed on a search which is made not containing any error) and that by reason of the clear search, H.M. Land Registry has not registered the burden of the covenant, the Court may rectify the register against that purchaser.[22]

The second problem (noting invalid covenants) arises where on first registration the policy of H.M. Land Registry is to enter covenants disclosed on the title unless it is plain that they are void for non-registration.[23] In this instance such entry does not give the covenant any validity it would not otherwise have. If it has not been registered as a Class D(ii) Land Charge and there has been a disposition of the burdened land which renders the covenant void against a successor as a purchaser for money or money's worth of the legal estate, the registered proprietor of that estate takes free, and may seek rectification of the register to remove the entry.[24]

(c) The practice of not entering the benefit of covenants on the title to the benefited land

4–19 A major difficulty which lies in the way of discovering whether a covenant may be enforced arises because of the policy of H.M. Land Registry of not normally entering the benefit of covenants on the register of title to the land benefited by the covenant.[25]

However, in view of the terms in which the policy is expressed, it is *possible* to secure the entry of the benefit in two classes of case. First, where there is a defined building scheme (as to which see Chapter 8 below). Secondly, where application is made with a certified copy of the deed imposing the covenant and a clear definition of the land benefited. Even so the entry will be in terms which do not guarantee the ability to enforce, for the standard form of entry will state that the covenants are only "expressed to be for the benefit" of the land in the title.

One other task which may be necessary in many cases is to ascertain whether one has the benefit of a covenant at all. If adjacent land is registered, searches of the registers of title to such land may reveal the existence of covenants burdening that land, the benefit of which may be enforceable, in accordance with the principles set out in chapter 8. If the land is unregistered the task will be impossible, unless you are within a defined building scheme, or where local knowledge establishes that there are covenants over a defined area, which might allow you to claim the benefit of them.

[22] *Horrill v. Cooper*, above. However, that decision may be criticised as introducing the equitable doctrine of notice into registered land, that doctrine having no place in such a system; the decision is currently being taken to the Court of Appeal by the defendant against whom rectification was ordered.

[23] See *Ruoff & Roper*, para. 12–21.

[24] *Kitney v. MEPC* [1977] 1 W.L.R. 981 at 994 *per* Buckley L.J.

[25] See *Ruoff & Roper*, para. 35–23.

(d) Cases where covenants are not identified specifically on the register

4–20 A registered title may be expressed to be subject to covenants but their precise identity is not known because either the land is registered with possessory or qualified title (as to which see paragraphs 4–08 and 4–09 above), or because no evidence or particulars of the covenants were produced on first registration, or subsequently. The model forms of entry on the charges register will refer to the fact that the land may be affected by covenants but no particulars can be given for the reasons stated. This is a problem in practice in that whether any restriction can be enforced may be uncertain for both the party with the potential benefit and the party potentially subject to these unspecified covenants.

From the point of view of the owner of the burdened land the course to take in such cases (apart from digging out the evidence of the covenants and their terms) is to insure. (See Chapter 18, below for insurance).

(e) Modification of covenants

4–21 Problems sometimes emerge when covenants are modified.

If this happens (whether by agreement or by order of the Lands Tribunal under section 84 of the Law of Property Act 1925), parties sometimes forget to record the modification by re-registering the D(ii) entry (unregistered titles) or by applying for variation of the Charges Register entry in the register of title to the burdened land. It is more unusual to "forget" in the case of a Lands Tribunal order. (In the rare instance where the benefit is noted the same process should be observed).[26]

It has been known to happen that the original covenants were not registered in the manner appropriate to the title burdened, *i.e.* whether registered or unregistered. Entering into an agreement to vary would appear to be an acceptance of the burden by a successor in title of the covenantor even though the covenants (in their initial form) would have been initially void against him for non-registration. He may be estopped from denying the validity of the covenant.[27] An earlier failure to register may, therefore, be "cured" by subsequent variation. For the practitioner the important point to bear in mind is the need to protect such a variation, once made, by registration.

[26] See chap. 16 for the discharge and modification of restrictive covenants, and para. 16–112 thereof for the manner in which orders should be dealt with.

[27] See *Taylors Fashions v. Liverpool Victoria Trustees Co. Ltd* [1982] 1 Q.B. 133.

Chapter 5

MAKING COVENANTS WORK: IS THIS COVENANT ENFORCEABLE?

5–01 This Chapter looks at the general question of *enforceability*. By this stage the covenant (which has been ascertained to exist) has been established as valid in the sense that it binds successors in title of the original covenantor.

We now have to look at whether a restrictive covenant can be enforced *by* and *against* those affected.

Setting the scene

5–02 Once you have discovered the existence and validity of covenants the next stage is to consider how they may be made to work.

As covenants are designed to operate as restrictions on the use and/or enjoyment of land, their function would be incapable of performance if they did not work. It is, therefore, obvious that the real question which arises is whether the covenant is capable of enforcement. This is a separate question from validity. As explained in the previous chapter, a covenant's validity is independent from its enforceability.

It is in the context of *enforceability* that the real difficulties as regards restrictive covenants are encountered by practitioners. This is partly because validity is confused with enforceability and partly because of the rules which apply to ascertain whether a covenant is enforceable or not.[1] It is remarkable in how many instances a prolonged inquiry as to enforceability can be short-circuited by the discovery that the covenant is void for want of registration.[2]

[1] This and subsequent chapters on the question of enforceability proceed on the assumption that any covenant under consideration is valid in the sense that it is properly registered according to the status of the title of the land burdened by it and is not unenforceable as a covenant which is illegal, or created by a body acting in excess of its powers, or unenforceable as being contrary to public policy, or contrary, for example, to Art. 85 of the E.C. Treaty. See Chap. 14 below, for certain types of covenant which pose problems of enforceability in the alternative sense in which that word is used.

[2] See the flowchart at pp. 6–7 above for a reminder.

Who is seeking to enforce the covenant against whom?

5–03 To answer the question "is this covenant enforceable?" the answer has to be given from the standpoint of both the potential plaintiff (seeking to enforce) and the potential defendant (resisting enforcement). Clearly the interests of each will differ; the former being concerned to prove enforceability and the latter the contrary.

There are four situations in which the question posed above arises. In each case whether the covenant works or not depends upon the application of a different set of rules.

5–04 The four situations are as follows:

(a) *Situation 1*
The original covenantee wishes to enforce against the original covenantor.

(b) *Situation 2*
The original covenantee wishes to enforce against a successor of the original covenantor.

(c) *Situation 3*
A successor of the original covenantee wishes to enforce against the original covenantor.

(d) *Situation 4*
A successor of the original covenantee wishes to enforce against a successor of the original covenantor.

Each situation is examined in the next four succeeding chapters.

Chapter 6

ENFORCEMENT OF COVENANTS BETWEEN THE ORIGINAL COVENANTING PARTIES

6–01 This Chapter looks at the rules which determine enforceability of covenants between the original parties.

Summary

6–02 As a general rule a covenant may be enforced by and against the original parties without exception.

In respect of non-executing parties they will both be bound and be entitled to enforce.

In respect of non-parties, only those within the ambit of a deed poll or section 56(1) can enforce, and non-parties cannot be bound.

The situation

6–03 The original covenantee wishes to enforce against the original covenantor.

The general rule

The covenant is enforceable by the covenantee and the covenantor is bound by virtue of the usual principles of privity of contract and by virtue of consideration having been given for the covenant.

Are there any problems with the general rule?

6–04 There ought to be no problem in practice with the general rule. But, as with all rules, they can contain exceptions.

Potentially tricky points can arise where the general rule may not be applicable. These are:

- whether a person *named* in the deed but who *is not a party* can claim the benefit of it;

- whether a party *named* in the deed but *who has not executed it* can enforce it, or be bound by it.

In practice, examples of these points may arise in the following manner:

You have a deed made between A and B whereby A covenants with B that he will not do certain things on his (A's) land. B can enforce against A.

But what if:

(a) the deed is a Land Registry transfer and B has not signed it;

(b) the covenant is for the benefit of C and he has not signed the deed;

(c) the covenant is not with B or C, but with the owners for the time being of the remainder of the X Estate, which B is selling off;

(d) A is not a party to the transfer, or if a party, he has not executed it?

For reasons which are explained below, dealing with each example in turn, the answers are as follows:

(a) B can enforce against A even though B has not executed it;

(b) C can enforce against A by virtue of the transfer being a deed poll;

(c) the owners for the time being of the remainder X estate if then in existence at the date of the deed can enforce by virtue of section 56(1) of the Law of Property Act 1925;

(d) As A is not a party to the transfer he cannot be bound by it. If he is a party but has not executed it he will be bound if he is in possession of the land burdened by the covenant.

Unless the reader needs to know the detailed background to and the reasons for these answers, he need not read further. In the vast majority of cases the covenant will be enforceable by an application of the general rule, and in the circumstances set out above. What follows is technical.

The technical points which cause problems in the application of the general rule

6–05 Before we can discover the reasons behind the answer to the two problems described at paragraph 6–04 above, we have to identify the type of deed which creates the covenant.

Even at the dawn of the next millenium the practitioner has to know the difference between two types of deed—albeit that the real difference in physical terms has been dormant for centuries. We also have to understand the effect of Law of Property Act 1925, s. 56(1).

The two technical points are:

(i) *The distinction between an indenture and a deed poll*

(ii) *The effect of Law of Property Act 1925, s. 56(1)*

6–06 (i) *indenture v. deed poll*

An indenture is a deed made *inter partes*. The classic instance being the usual form of conveyance of unregistered land, or a deed of covenant expressed to be made between A and B.

A deed poll is a deed made by one party only, as a unilateral act.[1] By virtue of section 56(2) of the Law of Property Act 1925 a deed *inter partes* has the effect of an indenture even though it is not indented, nor expressed to be an indenture. What this means is that a deed between two parties will operate as an *inter partes* deed however it is formally expressed.

6–07 (ii) *Section 56(1) of the Law of Property Act 1925*

This provides:

> "A person may take an immediate or other interest in land or other property or the benefit of any condition, right of entry, covenant or agreement over or respecting land or other property, although he may not be named as a party to the conveyance or other instrument"

It is this section which allows a third party to enforce a covenant where he is within the ambit of the covenant, *i.e.* the covenant must be made with him and it is not enough that the covenant may be for that person's benefit.[2] In the context of restrictive covenants, the formula often adopted, in order to take advantage of section 56(1), is to express the covenant to be with the owner or owners for the time being of defined property, so that there are, in effect words of covenant with those persons.[3]

The operation of section 56 is limited by the additional rule that the person claiming the benefit must have been in existence at the date of the deed creating the covenant.

[1] We are not concerned here with the old "physical" distinction between an indenture and a deed poll in that the former was made in two identical parts and "indented"; *i.e.* cut with a wavy line at the top or down the middle, whereas the latter was made in one part only. For the history see *Halsbury's Laws*, vol 12, para. 1303. These distinctions, curiously, survive the formal changes as regards execution by s. 1 of the Law of Property (Miscellaneous Provisions) Act 1989.

[2] See *Amsprop Trading Ltd v. Harris Distribution Ltd* [1997] 1 W.L.R. 1025.

[3] See Chap. 17 for drafting points and precedent at Appendix 7. This form of words allows adjoining owners who may have purchased adjoining plots *prior* to the conveyance containing the covenant to claim the benefit of the covenants if the covenant is expressed to be with them. See also *Re Shaw's Application* (1994) 68 P.&C.R. 591 where adjoining owners had the benefit under section 56(1) of a covenant to approve plans. That authority was, however, criticised by the Court in *Amsprop Trading* (above) and the stricter view that the covenant must be expressed to be with the person claiming the benefit of it prevailed. See also *Beswick v. Bewick* [1968] A.C. 58. See Chap. 8, para 8–22 for the problem posed if this form is not used.

The detailed answer to the problems in paragraph 6–04 **6–08**

With these distinctions in mind how does a covenant work in the circumstances posed in paragraph 6–04 above?

First, who can claim the *benefit* of the covenant?

By way of background, at common law, a person who was not a party to an indenture could not sue on it. That rule has been qualified by section 56(1), as explained above. But at common law a person who was within the ambit of a *deed poll* and entitled to the *benefit* of any covenant in it could enforce the covenant. The circumstances in which a person can claim to be within the ambit of a deed poll are the same as those which arise when considering whether a covenant is purportedly made with someone for the purposes of enforcement under section 56(1). That rule still applies, so in cases where covenants are imposed by a deed poll, the assistance of section 56(1) is not required.

The commonest example of a deed poll is the standard form of Land Registry transfer. As that operates as a deed poll, any covenants in it can be enforced by the covenantee, even though not a party to the transfer, or, if a party to it in the absence of execution by that party.[4]

The answer is, therefore:

- where the deed is *inter partes* and is, in effect, an *indenture*, section 56(1) will apply to allow the benefit to be claimed by persons who are not parties to an indenture, provided the covenant is purported to be made with them; *e.g.* the owners for the time being of the adjacent land;
- where a *deed poll* is used (*e.g.* a Land Registry transfer) a person within its ambit (*e.g.* defined as the covenantee(s) in the example just given) can claim the benefit of the covenant either at common law, or under section 56(1)—although a claim under the section is strictly unnecessary;
- those who are named as parties but who have simply failed to execute can take the benefit and enforce the covenants.
- *but*, a claim to the benefit of a covenant by a person who is not a party to the deed will not be possible where an indenture is used and where section 56(1) does not assist; *e.g.* where the covenant does not purport to be made with the person attempting to enforce it.

Secondly, who can be *bound* by the covenant? **6–09**

Fortunately, the rules here are simple.

- A non-party cannot be bound, and section 56(1) has no application as it concerns the *benefit* of the covenant only.

[4] *Chelsea & Walham Green B.S. v. Armstrong* [1951] Ch. 853; *Megarry & Wade*, p. 762; *Emmet*, para. 11.001/2.

- In the case of a deed of either variety (*i.e.* whether an *indenture* or a *deed poll*) which has not been executed by a party to it (the covenantor) the burden is enforceable against him.[5]

[5] In the sense that the burden of the covenant will be enforceable in equity against the non-executing party who has accepted the benefit of the deed (*e.g.* by going into possession of the land conveyed). *Formby v. Barker* [1903] 2 Ch. 539.

CHAPTER 7

ENFORCEMENT OF COVENANTS BY THE ORIGINAL COVENANTEE AGAINST A SUCCESSOR OF THE ORIGINAL COVENANTOR: MAKING THE BURDEN OF THE COVENANT RUN

7–01 This Chapter considers how the *burden* of a restrictive covenant can be made to run with the land and against successors of the original party who gave the covenant.

SUMMARY

7–02 For the burden of a restrictive covenant to be enforceable against successors in title of the original covenantor it must be shown that:

- the covenant is restrictive
- it protects adjacent land
- it is not a personal covenant
- it was validly granted
- it satisfies the notice or registration requirements so as to bind that successor.

THE SITUATION

7–03 The original covenantee wishes to enforce against a successor of the original covenantor.

THE GENERAL RULE

7–04 A covenant will only be enforceable against a successor of the original covenantor if it is:

(a) restrictive (according to the rules defining such a covenant) and

(b) if:

(i) the covenant has been taken to protect the covenantee's retained land which is so retained at the time of the conveyance and at the time of enforcement;
(ii) the covenant benefits that land as a matter of evidence;
(iii) the covenant is not a purely personal one between the original parties;
(iv) the covenantor who gave the covenant was competent to give it;
(v) the covenant satisfies the requirement of validity set out in chapter 4 above.

The conditions under (b) are referred to as "the five conditions".[1]

By way of an historical note, as these conditions for enforcement are the product of the Court of Equity (the common law refusing to allow the burden of a covenant to run with the land) only equitable remedies are available in respect of any breach.[2]

Encountering the five conditions in practice and satisfying them

7–05 Taking each in turn.

Condition No. 1

The covenantee must retain land at the date when the covenant is given or entered into and has retained land which is capable of benefiting at the time he seeks to enforce.[3]

The condition analysed:

(a) In most cases of freehold conveyancing where covenants are taken for the benefit of defined land of the vendor, the purchaser's successor will be bound and it will be easy for the vendor to show the land for the benefit of which the covenant was taken.

But there are three problems that can arise in practice:

(i) The first requires a knowledge of the order of conveyances by the covenantee if he was selling off plots one at a time.
(ii) The second concerns covenants taken for the benefit of the covenantee's leasehold estate.

[1] It is these conditions which are the product of the decision in *Tulk v. Moxhay*; see Chap. 3 above.
[2] See Chap. 15 post for remedies. In view of the ability of a modern Court to award not only injunctive relief, but also damages in lieu, the inability to obtain common law damages for breach in such a situation seems rather academic.
[3] *Millbourn v. Lyons* [1914] 2 Ch. 231. *LCC v. Allen* [1914] 3 K.B. 642.

(iii) Finally, there are the statutory exceptions to the rule.

(b) The three problems examined. **7–06**

(i) *Last man out escapes liability*
(See Appendix 6, Plan I)

A problem of enforcement arises where the covenant is imposed in the context of an estate type development and the enforceability of the covenant is being tested against the owner of the *last* plot to be sold off. That owner is a successor to the original covenantor.

Unless there is a scheme of development, or building scheme,[4] the common vendor who is the covenantee will not be able to enforce the covenant. This is because the common vendor retained no land when the last plot was conveyed.

This is not a common problem, although it can often arise unexpectedly, and may be overlooked, particularly when the full sequence of conveyances may not be known until litigation is commenced and at the stage of disclosure of documents under Part 31 of the CPR. The wise defendant in this situation should check at any early stage whether or not his predecessor was "the last man out". It is possible to detect the order of conveyances made by the former common vendor by using the right to obtain office copies of the registered titles in order to detect which plot was the last to be conveyed. This method will only work where the titles are few in number and easily identified. But in most cases armed with a plan of all the neighbouring houses, and a set of office copies, it is possible to work out in what order the sales off were made.

The only snag which can arise, and nowadays rather more frequently, is that in estates where the covenants were imposed in the 1930s or 1950s and the land was first registered at that stage, unless each title has a reference to the common form of covenants imposed by the common vendor, so that the order of sales can thereby be deduced, the modern computer generated certificates will omit historic entries. In theory those covenants should be there on the register (and if they are not they will not bind successors) but it is sometimes harder to get a complete picture with the modern form of register than the old manually compiled ones with entries crossed out in red. (Looking at Plan I it will be seen that D cannot be sued by A, B or C but may sue any of them).

(ii) *When the lease ends so does the liability.*
What sometimes happens is that a landowner will grant a lease of part of his land and covenants with the lessee to restrict the use, by the lessor, of his adjoining freehold land for the protection of the land demised.

The liability of the lessor's successors will only endure for the term

[4] See Chap. 8, para. 8–26, below.

of the lease.[5] It is, however, worth noting that in respect of covenants between landlord and tenant (and others with derivative interests in the reversion) the landlord's interest in that reversion removes the need to retain other land for the covenant to be enforceable. The same principle may also apply to mortgagees of the benefited land.[6]

(iii) *Can statutes be an exception to the rule?*
Numerous statutory exceptions exist in respect of the rule which requires the retention of land by the covenantee. These are dealt with at Chapter 10 below.

Condition No. 2

The covenant must benefit the covenantee's land as a matter of evidence when he comes to enforce.

7–07 **The condition analysed:**

(a) The condition raises three questions:

- Is the land for the benefit of which the covenant was taken sufficiently defined of ascertainable?
- Is that land capable of being benefited by the covenant?
- What does "benefit" mean?

(b) Taking each question in turn, the answers are:

Defining the land
There are two broad distinctions here.

- First, those cases where the words of the covenant specifically define the land for which the benefit runs.[7]
- Secondly, where the terms of the covenant confine the benefit to the land remaining unsold.[8]

In either case, extrinsic evidence should be capable of showing the extent of the land which is within the scope of the benefit on the face of the words used to identify the defined land. There is, sadly, a "hybrid" line of authority where it was unclear, as a matter of construction, as to what was comprised within the scope of the

[5] *Golden Lion Hotel (Hunstanton) Ltd v. Carter* [1965] 1 W.L.R. 1189. Questions may, of course, arise in such cases as to whether the lease in question has been extinguished, by merger, for example.
[6] See *Megarry & Wade*, p. 776.
[7] See *Lord Northbourne v. Johnston & Son* [1922] 2 Ch. 309 (the Shipcote Estate, Gateshead); *Re Ballard's Conveyance* [1937] Ch. 473 (the Childwickbury Estate, Herts.); *Marten v. Flight Refuelling* [1962] Ch. 115 (the Crichel Estate, Dorset); *Earl of Leicester v. Wells-next-the-Sea U.D.C.* [1973] Ch. 110 (the Holkham Estate, Norfolk); *Wrotham Park Estate Co. Ltd v. Parkside Homes Ltd* [1974] 1 W.L.R. 798 (the Wrotham Park Estate, Herts).
[8] *Marquess of Zetland v. Driver* [1939] Ch. 1; *Cryer v. Scott Bros. (Sunbury) Ltd* (1986) 55 P.& C.R. 183.

benefited land. Therefore, in some cases the drafting of the covenant may cause doubt to arise on its face, quite apart from the evidential requirement to identify the benefited land.[9]

Is that land capable of being benefited by the covenant?
The general rule was stated by Wilberforce J. in *Marten v. Flight Refuelling.*[10]

"If an owner of land, on selling part of it, thinks fit to impose a restriction on the user, and the restriction was imposed for the purpose of benefiting the land retained, the court would normally assume that it is capable of doing so. There might, of course, be exceptional cases where the covenant was on the face of it taken capriciously or not bona fide, but a covenant taken by the owner of an agricultural estate not to use a sold-off portion for other than agricultural purposes could hardly fall within either of these categories".[11]

What does this mean in practice? **7–08**

First, if it can be shown that the covenant relates to specified land of the covenantee, there is a (rebuttable) presumption that the covenant is capable of benefiting the land specified. It will be for the covenantor's successor to adduce evidence to show that this presumption no longer applies.[12] Invariably this will require expert evidence from land agents and valuers.

Secondly, where there is an issue as to what land was within the scope of the benefit of the covenant and whether it is capable of being benefited by it, there are no presumptions and the covenantee will have to produce evidence on both questions.[13]

The meaning of "benefit"

7–09 In the archaic language of lawyers the concept of the benefit conferred by a covenant may be reduced to the phrase "touch and concern". In modern parlance this is neither helpful or desirable.[14]

Benefit in modern terms means "preserve value" or "amenity".

Thus, unless the covenant preserves the value of the covenantee's land, it is not restrictive and is not enforceable against a successor of the covenantor.

Modern cases show that "value" may be preserved in a number of way, *i.e.*:

[9] See *Re Jeff's Transfer (No.2)* [1966] 1 W.L.R. 841; *Eagling v. Gardner* [1970] 2 All E.R. 838; *Allen v. Veranne Builder Ltd* [1988] N.P.C. 11.

[10] [1962] Ch. 115 at 136.

[11] See also Brightman J. in *Wrotham Park Estate Co. Ltd v. Parkside Homes Ltd* [1974] 1 W.L.R. 798 at 808, where he emphasised that it will be the reasonably held view of the estate owner (covenantee) which will prevail in the absence of the contrary being proved.

[12] Evidence for both sides was before the Court in *Marten v. Flight Refuelling*, above, but no evidence was placed before the Court in *Earl of Leicester v. Wells-next-the-Sea U.D.C.*, above, to contradict the evidence that the covenant in question was of benefit to the Holkham Estate.

[13] As occurred in *Newton Abbot Co-operative Society Ltd v. Williamson & Treadgold Ltd* [1952] Ch. 286.

[14] For a modern authority on the question in the context of landlord and tenant and petrol station ties see *Caerns Motor Services Ltd v. Texaco Ltd* [1994] 1 W.L.R. 1249.

- by protection from competing trades.[15] But note that personal covenants restricting types of trades or sales of branded goods, may not be enforceable against successors as a restrictive covenant, and they may be held to be unenforceable as an unreasonable restraint of trade, or infringing Article 85 of the E.C. Treaty.[16]
- by protection from certain forms of development—to include protection of a view.[17]

Condition No. 3

The covenant is not a purely personal one between the original parties.

7–10 (a) Whether a covenant is so regarded depends upon the date of the instrument creating it.

(b) The relevant periods are as follows, taking them in reverse historical order, on the footing that the more recent the covenant, the more likely it is going to be encountered.

(i) *Covenants entered into after December 31, 1925*
Subject to the contrary being expressed, Law of Property Act 1925, s. 79 will treat the covenant as having been entered into with the covenantor, his successors in title, and the persons deriving title under him. This section has been described as a mere "word saving" section.[18]

(ii) *Covenants entered into on or before December 31, 1925*
The answer depends on the words of the covenant and whether there are words which indicate that the covenantor's successors are to be bound. Thus not only will words such as "the covenantor for himself, his heirs, executors, administrators and assigns" allow the court to find that the covenant binds successors, but also the nature of the obligation placed on the covenantor will also indicate whether successors are to be bound. An example of the latter may be the obligation to "procure" that something be done or not done.[19]

Condition No. 4

The covenantor who gave the covenant was competent to give it.

7–11 The question whether the covenantor had the power to give the covenant arises infrequently. In most cases whether the power existed will be answered

[15] See the *Newton Abbot Co-operative Society* case, above.
[16] See Chap. 14 below.
[17] *Wrotham Park Estate Co. v. Parkside Homes* [1974] 1 W.L.R. 798; *Gilbert v. Spoor* [1983] Ch. 27.
[18] *Sefton v. Tophams* [1967] 1 A.C. 50 at 73.
[19] See *Re Fawcett and Holmes' Contract* (1889) 42 Ch. D. 150 for an example of the former and *Re Royal Victoria Pavilion Ramsgate* [1961] Ch. 581, for an example of the latter.

in the affirmative, and particular in the following cases where the question of *vires* may be raised.

(a) *Trustees for sale of land, personal representatives and tenants for life*

(i) **Covenants entered into on or after January 1, 1997.**

7–12

Save for pre-existing strict settlements, trustees or the personal representatives will be fully empowered to impose or accept restrictive covenants; Trusts of Land and Appointment of Trustees Act 1996, s. 6(1) and 18. The breadth of this power is only qualified by the overriding fiduciary duties owed by such persons and any express restrictions in the instrument from which the trustee or personal representative derives his power.

For pre-existing strict settlements the position is as before that date, as to which see below.

For charity trustees the new power extends to them in like manner as to trustees of private trusts.

(ii) **Covenants entered into before January 1, 1997.**

Unless the instrument from which the trustee or personal representative derives his power confers a wider power, the rules as to *vires* are as follows:

—Trustees for sale
—Personal Representatives
—Tenants for life and statutory owners

All have the power to grant or accept a covenant on the occasion of the sale of land vested in them; Settled Land Act 1925, s. 49(1).[20]

If the covenant is taken or imposed without a sale, or without an order of the Court under Trustee Act 1925, s. 57 or Settled Land Act 1925, s. 64, the covenant may be voidable only at the suit of a beneficiary, save that where a tenant for life takes or imposes a covenant other than within the power conferred by section 49(1), it will be void under section 18(1)(a) of that Act and will not bind the legal estate.

As to charity trustees, they have the same powers as the class described above by virtue of Settled Land Act 1925, s. 29, and to the extent that they do not, the scheme jurisdiction may supply it.[21]

(b) *Limited Companies*

7–13

Since the abolition of the *ultra vires* doctrine by Companies Act 1985, s. 35, a company entering into a covenant will be taken to have full power to do so.

[20] Applicable to trustees for sale by Law of Property Act 1925, s. 28(1) and to personal representatives by Administration of Estates Act 1925, s. 39(1)(ii).

[21] Charities Act 1993, ss. 26 and 36.

(c) *Bodies created by statute*

7–14 the existence of the power will depend upon the authority given to the body by the Act which constitutes that body. Most such bodies are empowered to enter into covenants. If in doubt ask for the statutory authority.

The most commonly encountered instance is that of local authorities, who have the wide powers conferred under Local Government Act 1972, s. 123.

As to the question whether the covenant interferes with the statutory purposes for which the land is held see Chapter 10 below.

7–15 (d) *Trustees in bankruptcy, liquidators and receivers*

Trustees in Bankruptcy

The bankrupt's property will vest in him under section 306 of the Insolvency Act 1986, so he will be bound by the covenant. In exercise of his powers under Schedule 5, Pt II, para. 9 to that Act he can impose or accept covenants over the land being sold.

Liquidators

Although the assets of the company do not rest in the liquidators of a company in a winding-up, the powers conferred by Schedule 5, Pt III, para. 6 of the Insolvency Act 1986 allow the liquidators to sell and, if necessary, impose or accept covenants. (See *Emmet*, para. 11.192)

Receivers

The powers in Schedule I to the Insolvency Act 1986 would appear to allow administrative receivers to impose or accept covenants on sale of any land in the name of the company. Receivers appointed by debenture holders or banks under mortgages would have the powers of the freehold owner and will usually have full power under the terms of their appointment to impose or accept covenants on sale.

7–16 (e) *Persons without the freehold legal estate*

(i) **Lessees**

The covenant is valid and binding for the duration of the term.[22]

(ii) **Parties with a contractual right only**

The covenant will be valid and will invariably bind the legal estate on completion.[23]

(iii) **Mortgagors**

Subject to any restrictions in the mortgage deed, they have the legal estate and can enter into covenants.[24]

[22] *Golden Lion Hotel (Hunstanton) Ltd v. Carter* [1965] 1 W.L.R. 1189.

[23] See *Re Rutherford's Conveyance* [1938] Ch. 396.

[24] But "tie" covenants may not survive the terms of the mortgage. See Chap. 14 below for the problems which commercial "tie" and related covenants can create as regards restraint of trade and infringement of Article 85 of the E.C. Treaty.

(iv) **Mortgagees in possession**
Subject to wider powers in the mortgage deed, the power to impose restrictions under Law of Property Act 1925, s. 101(2)(i) on sale.

Condition No. 5

The covenant satisfies the requirements of notice or registration **7–17**
Chapter 4 above deals with this rule.

To recap: unless the covenant is so registered, or (in the case of pre-1926 covenants) the successor to the covenantor has notice, he can take free from it if he is within the class of persons who may do so, *e.g.* a purchaser of registered land which would otherwise be subject to the covenant.

Chapter 8

ENFORCEMENT OF COVENANTS AGAINST THE ORIGINAL COVENANTOR BY A SUCCESSOR OF THE ORIGINAL COVENANTEE: MAKING THE BENEFIT OF THE COVENANT RUN

8–01 This Chapter considers how the benefit of a restrictive covenant can be made to run with the land in favour of the successors of the original covenantee who imposed the covenant.

Summary

8–02 For the benefit of a covenant to be enforceable by a successor of the original covenantee it must be shown that:

(a) The covenant was taken for the advantage of some land which it benefits as a matter of evidence; in the sense that any breach of the covenant would affect its value or amenity.

(b) The plaintiff is the owner of such land or has a sufficient interest in it.

(c) The benefit of the covenant has passed to the plaintiff by one of three means, *i.e.*

- annexation
- assignment
- the imposition of a scheme of development.

In respect of covenants created after December 31, 1925, it will usually be sufficient to show that the words of the instrument creating them do not exclude the statutory annexation effected by Law of Property Act 1925, s. 78. To that extent, the task of discovering whether the benefit of the covenant has run is now easier. If that section applies the practitioner does not have to consider any other rules for the passing of the benefit and much of this chapter can be ignored.

Where section 78 does not apply, in the case of pre-1926 covenants the technical rules for the passing of the benefit will depend upon:

- whether words of annexation are present in the instrument creating the covenant;
- whether the formalities of assignment have been satisfied;
- whether all the ingredients of a building scheme are present.

THE SITUATION

8–03 A successor of the original covenantee wishes to enforce against the original covenantor.

THE GENERAL RULE

A covenant will only be enforceable by a successor of the original covenantee against the original covenantor if the following requirements are met:

(a) That the covenant satisfies the requirement that the covenant was taken for the benefit of the land in which the plaintiff has an interest and that it does in fact do so (in the sense of "touching and concerning" it[1]).

(b) that the plaintiff is either the freehold owner of the benefited land, or has an interest recognised as one which gives him locus. Examples of the latter are:

- a contracting purchaser of the legal estate.[2]
- a beneficiary under a trust who is entitled to call for an assignment of the covenant, if not of the land which is benefited by it.[3]
- licensees who are "occupiers" within Law of Property Act 1925, s. 78.[4]
- a trustee in bankruptcy where the bankrupt's estate has vested in him pursuant to Insolvency Act 1986, s. 306.
- a person to whom the benefit will have passed by operation of law, such as a personal representative, under Administration of Estates Act 1925, s. 1.

(c) That the plaintiff has acquired the benefit of the covenant by one of three methods, namely:

- annexation either by virtue of the terms of the instrument creating the covenant, or by Law of Property Act 1925, s. 78 if the covenant was created after December 31, 1925;

[1] See Chap. 7, para. 7–09, above.
[2] See *Re Rutherford's Conveyance* [1938] Ch. 396.
[3] *Newton Abbot Co-operative Society Ltd v. Williamson & Treadgold Ltd* [1952] Ch. 286 at 291.
[4] This is by no means established; See *Re Da Costa* (1986) 52 P.&C.R. 99, where a licensee of land to which the benefit of a covenant had been annexed under Law of Property Act 1925, s. 78, had no locus to object to an application under s. 84(1) of that Act.

- assignment;
- the imposition of a building scheme, or scheme of development.

(d) That the covenantor as a potential defendant satisfies the requirements set out in Chapters 6 and 7 above, and is liable to be sued as an original covenantor.

(e) That the covenant is not personal to the original covenantee.

AN HISTORICAL NOTE ABOUT THE GENERAL RULE

8–04 The general rule set out above reflects the way in which Courts of Equity have defined how the benefit is to pass. Even though the benefit of a restrictive covenant can pass at common law under somewhat simpler rules,[5] the rules of equity (as summarised above) are now regarded as applicable in all actions and it is, therefore, these rules which have to be satisfied. It is the complexity of these rules which cause the major difficulty in determining the enforceability of restrictive covenants.[6] Although Law of Property Act 1925, s. 78, as interpreted in *Federated Homes Ltd v. Mill Lodge Properties*[7] has made the task of determining whether the benefit runs much easier in cases to which it applies (in practice the majority of covenants created after 1925) there are still areas where that section has no application and it is here that the rules are complex.

PRACTICAL PROBLEMS IN DECIDING WHETHER THERE THE BENEFIT OF A COVENANT IS POTENTIALLY ENFORCEABLE

8–05 Before analysing the rules which determine how the benefit can pass, as summarised under paragraph 8–03 above, we have to consider how the *potential* to enforce a restrictive covenant will manifest itself. In essence, what does the title of the potential plaintiff show?

Registered titles throw up the problem of knowing whether you have the benefit. Because of the policy of H.M. Land Registry of not generally entering the benefit of covenants on the land which is (potentially) benefited, there may be an initial difficulty in ascertaining whether the potential plaintiff has any cause of action at all on any covenant.[8] There is a difference in approach depending on whether the title is registered or unregistered.

[5] To the effect that the covenant was enforceable if (a) it touched and concerned the benefited land and (b) the covenantee and his successor had a legal estate in that land. Since 1926 that does not have to be the same legal estate; see Law of Property Act 1925, s. 78 and *Smith v. River Douglas Catchment Board* [1949] 2 K.B. 500.

[6] See *Megarry & Wade*, p. 780–1.

[7] [1980] 1 W.L.R. 594; see para. 8–16, below.

[8] See Chap. 4, para. 4–19 above.

Registered titles

8–06 The remedy where titles are registered lies in a degree of detective work which requires consideration of the following matters:

- look at what is registered on the Charges Register to see whether the covenants which bind the title give some clue as to the benefited land. Often the covenants are expressed to be for the benefit of the X estate or the Y land, and that may well include the land comprised in the title.
- if the manner in which the Land Registry have entered the covenants has been the "filed and sewn up" method (*i.e.* by referring directly to the instrument imposing the covenants) sight of a copy of that instrument will confirm the extent of the covenants and their format, thereby giving an indication of the location of the benefit. (The instrument should be with the Land or Charge certificate, or at least obtainable from the Registry by reference to the title number given).
- you may be in a situation where the vendor has given covenants in favour of the purchaser, and these may be shown on the title in the property register.
- if there is a building scheme, the policy of the Registry is to make an entry on the title referring to the existence of such a scheme, and its extent by reference to a plan.
- local knowledge may count for a lot where defined estates were developed by a common vendor and either a scheme or a set of like covenants is known to be enforceable.
- searching the neighbour's title (being the neighbour threatening to infringe) and obtaining a copy of his title, if registered, may well solve the problem as the burden should appear on his title.[9]
- retention of pre-registration deeds may for practical reasons be unwelcome, but may shed light on the extent to which the land has the benefit of covenants.[10]
- preparation of a "master plan" to show the dates of sales off by the common vendor. (See Appendix 6, Plan I for an example).

[9] It is assumed, of course, that this will not throw up the problem of a failure by H.M. Land Registry (or any other person concerned) to enter the burden of the covenants on the neighbour's title. See Chap. 4, para. 4–18 for the difficulty of enforcement this poses. The potential plaintiff may be left with an indemnity claim under Land Registration Act 1925, s. 83. For the general practice of the Registry as regards restrictive covenants see *Ruoff & Roper*, paras 35–20–35–25.

[10] The same problem is put slightly differently by *Preston & Newsom* at para. 2–13, n. 21, from the point of view of the owner of the burdened land who might consider whether there are persons who know of the covenant's existence. From the point of view of the former it would appear that he would be more likely than not to lie low and say nothing. But in the context of potential development land something may have to be said, if only to the insurers when an indemnity policy is required. See Chap. 18 below on insurance in this context.

Unregistered titles

8–07 In unregistered titles the documents of title will show the extent to which covenants have been taken for the benefit of the land. Although these are fast becoming a rarity, it is important to bear in mind that on first registration it may be possible to persuade H.M. Land Registry to enter the benefit on the title (see Chap. 4, para. 4–19 above).

Applying the general rule: the importance of the date of the covenant

8–08 Having located the instrument containing the covenant which is to be enforced, whether the covenant was taken on or before December 31, 1925 or after that date, will be of critical importance in determining the rules which apply in deciding the manner in which the benefit of the covenant will run.

In the case of covenants created *on or before December 31, 1925*, the instrument imposing it must be examined for signs of one of the following:

(a) Express or implied annexation of the benefit of the covenant.

(b) The creation of a building scheme.

In the case of covenants created on or before December 31, 1925, there may also be evidence of assignment of the benefit of the covenant, in the instruments transferring the benefited land or in separate deeds.

In the case of covenants created *after December 31, 1925* it is possible to enforce covenants of that age by satisfying one of the three conditions set out in paragraph 8–03(c) above.

But it may well be unnecessary to do so.

This is because of the effect of the *Federated Homes* case referred to at paragraph 8–16, below and by the use of Law of Property Act 1925, s. 78, which, in effect, achieves annexation of the benefit of the covenant without the need for special words of annexation, unless that section is excluded by words in the instrument imposing the covenant.

Thus, armed with (a) the instrument creating the covenant (b) evidence of devolution of the title since creation (including evidence of the assignment of the benefit of the covenant) and (c) knowing whether the covenant is pre- or post-January 1, 1926, the next stage is to examine in detail the means by which the benefit of the covenant can be transmitted in each case.

Applying the general rule: separating the easy from the hard parts

8–09 It is usually easy to decide whether or not four out of the five requirements of the general rule set out at paragraph 8–03 have been satisfied. In practice, therefore, the potential plaintiff usually can show:

- that the covenant touches and concerns his land;
- that he has sufficient interest to enforce;

- that the grantor can be bound;
- that the covenant is not personal to the original covenantee.

The hard part lies in satisfying the fifth requirement; namely that the benefit is vested in the successor by one of the three established methods.

- annexation;
- assignment;
- the imposition of a building scheme, or scheme of development.

The rest of this chapter will be directed at looking at how the fifth requirement can be met.

THE GENERAL RULE: ANNEXATION

8–10 Since 1980 and the decision in *Federated Homes v. Mill Lodge Properties*[11], it has been necessary to separate any discussion of annexation into two parts.

First, express annexation.

Secondly, annexation by Law of Property Act 1925, s. 78 (following the decision in *Federated Homes*).

Although, for reasons which appear below, the decision in *Federated Homes* has lightened the task of checking that the fifth requirement is met, it is still necessary to consider express annexation (and other means of passing the benefit) where *Federated Homes* may not apply.

For those cases where it is clear that *Federated Homes* and section 78 does effect annexation, it is not necessary to consider the technical rules of annexation, although, as paragraph 8–16 points out, it is still necessary to consider what land is within the scope of the benefit as annexed and whether it is in fact benefited. To that extent some of the dry and technical rules set out in paragraph 8–12 have to be satisfied.

Express Annexation

8–11 What does "annexation" mean and how do you recognise it?

(a) In its simplest form, annexation denotes words which attach the covenant to the property it is to benefit. The effect may be seen as similar to the effect of an easement being annexed to the land which is benefited by that easement. Once annexed it is there forever subject only to the Lands Tribunal's jurisdiction to discharge or modify under Law of Property Act 1925, s. 84. Unlike an easement, the benefit so annexed may be something of which the (potentially) proud owner

[11] [1980] 1 W.L.R. 594.

may be unaware; hence the poetic description of such a benefit as "a hidden treasure which may be discovered in the hour of need".[12]

(b) The essential thing is that the words of annexation (if they are to be construed as such) must (a) identify the land to be benefited and (b) show that the land so identified is intended to be benefited by the covenant. A covenant merely with "heirs, executors, administrators and assigns" is not enough to achieve annexation as there is no reference to any land.

(c) Examples:

(After the words of covenant)
"to the intent that the benefit may be annexed to and run with [the land of the Vendor shown on the plan annexed hereto edged green] [the X Estate] [and each and every part thereof]"
"[for the benefit of] [each and every part] [of the land adjoining or near to] [the land being sold with the benefit of the covenant]"[13]
"[for the benefit of] the Vendor's [adjoining or neighbouring] land",[14]
"to benefit and protect [each and every] [such] part[s] of the Vendor's land at X as shall for the time being remain unsold"[15]
a covenant with "QB his heirs and assigns owners for the time being of freehold properties in [Leicester Square]".[16]
"with intent that the covenant may enure to the benefit of the vendors their successors and assigns and others claiming under them to all or any of their lands adjoining."[17]
"with the vendors and his assigns owner or owners for the time being of the Vendor's X estate using that term in the broad and popular sense."[18]
"the covenants are to run with the lands of the Vendor."[19]

(d) *Other rules for annexation to be effective*
This is a dry and technical area of law and it is easy to get lost in the welter of authority which exists on the subject.[20]

But for those who need some relatively simple guidance on the annexation of pre-1926 covenants, or in cases of post-1925 covenants where *Federated Homes* does not apply, here are some rules which may assist.

[12] *Per* Simonds J. in *Lawrence v. South County Freeholds Ltd* [1939] Ch. 656 at 680. Whether a covenantor's successor, who finds that the treasure has been found and is threatened with enforcement of a supposed "extinct" covenant would regard this description as helpful, may be open to doubt. See n. 10 at para. 8–06 in this context.
[13] Held a valid form of words of annexation in *Rogers v. Hosegood* [1900] 2 Ch. 388.
[14] Words of annexation approved in *Russell v. Archdale* [1964] Ch. 38. See also *Re Selwyn's Conveyance* [1967] Ch. 674 for a variation on these words.
[15] Words of annexation approved in *Marquess of Zetland v. Driver* [1939] Ch. 1.
[16] Held sufficient words of annexation in *R. v. Westminster City Council, ex p. Leicester Square Coventry Street Association Ltd* (1989) 59 P.&C.R. 51. See also *Re Ballard's Conveyance* [1937] Ch. 473 where the covenant was with the vendor and "her heirs and assigns and successors in title owners from time to time of the Childwickbury Estate."
[17] The "classic formula" expressed in *Megarry & Wade* at p. 782.
[18] As in *Wrotham Park Estate Co. Ltd v. Parkside Homes Ltd* [1974] 1 W.L.R. 798.
[19] As in *Shropshire County Council v. Edwards* (1982) 46 P.&C.R. 270.
[20] For a full "academic" analysis see *Scamell*, p. 53–88.

Rule 1

8–12 If the benefited land is identified and if (but only if) the instrument containing the covenant shows that the land so identified is *intended* to be benefited by the covenant, annexation will be achieved.

This rule excludes from annexation personal covenants, or those which merely affect the covenanting parties in a personal capacity, such as certain "tie" covenants, so far as they may be enforceable. Another example where such an intention to benefit may not be present is in the case of the owner of the sub-soil of a highway.[21]

Rule 2

The form of words used to annex the benefit of a covenant is not critical (and see the various forms above at (c) above) but it must be possible to find either express words, or surrounding circumstances which allow the instrument containing the covenant to be construed as one which manifests an intention that the benefit should be annexed to the land retained by the covenantee.[22]

Rule 3

8–13 A covenant which is imposed to allow the vendor to exploit the benefit of it by assigning the benefit of it at a future date to individual purchasers, or by exacting further payments as the price of a release, will not be found to be annexed.[23]

Rule 4

In the case of covenants entered into between December 31, 1881 and December 31, 1925, s. 58 of the Conveyancing and Law of Property Act does not effect annexation where there is no express or implied intention to annex the benefit of the covenant in accordance with rule 2 above.[24] It is in different terms from section 78.

Rule 5

If rules 1 and 2 are satisfied, it is still necessary to identify the land to which the covenant is annexed.

Where plans are not used, and where words such as "adjoining" or "near to" or "adjacent" are found, this may prompt an inquiry as to what land was within the scope of those words at the time the covenant was taken.[25]

Rule 6

8–14 There is a rebuttable presumption that the covenant will allow the land (identified under rule 5 as the benefited land) to derive value from the

[21] *Kelly v. Barrett* [1924] 2 Ch. 379.

[22] Authority for rules 1 and 2 is found in modern form in *J. Sainsbury Plc v. Enfield Borough Council* [1989] 1 W.L.R. 590 at 595–597 and in *Robins v. Berkeley Homes* [1996] E.G.C.S. 75.

[23] As was found to be the case in *J. Sainsbury v. Enfield LBC*, above and in the earlier authority of *Chambers v. Randall* [1923] 1 Ch. 149.

[24] s. 58 is printed at Appendix 1. See *J. Sainsbury Plc v. Enfield LBC*, above, at 601 *per* Morritt J.

[25] See Chap. 7, above, para. 7–05. See *Wrotham Park Estate Co. Ltd v. Parkside Homes Ltd* [1974] 1 W.L.R. 798 at 806.

existence of the covenant. (In lawyers' words the land will be presumed in the absence of evidence to the contrary to be "touched and concerned "by the covenant).[26]

Evidence may, therefore, have to be adduced as to the extent to which the benefit can be shown to be of value to the land so identified.[27]

Rule 7

If the benefit of the covenant can be shown only to benefit a portion of the land identified as the land to which the covenant is annexed, it may be difficult to sever the covenant and treat is as annexed to that part of the land which derives value from it, but not to that part of the land which does not derive value.

This rule shows the danger of describing the benefited land in terms which are too wide; *e.g.* in terms of "the X estate".[28]

The rule will not apply where it can be said that the benefit of the covenant is annexed to *each and every part* of the benefited land. For in such a case the Court is entitled to find that the benefit of the covenant can be shown to run for the benefit of a particular part and there is no need to sever the good from the bad.[29]

In view of rule 8 below, since the decision in *Federated Homes*, is open to question whether, if as a matter of implication the covenant is annexed to each and every part of the benefited land, there will nowadays be a problem of the sort thrown up by *Re Ballard.* There may yet be an instance where rule 8 does not apply and, therefore, as a matter of construction, the covenant is annexed to the whole and the problem of severance will be present. But that, it is thought, will be rare.

Rule 8

8–15 It will generally be presumed that the benefit of a covenant will be annexed to each and every part of the land for which it is expressed to be taken.

Quite apart from potentially solving problems of severance referred to under rule 7, the rule will avoid the need for argument on the question whether, in cases where the retained land has been subdivided since the covenant was taken, the potential plaintiff has the benefit vested in him as the owner of such a part. The general rule will be that he does.[30] The rule will be displaced if there is clear evidence to show, as a matter of

[26] See Chap. 7, para. 7–09 above for the main authorities, and see *Cryer v. Scott Brothers (Sunbury) Ltd* (1986) 55 P.&C.R. 183, where the presumption was upheld.

[27] As it was in the *Wrotham Park* case, above.

[28] This was the result in *Re Ballard* [1937] Ch. 473, where the Court refused to sever a covenant annexed to the Childwickbury Estate amounting to 1700 acres, where the benefit of the covenant was shown (on uncontradicted evidence) not to extend over the whole of the area. The same problem is encountered in restraint covenant cases, where the Court will not sever where the effect would be to alter the nature of the covenant. See Treitel, *The Law of Contract*, 9th ed., p. 461–465) for the Court's approach in that area.

[29] As in *Marquess of Zetland v. Driver* [1939] Ch. 1.

[30] This rule is derived from *Federated Homes Ltd v. Mill Lodge Properties Ltd* [1980] 1 W.L.R. 594 at 606 *per* Brightman L.J., his dictum being supported by the other members of the Court of Appeal at 607–8.

construction of the instrument containing the covenant, that the covenant is taken for the benefit of the land expressed as a whole only.[31]

Annexation under Law of Property Act 1925, s. 78: the effect of Federated Homes

(a) In practical terms the enforcement of post-1925 covenants, where the potential plaintiff and the potential defendant are both freehold owners and where the concept of benefit can plainly be shown, will not now be a problem. **8–16**

This is because since the decision in *Federated Homes v. Mill Lodge Properties*[32]. Provided the plaintiff can rely upon Law of Property Act 1925, s. 78, the other means by which the benefit had to be vested in the plaintiff do not have to be satisfied.

This means that proof of either express annexation, assignment, or building schemes does not have to be shown if the covenant satisfies section 78. That section achieves what has been referred to as "statutory annexation" when it applies.

(b) Section 78(1) runs as follows:

> "A covenant relating to any land of the covenantee shall be deemed to be made with the covenantee and his successors in title and the persons deriving title under him or them, and shall have effect as if such successors and other persons were expressed." For the purposes of this subsection in connexion with covenants restrictive of the user of land 'successors in title' shall be deemed to include the owners and occupiers for the time being of the land of the covenantee intended to be benefited."

(c) There will, however, be a question mark over enforceability where section 78 is excluded expressly or by implication by the terms of the instrument imposing the covenant, and in cases where, owing to the order of conveyances, the plaintiff is unable to show that his land was owned by the common vendor when the defendant gave the covenant. In the latter case the question of whether a building scheme exists will be vital to the plaintiff's right to enforce. So there are still cases where section 78 will not provide the answer to the question whether the covenant is enforceable. **8–17**

(d) Section 78 will only apply so as to permit a plaintiff relying on it to enforce a covenant if the flowing requirements are met: **8–18**

(i) The covenant must have been made after December 31, 1925.
(ii) The covenant must be one which was entered into at a time when the covenantee had land and the covenant must be one

[31] *Preston & Newsom* at paras 2–20–2–26 contains a detailed analysis of the pros and cons of the effect of rule 8.
[32] [1980] 1 W.L.R. 594.

which "touches and concerns" that land; see paragraph 7–09 above.

(iii) The covenant must "relate to" the land of the covenantee, or at least to part of it. Note the use of those words in section 78(1). Following a dictum of Brightman L.J. in *Federated Homes*, "relate to" has the same meaning as "touch and concern".[33]

(iv) The potential plaintiff, seeking to enforce its reliance upon section 78 must have an interest in that land, either as a freehold owner, or as a person with the right to call for the legal estate, or as an occupier; see paragraph 8–03 above.[34]

(e) It also seems to be the case that notwithstanding the effect of section 78, the potential plaintiff still has to satisfy some of the rules set out at paragraph 8–12 above. The rules which still have to be satisfied in respect of covenants to which section 78 applies are:

Rule 5—identifying the land to which the covenant is annexed.
Rule 7—the problem of severance as modified by rule 8.
Rule 8—annexation to each and every part in the absence of a contrary indication.

8–19 (f) Section 78 may be excluded by words which make it plain that there is to be no annexation, or that it is to be limited. One example would be where the benefit is not to pass unless expressly assigned.[35]

(g) It is an open question whether it is possible to satisfy section 78 and the requirement that the covenant must relate to the land of the covenantee where there are no actual words in the instrument which expressly or by implication identify that land. Is the requirement the same as in rules 1 and 2 above, namely that there must be something in the instrument which allows the Court to identify the land to which the covenant relates? Or is it possible to adduce evidence from outside the instrument to allow such identification? The author's view is that the task is in reality no different from that carried out in cases where section 78 does not apply. There must be something by way of evidence to show which land is benefited by the covenant to which it must, if section 78 is to have any effect, relate. Whether that evidence comes from the instrument, or is extrinsic to it should not matter, although there must be something in the extrinsic evidence which will allow the Court, on the balance of probabilities, to find that the

[33] At 605 B-C.

[34] A licensee may not be within the scope of s. 78. He did not have locus to object to an application under s. 84(1) where he was the licensee of land to which annexation had been effected under s. 78 in *Re Da Costa's Application* (1986) 52 P.&C.R. 99.

[35] As in *Roake v. Chadha* [1984] 1 W.L.R. 40, where the Court refused to accept that s. 78 had a mandatory operation, even though the express words in s. 79 ("unless a contrary intention is expressed") are not found in s. 78. The express words of the covenant were against automatic annexation under s. 78. An argument based on implied annexation under Law of Property Act 1925, s. 62 also failed; see the report at p. 47. See also *Robins v. Berkeley Homes* [1996] E.G.C.S. 75 for an important analysis of the manner in which section 78 will apply so as to annex the benefit of a covenant.

covenant relates to certain land.[36] It would seem that the automatic effect of section 78 does allow a broader approach to the question of identifying the land and avoids the need to search for the requisite intention, which is supplied by the section.

(h) Two final points under this paragraph. **8–20**

(i) It seems reasonably clear from such authority as there may be that annexation cannot be achieved by contending that Law of Property Act 1925, s. 62(1), effects annexation by the general words which apply on a conveyance of land.[37]

(ii) It is unclear whether unilateral action by the covenantee (who has the benefit by assignment) to "annex" the benefit of the covenant, without the consent of the covenantor can be effective.[38]

The General Rule: Assignment

What is assignment?

(a) This is the process whereby the benefit of a covenant (being in essence the right to sue which is a form of chose in action) can be passed by an express form of words which show that A (the assignor) intends to and does assign the benefit of the covenant to B (the assignee). **8–21**

(b) Since *Federated Homes* (see paragraph 8–16 above), the need to prove assignment of the benefit of a covenant is limited to cases where covenants were entered into before 1926, or in the case of post-1925 covenants, where section 78 is excluded.

How will assignment be revealed?

(a) The title should show that in each instrument by which the freehold land benefited has passed, there has been an express reference to the benefit of the covenant and that it is to pass to the assignee. If there is no such reference, and unless annexation is found, the benefit of the covenant will not pass. **8–22**

(b) In unregistered titles the deeds forming the evidence of title back to the root, or beyond if the covenant is earlier, will indicate one way or another whether there is evidence of assignment of the benefit.

[36] Compare the approach adopted by the Court in *J. Sainsbury Plc v. Enfield LBC* [1989] 1 W.L.R. 590, referred to at paragraph 8–12 under rule 2 above.

[37] *Roake v. Chadha*, above; *Kumar v. Dunning* [1989] Q.B. 193.

[38] This concept was referred to in *Federated Homes*, above, by the first instance Court and the Court of Appeal as "delayed annexation by assignment" but no approval to this concept was given by either Court; see [1980] 1 W.L.R. at 603 H. For a full discussion see *Scamell*, pp. 84–88 and *Megarry & Wade* p. 789.

(c) In registered titles, it may be more difficult to detect whether there has been such assignment. As explained in paragraphs 4–19 and 8–06 above, because the general policy of H.M. Land Registry is not to enter the benefit of covenants on the benefited land in most cases, detection will require an examination of the transfers whilst the land has been registered (copies should have been filed with the register by HMLR) and an examination of the deed inducing registration (copy kept likewise) and any pre-registration deeds of earlier vintage subsequent to the taking of the covenant.

What other technicalities are there for an assignment to be valid?

8–23 (a) In theory whether assignment of the benefit has been achieved ought to be a simple affair, but a number of highly technical rules have developed in this context, and the following rules have to be observed before it can be said that the benefit of the covenant has passed by assignment.

(b) These rules are normally only applicable when it is an assignee of the covenantee who is suing a successor of the covenantor, the latter only being liable if the covenant satisfies the *Tulk v. Moxhay* requirement that it is a restrictive covenant which touches and concerns the covenantee's land. (See Chapter 7 above).

(c) In cases where the original covenantor is being used by an assign of the covenantee, the latter need only prove the fact of the assignment to him.

(d) The rules where successors in title are suing and being sued, are, therefore as follows:

Rule 1

8–24 The covenant must have been taken for the benefit of ascertainable land of the covenantee which is capable of being benefited by the covenant.

This rule follows the requirement in annexation (as to which see paragraph 8–11 above). However, in view of the fact that in the instrument creating the covenant there will be no words of the type found where there has been annexation to identify the land benefited, there will have to be other evidence adduced of the circumstances surrounding the taking of the covenant. Sometimes this evidence may be difficult to establish, particularly where the covenants are old, but that may be seen as the penalty for not annexing the benefit.[39]

Rule 2

The assignment must be made at, or substantially at, the same time

[39] See *Miles v. Easter* [1933] Ch. 611. See *Newton Abbot Co-operative Society Ltd v. Williamson & Treadgold* [1952] Ch. 286 for the approach to the question of an intention to benefit as shown from the circumstances and *Marten v. Flight Refuelling* [1962] Ch. 115 for the "broad and reasonable view" to be taken as to the identity of the land to be benefited.

as the conveyance of the benefited land or if made at a later date, it will be effective if made to satisfy the outstanding equitable right in the assignee to have the assignment perfected.[40]

Rule 3
An assignment may be made in respect of part of the benefited land.[41]

Rule 4
There must be a complete chain of assignments.[42] A separation of the title to the land from the benefit of the covenant is fatal. **8–25**

Rule 5
The assignment must comply with Law of Property Act 1925, s. 53(1)(a) and must, therefore, be in writing and signed by the assignor or his agent in order to be valid.

(e) The extent to which an assignment has to comply with Law of Property Act 1925, s. 136(1) seems debatable, and although that section requires notice to be given to the owner of the burdened land, it seems in practice that this is not done. A failure to comply should not affect the right of the assignee to enforce, provided he gives notice under section 136 prior to bringing any action on the covenant.[43]

THE GENERAL RULE: SCHEMES OF DEVELOPMENT

What's in a name?

8–26 Conveyancing arrangements which are sometimes encountered where the original developer has decided to set up a comprehensive scheme of covenants which are designed to be enforceable by and against all the owners from time to time of land on the estate governed by the scheme. The schemes are variously called "schemes of development" and "building schemes". In this chapter the former name will be used.

Why are schemes of development used?

8–27 (a) A person seeking to enforce a covenant must show that he has the benefit of the covenant. The earlier chapters have shown that unless he is the original covenantee, or unless he has the benefit of an assignment or the annexation of the covenant to his land (expressly

[40] *Miles v. Easter*, above at 632 *per* Romer L.J.
[41] *Russell v. Archdale* [1964] Ch. 38.
[42] *Re Pinewood Estate Farnborough* [1958] Ch. 280. For a detailed analysis of how there may be assignment by implication, see *Scamell*, pp. 102–106. While the latter point is open to doubt, practitioners can only safely rely on the complete chain of assignments.
[43] See Treitel, *Contract* (9th ed.) p. 596–7 for the formal rules governing assignments under s. 136. In the rare cases where a chain of express assignments have to be relied upon, the important point for the practitioner is to give written notice of the assignment before action is brought; notice to the covenantor in some other way (*e.g.* by discovery in the action) has been held not to be good enough; see Treitel, above, at 597.

or by statute), he will be unable to enforce the covenant apparently in his favour.

(b) This is because of the "before and after" problem. This manifests itself in two ways, depending on the order and form of the conveyance from the common vendor who took and imposed the covenants. Commonly, an estate is developed by sales of individual plots and the vendor takes a covenant from the purchaser of each plot, for the benefit of the vendor's unsold land, to the effect that the purchaser will comply with a set of covenants designed to preserve the appearance and amenity of the estate. (See Appendix 6; plan 1).

This produces a series of conveyances or transfers, each diminishing the land of the covenantee vendor, until by the last disposition there is none left. This situation produces the two problems referred to below.

Problem No. 1

8–28 The intending plaintiff's title is derived from a conveyance by the common vendor which is earlier than the potential defendant's title derived from the same vendor.

Example

(See Appendix 6: plan I)

The common vendor (V) sells the Chesney Wold estate imposing covenants on each transfer for the remainder of that estate belonging to the vendor. A's predecessor acquires title from V on January 1, 1990. B's predecessor acquires title from V on March 1, 1990. A wishes to sue B for breach of covenant by B on his land. C also wishes to sue B, having acquired title on November 1, 1989.

The problem

A's covenant is with V made on January 1, 1990 and the benefit is annexed to V's land at that date. But on March 1, 1990 V did not own A's land and B covenanted only with V for the benefit of the remainder of the estate.

Unless the covenant is expressed to have been made with and for the benefit of those who have already bought and not just V, B can say that the covenant was not with anyone other than V, and was not made with A.[44]

The irony in this situation (described as "Gilbertian" by Stamp J. in *Re Jeff's Transfer* is that B can sue A for breaches of covenant on A's land. This is because B has the benefit of the covenant A gave V which was annexed to the remainder of the Chesney Wold estate on January 1, 1990, and part of which was bought by B on March 1,

[44] Law of Property Act 1925, s. 56 may be thought to be a way round this problem in the sense that the section extends the scope of the benefit of the covenant to the earlier purchaser. But A is not within the ambit of any covenant given by B to V; see Chap. 6, para. 6–07 above.

1990. C, who took title from V on November 1, 1989, cannot sue A or B, but may be sued by either of A or B.

Problem No. 2

8–29 This problem is less often encountered than problem No. 1, and is caused by the failure of the common vendor to annex the benefit of the covenants being imposed when the estate is being sold off to each and every part of that estate, or to have express assignments of the benefit. In view of the decision in *Federated Homes* (see paragraph 8–16 above) it is unlikely that this problem will emerge in the case of post-1925 covenants, since they will be presumed (in the absence of words to the contrary) to be annexed to each and every part of the covenantee vendor's estate by Law of Property Act 1925, s. 78 and as a general principle of construction.[45]

Example

See Appendix 6, plan I

As in problem No. 1 above, V is selling off the Chesney Wold Estate, but the forms of conveyance of each plot do not annex the benefit of the covenant to each and every part of the remainder of the unsold estate. There are no express assignments. A's predecessor acquired his title from V on March 1, 1990. B's predecessor acquired his title from V on January 1, 1990. A wishes to sue B for breach of covenant on B's land.

The problem

A cannot sue B because B's covenant was given to V for the benefit of the whole of the Chesney Wold estate unsold on January 1, 1990, and not just the part A acquired on March 1. The benefit of B's covenant is not, therefore, annexed to A's land and in the absence of a chain of assignments of the benefit of the covenant from V to A, A cannot enforce against B. By a twist of the same irony which arises in problem No. 1, B cannot sue A for the reasons stated under that heading.

(c) The two problems show that dates in the order of conveyances and their form are going to be of critical significance in many cases. Without the "right" order of sales off, or forms of annexation, or assignments, it may be possible to enforce against an earlier purchaser, but not a later one. But the same, later, purchaser can enforce against the earlier purchaser.[46] But in some cases (*e.g.* under problem No. 2) neither can enforce.

(d) The difficulty can be at its most acute where the potential defendant's title is, historically, the last sale off by the common vendor. All the

[45] See *Allen v. Veranne Builders* [1988] N.P.C. 11 and *Robin v. Berkeley Homes* at n. 35 above; and see r. 8 at para. 8–15 above.

[46] See the observations of Stamp J. in *Re Jeff's Transfer* [1966] 1 W.L.R. 841 at 847–8, referred to by Goff J. in *Page v. King's Parade Properties Ltd* (1967) 20 P.&C.R. 710 at 718.

potential plaintiffs will, therefore, be prior and there can have been no land retained by the common vendor to which the covenant could have been annexed. The covenants given by the owner of the last plot cannot be enforced by the prior plot owners.[47]

(e) It should be apparent at this stage that in view of the importance of the order of sales off by the original common vendor, if the plaintiff is to enforce without knowing that order, he takes the risk that until service of the defence, he may be ignorant of the order. It should be possible to discover at an earlier stage whether the defendant's title is derived from an earlier or later sale off, by examining the defendant's register of title at H.M. Land Registry. The detective work and the use of a master plan referred to at paragraph 8–06 above will be required. This should refer to the covenant imposed by the common vendor and the date of the conveyance imposing it will tell the plaintiff whether it is before (bad news) or after (good news) the defendant. If the title is unregistered then it is a wise precaution to seek early disclosure of the potential defendant's title; the latter can hardly object in view of the fact that if the title deduced shows an earlier sale off that will be an end of the action, and if later, such title would have had to be deduced as part of the discovery in the action in any case. The same point is also true to the extent that the form of words in the conveyance imposing the covenants, or the presence or absence of assignments will indicate whether there is an additional problem is establishing that the potential plaintiff has the benefit of the covenants at all.

Enter—the scheme of development

8–30 The scheme of development is designed to avoid these problems and difficulties of enforcement. Where a scheme exists, all owners of plots within the scheme can enforce and be enforced against, irrespective of the order in which the common vendor sold those plots and irrespective of the formalities regarding annexation and assignment of the benefit of covenants.

A word of caution: schemes of development are rare.

It is tempting to see schemes of development around every corner when examining titles of building estates. In fact they are rare beasts and are far less encountered than might be supposed.

What is required for a valid scheme of development?

The requirements are:

8–31 (i) Both the plaintiff and defendant derive title from a *common vendor*.

[47] See the "last man out" scenario at para. 7–06 above.

(ii) Prior to selling the land to which the plaintiff and defendant are entitled, the common vendor laid out the estate (or a defined portion of it) for sale in *lots*, subject to *restrictions intended to be imposed on all the lots*. Those *restrictions*, although they may vary in details as to particular lots, *are consistent* and consistent only with some general scheme of development.

(iii) The restrictions are intended by the common vendor to be and are *for the benefit of all the lots intended to be sold*, whether or not they are also intended to be and are for the benefit of other land retained by the common vendor.

(iv) That both the plaintiff and defendant (or their predecessors in title) purchased their lots from the common vendor on the footing that the restrictions subject to which the purchases were made were *to enure for the benefit of the other lots* included in the general scheme, whether or not they were to enure for the benefit of other lands retained by the vendor.[48]

In many cases the existence of a scheme will be obvious, at least where it is well established that such a scheme affects properties within a given area. In addition, the registered title of a plot owner may contain an entry (usually in standard form) referring to the fact that the land in the title falls within the area covered by a building scheme constituted by a conveyance of given date. The policy of H.M. Land Registry is to enter notice of such schemes on the titles affected where they are established.[49] HMLR records and titles are kept in such a way that on first registration of a plot within the area of a scheme, that even will "trigger" the making of the appropriate entry.

8–32 Whether a scheme of development exists or not is a question of fact to be determined from the terms of the titles and the relevant circumstances surrounding the sales by the common vendor to the various purchasers. Thus, where there is a question as to the existence of a scheme the burden lies on the party seeking to establish it as a matter of fact within the principles set out at paragraph 8–31 above.[50]

Where the existence of a scheme is not clearly established, the following points should be considered when examining whether the four main elements set out at paragraph 8–31 are satisfied.

(i) Is there any doubt as to the common vendor test being satisfied?

- it may not matter if during the course of the sales under the

[48] These four sub-headings are taken from the words of Parker J. in *Elliston v. Reacher* [1908] 2 Ch. 374 at 384. His classification was described by Browne-Wilkinson V.-C. as the "*locus classicus*" in *Allen v. Veranne Builders* (1988 N.P.C. 11). It is equally the case that the modern approach has been to discern the existence of a scheme from the "wider rule" which forms the basis of such schemes, which is itself founded on the intention of the parties that the various purchasers are to have rights inter se; see *Baxter v. Four Oaks Properties Ltd* [1965] Ch. 816 and *Re Dolphin's Conveyance* [1970] Ch. 654 at 663 *per* Stamp J.

[49] See *Ruoff & Roper*, para. 35–24 for the practice.

[50] *Jamaica Mutual Life Assurance Society v. Hillsborough Ltd* [1989] 1 W.L.R. 1101.

scheme, the identity of the "common" vendor changes;[51]
- the identity of the common vendor may be a matter of inference from the title.[52]

(ii) Is the area of the scheme defined, and how is it defined?

- consider the use of maps; clear evidence of the land to which the scheme relates is essential;[53] (See Appendix 6, plan II).
- local knowledge may assist in explaining plans;[54]
- are there solicitors with knowledge of the extent of the area?[55]

(iii) What evidence is there of prior lotting?

- recent authority suggest that this is not essential.[56]

(iv) There must be evidence that it was intended that the purchasers of the lots are to have mutual rights and obligations. "Reciprocity of obligations between purchasers of different plots is essential".[57]

- lack of uniformity in the covenants is fatal to a scheme; some variation may be acceptable within a scheme (*e.g.* in a mixed scheme user covenants may vary) but unless there is substantial uniformity the essential ingredient of uniformity will be missing.[58]

Problem areas in schemes of development

8–33 Within the rules which apply to schemes of development there are areas where problems arise in practice. These are:

(i) Sub-schemes.

(ii) The sub-division of lots after the original sale.

(iii) The effect on the scheme of the unity of ownership of plots.

(iv) The existence of the power to waive and vary the covenants.

(v) Problems of non-registration of covenants within a scheme.

(vi) Changes in the neighbourhood and the effect of acquiescence in breaches.

Dealing with each in turn:

[51] As it did in *Re Dolphin's Conveyance* above at n. 48.
[52] As it was in *Re Elm Avenue* [1984] 1 W.L.R. 1398 at 1406.
[53] *Jamaica Mutual Life Assurance Society v. Hillsborough Ltd* above at n. 50.
[54] As did the solicitor's clerk in *Page v. King's Parade Properties Ltd* (1967) 20 P.&C.R. 710, when dealing with the Marine Park Estate at Bognor Regis.
[55] As were the solicitors acting for the plaintiffs in *Allen v. Veranne Builders Ltd* who had extensive knowledge of the conveyancing history of the Winderness Estate near Sevenoaks in Kent.
[56] See *Baxter v. Four Oaks*; *Re Dolphin*, above at n. 48.
[57] *Jamaica Mutual Life v. Hillsborough Ltd*, above, at 1106 *per* Lord Jauncey.
[58] See *Kingsbury v. Anderson* (1979) 40 P.&C.R. 136; *Emile Elias & Co. Ltd v. Pine Groves Ltd* (1993) 66 P.&C.R. 1, for examples of where the uniformity was lacking.

(i) Sub-schemes

8–34 These arise where, for example, A and B as two plot owners agree a set of covenants between themselves to replace the scheme covenants. These covenants will not affect the ability of the other plot owners to enforce the scheme against A and B, and vice versa. But A and B cannot enforce the head scheme between themselves.[59] Sub-schemes are sometimes found to have arisen where the common vendor sells more than one plot to a purchaser (A) who then sells off each plot separately to B, C and D, imposing covenants on each of B, C and D. The head scheme covenants into which A entered with the common vendor cannot be enforced by B, C or D between themselves. But B, C and D can enforce the covenants each entered into with A, assuming that the benefit can be shown to be enforceable on the usual principles; *e.g.* section 78. The head scheme may still be enforceable by persons neighbouring B, C and D's land against any of them in view of A's covenants with the common vendor.

(ii) Sub-division of plots

8–35 In many estates which were developed in the spacious days prior to the last War, and particularly at the turn of the century, the acreage devoted to each house plot was, by modern standards, generous. There is often a later subdivision of the lot. Alternatively, A may acquire two or more lots from the common vendor, and then sell them on as individual lots: see above. In both instances the authorities suggest that, in the absence of an intention expressed at the time of division (*e.g.* by the creation of a sub-scheme) the scheme will operate so as to bind and allow the enforcement of it by and against all the sub-purchasers.[60]

(iii) Unity of ownership of plots and subsequent severance

8–36 While there is unity of ownership (sometimes referred to a "unity of seisin") the covenants are unenforceable by virtue of the fact that the owner of the united plots can hardly sue himself in respect of his activity on one of the plots he owns. When the ownership is divided up the covenants become enforceable again.[61]

(iv) The power to waive and vary the covenants

8–37 There is a conflict in the authorities as to whether the insertion of such a power is consistent with the existence of a scheme, or whether the existence of such a power is such as to negative the concept of mutuality. The modern view seems to be that the existence of such a power will not prevent a scheme

[59] *Knight v. Simmonds* [1896] 1 Ch. 653, explained by Megarry J. in *Brunner v. Greenslade* [1971] Ch. 993 at 1001.

[60] See *Brunner v. Greenslade*, above, approved by the Privy Council in *Texaco Antilles Ltd v. Kernochan* [1973] A.C. 609 at 626 *per* Lord Cross.

[61] See *Texaco Antilles Ltd v. Kernochan* above. The position is different where no scheme of development exists; see, *Re Tiltwood* [1978] Ch. 269, referred to at Chap. 13, below.

from existing.[62] There is a subsidiary point which is whether the power to waive, or vary (or give consent in certain cases) must be exercised by the named vendor, or may be exercised by his successors and assigns.[63] It may also be the case that the vendor, if a company, is defunct. In that case it may be necessary to consider applying to the Bona Vacantia department of the Treasury Solicitor for consent, assuming it is not possible to restore the vendor company under chapter VI of the Companies Act 1985.

(v) Problems of non-registration of covenants in schemes

8–38 As explained in Chapter 4 above, in the case of registered and unregistered land, for a restrictive covenant created after 1925 to be enforceable against the defined classes of successors in title to the original covenantor, it must be registered in accordance with the rules set out in that Chapter.

Covenants taken and imposed in the context of a scheme of development are required to be registered in exactly the same way. But unlike covenants taken to protect one piece of land, or in a no-scheme world, the failure to register post-1925 covenants in a scheme can lead to rather more damaging consequences. In essence, the failure to ensure registration will cause gaps to arise in the ability of plot owners to enforce, thereby weakening the overall effect of the scheme; the term "haphazard islands of immunity" comes to mind.[64]

(vi) Changes in the neighbourhood and the effect of acquiescence in breaches

8–39 It would seem that there would have to be a radical failure to have observed the scheme for covenants in it to be unenforceable, and whilst acquiescence may affect the remedy, it would not follow that such conduct would lead a Court to find the covenants unenforceable as such.[65]

At an early stage in considering the "unity" of the scheme, evidence should be prepared to test how far the scheme is, or is not intact. Quite apart from planning records and visual records and the Ordnance plan, the use of transparent overlays will show, one way or the other, how far the original scheme has been observed. These can be a dramatic demonstration in many cases of how piecemeal departures over a large area of the original scheme has destroyed the unity of it. It is always going to be a matter of fact and degree how far departures from the scheme will affect the Court's willingness to grant injunctive relief. It is suggested that in cases where there is clear

[62] See *Re Wembley Park Estate Co. Ltd's Transfer* [1968] Ch. 491, for a collection of older authority on the subject, and see *Re Elm Avenue*, above, *Allen v. Veranne Builders Ltd*, above, and *Re Bromor's Application* (1995) 70 P.&C.R. 569, for more modern authority in support of the view that such a power does not negate a scheme. In practice the existence of such a power is just one matter to be looked at in the context of the whole in deciding whether a scheme exists.

[63] If there are no words in the relevant deed to include successors and assigns, the power would appear to be personal to the vendor; *Bell v. Norman C. Ashton* (1956) 7 P.&C.R. 359. See Chap. 14, para. 14–10, below.

[64] The words used by Megarry J. in *Brunner v. Greenslade*, above. For an example of the effect of a failure to register see *Freer v. Unwins* [1976] Ch. 288, and see *Emmet*, para. 19.043 for a discussion of this problem.

[65] See *Knight v. Simmonds*, above; *Bell v. Norman C. Ashton Ltd*, above; *Chatsworth Estates v. Fewell* [1931] 1 Ch. 224; *Robins Ltd v. Berkeley Homes* [1996] E.G.C.S. 75.

evidence of a departure from the scheme, declarations as to non-enforceability may be an option under Law of Property Act 1925, section 84(2) (see Chapter 16 below) and the Lands tribunal may be more willing to modify or discharge under section 84(1) than in cases where the scheme is still tightly enforced and intact.

Chapter 9

ENFORCEMENT OF COVENANTS BY A SUCCESSOR OF THE ORIGINAL COVENANTEE AGAINST A SUCCESSOR OF THE ORIGINAL COVENANTOR: MAKING BOTH THE BENEFIT AND THE BURDEN OF THE COVENANT RUN

9–01 This Chapter looks at the enforceability of covenants between successors to the original parties, not only as regards the benefit of the covenant, but also as regards the burden.

Summary

9–02 In cases where enforcement of restrictive covenants is by and against successors in title to the original parties, the rules which apply to the passing of the benefit and of the burden of the covenant have to be complied with. In essence this chapter pulls together the rules in the last two chapters.

The situation

9–03 A successor of the original covenantee wishes to enforce against a successor of the original covenantor.

The general rule

(a) The plaintiff must show that he has *the benefit* of the covenant in accordance with the rules set out in Chapter 8 above.

(b) He must also show that the potential defendant is *liable* in that the covenant is:

- valid and binding in accordance with the rules in Chapter 4; and
- enforceable against him in accordance with the rules in Chapter 7.

As this situation is often the most commonly encountered when covenants are being enforced the checklist below, which also summarises the rules for validity and enforcement, can be used. The flowchart at pages 6–7 will also assist.

CHECKLIST

9–04

(a) Is the covenant binding on the potential defendant as a properly registered covenant (or one to which the doctrine of notice applies?). (Chapter 4).

(b) Is the covenant restrictive, not being purely personal, and was it taken to protect the covenantee's retained land? (Chapters 3 and 7).

(c) Does the covenant satisfy the presumption that it benefits land owned by the potential plaintiff? (Chapter 7).

(d) Can the potential plaintiff show that he has the benefit of the covenant by any of the methods set out in Chapter 8? In particular can he show that he has the benefit under Law of Property Act 1925, s. 78?

(e) If the parties' properties are not within a scheme of development are there problems with the order in which the parties' predecessors' titles were conveyed by the common vendor? If the plaintiff's title is derived from a conveyance from that vendor which is earlier than the defendant's title, the plaintiff may be unable to enforce, unless the words of the covenant extend to prior purchasers from the common vendor. Is the potential defendant "the last man out", for if he is and in the absence of a scheme, there was no land retained by the common vendor when the defendant's predecessor purchased and gave covenants? (Chapters 7 and 8).

(f) Is this a case where special statutory rules apply which allow the benefit to be enforced even though no land is retained? (Chapter 10, below).
(Refer also to the checklist at pages 8 and 9 if necessary).

CHAPTER 10

RESTRICTIVE COVENANTS AND PUBLIC AUTHORITIES

10–01 This Chapter considers the special rules which apply to restrictive covenants which are created by public authorities acting under statutory powers.

INTRODUCTION

10–02 Special rules govern the enforceability of covenants and other agreements of a similar nature entered into by local and other public authorities, and other bodies with powers derived from statute.

The aim of these special rules is to avoid the problems inherent in enforcing restrictive covenants which private law poses. The principal problem being the inability of a successor of the covenantee to enforce if it possesses no interest in land capable of benefiting from the covenant.[1] The other difficulty, but lying outside the field of restrictive covenants, is that of the general inability of successors in title to enforce *positive* covenants. Although the subject of positive covenants is outside the scope of this book, it is mentioned if only to demonstrate how Parliament can legislate to overcome the shortcomings of common law and equity, albeit in a limited context.

It should be relatively easy to spot where these special rules apply. The deeds or agreements in which the covenants are contained will invariably be made expressly under the statutory authority conferring the power to make them. The purpose of this chapter is to identify the statutory provisions which specify the manner in which covenants entered into under them are enforceable.

THE SCHEME OF THE LEGISLATION

10–03 In view of the need to allow enforcement where the covenantee (*i.e.* in these instances the public authority) has retained no land capable of benefiting from the covenant and a successor to that authority is the enforcing party, Parliament has adopted two methods to allow such enforcement, each based on a "fiction".

[1] See Chap. 7, para. 7–05 above

The first is to assume that the authority/covenantee has adjacent land and that the covenant is taken for the benefit of it.

The second is to deem successors to be the original covenantor for the purposes of enforcement.

In some instances the statute incorporates both fictions, or adopts a further variant which treats the ability to enforce positive covenants as if they were negative.

THE LEGISLATION

10–04 This divides itself into three broad categories:

(i) Agreements made with local planning authorities under the Town & Country Planning Act 1990 and its predecessors.

(ii) Agreements made with local and other public authorities for the purpose of enabling those authorities to carry out their statutory functions, *e.g.* in respect of roads or housing.

(iii) Agreements made with other bodies where specific statutory provisions allowing enforcement apply.

It will be a matter of construction of the statute as to whether the general law is applicable (so that the covenant may be unenforceable for the reasons summarised in paragraph 10–02 above), or whether the statute creates a statutory scheme which may be enforced without the restrictions of the general law.[2]

The legislation is set out in paragraph 10–06 below. But before coming to it, there is one area which can affect the ability to enforce and that is the question whether the covenant taken is within the powers of the body imposing it. Is the covenant *ultra vires*?

A NOTE ON *ultra vires*

10–05 One of the spectres which occasionally appears in the context of bodies upon which limited powers are conferred is that of the limit of those powers. In the particular context of restrictive covenants, this means that the body may not impose restrictions which conflict with the purpose for which the acquisition is made.[3]

But the effect of the rule may be less draconian by virtue of:

[2] See *Peabody Donation Fund v. London Residuary Body* (1987) 55 P.&C.R. 355 for an example of how a statute may be construed so as to give effect to conditions entered into under the Act as part of a statutory scheme.

[3] See *Ayr Harbour Trustees v. Oswald* (1883) 8 App. Cas. 623; *Re South Eastern Railway Co. & Wiffin's Contract* [1907] 2 Ch. 366; *Stourcliffe Estates Co. Ltd v. Bournemouth Corp.* [1910] 2 Ch. 12; *Re Heywood's Conveyance* [1938] 2 All E.R. 230; *Earl of Leicester v. Wells-next-the-Sea U.D.C.* [1973] Ch. 110.

(a) The principle expressed in the authorities that the covenant will not be *ultra vires* and therefore will be binding even if that covenant prevents the covenantor from exercising other statutory powers in respect of the same land.[4]

(b) The wide power conferred by Local Government Act 1972, section 123 giving principal councils power to dispose of land held by them in any manner they wish (subject to the restrictions set out in that section).[5] In practice the width of this power will prevent an *ultra vires* argument being available where covenants are being imposed on disposal.

Finally, the existence of a covenant to use land acquired by a public authority for certain statutory purposes will not prevent that authority from using the land for other statutory purposes at a future date. It may then be open to the authority to consider exercising its powers to pay compensation in respect of any breach under Town & Country Planning Act 1990, s. 237 or to apply to release or modify under Law of Property Act 1925, s. 84.[6]

The legislation

10–06 *Section 106 of the Town & Country Planning Act 1990.*[7]

For the full treatment of this section reference should be made to Volume 2 of the *Encyclopedia of Planning* and Volume 5 for DOE Circular 1/97.

In the context of the enforceability of covenants entered into under this section, the following points should be noted:

- as a generic class "section 106 agreements" will be readily identifiable by virtue of the fact that they will declare on their face the authority under which they are made.
- the current terms of section 106 have been in force since October 25, 1991 and, therefore, only agreements entered into after that date are

[4] See *Stourcliffe Estates v. Bournemouth Corp.*, above, where the covenant against the erection of certain structures validly prevented the construction of public lavatories under statutory authority, whilst not interfering with the main purpose of the acquisition of land as a public park. See also *Cadogan v. Royal Brompton Hospital National Health Trust* [1996] 2 E.G.L.R. 115, where the covenant restricted the use of the site to one type of hospital and *Thames Water Utilities v. Oxford City Council* [1998] E.G.C.S. 133 where the use of a football stadium in breach of covenant was not authorised by section 237 of the Town and Country Planning Act 1990. (See Chap. 12, below).

[5] This power extends to those "principal councils" defined by s. 270(1) of the 1972 Act, being county, borough, district and London borough councils and is also extended to include joint authorities in London and elsewhere and police authorities; see s. 146A of the 1972 Act.

[6] See *Marten v. Flight Refuelling* [1962] Ch. 115 at 151–3; *Earl of Leicester v. Wells-next-the-Sea U.D.C.*, above, at 127; see Chapter 12, below, as to the exercise of powers under s. 237 and related legislation.

[7] Printed at Appendix 2, below.

caught by its terms. By subsection 3 any person deriving title from the original covenantor will be bound.[8]

- the immediate predecessor of the present version of section 106, which will apply to agreements entered into after August 14, 1990 but before October 25, 1991 was different in that subsection 3 included the "fiction" of the notionally adjacent land, which the agreement benefited. In view of the terms of the subsection there appears to be an irrebutable presumption that the "notional" adjacent land is capable of being benefited by the agreement.[9]

- the statutory predecessors of section 106 of the 1990 Act were:

Town & Country Planning Act 1971, s. 52 in force from April 1, 1972
Town & Country Planning Act 1962, s. 37 in force from April 1, 1963
Town & Country Planning Act 1947, s. 25 in force from July 1, 1948
Town & Country Planning Act 1932, s. 34 in force from April 1, 1933
Agreements made under these statutes during the period for which they were in force will still be encountered and as regards enforcement, the principles are the same as under the original terms of section 106. Each incorporates the "fiction" of adjacent and benefited land.

Other legislation[10]

Of general application: **10–07**

- Highways Act 1980, s. 35
- Wildlife & Countryside Act 1981, s. 39
- Local Government (Miscellaneous Provisions) Act 1982, s. 33
- Pastoral Measure 1983, s. 62

Of more specific application:

- National Trust Act 1937, s. 8 and the restriction imposed on applications under Law of Property Act 1925, s. 84 by National Trust Act 1971, s. 27
- Green Belt (London & Home Counties) Act 1938, s. 22
- City of London (Various Powers) Act 1960, s. 33

[8] For the definition of a person deriving title see s.336(8) of the 1990 Act. This would not appear to include a squatter in view of the fact that his title arises in spite of the title of the dispossessed (paper) owner. There appears to be no authority where a squatter as "successor" to a covenantor has been the subject of proceedings to enforce a s. 106 Agreement. Would a local planning authority in those circumstances have to show the existence of land capable of being benefited by the terms of the covenant in the agreement according to private law principles? *Re Nisbet & Pott's Contract* [1906] 1 Ch. 386 decided that a squatter can be made liable upon covenants affecting the land in respect of which he is in possession.

[9] See *Gee v. National Trust* [1966] 1 W.L.R. 170. That case concerned s. 8 of the National Trust Act 1937. Lord Denning M.R. favoured this approach, but the other members of the Court of Appeal reserved their opinions on it.

[10] Printed at Appendix 2.

- Leasehold Reform Act 1967, s. 19 and the Leasehold Reform Housing and Urban Development Act 1993, Pt IV.
- National Parks and Access to the Countryside Act 1949, s. 16
- Countryside Act 1968, s. 15
- Greater London Council (General Powers) Act 1974, s. 16
- Ancient Monuments and Archaeological Areas Act 1979, s. 17
- Housing Act 1985, s. 609

Registration of agreements with local authorities

10–08 Section 1 of the Local Land Charges Act 1975 makes provision for the registration of prohibitions or restrictions on the use of land binding on successive owners of the land affected.

Section 1 applies to those covenants imposed by local authorities, Ministers of the Crown, or Government departments. It also applies to those covenants which are expressly made local land charges by the legislation conferring power on the body concerned to enter into them. (For example, Town & Country Planning Act 1990, s. 106(11).

Excluded from the class of local land charges are those covenants entered into by a public body which are taken for the benefit of land owned by it: section 2 thereof. These have to be protected by registration in the usual way.[11]

10–09 Failure to register a local land charge which is properly registrable has the following consequences:

(a) *Covenants entered into before August 1, 1977*
If unregistered, void against a purchaser for money or money's worth of a legal estate in the land affected.[12]

(b) *Covenants entered into on or after August 1, 1977*
If unregistered, enforceable, but a purchaser for valuable consideration who has made a search of the local land charges register and has a "clear" certificate, has a compensation claim against the registering authority.[13]

There are, however, some covenants which must be registrable to be enforceable, in which case the statutory provision to that effect overrides section 10.[14]

10–10 In respect of post-August 1, 1977 covenants which are *not* registered as local

[11] See Chap. 4 above.
[12] Land Charges Act 1925, s. 15(1). See *MHLG v. Sharp* [1970] 2 Q.B. 223 for an instance of the effect of an erroneous clear search under that Act.
[13] Local Land Charges Act 1975, s. 10. Note the definition of "purchaser" in subs. 3(a) and the definition of the time by which the search has to be made by subs. 3(b). Note also s. 11 of that Act as regards claims made by mortgagees and other limited owners. August 1, 1977 was the commencement date of the Act. See *Emmet*, para. 10.058 for the compensation provisions.
[14] See, for example Leasehold Reform Act 1967, s. 19, printed at Appendix 2.

land charges, does it matter whether the title to the land affected is either registered, or unregistered?

It should not in practice matter for the following reasons.

(a) *Unregistered land*
Enforceability will depend upon whether a bona fide purchaser for value has notice, or not.

(b) *Registered land*
The same principle should apply. Even though the class of overriding interests includes "rights under local land charges unless and until registered or protected on the register in the prescribed manner" (Land Registration Act 1925, s. 80(1)(i)), the mere status as an overriding interest does not affect the inherent quality of a covenant as an equitable interest, and enforceability will still depend on notice.

SUMMARY

10–11 Provided the body imposing the covenant under statutory authority is within its powers, a covenant so imposed will have its own special force.

The problems of enforcement of private covenants which are present where either no land has been retained by the covenantee, or as between successors in title, are avoided.

In any case where covenants are imposed by statute, regard must be had to the statute, not only for the manner in which the covenant is to be regarded as enforceable, but also as to whether such a covenant is to be protected as a local land charge, or in some other way.

In most cases the covenants imposed by statute will be registrable as local land charges. Even if they are unregistered, they will be enforceable against a bona fide purchaser for value with notice if created after August 1, 1977.

CHAPTER 11

ACQUISITION OF LAND FOR PUBLIC PURPOSES AND THE EFFECT ON RESTRICTIVE COVENANTS

11–01 This Chapter looks at the relationship between the acquisition of land by public authorities and restrictive covenants on that land or neighbouring land.

INTRODUCTION

11–02 There are two issues which arise in practice where land, which is subject to restrictive covenants, has been acquired under compulsory powers, whether invoked, or by voluntary agreement.[1]

These are:

(a) What is the effect of the acquisition upon the covenant?

(b) What, if any, relief can the covenantee obtain in respect of a breach of the covenant? What is the effect of any claim for relief on the covenant?

In addition there are two further questions which arise in this context, namely:

(a) What is the effect on a restrictive covenant to which the land is subject of a sale onwards by the acquiring authority of the land compulsorily acquired?

(b) What powers do local authorities have to override covenants in respect of land acquired or appropriated by them for planning purposes?[2]

[1] Note the important point that the principles will apply whether the acquisition is by exercise of the statutory powers, or by voluntary agreement. *Kirby v. School Board for Harrogate* [1896] 1 Ch. 437. See Local Government Act 1972, s. 120 for powers of local authorities to acquire land by agreement under compulsory powers. Care should also be taken to examine the Act under which the power to acquire is being exercised to ascertain on what basis compensation is payable and whether Compulsory Purchase Act 1965, s. 10 applies even where the acquisition is by agreement. (For example, see Telecommunications Act 1984, s. 40).

[2] See Chap. 12, below.

The effect of the acquisition upon the covenant

11–03 The rule is that the covenant continues in existence as a burden on the land acquired. It is not discharged, or overridden.[3]

What relief can the covenantee obtain?

11–04 The rule is that the covenantee cannot obtain relief which would prevent the statutory purpose being carried out for which the acquisition took place. Nor can the covenantee obtain damages.

The only remedy for the covenantee is to claim compensation under Compulsory Purchase Act 1965, s. 10 for "injurious affection".[4] An injunction will not lie to restrain a breach if that would interfere with the purpose for which the land is being used under the statute for which it was acquired. However, if compliance with the covenant will not interfere with the discharge of the statutory body's functions, an injunction may lie to enforce. For example an obligation to submit plans for consent prior to building may be enforceable by injunction.[5]

It may be appropriate for the covenantee to establish by means of a declaration under Law of Property Act, s. 84(2) whether or not he has the title to sue for that relief, if there is doubt as to whether the benefit of the covenant is vested in him.[6]

In what circumstances will a claim lie for injurious affection where the carrying out of the statutory purpose has broken the covenant?

The covenantee must show:

11–05

(a) that what is being done would be a breach of covenant (but for the protection of the statutory acquisition);

(b) that he has the benefit of the covenant, *i.e.* the ability to sue;

(c) that damage has already occurred; prospective loss would appear not to be within the scope of "injurious affection". Damage means diminution in the value of the land and does not allow a "ransom" element.[7]

[3] See *Re 6, 8, 10 and 12 Elm Avenue New Milton, ex p. New Forest D.C.* [1984] 1 W.L.R. 1398 at 1405 *per* Scott J., and the earlier authorities cited therein.

[4] *Brown v. Heathlands Mental Health National Health Service Trust* [1996] 1 All E.R. 133 at 136 *per* Chadwick J. This authority conveniently collects the earlier authorities on this question. See also *Cadogan v. Royal Brompton Hospital National Health Trust* [1996] 2 E.G.L.R. 115 and *Thames Water Utilities Ltd v. Oxford City Council* [1998] E.G.C.S. 133. See also n. 1, above. For the nature of a claim for "injurious affection" and its scope see *Halsbury's Laws of England* (4th ed.) vol. 8(1), paras 353–358.

[5] *Cadogan v. Royal Brompton Hospital NHS Trust*, above.

[6] See Chap. 16, below, for applications under s. 84(2).

[7] *Wrotham Park Settled Estates v. Hertsmere B.C.* [1993] 2 E.G.L.R. 15.

FOR WHAT LOSS IS COMPENSATION GIVEN?

11–06 The compensation payable under section 10 will extend to injurious affection resulting from:

(a) the execution of the works carried out by the acquiring authority, *e.g.* building works on the adjacent (burdened) land, and, potentially,

(b) the use of the land or the works for the purposes for which it was acquired.[8]

WHAT IS THE EFFECT OF A CLAIM UNDER SECTION 10 UPON THE COVENANT?

11–07 There appears to be no decided authority on this question.

The view expressed by one text book is that a claim under section 10 will extinguish the covenant.[9]

> Another makes the distinction between those cases where compensation has been awarded under section 10 on a "permanent" non-compliance basis and those where the non-compliance is temporary.[10] It is hard to see where the distinction between these two forms of compensation lies.

If compensation is awarded for the breach, that would seem to put an end to the enforceability of the covenant; at least while the statutory purpose for which compensation is made is being carried out. In most cases that would be regarded as putting an end to the right to enforce the covenant. But the covenant does not cease to exist merely because it is unenforceable.[11]

In view of the uncertain nature of this area of the law, in an attempt to give some guidance to the practitioner encountering it, the following points may assist:

[8] *Brown v. Heathlands Mental Health NHS Trust*, above, at 139 *per* Chadwick J. However, this part of the decision does not sit easily with the authority of *Wrotham Park v. Hertsmere BC*, above, which was not cited in *Brown*. In *Thames Water Utilities Ltd v. Oxford City Council* [1998] E.G.C.S. 133, H.H. Judge Rich Q.C. (sitting as a Judge of the High Court) declined to follow the reasoning of Chadwick J. in *Brown* and held that compensation under s. 10 could not be recovered for the use of land or the works. Until the Court of Appeal gives a ruling there are, at the time of writing, two inconsistent High Court decisions on this point.

[9] *Preston & Newsom*, para. 3–36, referring to *Ellis v. Rogers* (1885) 29 Ch. 661. That was a case where the land compulsorily acquired by a railway company was burdened by covenants and the plaintiff in the action had the benefit of an agreement that the railway company would grant leases over the land to the plaintiff. The plaintiff agreed to assign the benefit of the agreement to the defendant. The plaintiff and the defendant both (erroneously) thought that the effect of the compulsory acquisition was to free the land from the covenants. The *obiter* dictum of Kay J. at 666 is the nearest one gets to a statement that the effect of (what is now) a payment under s. 10 is to free the land from the burden of those covenants. The Court of Appeal held that as a matter of title, the existence of the covenants prevented the plaintiff from enforcing the contract.

[10] *Scamell*, p. 200.

[11] The covenant may be regarded as suspended in such a case; see *Bird v. Eggleton* (1885) 29 Ch. D. 1012.

(a) If the covenantee has already received compensation under section 10 for the effect of the injurious affection and the statutory purpose is *still* being carried out by the acquiring authority, in practical terms it cannot be possible for the covenantee to claim "second time round" for the same injury.[12]

(b) The same principle expressed under (a) should apply if the acquiring authority transfers the land to a third party.

(c) If the acquiring authority carries out a *different* activity which amounts to a breach of covenant, it may be possible to argue that the covenant is still effective to allow a section 10 claim.

(d) If the different activity is carried out by a successor to the acquiring authority it would seem that the covenant is fully enforceable in the sense that all civil law remedies will be available.[13]

Sales onwards and other transfers by the acquiring authority

11–08 It may well be that the acquiring authority has decided that the land acquired is surplus to requirements. One of two things will usually happen.

(a) There will be a sale to a third party (invariably after the land has been offered back to the original owner from whom it was acquired).[14] Sales by a local authority may be under Local Government Act 1972, s. 123, or under Town & Country Planning Act 1990, s. 233 where land has been held for planning purposes.

(b) There will be an exercise of the power to appropriate the land for any purpose for which the land may be acquired, if the land is vested in a local authority, under Local Government Act 1972, s. 122, or if held for planning purposes, under Town & Country Planning Act 1990, s. 232.

11–09 If (a) occurs there seems no reason why the covenant should not continue to be fully enforceable with all the usual civil law remedies at the covenantee's disposal.

However, by virtue of Local Government Act 1972, s. 131(1)(a), sales under section 123 cannot be made in breach of a covenant against alienation, although a sale which required the purchaser to carry out works in breach of covenant would be permitted under that section, albeit without prejudice to the covenantor's remedies.[15] Sales under Town & Country Planning Act, s.

[12] The objection might be put on the footing of "issue estoppel", or simply on the basis that there would be double recovery for the same loss.
[13] *Marten v. Flight Refuelling* [1962] Ch. 115, at 152.
[14] See DOE Circular 6/93 para. 19 and circular letter of October 30, 1992, reproduced in Vol. 5 of the *Planning Encyclopedia*, para. 4–912/1; "the Crichel Down" rules.
[15] See *R. v. Westminster City Council, ex p. Leicester Square Coventry Street Association* (1989) 59 P.&C.R. 51. (Proposal to erect electricity substation under the Square).

233 are without restriction and, in any event, in respect of land held by local authorities for planning purposes, they have the power to override any covenant under section 237 of that Act. As to the scope of that power, see Chapter 12 below.

If (b) occurs section 122(4) of the 1972 Act will treat any work done on the land after the appropriation as if it had been done under the original authority to acquire and any claim by the covenantee will be limited to the remedy under Compulsory Purchase Act 1965, s. 10; *i.e.* injurious affection.[16]

THE EFFECT OF COMPULSORY ACQUISITION OF THE BENEFITED LAND

11–10 Finally, what is the effect of compulsory powers on a covenant which is annexed to the land (*i.e.* is there to benefit that land)?

(a) The general rule is that where powers are given to acquire land compulsorily, the whole of the land and the interests in it must be taken. This means that the acquiring authority will have the same right to enforce as any other owner. The rights of the original owner will be extinguished as part of the price paid for the land.[17]

(b) Some statutes confer specific power to take an interest in land without acquiring the freehold, but restrictive covenants do not appear to fall within the class of interests to be acquired.[18]

(c) There are some statutory provisions which confer power on the acquiring authority to acquire certain *adverse rights* over land only, including restrictive covenants. In such cases it is clear that the acquisition of the right (for which compensation is given) causes it to be extinguished.[19]

SUMMARY

11–11 Acquisition of land which is subject to restrictive covenants does not extinguish them but alters the way in which the person with the right to enforce that covenant can do so.

The normal civil remedies of an injunction or damages may not be available. Instead statutory compensation is awarded for injurious affection. In some cases an injunction may still lie if its grant will not hinder the carrying out of the purpose for which the land was acquired.

[16] This appears to be the case from the *obiter* dictum of Scott J. in *Re Elm Avenue*, above, at 1404. Chadwick J. declined to express a view on this point in *Brown*, above.

[17] See Compulsory Purchase Act 1965, s. 23(6). This principle must not be confused with the effect on the adjoining land of the covenantee (not being acquired) of a payment of compensation under s. 10 of that Act; see para. 11–06, above.

[18] See, *Halsbury's Laws*, vol. 8(1) and, see for example, Highways Act 1980, s. 250 giving power to acquire rights over land, but this does not appear to include a right in the nature of the benefit of a restrictive covenant.

[19] For example, Requisitioned Land and War Works Act 1945, ss. 33 and 39.

The effect of an award of compensation may or may not affect the future right to enforce the same covenant in respect of which that compensation was granted. The amount of compensation will reflect the effect of the carrying out of the work (in breach) on the land acquired and, potentially (*i.e.* with less certainty as a matter of law) the effect of the use (in breach) of the land acquired upon the land with the benefit of the covenant.

Where land is sold on by the acquiring authority the same principles will in most cases apply in respect of any activity carried out by the purchaser which is in breach of covenant.

Where land which has the benefit of a covenant is compulsorily acquired, the right to enforce will usually pass to the acquiring authority.

Chapter 12

THE POWER OF LOCAL AND OTHER AUTHORITIES TO OVERRIDE RESTRICTIVE COVENANTS

12–01 This Chapter considers the powers given to local authorities (and other bodies so empowered) to override restrictive covenants which would otherwise prevent the use of land vested in them.

Introduction

12–02 Whereas Chapter 11 has been concerned with the effect of the acquisition of land under compulsory purchase powers upon covenants which burden or benefit that land, or upon neighbouring land, in this chapter consideration is given to the ways in which local authorities (and other bodies) can avoid the effect of restrictive covenants which might otherwise act as a fetter on their plans for the use of the land vested in them. The effect of Town & Country Planning Act, s. 237 should not be overlooked. It is particularly important in the context of redevelopment by local authorities of land which they have acquired or appropriated for planning purposes, and may benefit those who derive title from such authorities.

The statutory provisions

These are:

12–03 Town & Country Planning Act 1990, s. 237[1]

This power is quite frequently encountered.

Requisitioned Land and War Works Act 1945, ss. 33–38

This power is much less frequently encountered.

[1] Printed at App. 2. Applicable to the wide class of "local authorities" defined by s. 336(1) and (10) of the 1990 Act.

SECTION 237 OF THE 1990 ACT

12–04

(a) This allows local authorities which own land acquired, or appropriated by them for planning purposes to override restrictions (and other rights) where development is carried out in accordance with planning permission.[2] It is important that if there is to be an appropriation, it is valid, and for planning purposes. An appropriation to sell land for redevelopment would not be a valid appropriation and section 237 could not, therefore, be invoked.[3] It is important to note that this power should only be exercised in cases where it is necessary to interfere with rights of third parties which are known to exist; in other words some care should be given to a consideration of the necessity in each case of exercising the power in view of the effect on third party rights. If care is not taken the exercise of the power will be judicially reviewable, with all the delay that will mean for the authority concerned and, no doubt, the developer waiting to pay a hefty price to the hard pressed authority.[4]

(b) Compensation is payable under subsection (4) on an "injurious affection" basis.[5]

(c) Significantly, the development which allows the covenant to be overridden may be a second or subsequent redevelopment.[6]

(d) The power to override extends to "a person deriving title under" the local authority, if the work for which the planning permission exists is done by that person. That is important in the context of sale by local authorities of land which they have acquired or appropriated for planning purposes, to third parties, who then have the benefit of the section, albeit subject to the obligation to pay compensation. (Subsection 5 places the liability on the local authority in those circumstances; no doubt a local authority will secure its position *vis-à-vis* the purchaser by means of an indemnity or bond). It appears from the *Barbers* case[7] that where the section is being used by a

[2] For the wide scope of "planning purposes" see ss. 226 and 246 of the 1990 Act.

[3] As occurred in *Sutton LBC v. Bolton* [1993] 2 E.G.L.R. 181.

[4] See *R. v. Leeds City Council, ex p. Leeds Industrial Co-operative Society* (1996) 73 P.&C.R. 70, for authority for the need for care in the exercise of the power and for an example of the problems created by judicial review applications which can hold up development plans.

[5] See Chap. 11 above. See *Ward v. Wychavon D.C.* (1986) 279 E.G. 77, for a claim under the predecessor to this section (1971 Act, s. 127) for loss arising from interference to an easement, which on the facts failed. But note that the acts of the authority causing the compensation to be payable must be ones which fall within s. 237. If they do not, no compensation will be payable; *Thames Water Utilities Ltd v. Oxford City Council* [1998] E.G.C.S. 133 and see Chap. 10, para. 10–05, above.

[6] *R. v. City of London Corporation, ex p. Barbers' Company* (1996) 95 L.G.R. 459.

[7] See n. 6 above. This is an important case in that a local authority, acting within the terms of planning permission, can use s. 237 to acquire adverse rights on any number of developments, of the same site and the benefit of that section can be used by developers who have acquired the site from such an authority, within the limit expressed in the text, itself based on the provisional view of Dyson J. expressed at p. 466 of the Report.

person deriving title from the local authority, the work done by it must be related in some way to the planning purpose for which the land was acquired or appropriated. Thus if land was acquired or appropriated for housing purposes, the person deriving title could not claim the benefit of section 237 if the redevelopment was for offices.

(e) Because compensation is based on an "injurious affection" measure, a "ransom" element will not be recoverable.[8]

SECTIONS 33–38 OF THE 1945 ACT

12–05 (a) Whilst not often encountered in practice, these provisions allow the Ministry of Defence the right to acquire a restrictive covenant which might otherwise hinder the use of land for MOD purposes.

(b) Compensation is payable in accordance with the Land Compensation Act 1961; s. 39 of the 1945 Act.

[8] See *Wrotham Park Settled Estates v. Hertsmere B.C.* [1993] 2 E.G.L.R. 15. See also *Thames Water Utilities Ltd v. Oxford City Council*, above, for authority on the limit to the amount recoverable and the heads of damage within an injurious affection claim. In that case the effect on the plaintiff's land of the subsequent use of the buildings and development authorised under s. 237 was not something which could be within a compensation claim under that section. See Chap. 11, para. 11–06 above. The law is developing here in an uncertain fashion and at present lacks clarity.

CHAPTER 13

EXTINGUISHING RESTRICTIVE COVENANTS

13–01 This Chapter examines the circumstances in which restrictive covenants will cease to be enforceable by virtue of their discharge or extinguishment.

INTRODUCTION

13–02 In some cases it should be obvious that a covenant has ceased to bind land; for example where there is an order of the Lands tribunal for the discharge of a covenant. In other cases it will be less obvious; for example where a breach of covenant has been acquiesced in for many years so that the covenant is, in effect, abandoned.

The following events will cause restrictive covenants to be regarded as discharged or extinguished.

(a) By the absence of a competent plaintiff or defendant.

(b) By express release.

(c) By operation of law.

(d) By an order of the court under Law of Property Act 1925, s. 84(2).

(e) By an order of the Lands Tribunal under Law of Property Act 1925, s. 84(1).

(f) By virtue of Town & Country Planning Act 1990, s. 237.

Taking each in turn, the principles are as follows.

THE ABSENCE OF A COMPETENT PLAINTIFF OR DEFENDANT

13–03 It is clear that when using the flowchart at pages 6 and 7 above, there will be circumstances where a restrictive covenant ceases to be enforceable as result of either the inability of the plaintiff to show that he has the benefit of the covenant, or the defendant's ability to show that he is free from its burden.

In cases of pre-1926 covenants it will often happen that where the benefit of covenants has not been expressly annexed, and where there is no chain of assignments, the benefit will be lost. No-one can sue on the covenants. In view of the effect of the *Federated Homes* decision on post-1925 covenants, that situation will be rarer in the case of such covenants.[1]

There are also cases where the covenants can be regarded as discharged because of the failure over many years to enforce the covenants. Thus where breaches have gone unchallenged, the covenants can be regarded as lost by abandonment.[2]

13–04 It sometimes occurs that a court refuses an injunction to enforce a restrictive covenant. If that happens, the covenant is *de facto* unenforceable—at least between the parties to the action. It is open to the victor to apply under Land Registration Act 1925, s. 50(3), if the title to the burdened land is registered, for the entry of the covenant to be cancelled (or for the order of refusal to be noted on the title). In practice H.M. Land Registry is reluctant to cancel the entry in view of the problem of satisfying itself that all those with the benefit are bound; see paragraph 13–06 below. It seems that the Land Charges Registry is likely to be as reluctant, and there is no equivalent provision in the Land Charges Act 1972, although Land Charges Rules 1974, r. 10 allows vacation where the charge can be shown to be "discharged . . . or of no effect". The problem with satisfying the Land Charges Registry is the same as that referred to above in cases of registered titles and at paragraph 13–06 below.[3]

By express release

13–05 It is open to the person having the benefit of a covenant to release it, expressly, in writing and ideally (to avoid any claim that there is a want of consideration) by deed.[4]

Whether or not a release is coupled with a variation it is important to remember to apply to alter the registration of the original covenant. If the title to the burdened land is registered the entry in the Charges Register has to be modified. If title to the burdened land is unregistered, there needs to be a new registration of a Class D(ii) land charge against the estate owner of the burdened land (where there is a modification), coupled with an application to vacate the old Land Charge. But see the next paragraph for the difficulty in securing a cancellation of the old registration.

13–06 Where the title to the burdened land is registered the policy of H.M. Land

[1] See Chap. 8, para. 8–16 above.

[2] See *Hepworth v. Pickles* [1900] 1 Ch. 108, applied in Att.-Gen. of *Hong Kong v. Fairfax Ltd* [1997] 1 W.L.R. 149.

[3] Land Charges Act 1972, s. 1(6) permits vacation pursuant to an order of the court, but that requires the court to be satisfied that all potentially able to enforce the covenant are before the court in an action where an injunction is refused, or where the court has made an order under s. 84(2).

[4] As to writing which is required for "interests in land" see Law of Property Act 1925, s. 53(1)(a). The benefit of a restrictive covenant is such an interest: *LSWR v. Gomm* (1882) 20 Ch.D. 562 at 581. As to the formalities governing deeds see Law of Property (Misc. Prov.) Act 1989, s. 1.

Registry is normally to note the deed of release on the register and not to cancel the original entry.

This is because the Registry takes the view that it is difficult in the vast majority of cases to show that all those with the benefit of the original covenant have been party to the release or modification.[5] The same view is taken by the Land Charge Registry at Plymouth when dealing with applications to cancel the old land charge registration.

It is obvious that any release or modification will only be effective if all those who are known to have the benefit of the covenants which are the subject of it are parties.

A deed will not be required where all those entitled to the benefit of the covenant have (expressly or impliedly) by their acts or omissions agreed to the discharge or modification of the covenant and the Lands Tribunal so orders under Law of Property Act 1925, s. 84(1)(b).[6]

By operation of law

13–07 Where the whole of the burdened and the whole of the benefited land become vested in one person who then owns the freehold of the two parcels (free from any leasehold or other interest which might be entitled to enforce covenants which ran for the benefit of one of the parcels and bound the other) the covenant which benefited and burdened the respective parcels comes to an end, and will not be revived on a subsequent severance unless recreated by the common owner.[7] The unification of the freehold ownership in the two parcels of land is sometimes referred to as "unity of seisin".

Where only part of the freehold of the burdened land becomes vested in the freehold owner of the whole of the benefited land (free from any third party right to enforce) the extinguishment of the covenant is confined to the part of the burdened land which is vested in the common owner. He can still enforce against that part of the burdened land not vested in him.[8] Unless recreated on a division, the covenants are, therefore, extinguished as to those parts in common ownership.[9] There is no automatic revival on severance.

Where part of the benefited land and the whole or part of the burdened land come into common freehold ownership (free from any third party right to enforce), the same result occurs as under the previous paragraph. In other words, as to those parts where burden and benefit are united, there is extinguishment without automatic revival on severance. As to those parts where there is no unity the covenants remain in force.[10]

13–08 Where a scheme of development applies there is extinguishment on unity of ownership (in accordance with the rules stated above), but there is an automatic revival on severance, unless:

[5] For the Registry's practice see *Ruoff & Roper*, para. 35–25.

[6] See Chap. 16 below.

[7] *Texaco Antilles v. Kernochan* [1973] A.C. 609.

[8] *Cryer v. Scott Bros. (Sunbury) Ltd* (1986) 55 P.&C.R. 183 at 188.

[9] *Re Tiltwood* [1978] Ch. 269.

[10] *Re Tiltwood*, above.

(a) The entirety of the land subject to the scheme comes into common ownership. This is an unlikely event.

(b) Where the parties to the severance agree that the scheme covenants are no longer to apply and agree to enter into new covenants, thereby creating a sub-scheme.[11]

(c) Where there is some other reason to conclude that the original covenants are not to be regarded as having revived, even if there is nothing in any conveyance severing the formerly united properties. One example is where during the unity of seisin a breach of the scheme covenant is committed on one of the plots. The plot is then sold and the breach continued by the new owner. The person who retains the other plot cannot, it seems, sue the new owner for breach even though the owners of other plots (not affected by the unity of seisin) could sue to enforce the scheme covenants. The rationale for this example of the exception to the usual rule in scheme covenants appears to be based on the ground that it would be a derogation from the grant of the vendor to sue his purchaser for breach of a covenant of which the vendor had himself been in breach. Whether this is the rationale, or whether some other ground could be used to justify the rule (*e.g.* estoppel), it is the case that where there are circumstances which indicate that the scheme covenants are not to apply, they will not be revived where there is a severance of the formerly united properties.[12]

WHAT IS RE-CREATION?

13–09 In cases of unity of seisin followed by severance, other than where schemes of development are involved, what is required to re-create the covenant?

An express affirmation or confirmation of the covenants should ideally be used to ensure revival. In the conveyance or transfer reference should be made to the original covenants, the fact of unity of seisin and the fact that it is intended that the covenants (formerly extinguished) are intended by the parties to be revived.

A suggested form of words in the operative part of any conveyance or transfer to avoid any doubt is:

> "The parties intend that the covenants referred to at clause [] are hereby expressly confirmed to be binding between the parties as if they had never been extinguished and to the intent that the benefit and burden thereof shall run with and bind the land so expressed to be benefited and burdened in accordance with the terms of [the instrument originally imposing the covenants]"[13]

[11] See Chap. 8, para. 8–34 above and *Knight v. Simmonds* [1896] 1 Ch. 653.

[12] See *Texaco Antilles Ltd v. Kernochan*, above, at 625, *per* Lord Cross, and at 626, affirming *Brunner v. Greenslade* [1971] Ch. 993, on the general rule applicable to revival of scheme covenants on severance.

[13] See Appendix 7 at A7–05, below, for further drafting suggestions.

It is debatable whether either a mere assignment of the benefit (where the common owner is disposing of the benefited land), or a mere expression that the burdened land is conveyed "subject to" the original covenants (when the burdened land is being disposed of by the common owner) will be sufficient to effect re-creation. Such expressions may not be an adequate indication of an intention to re-create.

OTHER MEANS BY WHICH COVENANTS ARE EXTINGUISHED

By an order of the court under Law of Property Act 1925, s. 84(2) **13–10**

See Chapter 15 below for the manner in which land may be freed on restrictive covenants under this provision.

By an order of the Lands tribunal under Law of Property Act 1925, s. 84(1)

See Chapter 16 below for the manner in which this jurisdiction is exercised.

By the exercise of powers under Town & Country Planning Act 1990, s. 237

See Chapter 12 above for the operation of this section.

Where a Court has refused an injunction and all parties capable of enforcing the covenant are before the Court **13–11**

As explained at paragraph 13–04 above, it is possible to ask for the notice of the entry of the covenant on the register of title or the land charge entry to be cancelled or vacated, following the court's refusal to enforce a covenant, but as explained there and at paragraph 13–06 above, there may be difficulties in proving that all persons with the benefit are bound. If it is so possible, there is no reason why the covenant should not be regarded as at an end.

Where statutory provisions or orders under statutory powers override the covenant **13–12**

For example:

(a) Orders of the county court under Housing Act 1985, s. 610 allowing subdivision of houses, even if contrary to covenant.

(b) The terms of the Allotments Act 1950, s. 12 allowing the keeping of hens or rabbits on any land (*i.e.* not just allotments) and structures to house them, even if contrary to a covenant, other than by way of trade or business and provided no nuisance is committed.[14]

[14] Statutory provisions are at App. 2. The terms of s. 12 are a legacy of the Second World War and the campaign during it to encourage self-sufficiency in the provision of food; rabbits then being a cheap and easy way of providing part of the diet when meat was strictly rationed!

Note that there is no extinguishment where covenants are acquired as part of the acquisition of land under statutory powers; see Chap. 11, para. 11–03 above and paragraph 11–07 for the effect of a payment under Compulsory Purchase Act 1965, s. 10 which does not, it is thought, extinguish the covenant.

CHAPTER 14

THE CONSTRUCTION OF RESTRICTIVE COVENANTS

14–01 This Chapter looks at the principles of construction which apply to restrictive covenants and the way in which certain covenants are construed. The purpose of this chapter is not to provide a textbook on interpretation, but rather to highlight the main principles and some of the problems which the more commonly encountered covenants present.

GENERAL PRINCIPLES OF CONSTRUCTION

14–02 The construction of restrictive covenants is carried out by a court in the same way as with any other words which are intended to have a specific meaning in a document. As a general rule, the aim of the court is to ascertain the intention of the parties from the words used, considering those words in the light of the factual circumstances in which they appear; the last factor is sometimes referred to as the "factual matrix".

Recent authority suggests that the process of construction may require a wider search for the meaning of words and thus it may be permissible, within limits, to look at any evidence which would have affected the way in which the language of the document would have been understood by a reasonable man. The limits to such a process exclude previous negotiations and expressions of subjective intent; such evidence may only be admissible in an action to rectify.

14–03 If the words are clear their meaning should be plain by application of the principles set out above. Equally if the wrong words or grammar are used the court is not obliged to attribute to the parties an intention they could not have had.[1]

In the specific context of restrictive covenants the words used should make it plain that the purpose is to govern the use of land by means of a restriction. It may sometimes be less than obvious how that is to be achieved (*e.g.* in the

[1] For a full guide to interpretation see Lewison, *The Interpretation of Contracts*, (2nd ed.). For the "modern" approach see the House of Lords' decisions in *Mannai Investment Co. Ltd v. Eagle Star Life Assnce. Co. Ltd* [1997] A.C. 749 and *Investors Compensation Scheme Ltd v. West Bromwich Building Society* [1998] 1 All E.R. 98. The law is developing in this area and there is a degree of conflict over how far the approach of the House of Lords can or should be followed.

context of consents) but in most cases the problems of construction should be more easily resolved than in some other areas, such as commercial contracts.

SPECIFIC QUESTIONS OF CONSTRUCTION WHICH ARISE IN THE CONTEXT OF RESTRICTIVE COVENANTS

The following questions frequently arise.

14–04 *Are the words of the covenant aimed at protecting the land of the covenantee*

Do the words of covenant used affect the value of the land to be benefited, or amenity in the sense of "touching and concerning it" or are they aimed at protecting some other interest, such as trading interest only and protection from competition?[2]

- If of the former type, the covenant will have all the qualities of an equity binding the covenantor's land, the benefit of which is capable of running with the covenantee's land. If of the latter type, it may be binding only between the original parties.
- Certain types of covenant, such as tie covenants, or those directed at restrictions on the brand identity, or manufacturer of goods to be sold from land may be affected by the rules which make such covenants unenforceable, or void, either as an unreasonable restraint of trade, or as infringing Article 85 (and in some cases Article 86) of the E.C. Treaty. This is a complex and developing area of law where space does not permit a full analysis. However, the practitioner should be aware that such covenants may not be enforceable, or valid, between the original parties and successors. The present law appears to be that if land is already encumbered with such covenants and the purchaser acquires the land subject to them, the restraint of doctrine will not apply.[3] However, if the land is acquired and only later is the covenant imposed, the restraint of trade doctrine may apply and the reasonableness test will apply to that material covenant.[4] The distinctions are fine ones and may not be entirely logical. Moreover, in any case it is open to raise invalidity under Articles 85 and 86 of the E.C. Treaty, but in order to succeed on that ground it has to be proved that the covenant in question has a particular economic effect (*i.e.* the prevention, etc. of competition within the terms of Article 85) at the time when its validity is being considered. There is no automatic invalidity and in many cases a successful challenge to a "tie" covenant will require a mass of economic data concerning the trading methods of the covenantee (*e.g.* the brewery, or tyre manufacturer) and the effect of the covenant on the covenantor (*e.g.* the tenant of the pub, or the owner of the tyre-

[2] Restraint covenants of the type considered in *Esso Petroleum Co. v. Harper's Garage* [1968] A.C. 269, may be an example of the latter.

[3] See the *Esso Petroleum* case, above.

[4] See *Alec Lobb (Garages) Ltd v. Total Oil (GB) Ltd* [1985] 1 W.L.R. 173.

fitting bay).[5] It has yet to arise, but there is no reason in theory why a "tie" covenant could not be the subject of an application under Law of Property Act 1925, s. 84(1).

Are the words of the covenant truly restrictive?[6]

14–05 *Are the words sufficiently certain so as to be enforceable?*

- Covenants which affect "amenity" may be attacked for being too broad, although in general the court will try to give effect to the words used.[7]
- The "blue pencil" test may be used to remove those parts which are too uncertain.
- Where the uncertainty is clearly an error of drafting, the court may enforce the true intention of the covenant and ignore words in accordance with the "modern" approach to construction referred to at paragraph 14–02 above.

14–06 *Are there any limits on the scope of the persons who can sue or be sued on the covenants?*

- Are there words limiting the effect of Law of Property Act 1925, ss. 78 and 79 which would otherwise permit full enforcement of post-1925 covenants?[8]
- If the covenant was made before 1926 are there any indications that the covenant was purely personal, or in some other way limited to the original parties?

Is the original covenantor liable for the acts and omissions of subsequent owners and occupiers?

14–07

- The general rule is that where A covenants for himself, his executors, administrators and assigns that he will or will not do a particular act, A does not thereby covenant that he is to be liable for the acts of those persons. The words describing the class of persons after A's name are merely there to show that the covenant is to run with the land. Strictly speaking, in view of the terms of sections 78 and 79 of the Law of

[5] See *Passmore v. Morland plc* [1998] 4 All E.R. 468 and *Inntrepreneur v. Price* [1998] E.G.C.S. 167 for the way in which alleged infringement of Art. 85 is treated and *Gibbs Mew plc v. Gemmell* [1999] 01 E.G. 117, for the way in which alleged infringement of Art. 85 is treated. In this context block exemption under Art. 85 (*e.g.* Reg. 83/84 as to beer tie agreements) may be relevant. See Treitel, *Contact* (9th ed.,) pp. 412–435 for full treatment of the restraint of trade doctrine and *Practitioners' Handbook of European Law* (1998) Chap. 12 for a full treatment of Art. 85, and Art. 86, which too can be relevant in some cases of economic restraint.

[6] See Chap. 3 above.

[7] See *National Trust v. Midlands Electricity Board* [1952] Ch. 380, for an example of the court's refusal to enforce covenants which were directed at preserving the amenities of the Malvern Hills. Whether the same decision would be reached today is open to doubt.

[8] See Chap. 7, para. 7–10 and Chap. 8, para. 8–16 above.

Property Act 1925, those additional words are unnecessary after 1925, but in many cases they are still used and in respect of pre-1926 covenants those words are necessary and have the effect described in the last sentence.[9]

- But in some cases A may covenant in such a way as to effectively warrant performance of the covenant by his successors, *e.g.* by the use of the word "permit" considered at paragraph 14–18 below.
- Irrespective of the words of the covenant, A may be liable in tort where he transfers land to B in circumstances where he knows that B will use the land transferred in breach. This consequence may also follow such a transfer where a covenant is directed against a certain use of the land being permitted. A may be liable for permitting it even though it is B who has caused it.[10]
- Where the covenant contains an express provision excluding the liability of the covenantor after parting with all interest in or possession of the burdened land, that should put an end to the covenantor's liability. The scope of such a clause may, however, depend upon the terms of the covenants and what has been disposed of by the covenantor. If there is a disposal of the freehold and the covenants do not contain any warranty of performance by the covenantor, the clause may be regarded as unnecessary. If there is a warranty of performance in the covenants and the covenantor has merely given up possession of the land he may be liable for the acts of licensees. Further, if the covenants are in terms that a certain use is not to be permitted he may be liable for the acts of others if he has not disposed of all interest in the land. The solution to the problem of whether a clause excluding liability after disposal is effective is to look at (i) the provision limiting liability to determine its scope; (ii) the covenants themselves to see whether any warranty of performance is given (*e.g.* by the use of the words "permit" or "suffer"); and (iii) whether the covenantor has given up his freehold or merely possession.[11] Clearly a tightly worded clause will avoid liability on the disposal of *any* interest on the burdened land *and* on the giving up of possession of it.

Liability for the acts or omissions of earlier owners or occupiers.

14–08

- Unless the present owner has acquired the burdened land with notice of a registered[12] pending action or a writ or order affecting that land, he will not be liable for the acts or omissions of his predecessors. This

[9] *Powell v. Hemsley* [1909] 1 Ch. 680; the point did not arise on appeal at [1909] 2 Ch. 252.

[10] *Sefton v. Tophams* [1965] Ch. 1140, and see para. 14–18 below on the effect of the word "permit".

[11] See *Ives v. Brown*, unreported, March 6, 1997, CA for a case where the question of construction arose on the issue whether merely giving up possession (as opposed to disposing of the freehold) was enough to avoid liability.

[12] Registered in unregistered titles under Land Charges Act 1972, ss. 5 or 6, and in registered titles, under Land Registration Act 1925, s. 49.

rule appears to apply only to single breaches, *e.g.* a past breach as to user which has ceased.

- However, in some cases the breach may be in the nature of a continuing one which may render the present owner liable for the sins of his predecessor, *e.g.* the use of a building in breach of covenant which continues.
- It may be that the covenant is directed at a particular act (*e.g.* directing that only a particular class of building be erected) and there is some authority for saying that the person who acquires the land on which a building has been erected in breach is not liable by virtue of his mere acquisition. However he may be liable if he uses it in breach or if he participates in the breach by acquiring property (which is the source of the breach) in the course of construction.[13]
- The last distinction seems a fine one; it may be that a modern court would look at the question of whether the present owner was in breach more broadly, both as a matter of construction and as a matter of determining the nature of the breach. In many cases no modern purchaser will unwittingly acquire land where it is plain that some breach of covenant has occurred without the protection of an indemnity from the vendor or insurance. In such cases the construction of the covenant alleged to have been broken will be crucial in determining the risk.

The problems of consents.

Two problems emerge: **14–09**

(i) Who is to give consent?
(ii) Is there to be an implication (in the absence of express words) that consent is not to be unreasonably withheld?

Dealing with each question in turn

(i) Who is to give consent?

- In the absence of words indicating that the consent may be given by successors in title, the granting of consent has been regarded as personal to the original party.[14] This principle is one which can cause much difficulty. On the one hand, a wide construction of "the vendor" will admit successors as persons whose consent should be obtained. On the other hand, if the words are so limited in **14–10**

[13] *Powell v. Hemsley*, above at n. 9. *Wrotham Park Estate Co. Ltd v. Parkside Homes Ltd* [1974] 1 W.L.R. 798.

[14] See *Mayner v. Payne* [1914] 2 Ch. 555; *Bell v. Norman C. Ashton Ltd* (1956) 7 P.&C.R. 359; which are both examples of a narrow construction. In *Wrotham Park*, above, the parties conceded that the word "the vendor" meant his successors. In the context of *Mannai Investments* (see n. 1, above) it is frankly hard to believe that such a narrow view would now prevail. In *Hale v. Bellway Homes* [1998] E.G.C.S. 83, an opportunity arose to decide the point, but sadly the parties agreed to defer consideration of it, so the point remained undecided.

scope, why should a wider meaning be given? A modern court might well apply the principles set out at paragraph 14–02 above, in view of the commercial purpose behind such consent provisions, but on such authority on this point as there is, a narrow construction may prevail.

- Problems can arise in particular in the context of schemes of development where consents are required for the modification of scheme covenants, or for consents to works. The scheme may become unworkable if there is no-one whose consent can in practice be obtained, or if there is lengthy argument over whose consent is required.
- It will usually be sufficient to identify the owner for the time being of the unsold part of the original covenantee's land rather than have to approach his successors, as owners of the plots on the whole estate.[15] But even this point is not free from doubt. Even if the persons whose consent is required are numerous (as successors in title to the common vendor) there may be no reason why, as a matter of construction, their consents are not to be obtained.[16]
- Restrictions on the titles to registered land can sometimes be used to reinforce covenants, particularly where consents of third parties are required. They are more commonly used where positive obligations are imposed, but in any case care must be taken to ensure that there is going to be some means of obtaining a consent (thereby lifting the restriction) in the event that the named party is dead, or no longer in existence. In the latter class limited companies can be particularly dangerous in that once they are in liquidation or wound up or struck off it is can be a complex task to take steps to require the company to grant the consent.[17]
- The only solution to many of these problems may be declaration under Law of Property Act 1925, s. 84(2), or under the inherent jurisdiction of the Court; see Chap. 15, below.

(ii) Is there to be an implication of reasonableness in the giving of consent?

14–11

- Unless those who are required to consider whether or not to give consent have an existing duty to act in good faith, there will be an implied obligation not to withhold consent unreasonably.
- Where the consent required relates to a "general" matter (*e.g.* to a particular trade) there may be no implication as to reasonableness.
- However, where the consent is required for a specific matter (*e.g.* plans for a building) reasonableness will be required for otherwise business efficacy could not be given to such a condition if it was

[15] See *Everett v. Remington* [1892] 3 Ch. 148; *Cryer v. Scott Bros. (Sunbury) Ltd* (1986) 55 P.& C.R. 183.

[16] In *Hale v. Bellway Homes*, above, over 100 successors to the original vendor were, arguably, in a position to grant or withhold consent.

[17] See the precedents at App. 7 below and see Chap. 8, para. 8–37, above.

open to the covenantee to refuse consent to plans "which are free from any tenable objection."[18]

- It is obvious that where the terms of the instrument show that the implication is meant to be excluded (*e.g.* where some covenants in the same instrument are expressly qualified and others are not) the implication will not be made—unless there is clearly an error of drafting.[19]
- The Lands Tribunal has no jurisdiction to add the implication as to reasonableness, if not present, as that would amount to a rewriting of the original covenant.[20]
- It is open to question as to whether any liability can attach to the grantor of consent for the consequences of any wrongful delay or refusal of consent. Unlike the position under section 1 of the Landlord and Tenant Act 1988, there is no statutory duty on the grantor and it may be that the position here is the same as under the law of landlord and tenant prior to the commencement of that Act, where no liability for the consequences of delay or refusal lay on the landlord.[21]

QUESTIONS OF CONSTRUCTION WHICH ARISE FROM CERTAIN TYPES OF RESTRICTIVE COVENANT AND THE WORDS USED IN THEM

14–12 In this part of the chapter there is a selection of the words and phrases which appear to be the most frequently encountered in practice and which raise problems. It should be noted that following the application of the general principles set out at paragraph 14.1 above, the meaning of words must be dependant on their context and the circumstances in which they are found. To this extent, whilst it is tempting to use statutory definitions in some instances, such definitions can only be regarded as a starting point, if that.[22]

(a) Covenants directed against buildings and the like.

14–13 "building" denotes something enclosing an air space, and that is the true meaning in many cases. It can also mean

[18] *Per* Megarry V.-C. in *Clerical Medical and General Life Assurance Society v. Fanfare Properties*, unreported, 1981, cited in *Cryer v. Scott Bros (Sunbury) Ltd*, above.

[19] See *Hale v. Bellway Homes* [1998] E.G.C.S. 83. For other authority on the question of the implication of reasonableness see *Price v. Bouch* (1986) 53 P.&C.R. 257, and *King v. Bittlestone*, unreported, October 22, 1997, Blackburne J.

[20] *Re North's Application* (1997) 75 P.&C.R. 117.

[21] *Norwich Union v. Shopmoor* [1997] 1 W.L.R. 531 and *Footwear Corp. v. Amplight Properties* [1999] 1 W.L.R. 551 for the landlord and tenant position.

[22] For example, the definition in the Leasehold Reform Act 1967 s. 2(1) of "house" is designed to exclude flats, which by that Act were outside the enfranchisement legislation. For a collection of definitions against many of the words which appear below reference should be made to Stroud's *Judicial Dictionary*; although a note of caution in applying specific statutory definitions to such words in the context of restrictive covenants should be borne in mind when using Stroud.

hoardings and depending on the context, walls.[23] The definition has included a substantial brick barbecue,[24] a bay or bow window in advance of a house and a glazed lean-to.

"house" — denotes a permanent building for habitation. The word can include a building containing residential flats if no qualification is give to the word; as to which see "single" or "single private" dwelling house below.[25]

"dwelling house" — this may be more restrictive than "house", requiring personal habitation and excludes non-residential use. There may, however, be multiple occupation.[26]

"a single dwelling house" — this is even more restrictive than "dwelling house" used alone, for it prevents sub-division and multiple occupation.[27]

"a private dwelling house" — as in the last example, multiple occupation will be in breach.[28]

14–14 "a single private dwelling house" — the word "single" may define the use which may be made of the dwelling house (*e.g.* "to use any building erected on the land as a single private dwelling house") or it may define the number of dwelling houses which may be built on the land, *e.g.* not to use the property conveyed or any part of it for any purpose other than that of a single private dwelling house.[29] This latter type of covenant will prevent the erection of further dwelling houses where one is already built on the burdened land. There appears to be no authority on the question whether, if one house is built straddling two plots (each subject to a restriction limiting each plot to one house), a subdivision of one plot would allow the building of one house on the plot so sub-divided. The diagram below shows what is meant in practice. The answer (depending no doubt on the construction of the

[23] In *Urban Housing Co. v. Oxford City Council* [1940] Ch. 70 a wall was held not to be a building in the context of the covenants in that case.

[24] *Windsor Hotel (Newquay) v. Allan, The Times*, July 2, 1980.

[25] See *Kimber v. Admans* [1900] 1 Ch. 412.

[26] See *C&G Homes v. Secretary of State for Health* [1991] Ch. 365 for an example of where use of this word alone would have allowed multiple occupation of a house by persons in care. However, if stress is placed on the article "a" that may restrict the covenant and exclude multiple occupation; *Berton v. Alliance Economic Investment Co.* [1922] 1 K.B. 742.

[27] *Barton v. Keeble* [1928] Ch. 517.

[28] *Barton v. Keeble*, above. In C&G Homes v. Secretary of State for Health [1991] Ch. 365, it was held that the use of a house for persons in care was a breach of such a covenant, although it might not have been a breach if the covenant had been merely to use the property as a dwellinghouse.

[29] *Re Enderick's Conveyance* [1973] 1 All E.R. 843.

precise covenant in question) is that the erection of the additional house on that part of plot B which is sold off is a breach, in that the entirety of plot B has two houses on it even though it might be said in pure mathematical terms that there are one and half houses on it; that would still be a breach, being more than one.

The diagram shows how this problem arises in practice.

"structure" or "erection" — potentially wide in scope; wider than "building"; can include poles, fences and walls. Potentially this can include diving-board, grab-handles and other superstructures associated with outdoor swimming pools.[30]

"bungalow" — means a building where the walls, save the gables, are no higher than the ground floor and where the roof starts at a point not substantially higher than those walls.[31]

(b) Land use generally

14–15

"agricultural" purposes — statutory definitions are wide in their scope, *e.g.* Town & Country Planning Act 1990, s. 336(1); a similar definition in Agricultural Tenancies Act 1995, s. 38(1). Greenhouses used for trading purposes have been non-agricultural for rating purposes. It is possible for the words "agricultural land" to exclude a farmhouse with its garden in the context of inheritance tax.[32] The main point to watch when using covenants aimed at preserving an agricultural use is that the land or buildings which are being used for such a purpose are not themselves productive of nuisances or annoyances;

[30] For poles see *National Trust v. Midlands Electricity Board* [1952] Ch. 380; for walls and fences see *Urban Housing Co. v. Oxford City Council* [1940] Ch. 70 at 82. For "structure" see *Hobday v. Nicol* [1944] 1 All E.R. 302 and see the *OED* definition. For "erection" see *Long Eaton Recreation Grounds Co. Ltd v. Midland Railway* [1902] 2 K.B. 574; railway embankment.

[31] *Ward v. Paterson* [1929] 2 Ch. 396.

[32] See *Starke v. IRC* [1994] 1 W.L.R. 888.

see below for those words. In this context it is often useful to consider specific agricultural activities such as intensive pig rearing, or battery hen-houses, which may themselves be capable of creating a nuisance, and if they are to be proscribed, the covenant should be drawn to say so.[33]

"annoyance" or "nuisance" — words which include within their meaning a wide category of conduct. "Annoyance" may be wider then "nuisance".[34] Mere economic loss caused by reduced marketability of property will not amount to a "nuisance, annoyance, danger or detriment".[35] Under this head may also be brought the notion of an "offensive" use of the land; whether as part of a trade or business or some other use. It will be a question of fact whether what is being done is offensive in all the circumstances. How far the authorities in the nineteenth century are of much assistance is open to doubt. The modern test will invariably be one based on the nature of the locality and the environment generally in which the conduct occurs. A fried fish shop or takeaway in some parts of a town may not be offensive, whereas it may be in other parts of it. It is sometimes the case that the covenant is expressed so that it is for a third party to say whether in his opinion an annoyance, etc. has been caused. In such cases, whilst the third party is not acting in a judicial capacity, he must act bona fide in forming a view as to whether the act complained of has occurred.[36]

14–16 "trade or business" — there is a distinction between these two words. Trade is a wider word than business. In practice and ignoring some of the "Victorian" distinctions, it will be a question of fact and degree whether what is being done falls within either of those words. It is often the case that the words are found in conjunction with the obligation to use the property only as a private dwelling house. In such

[33] See *Jobson v. Record* (1998) 09 E.G. 148 for authority (in the context of the construction of an easement) that storage of cut timber (not grown on the land served by the easement) was not an agricultural purpose.

[34] *Ives v. Brown* [1919] 2 Ch. 314 at 321. In the case of nuisance covenants one has to prove private nuisance, being an unlawful interference with a person's use or enjoyment of land. That may be difficult to prove; see *Hunter v. Canary Wharf* [1997] A.C. 655 for an instance where no cause of action lay for interference with television reception.

[35] *C&G Homes v. Secretary of State for Health* [1991] Ch. 365.

[36] *Zetland v. Driver* [1939] Ch. 1. It is unlikely that a decision in such a case would be judicially reviewable, but it would be open to the person alleging breach to sue for an injunction restraining it and, if necessary for a declaration that the decision of the third party is ineffective; see *R. v. Disciplinary Committee of the Jockey Club, ex p. Aga Khan* [1993] 1 W.L.R. 909.

cases what may be done may well not amount to a trade, or even a business (*e.g.* using property as a charitable boarding institution) but will be a breach of the dwelling house covenant. Likewise payment may not be an essential ingredient of carrying on a business. But it will be for a trade to be carried on.[37]

"not to let the property for a [particular] trade" or "other than for [a particular trade]" — there must be a substantial degree of identity where a prohibited trade is threatened. Where a covenant is restricted to a certain trade by way of user it will be a question of fact whether the user falls within the permitted description.[38] Note the constraints of the law referred to at paragraph 14.2.1 above in the context of restraints of trade and the E.C. Treaty.

(c) *Covenants requiring the submission of plans*

14–17 "to submit plans of any proposed building or alteration" — this will be treated as a negative covenant and as an obligation not to build, etc. until plans, etc. are approved.[39] "Alteration" admits of a wide variety of meaning.[40]

"with the consent of the vendor and his successors" — see paragraph 14–09 above for the problems associated with consent provisions.

(d) *"permit" and "suffer"*

14–18 "permit" — means the giving of leave for an act to be done (or prevented) which the person permitting has power to cause to be done or prevent. "Permit" should only be used in covenants where the original covenantor has the power to control his successor. In ordinary sales of freeholds from A to B, A will have no control over B once A has sold up. But where used, the covenantor can be made liable for his successor's breach.[41] An answer to such a claim might be (as between successors to the original covenantor and covenantee) that a restrictive cov-

[37] For a recent consideration of this type of covenant see *C&G Homes v. Secretary of State for Health*, above at 380–384 *per* Nourse L.J. For a collection of authorities under the general heading of trade or business see *Preston & Newsom*, paras 6–23–6–26.

[38] *Rother v. Colchester Corporation* [1969] 1 W.L.R. 720. On the remedy for breach of a covenant to use for a certain trade see *Co-operative Insurance society Ltd v. Argyle Stores (Holdings) Ltd* [1998] A.C. 1, and see Chap. 15, para. 15–26, below.

[39] *Powell v. Hemsley* [1909] 1 Ch. 680. But note from that case the fact that if a breach of such a covenant occurs, a successor in title of the covenantor in breach will not be liable.

[40] See *Preston & Newsom*, para. 6–15 for a collection of authority; reference can also be made to authority in landlord and tenant cases on covenants in leases not to alter.

[41] See *Sefton v. Tophams* [1967] 1 A.C. 50.

enant cannot require the expenditure of money, so A can hardly be required to take action preventing the occurrence of a breach by B which A has allegedly permitted.

"suffer" — this may have a wider meaning than permit.[42] This may require the taking of legal proceedings to prevent the breach by the successor, notwithstanding the argument (at least as between successors to the original covenantor and covenantee) that the covenant should not require expenditure.[43]

(e) Breach "by association"

14–19 Where, for example, a covenant is directed against the use of land for a business, or where a specific use is proscribed, it may be possible to be in breach where use of the land is closely associated with the activity in the covenant, if what is being done could be said to fall within the words of the covenant. However, there must be something being done which on any reasonable view amounts to a breach. Thus, use of land for access to a business will not amount to use of that land as a business, and use of land as a landscaped area for a superstore will not amount to breach of a covenant against food retailing.[44]

(f) Covenants relating to rights of light

14–20 These covenants are sometimes encountered when consideration is being given to development in conurbations. They pose particular problems in view of the complexity of the law of light.[45] In the context of their existence as restrictive covenants the following short observations may assist in understanding their effect.

(i) Covenants may be imposed so as to prevent the acquisition of light by or against neighbouring properties. Depending upon the words used, if effective, they will prevent acquisition of a right to light by the principal means of implied acquisition, these being prescription under the Prescription Act 1832, or (outside the City of London) by the application of the doctrine of Lost Modern Grant. Some covenants allow development by the owner of the land with the benefit of the covenant without regard to interference with any light received by his neighbour, and subject to the covenant. Other covenants restricting

[42] *Barton v. Reed* [1932] 1 Ch. 362 at 375.

[43] See *Barton v. Reed*, above, and *Berton v. Alliance Economic Investment Co.* [1922] 1 K.B. 742. For a longer analysis of the effect of the words permit and suffer see *Preston & Newsom*, paras 6–61–6–76.

[44] See *Elliott v. Safeway Stores* [1985] 1 W.L.R. 1396; *Co-operative Retail Services Ltd v. Tesco Stores Ltd* (1998) 76 P.&C.R. 328, for examples of each occurrence.

[45] See Gale, *Easements*, Chap. 7 for the law of light.

building will also determine whether and if so, to what extent building is permitted within defined limits. Such covenants may be designed to protect rights of light so that any future building must conform to the restrictions in the covenant.

(ii) Covenants against building may be either restrictive, or permissive. If restrictive, that operates as a restrictive covenant and any breach is actionable. (*e.g.* a covenant that A is not to build more than 50 feet above a datum line; or that A is only to build within the terms of certain plans). A permissive deed is one where the covenant gives liberty to build to a certain height or within a certain envelope. In such a case any building which exceeds the permission will not be actionable as such. It will only be actionable if it can be shown that the excess is an actionable interference with the light enjoyed by the dominant owner.[46]

(iii) A covenant may restrict the covenantor's right to build, and may also allow the covenantee a right to build to any height (or only to a defined height), whether or not that interferes with the covenantor's enjoyment of light. Such a covenant is not only restrictive, but also prevents any acquisition of light by prescription under the Act (or by lost modern grant) by the covenantor's property.[47]

[46] See Gale, above, on what is and what is not an actionable interference with the easement of light.

[47] *Haynes v. King* [1893] 3 Ch. 439.

Chapter 15

LITIGATION AND RESTRICTIVE COVENANTS

15–01 The previous chapters of this book have been concerned with setting the scene for this chapter, which deals with the actions and remedies which relate to restrictive covenants. It is such proceedings which determine the meaning of a covenant, whether and how it can be enforced and what remedy lies for breach of it.

The chapter is divided into three parts.

Part I: Applications for a declaration under Law of Property Act 1925, s. 84(2) or for a declaration of right under the inherent jurisdiction of the Court.

Part II: Actions for an injunction.

Part III: Actions for damages, either at common law, or in lieu of an injunction.

Part I: Applications for a declaration under Law of Property Act 1925, s. 84(2)

15–02 The text of Law of Property Act 1925, s. 84(2) runs as follows:

> "The court shall have power on the application of any person interested—
> (a) to declare whether or not in any particular case any freehold land is, or would in any given event be, affected by a restriction imposed by any instrument; or
> (b) to declare what, upon the true construction of any instrument purporting to impose a restriction, is the nature and extent of the restriction thereby imposed and whether the same is, or would in any given event be, enforceable and if so by whom."

There are certain features as to the scope of section 84(2) which should be noted:

15–03

- The terms of section 84(2) are broad and provide a potentially useful means by which the validity or enforceability of covenants can be tested. In particular the jurisdiction allows covenants which are plainly unenforceable to be "cleared off". However, as will be seen below the difficulty in finding all those entitled to enforce may prove an expensive and time consuming business. Because the section operates *in rem*, (*i.e.* directly upon the property benefited by the covenant) the Court will require evidence that all those potentially affected have been notified of the intention to apply under section 84(2). The procedural steps required before a final hearing are off-putting in cases where the benefit of a covenant may be annexed to a wide or uncertain area. It is often the case that, rather than use section 84(2), insurance (see Chapter 18) will be considered a cheaper option, particularly where the time taken to complete an application under section 84(2) would be unacceptable to a developer. It may also be the case that in view of the decision in *Greenwich Healthcare NHS Trust v. London & Quadrant Housing Trust*,[1] a declaration of right under RSC, O. 15, r. 6, (CPR, Sched. 1) could be obtained as an alternative to potentially long-winded proceedings under section 84(2); this remedy is dealt with at paragraph 15–19 below.

- The section applies to leases granted for a term of over 40 years of which 25 years are expired: section 84(12).
- Covenants over land given for charitable and public purposes are within the scope of section 84(2).
- Covenants over Royal and other land within section 84(11) are within the scope of section 84(2).
- Covenants entered into under statutory authority are within the scope of section 84(2), even though they may not be within the scope of the Lands Tribunal's jurisdiction under section 84(1).[2]
- An Order under section 84(2) operates *in rem* by virtue of section 84(5); in effect it binds the land benefited by the restriction and all persons capable of being entitled to the benefit whether they are parties, or whether they have been informed of the proceedings or not. It is this provision which explains why such care has to be taken to identify all those with the benefit of the covenant.

When can section 84(2) be used?

15–04 (i) Where it is necessary to "clear off" restrictions which, on their face are unenforceable because:

(a) the benefit of the covenants (which are not annexed to the benefited land) has not been assigned;
(b) where the annexation of the benefit is to the whole of the benefited land rather than to each and every part of it;[3]

[1] [1998] 1 W.L.R. 1749.
[2] For example National Trust Act 1971, s. 27, in App. 2, below.
[3] This is unlikely to arise often since the dictum in *Federated Homes v. Mill Lodge Properties* [1980] 1 W.L.R. 594, to the effect that the benefit runs with each and every part of the benefited land; see Chap. 8, para. 8–15 above.

(c) where the benefited land cannot be ascertained;[4]
(d) where a scheme of development has been invalidly created;
(e) where some other point of construction of the covenant makes it doubtful that the covenant can be enforced:
(f) where notwithstanding the apparent unenforceability of the covenant (or the difficulties therein), insurance is not an option.

(ii) Where it is necessary to resolve some question of construction. For example:

- whether the giving of consent should be qualified by an implied term as to reasonableness, and if so, by whom it should be given.
- whether an activity would be in breach of the covenant.

15–05 (iii) Where it is necessary to resolve some question as to enforceability or construction even though the question is only likely (if at all) to arise at as future date or on future events which have yet to happen. This is an exception to the general rule that the Courts will not grant declarations on "hypothetical" questions. It is in the nature of the jurisdiction under section 84(2) that future questions may arise. For developers wanting an answer to the effect of covenants in given events to happen in the future, the jurisdiction is, therefore, potentially useful.[5]

Who can apply?

15–06 Section 84(2) states that "any person interested" can apply. That comprises a wide class of persons and will include:

- the owner of the freehold (or leasehold) burdened land
- the owner of the freehold (or leasehold) benefited land
- a mortgagee of any of the above
- a person contractually entitled to the burdened or benefited land[6]

How is the application to be made?

15–07

- By application in the Chancery Division of the High Court, either in London, or in the most convenient Chancery Registry outside London.[7]
- The relief sought will need to be tailored to the precise ground on which

[4] As in n. 3 above, this is unlikely to arise often since *Federated Homes* effected statutory annexation under Law of Property Act 1925, s. 78 in respect of post-1925 covenants. But the point may still arise in respect of pre-1926 covenants, as it did in *J. Sainsbury v. Enfield LBC* [1989] 1 W.L.R. 590, which was an application under s. 84(2).

[5] See para. 15–19 below as to the jurisdiction to grant declarations or right which may be an alternative to an application under s. 84(2) in appropriate cases.

[6] As in *J. Sainsbury v. Enfield LBC*, above.

[7] Under Pt. 8 of the CPR would appear to be appropriate, subject to the terms of any Practice Direction not promulgated at the time of writing.

the application is being made. There may also need to be relief by way of an order that the entries of the covenants at the Land Charges Registry, or on the titles of the affected properties, if registered, be vacated or in some other way dealt with so as to reflect any order made in the application.

- By counterclaim in proceedings to enforce by injunction; see paragraph 15.4.2 below.

Who should be the respondent?

- Anyone who has an arguable claim to the right to enforce the covenant, *e.g.* the original covenantee. It may be that such a person may take the view that he is not entitled to enforce—but initially at least such a person should be joined.[8] **15–08**

- Anyone who is an objector under the procedure set out below—even if at the stage of joining them it is unclear whether they have the right to enforce.

Defining who might be a respondent

15–09 As indicated at paragraph 15–03 above, one of the features of an application under section 84(2) is the need to ascertain who is entitled to enforce the covenant, and to ensure that if opposing, they can be heard at any hearing. In some cases the scope of such a class and the identity of its members may be limited and easy to define; in others it may be hard to define the class for a number of reasons, not the least of which may be the difficulty of identifying the land benefited by the covenant.

To this end, the practice has developed of sending a "circular" to all those potentially entitled to enforce with the aim of weeding out those who are not so entitled and those who do not oppose the application, leaving a "rump" of objectors who will be respondents to the summons.

As will be seen the task of preparing for the despatch of the circular, and its terms and the follow-up to it is not an easy one. In many cases the alternative of insurance may be far more attractive, or even a declaration under the inherent jurisdiction. But in other cases there may be no alternative to seeking relief under section 84(2) with all the preparation that it entails.

The "circular" and its preparation and use

15–10 The following steps should be taken to identify who should be respondents to the summons (in addition to the original covenantee if applicable).

[8] *Re Sunnyfield* [1932] 1 Ch. 79. That was an example of a case where the original covenantee took the view that it was not entitled to enforce the covenants.

Step I

15–11 Ascertain the full extent of the land which may have been capable of benefiting from the covenant. In effect this is the whole of the covenantee's land at the date of the instrument creating the covenant which is the subject of the application under section 84(2). If the application relates to a scheme of development the benefited land will include the whole of the estate subject to the scheme. If the covenant is annexed by reference to a plan that will make the task much easier. It is at this stage that the text of the original instrument does need to be examined in order to see how the benefit of the covenant has been annexed, or if not, by what means the benefit of the covenant is expressed to pass. In the latter case the area may be undefined, and it may be very difficult to see what land is capable of benefiting.

Step II

Try (as best one can) to ascertain who owns each and every part of the land identified at Step I. (Use, for example, index map searches, electoral roll, Kelly's *Directory*).

Step III

15–12 Send to each of the persons identified at Step II a form of letter ("the circular") which should state:

(a) The identity of the client's property and the covenants which are the subject of the application.

(b) What is proposed by way of development (for example) which would potentially be a breach of covenant. (If planning consent has been obtained, refer to that).

(c) That the client has been advised that the covenant is no longer enforceable (or has a certain meaning) which has led the client to consider making an application under Law of Property Act 1925, s. 84(2), for a declaration that the covenant is no longer enforceable (or has a certain meaning to the effect that the proposed development would not be a breach of it, as the case may be).

(d) That the addressee is asked to say whether he wishes to consent to an order being made in form requested in the proposed application, or if he wishes to object and thereby be a respondent to it. If the course of objection is proposed the addressee should be informed that he will in due course have to say on what basis he claims the right to enforce the covenant. That may have to be done by his solicitor and production of his title will be required. It is sometimes the practice to send a second letter to any objector (once the form expressing a lack of consent is received) asking for particulars of the manner in which the benefit is vested in the objector and disclosing the evidence of title on which that assertion is based.

(e) There should be enclosed with the letter:

- a copy of the draft application[9] and such other evidence as is relevant in support to enable the addressee to decide how he is to respond;
- a form of consent or objection with spare copies for co-owners.

(f) The addressee should be asked to identify any other person having an interest in the land at the address given, *e.g.* a tenant or a mortgagee.

(g) A time within which a response should be given and an invitation to take legal advice on the letter should be included; a s.a.e. is a tactful enclosure.

(A draft form is at A7–06).

Step IV

15–13 Having allowed for the response time to the initial letter, chasers and other letters to mortgagees, etc., it will be possible to say how the application should proceed and against whom. One of four situations will, probably, emerge.

(i) It is impossible to identify those who may be entitled to enforce from initial research and/or from the response to the circular.

(ii) All consent to the application.

(iii) None consent to the application.

(iv) Some do and some do not consent to the application, or at least some are silent.

Step V

15–14 Those who are to be respondents will be all those under (iii) and those objecting under (iv). If they are numerous and appear to have an identity of interest a representation order may be advisable under CPR, Sched. 2, incorporating RSC, O. 15.

Making the application

15–15 (i) you will need to put the affidavit in support of the application into final form. No affidavit can ever be the same as another, but some pointers as to contents are:

- exhibit the best evidence of the instrument imposing the covenant which is the subject of the application. In registered titles the pre-registration deeds may still be located, and the District Registry at which the register of title is maintained should have filed a copy of the instrument. It is sometimes unsafe to rely on what is on the register itself in view of the (unnoticed) errors that can occur in copying at first registration;

[9] After April 1999, an application under Pt 8 of the CPR would seem to be appropriate. See n. 7 above.

- a large scale plan to identify the burdened and (potentially) benefited land at the date the covenant was imposed; if a scheme covenant show the extent of the area covered by the scheme. The better the plan the clearer your case will be. Bad small scale photocopies with smudges and thick lines are no use!
- show the devolution of title to the respondents, so far as revealed, at this stage. It is this point which makes it desirable as early as possible to get the potential objectors to show their title in order to show how they claim the benefit of the covenant. The circular can make this request, but invariably such a request is only likely to produce results once solicitors are instructed on behalf of respondents. In many cases the production of title will show the absence of annexation or a scheme and the absence of a chain of assignment, thereby leading the respondent to concede that he is not entitled to object. Unless there has been progress on this aspect of the application at an early stage, the affidavit may be unable to state on what basis the respondents seek to assert the right to enforce;
- exhibit the circular, and all responses, if necessary explaining the research which went into the compilation of the list of addressees;
- where no responses have been received identify those cases, showing that the recorded delivery "advice of receipt" service has been used. Where inconclusive replies have been received, exhibit those. In each case it may be that further enquiries are being made to clarify whether there will or will not be objections, in which case say so.
- explain what is being proposed by way of development, etc., which causes the application to be made. If there is to be a declaration defining the nature and extent of the covenant say what is relied upon in support of the declaration sought.

(ii) Draw the originating summons in its final form, issue and serve on the respondents.

(iii) If there are no objections, or if there is no evidence as to who has the benefit of the covenant, you can make the application *ex parte*.

(iv) It may be necessary once the application is made and there are doubts over the right to enforce by any of the respondents to seek specific orders for the disclosure of title documents, *e.g.* where chains of assignment are being relied upon, where are the assignments?

Important points to remember about applications under section 84(2).

15–16

- it is easy to under-estimate the difficulties which this type of application can present. In applications based on the inability of anyone to enforce, the burden on the plaintiff is a heavy one. He must show that either there was no annexation of the benefit of the covenant (difficult since *Federated Homes* in respect of post-1925 covenants), or no chain of assignment of the benefit (a fact which may not be plain until titles are disclosed after the application is brought), or no effective scheme of development, or the fact that there is no land capable of being benefited by the covenant, or that by virtue of a failure to register, the covenant is not binding. The guiding rule is:

> "The Court ought to be clear that the property is not burdened by restrictions."[10]

This is the practical consequence of an Order made under the section operating *in rem*; see paragraph 15–03 above.[11] Hence the need for clear evidence in support of the application.

- Even where all that is being sought is a declaration as to construction, the plaintiff still has to satisfy the Court that all parties who have an interest in one or another of the forms of construction which could be put forward, are there to do so. In some cases it may be necessary for the representative of the "active" opponents to address the court at the hearing on behalf of the non-appearing (but not consenting) opponents to ensure that all views are known.[12]

- The circular and subsequent steps taken in response to it should be aimed at eliciting proof of entitlement, or lack of entitlement, to the benefit of the covenant which is the subject of the application. There is a danger in drafting a circular which merely asks for approval or disapproval of a particular development. An expression of approval in such a case will not be evidence of a lack of entitlement to the benefit and the applicant will therefore fail to obtain a declaration that certain covenants are not enforceable.[13]

Orders made under section 84(2)

15–17 Apart from the obvious form of the declaration which will be sought as to the enforceability or effect of the covenant, the Order may have to deal with the manner in which the burden of the covenant is protected by registration. The practice appears to be as follows:

- If the Order simply declares the construction of the covenant it seems unlikely that any change must be made to the registration, although it will be kept with the deeds (unregistered titles) and in registered titles it might be prudent to lodge a copy at the District Land Registry where the title to the burdened land is maintained and the Order may be noted

[10] *Per* Scott J. in *Re Elm Avenue New Milton* [1984] 1 W.L.R. 1398 at 1407. In that case the plaintiff had to show that there was no scheme of development affecting the land, which it failed to do on the evidence.
[11] For an example of the evidential difficulties see *Re Wembley Park Estate* [1968] Ch. 491.
[12] As occurred in *Re Tiltwood* [1978] Ch. 269.
[13] This is what seems to have gone wrong with the circular in *Re Elm Avenue*, above, although from the report it is not clear precisely why; see *per* Scott J. at 1407. The burden is on the applicant to "clear off" opponents by showing they do not have the benefit, and not that they are merely happy with the development proposed.

against that title. The latter course should be taken in the rare case where the benefit of the covenant is entered.

- If the Order is to the effect that the land is no longer affected by the covenant (*e.g.* because of unity of seisin) or if the Order is to the effect that there is no-one entitled to enforce the covenant, the ability to change the registration will depend upon whether all the burdened land was within the application, or was not.

- If all the burdened land is within the application and if the Court is satisfied that the land is no longer affected by the covenant, or no-one is entitled to enforce the covenant which is the subject of the application, or if all persons with the benefit consent, if the title is unregistered the Court can order vacation of the land charge protecting that covenant under Land Charges Act 1972, s. 1(6), or where the title to the burdened land is registered, modification of the register under Land Registration Act 1925, s. 50(3). As the order operates *in rem*, all titles which would (but for the order) have the benefit of the covenant are affected, so the Land Charges Registry and H.M. Land Registry will only vacate an entry where the Order is made in the circumstances set out at the start of this paragraph.

- If other land is still potentially bound, the owner of that land can still be bound and, therefore, vacation of the Land Charge protecting the burden of the covenant over that land will not be ordered. In registered titles there seems no reason why *as regards the title before the court* an order should not direct modification under either section 50(3) or rectification under section 82 of the Land Registration Act 1925.

Costs of applications under section 84(2)

15–18 Although the usual judicial discretion in matters of costs will apply in applications under section 84(2), because the aim of the applicant in bringing an application under section 84(2) is to "clean up" his title as regards the covenants upon it, which is for his benefit, a practice as to costs in such applications has developed which in simple terms means that the discretion will usually be exercised in the manner described below. No doubt there will be cases where circumstances will require the exercise of the discretion differently, but the practice appears to be as follows:

- The plaintiff will usually be expected to pay his own costs of the application;

- The plaintiff will usually have to pay the respondents' costs down to the time when they are able (on a full appreciation of the matter) to decide whether or not to oppose. If they oppose thereafter, unsuccessfully, they will bear their own costs thereafter—but will not be ordered to pay the plaintiff's costs. If they are successful in opposing, the plaintiff will pay the respondents' costs.[14]

- If the application succeeds on a novel point of law the plaintiff may be ordered to pay the respondents' costs of the application in its entirety.[15]
- There is sometimes a distinction drawn between the scale of costs to which the respondent may be entitled. The indemnity basis is usually chosen down to the time when the respondent had the opportunity to make a final assessment of merits; thereafter the standard basis is chosen. (See CPR, Pt 44, r. 44.4).

An action for a declaration of right

15–19

(a) Circumstances may arise where, for various reasons it is necessary to know whether a covenant is enforceable or not, and in particular whether an injunction will lie at the suit of any person potentially entitled to that remedy. The major difficulty in many cases is obtaining the right amount of knowledge to enable a decision to be taken as to whether a covenant is enforceable or not (and by means of an injunction in particular) is the difficulty in finding out who has the benefit of the covenant and thus who has the right to enforce. Furthermore, as has been pointed out above, the nature of an application under section 84(2) hardly endears itself to those where time is of the essence and development decisions depend upon the availability of borrowed money.

(b) There will be cases where it is possible to ascertain who has the benefit of the covenant and to avoid a period of damaging uncertainty, or a period which might put paid to the plans of a developer, or an unwarranted ransom demand, a declaration is required that specified persons are not entitled to enforce a covenant by means of an injunction or damages.

(c) Such cases will be rare, but there is no reason why the option of seeking a declaration of right should not be considered. In cases set out in (b) above, particularly where neither agreement nor objection is received from those entitled to the benefit, such a course may well be appropriate. However, the need to ascertain those who have the benefit of the covenant must be stressed. For unless all those so entitled are caught by any declaration the order will be useless; others not bound could still enforce, and the order does not operate in rem unlike an order under section 84(2).[16]

[14] *Re Jeffkins' Indentures* [1965] 1 W.L.R. 375.

[15] *Re Tiltwood* [1978] Ch. 269; but this is by no means automatic and there have been cases where this has not occurred.

[16] See *Greenwich Healthcare NHS Trust v. London and Quadrant Housing Trust* [1998] 1 W.L.R. 1749, where an application for a declaration that (*inter alia*) certain covenants were not enforceable by injunction, or by a claim for damages was granted in accordance with the principles set out above. The case is a useful one in respect of troublesome easements, for there is no jurisdiction to discharge or vary them, and declaratory relief may be the only way of protecting against latent objections to varying their terms.

Part II: Actions for an injunction

Introduction and preliminary steps

15–20 This is not a litigation handbook, and, therefore, some knowledge will be assumed as to civil litigation and the remedies of an injunction. The *White Book* and other guides can be used to fill the gaps where extra assistance is required. What is emphasised in Part II (and in Part III where damages are discussed) is the aspect of these remedies which have a particular bearing in the context of restrictive covenants.

15–21 Before contemplating bringing an action for an injunction ask yourself the following questions; it is all too easy to forget them in the hurly-burly of threatened litigation, and they are better asked at an early stage than later on when the costs penalties of changing course may be severe.

- If you are acting for the potential plaintiff, is he entitled to *the benefit* of the covenant by the means set out in Chapter 8? (Look at the summary of Rules at page 10 and the flowchart on pages 6–7).

- Whether you act for the potential plaintiff, or defendant (and this question may be more important if you act for the latter) is the defendant *bound* by the covenant? Is the covenant protected by registration if he is not the original covenantor? Is it a covenant where the burden runs? *e.g.* check that it is not a purely personal or trading covenant. Look at the summary to Chapter 4 at page 12.

- Has there been a *breach*, or what is threatened going to be a breach, and to what extent? A one inch incursion (even if measurable) into a "buildings free" zone may not be a very strong basis on which to launch expensive injunction proceedings. Look at Chapter 14 on construction of the words of the covenant. Is there any sense in seeking a declaration under section 84(2) or under the inherent jurisdiction, considered in Part I above?

- *How far has the potential defendant gone?* If he has gone too far in building in breach and your client has stood idly by, you will probably not get an injunction.

- *Can you afford to sue or defend?* This is not just a question of costs, but the question touches upon the *undertaking in damages* a plaintiff will have to give if he is to get an interim injunction (see 15–29 below) and the likely damages a defendant may have to pay if he is found liable in a case where damages are the remedy ordered by the court.

- *Can your client avoid litigation by other means?* Self help may be out, but what about arbitration, mediation, ADR and all the other modern (if not fashionable) alternatives to litigation?

General principles as to the grant of injunctions when enforcing restrictive covenants

15–22 (a) An injunction will be granted (almost) as a matter of course to restrain a breach of a restrictive covenant. In the older authorities the Court said that speaking generally, it had "no discretion" but to grant such relief, but the modern approach is for the Court to recognise that it has a discretion in the award of the remedy, whilst regarding such relief as the "natural" remedy for breach of a restrictive covenant. The discretion extends to the terms on which an injunction will be granted.[17]

(b) For an injunction to be granted it is not *necessary* for the plaintiff to prove pecuniary loss as a result of the actual or threatened breach, but it may be *desirable* to do so. Prima facie he is entitled to the remedy on proof of breach alone. However, in terms of whether damages in lieu of an injunction will be awarded, the question of loss will be relevant, and the modern approach to the exercise of the discretion will inevitably involve a consideration of the loss caused by breach.[18]

Specific factors which will hinder or prevent the grant of an injunction.

15–23 (a) Delay or acquiescence. Time is "of the essence" if not in legal then in factual terms when seeking injunctive relief. Varying degrees of delay and acquiescence will inevitably exist. At one end of the scale is permission openly granted to break the covenant, or allowing a breach in full knowledge of it, or years of delay in seeking to enforce the covenant. At the other end of the scale is conduct which is equivocal, or trivial in terms of time. Failing to object to planning applications for development potentially in breach may fall more into the latter than the former camp; although generalisations can hardly be drawn too far even from this example. Modern authorities show that the Court will look at all aspects of the parties' conduct before deciding whether such conduct disentitles the plaintiff from obtaining injunctive relief. The test of whether the plaintiff should or should not be so entitled by his conduct has been described as one which requires the question to be asked "would it be dishonest or unconscionable" for the plaintiff to enforce by means of an injunction?[19] Under this head may also be placed the various categories of estoppel which would prevent enforcement.

[17] For an example of the old approach, which must now be regarded with caution, see *Osborne v. Bradley* [1903] 2 Ch. 446, and for the modern approach to the exercise of the discretion, *Gafford v. A.H. Graham*, (1998) 77 P.&C.R. 73.

[18] See para. 15–4 below.

[19] See *Shaw v. Applegate* [1977] 1 W.L.R. 970 at 980; *Gafford v. A.H. Graham*, above. The latter authority decided that the defence of acquiescence is to be given equal weight in cases whether the plaintiff is suing to enforce the covenant at law as an original covenantee or in equity as a successor in title; for the distinction see Chap. 8, para. 8–04 above and paras 15–34 and 15–37, below.

(b) Past failures to enforce which have led to a change in the neighbourhood may have deprived covenants of their purpose and thereby lessened the prospect of injunctive relief being granted. The Court will not restrain a breach where little purpose would be served in specific enforcement.[20]

Applications by the defendant to stay the proceedings for an injunction

15–24 (a) The defendant, considering that he has a fair chance of applying to the Lands Tribunal for the discharge or modification of the covenant which is sought to be enforced, may apply for a stay of the injunction proceedings under Law of Property Act 1925, s. 84(9) and for the leave to apply to the Lands Tribunal under section 84(1) of that Act. (A classic instance of this is where a radical change in the neighbourhood has occurred).[21] But a defendant who wishes to take this course must undertake to proceed with his application to the Lands Tribunal forthwith and with due diligence, if not under a defined time table, and the plaintiff will be given liberty to apply to discharge such a stay if the defendant proves sluggish, or if for any other reason he needs to press on with the injunction. Each party will have to give an undertaking as to damages as a term of such a stay.[22] Bearing in mind the timescale of a fully contested application in the Lands Tribunal, and the potential exposure on the undertaking in damages, few defendants will want to stay the injunction proceedings by this route. Most will want to fight the injunction proceedings at the interlocutory stage, or settle on terms. This is particularly the case where the defendant is a developer.

(b) A defendant may wish to seek a declaration (by way of counterclaim in the injunction proceedings) under section 84(2) or under the inherent jurisdiction (see Part I above) as part of his defence if there is a live prior question on the effect, or enforceability of the covenant which the plaintiff seeks to enforce; it may well be that the determination of the issue raised under section 84(2) will require a stay of the injunction proceedings. In many cases the question of the effect or enforceability of the covenant can be raised without the need for such a formal step to be taken as such questions can be determined (at least as between the parties) by the Court in reaching a decision as to whether any remedy should be granted. Clearly if the covenant is unenforceable, or if the construction of it leads to the conclusion that there has been

[20] See *Robins v. Berkeley Homes* [1996] E.G.C.S 75 for a modern example of where this argument failed in respect of the Camden Park Estate, Chislehurst, Kent. See also, *Knight v. Simmonds* [1896] 2 Ch. 294; *Bell v. Norman C. Ashton Ltd* (1956) 7 P.&C.R. 359. Note the power to cancel entries of covenants where injunctions are refused referred to in Chap. 13, para. 13–04 above.

[21] For the precise grounds on which such an application to the Lands Tribunal would be made see Chap. 16, below.

[22] See *Hanning v. Gable-Jeffreys Properties* [1965] 1 W.L.R. 1390; *Shepherd Homes Ltd v. Sandham* [1971] Ch. 340 at 353.

no breach, the plaintiff will fail in his action for an injunction, if not damages.

What sort of injunction is needed?

15–25 There are two types of injunction which can be granted:

- *prohibitory*—being an injunction which restrains a breach which is either anticipated or threatened[23] (such as a building which is about to go up) or continuing and which is required to stop (*e.g.* trading in breach)
- *mandatory*—being an injunction which requires a positive act to be done by the defendant, such as the pulling down of a building.

The problems posed by breaches of covenant and the need to seek mandatory relief

15–26 It should be clear that anyone who delays beyond a point where prohibitory relief will serve no purpose (as in cases of building in breach) will have to face the prospect of seeking mandatory relief. That is not an attractive prospect in many cases as the Court will be reluctant to grant such relief.[24] This point reinforces that made at paragraph 15–23 above regarding the importance of a quick response to breaches of covenant.

In many restrictive covenant cases the Court will refuse mandatory relief because of the extreme effect of such an order; to order demolition of erected houses might well be "an unpardonable waste of much needed houses"[25] and even a fence may not be ordered to be removed, at least at the interlocutory stage.[26] In some cases however, a mandatory order will be made ordering the demolition of a house where special factors apply; such as the preservation of a sea view protected by the covenant.[27] It is also relevant to note that in rights of light cases the Court will be prepared to order demolition or partial demolition of buildings causing an interference with light, at least in cases of

[23] Those who have the Latin used to refer to this as a "*quia timet*" (that which is feared) injunction; at least until April 26, 1999.

[24] See *Morris v. Redland Bricks* [1970] A.C. 652 for the general principles on which the Court will act when applications are made for mandatory relief. In *Gafford v. Graham* (1998) 77 P.&C.R. 73 the Court of Appeal refused to grant mandatory relief seeking the removal of a riding school where the plaintiff had stood by and failed to prevent its erection by seeking interlocutory relief at an early stage. By the trial date the building had been up for over 7 years.

[25] *per* Brightman J. in *Wrotham Park Estate Co. Ltd v. Parkside Homes Ltd* [1974] 1 W.L.R. 798 at 811.

[26] See *Shepherd Homes Ltd v. Sandham* [1971] Ch. 340, where a five month delay in seeking removal of the fence was also a factor in refusing a mandatory injunction. For "interim" injunctions see para. 15–30 below.

[27] *Wakeham v. Wood* (1981) 43 P.&C.R. 40.

bad interference.[28] The same practice should apply where the effect of breach of covenant is extreme.[29]

At what stage should an injunction be sought?

15–27 The answer is always given—"as early as possible". But the tactical decision to seek early relief requires consideration of two matters:

15–28 (a) *Will simply issuing a claim form with a claim for an injunction be enough, or do I need to seek interim relief under Part 25 of the CPR?*

To answer this question, consider the following examples.

(i) The defendant (alleged to be in breach of covenant) may be engaged in speculative development with borrowed money and he may be on a tight contract with builders. The mere issue of a claim form may force him to stop acting in breach and sue for peace. If the claim form is registered as a pending land action[30] that will have to be explained to purchasers and the defendant's bank, for anything which threatens the speed at which the development can be completed will be bad news for the defendant and his bank.

(ii) The defendant is trading in breach of covenant and will continue to do so notwithstanding the issue of the writ.

In both cases the plaintiff runs a risk if he does not seek interim relief. In the first case it is tempting to think that the plaintiff can simply wait until trial, but in the meanwhile, the defendant can seek to strike out the plaintiff's action as an abuse of the process where it is plain that either the plaintiff is only after damages, or where the prospects of obtaining injunctive relief are remote. The plaintiff may be forced to elect whether to move for interim relief, or suffer a striking out. In the second case the conduct of the defendant will clearly require an application for interim relief, but in that case, if not in the first, the plaintiff has to consider the problem of the undertaking in damages.[31]

[28] For a recent example see *Deakins v. Hookings* [1994] 1 E.G.L.R. 190, where an upper floor extension was ordered to be cut back; anyone at the bus station in Wimbledon who sees a building where the upper storey looking like a quarter of cheese will be looking at the *locus in quo* of that case!

[29] As to the practice of the Court in granting mandatory injunctions in the context of covenants to carry on a trade or business, and the general policy of refusing such relief where it would require such a trade, etc., to be carried on, see *Co-operative Insurance Society Ltd v. Argyle Stores (Holdings) Ltd* [1998] A.C. 1.

[30] In registered titles use a caution under Land Registration Act 1925, s. 54 or in unregistered titles register a pending land action under Land Charges Act 1972, s. 5; see *Ruoff & Roper*, para. 36–06.

[31] For conflicting authority on whether the plaintiff should be forced to seek interim relief see *Blue Town Investments Ltd v. Higgs & Hill plc* [1990] 1 W.L.R. 696 (where the plaintiff was so forced in a right of light case) and *Oxy-Electric Ltd v. Zainuddin* [1991] 1 W.L.R. 115 (where the Court refused, where a breach of covenant was alleged, to require the plaintiff to make such an election). In *Vardy v. Banner New Homes*, unreported, 1998, the Court preferred the latter authority, largely because the striking factors of delay and lack of merit in the plaintiffs' claim which were present in the former case were not present in the instant case.

(b) *The problem of the undertaking in damages*

15–29 The usual practice when seeking interim relief is that the Court will require the plaintiff to undertake to pay the defendant the loss which it has suffered should it turn out at the trial that the injunction obtained on an interim basis is not to be made final.[32] This may be a heavy burden for a plaintiff to bear and although there are exceptions, any plaintiff contemplating enforcement of covenants by injunction must be prepared to give such an undertaking. The counterpart to this predicament lies in the fact that a defendant who is faced with a claim for an injunction without any interim application being made, will not be able to recoup any losses pending trial owing to the uncertainty of his position. But that uncertainty "is no more than a necessary consequence of the existence of a claim which has not yet been adjudicated."[33]

What the plaintiff may have to contemplate is the "David and Goliath" situation of having to give an undertaking for many thousands of pounds in a case where the defendant is a builder, or developer and there are penalties on the contract and other costs following a delay in the execution of the projected development.

What is clear is that any case of anticipated enforcement of covenants *the plaintiff must be forewarned of the generally accepted need to give an undertaking in damages as the price of obtaining an injunction.* Moreover, it is not acceptable to avoid this issue in all cases by not seeking interim relief in view of the risk that either the defendant will simply carry on regardless, or may seek to put the plaintiff to his election or face being struck out.[34] *The defendant should be warned that unless he can obtain an undertaking in damages from the plaintiff (which is of some value) he will be out of pocket if at trial it turns out that the interim injunction should not have been granted.*

What do you have to show the Court in order to obtain an interim injunction in restrictive covenant cases?

15–30 (a) In most respects applications for interim injunctions to enforce restrictive covenants are no different from other types of application for injunctions. You have to satisfy the Court that[35]:

[32] For detail of the practice on the undertaking as to damages see Goldrein & Wilkinson, *Commercial Litigation—Pre-emptive remedies*, (3rd ed.) p. 120. For the nature of the undertaking and its enforcement, see *Cheltenham & Gloucester B.S. v. Ricketts* [1993] 1 W.L.R. 1545. For the practice and the problems thrown up by impecunious and legally aided plaintiffs see CPR, Pt 25 and Pt 25 of the Practice Direction and *Allen v. Jambo Holdings* [1980] 1 W.L.R. 1252.

[33] *per* Hoffmann J. in *Oxy-Electric v. Zainuddin*, above, at 120.

[34] It should not be forgotten that it is a rule of practice (at least in the Chancery Division) that even where the defendant accepts that he should be bound by an interim order until trial and gives an undertaking not, for example, to do the acts alleged to be in breach of covenant, the plaintiff must still give the undertaking in damages; at least in case where the plaintiff would otherwise be required to give it, or unless the contrary is agreed.

[35] See CPR, Pts 23 and 25 and the test based on *American Cyanamid v. Ethicon* [1975] A.C. 396.

(i) there is a serious question to be tried;[36]
(ii) that the balance of convenience dictates the grant of the injunction;
(iii) that the plaintiff can give the undertaking in damages.

(b) In restrictive covenant cases, unless it is plain that the plaintiff does not have the benefit of the covenant, or that the defendant is not bound, there will usually be no dispute that there is a serious question to be tried. (It is, however, remarkable that in so many cases the question of whether the covenant is protected by registration is overlooked until the last minute, and only then does one side or the other realise that the covenant cannot be enforced).

(c) As to the balance of convenience, in cases where the injunction is restraining building there is less room for argument than in a case where a trade is being carried on—albeit in breach.

(d) The courts do not like defendants trying to "steal a march" on the plaintiff and will take such conduct into account when deciding whether to grant the interim injunction.

(e) It is much harder to persuade a court to grant a mandatory injunction on an interim basis, for in order that the court can do so it must be as certain as it can be that at the trial it will appear that the mandatory interim injunction was rightly granted. A modern view has been expressed in the sense that the court should consider whether the *injustice* suffered by the defendant in a case where the injunction turned out to be wrongly granted is greater than the injustice suffered by the plaintiff, if at trial it turned out that he was entitled to a mandatory injunction, having been refused it at the interlocutory stage.[37] In cases concerning covenants it may be difficult to assess where the greater injustice lies; where a building is to be knocked down the contrast between the two situations is extreme. In other cases (such as a breach of covenant relating to a wall) the contrast will be far less. In many cases money can satisfy the plaintiff, thereby making it less likely that a mandatory injunction will be granted.

How to obtain an interim injunction

15–31 Reference should be made to the *White Book* for the practice and the forms required.[38]

[36] Unless there is prima facie evidence of breach (actual or threatened) the Court will dismiss the application; see the flowchart at pp. 6 and 7 above; see also *Harbour Park Ltd v. Arun D.C.* [1998] E.G.C.S. 150 for a case where there was no prima facie evidence of breach.

[37] See *Shepherd Homes v. Sandham*, above. For the "injustice" argument see *Films Rover Ltd v. Cannon film Sales Ltd* [1987] 1 W.L.R. 670.

[38] Reference should be made to the CPR in force from April 26, 1999, in particular Pts 23 and 25 and the practice direction(s) thereto.

Costs of applications for interim injunctions

The usual practice is:

15–32

(a) If the plaintiff succeeds in obtaining interim relief he will get his costs as "plaintiff's costs in the cause", *i.e.* if he wins at trial he gets the costs of the interim application (and presumably the other costs of the action), but if he loses at trial he does not have to pay the defendant's costs of that application, although the plaintiff may have to pay the defendant's others costs of the action.

(b) If the plaintiff loses his application for interim relief the order will be "defendant's costs in the cause". Thus if the defendant wins at trial he will get the costs of the interim application (and presumably the other costs of the action) from the plaintiff. If, however, the plaintiff wins at trial and gets an injunction he will get the costs of the action, but not his costs of the interim application.

The "usual practice" can only be a general guide in view of the discretion as to costs. In some cases the Court may be persuaded to reserve the question of costs over to trial. In other cases the costs may simply be order to be "in the cause" so that whoever wins at trial will get all his costs including the costs of the interim application. There is also the factor of open pre-action offers of undertakings and "Calderbank" letters which may affect the way in which the Court will deal with costs at this stage—if not later at trial.
(See CPR, Pts 36 and 44).

PART III: ACTIONS FOR DAMAGES, EITHER AT COMMON LAW, OR IN LIEU OF AN INJUNCTION

15–33

The grounds upon which damages for breach of a restrictive covenant may be awarded are:

(a) for breach of covenant at *common law*;

(b) for breach of covenant *in equity* where damages are awarded in lieu of an injunction.

It is worth noting that the original covenantee still has the right to claim damages for breach of covenant even though he may have sold the benefited land, by virtue of his contract with the covenantor. But such damages will be nominal only and it is unlikely in practice that anyone will bother to take such action.

Why is there a difference?

15–34

The difference arises because of the historical distinction between the ability to enforce covenants at common law (*e.g.* between original parties, or where the original covenantor was being sued by an assignee of the benefit—the benefit running at common law) and the ability to enforce covenants in equity, which enabled the burden of the covenant to run. In the case of covenants enforceable at common law, damages were historically the only remedy, although since the fusion of law and equity in 1875 an injunction will also lie. In the case of covenants enforceable in equity, only equitable remedies lie, which consist of the injunction and since 1858, damages in lieu thereof.[39]

Does the difference matter?

15–35 It should not do, and in the vast majority of cases it does not, but there can be a distinction in some cases.

As will be seen below, where damages are awarded at common law for breach of covenant, such damages can only compensate for past breaches of covenant, and in practical terms this means the diminution in the value of the benefited land by reason of the breach. In contrast, when assessing damages in lieu of an injunction the court can take into account not only the effect of future breaches of covenant but also the fact that there is value in the ability to claim an injunction which in turn translates into the price of a release.

However, the contrast has now become muted, as recent authority has suggested that a similar measure to that available in lieu of an injunction, may be applied in cases where *common law* damages are being sought. An instance of this new approach is where mere diminution in value would not be truly compensatory and where such damages *could* have been awarded in equity in lieu of an injunction.

The principles to be applied in awarding damages.

15–36 The last paragraph shows that a distinction between damages at common law and in equity can emerge which is unhelpful and makes an understanding of this part of the law of covenants difficult.

From the point of view of the practitioner it is suggested that there should be no distinction and whether the plaintiff is suing to enforce as an original covenantee, or as a successor, against an original covenantor, or a successor, the principles governing an award of damages should be the same.

15–37 It seems from recent authority[40] that the courts will no longer regard whether the plaintiff is suing at common law or in equity as a distinction of importance when it comes to the assessment of damages. This is a sensible approach.

On the basis of such recent authority, the principles of assessment can be stated thus:

(a) It is axiomatic that any award of damages for breach of covenant should be compensatory in its aim, based on the theory that the

[39] See Chap. 7, para. 7–04 above for the distinction between the common law and equitable rules as to the enforceability of covenants.

[40] *Gafford v. Graham* (1998) 77 P.&C.R. 73.

plaintiff should be put into the position he would be in had the covenant been observed or performed.[41]

(b) Prima facie the measure will be based on the diminution in value of the benefited land by reason of the breach, whether past or continuing. However, in this context the concept of "parasitic" damages should not be ignored. Damage to part of a piece of land may in fact cause the whole to be diminished in value. This is a concept which is well-known in interference with light actions (easements) and there is no reason why a similar approach should not be adopted where a breach of covenant is the subject of the claim.[42]

(c) There may, however, be cases where the measure at (b) is not compensatory, either because it does not take full account of what the plaintiff has lost or what he would have had if the covenant had been observed. The latter alternative may be translated into the right to enforce the covenant at any time by means of an injunction.

(d) In cases falling within (c) the Court may award the plaintiff a sum which represents the amount the defendant would reasonably be willing to pay to secure the release from the covenant. That sum may be calculated by reference to a percentage of the defendant's profit, or by reference to some other benefit which accrues to the defendant from a release, *e.g.* a percentage of the uplift in value of his land freed from the covenant.

(e) An award under (d) is capable of being made both at common law and in equity. At common law such damages reflecting the price of a release can only be awarded where they are compensatory and if they could have been awarded in equity.

(f) A plaintiff cannot recover damages based on the price of a release if at the date of the writ the Court *could not* have awarded an injunction as matter of jurisdiction, *e.g.* because it was not sought, or because the persons to whom any injunction would have been directed were not parties.[43] If the Court *could* have granted an injunction, but *chose not to do so* because, for example, such an order would have been oppressive to the defendant, or because of the plaintiff's conduct, the measure under (d) is available.[44]

[41] See *McGregor on Damages*, (16th ed.), para. 810 for the general principle, and paras 1007–1011 for a discussion of the principles applicable to restrictive covenants.

[42] See 39 Conv. [N.S.] 116; Hudson "*Parasitic Damages for Loss of Light*".

[43] As in *Surrey County Council v. Bredero Homes* [1993] 1 W.L.R. 1361, where the houses built in breach had been sold off by the defendant prior to the action, and the house owners were not parties; the court could not have awarded an injunction to the plaintiff in such a case, even if it had sought it, which it did not.

[44] For authority on the principles in this paragraph, see, *Wrotham Park Estate Co. v. Parkside Homes*, above, *Jaggard v. Sawyer* [1995] 1 W.L.R. 269, and *Gafford v. Graham*, n. 40, above. The rationale of refusing damages based on the price of a release expressed in *Surrey County Council v. Bredero Homes* (above) was rejected by the Court of Appeal in the last two cases referred to above.

(g) As a matter of pleading, it is not necessary to claim either damages in lieu of an injunction (if he is really seeking an injunction) or an injunction (if he is really seeking damages in lieu—the chances of obtaining an injunction being remote) expressly in the claim form and particulars of claim within CPR, Pts 7 and 16. What is required is a clear indication of whether the plaintiff is seeking damages for past injury, or damages in substitution for an injunction; if the latter it would be sensible to put forward how the price of the release is calculated.[45]

If damages are assessed as the price of a release, what will be the measure?

15–38 (a) The starting point is to look at the anticipated net profit to be made from the development in breach. (Alternatively, the net development value of the land, that being the amount by which the value of the land is increased by virtue of the freedom from the covenant).

(b) The percentage to be applied to that is conventionally expressed as the "Stokes" percentage, that being one third of the net profit or uplift.[46]

(c) the percentage is not, however, immutable. The following fluctuations are recorded in the reported authorities:

"High Water Mark"
50 per cent

(*Re SJC Construction Co. Ltd's Application*[47]
"Low Water Mark"

5 per cent
Wrotham Park Estate Co. v. Parkside Homes[48].

(d) In other cases it may be difficult to apply a crude *Stokes* percentage and other measures are taken. In *Gafford v. Graham*[49] the Court of Appeal made an award of £25,000 based on the income generated by the business being carried in breach and the marriage value between the land and the business, that being a realistic guide to what the plaintiff would have demanded for a relaxation of the covenants. In *Jaggard v. Sawyer*[50] the sum awarded as a fair ransom price was £6250, where the injury to the plaintiff was small and where there was no element of speculative development.

[45] *Jaggard v. Sawyer*, above, at 285 *per* Millett L.J. The clearer the case is put as regards damages in the particulars of claim the better.
[46] See *Stokes v. Cambridge Corporation* (1962) 13 P.&C.R. 77.
[47] (1975) 29 P.&C.R. 322. An application to modify a covenant under Law of Property Act 1925, s. 84(1) where the issue was the compensation payable for such modification; see further Chap. 16, below.
[48] [1974] 1 W.L.R. 798.
[49] (referred to at n. 40 above).
[50] Above, at n. 44.

(e) In practice the plaintiff should be warned against over-estimating his expectation of recovery of a "Stokes" payment, whilst at the same time being advised that a "Stokes" percentage is at least a starting point. From the defendant's point of view he may be concerned, particularly in the context of speculative development, where time and money is at a premium, to reach a quick settlement, and he can at least point to the low percentage in *Wrotham Park*. It may be that if there have been payments in settlement of claims by other parties entitled to enforce these can be used as a precedent to show what the "market value" of the release will be.[51] In practice both sides need to get their respective surveyors together to see if a sum can be agreed.

Finally, a warning on tax.

15–39 (a) The *tax treatment* of payments for a release (or damages for breach) should never be forgotten—whether for capital gains tax, or income tax. The moral here is to consult a tax specialist, as the complete details of potential charges to tax and traps for the unwary are beyond the scope of this book.

But here are some short reminders of what to look for.

(b) First, the tax treatment may not vary even if the release is paid as damages, as opposed to a consensual price for a release. In principle whether a sum is paid in compromise of a claim under an agreed Order or as a result of terms (*e.g.* in "Tomlin" Order), or is paid under an Order of the Court where no agreement was present, the capital sum may be liable to capital gains tax.[52]

15–40 (c) Secondly, and in summary, practitioners should be aware of the following tax consequences of a release:

Capital gains tax

The release of the covenant will be a disposal of an asset, unless it is possible to claim principal private residence exemption.[53]

Income tax

The real trap here may be the treatment of the release as taxable under ICTA 1988, s. 776, which although seemingly bringing into charge artificial transactions in land, has brought into charge perfectly innocent transactions which could include releases of

[51] This was the approach adopted in *Marine & General Mutual Life Assurance Society v. St James' Real Estate Co. Ltd* [1991] 2 E.G.L.R. 178,(a right of light claim) where the court used a figure reached in settlement with another person affected as good evidence of the "ransom" price.

[52] See McGregor, *Damages*, (16th ed.), paras 614–617.

[53] See TCGA 1992, ss. 21(1) (what is an asset) and s. 222 (for principal private residence exemption). A release may also be chargeable under TCGA, s. 22(1)(a) as a disposal when a capital sum is received in return for exercising or not exercising a right. See also *Emmet*, Chap. 29. The cost is not an allowable expense for capital gains tax purposes; *Garner (I.T.) v. Pounds Shipowners and Shipbreaking Ltd* [1998] B.T.C. 495.

rights under covenants. It is, however, possible to ask for clearance under ICTA, s. 776(1).[54]

VAT

In view of the exemption provisions contained in Schedule 9 (Group 1) to the VAT Act 1994 it is not thought likely that a release would attract VAT if granted by a trader in the course of his business. But as with any tax point it is wise to check.

When will damages in lieu of an injunction be granted?

15–41 (a) When the Court has jurisdiction at the date of the writ to grant an injunction, it can give damages in lieu, governed by the circumstances in existence at the date of the hearing, or if later, the date of the inquiry as to damages.[55]

(b) The discretion to grant such damages is governed by the following "good working rule" setting out the circumstances in which damages in lieu may be given:

(i) where the injury to the plaintiff's legal rights is small;
(ii) one which is capable of being estimated in money;
(iii) one which is capable of being compensated by a small money payment;
(iv) one in which it would be oppressive to grant an injunction.

(c) Other factors which may incline the court more towards the grant of an injunction than against it (even though the four factors above are present); for example where the defendant has tried to steal a march on the plaintiff.[56]

(d) But care must be taken to advise a defendant that the idea that he has the right to "buy off" the plaintiff with an offer of damages is wrong. It will fall to the defendant to show why the plaintiff's prima facie right to an injunction should not be granted. In effect the defendant must show that it would be oppressive to award an injunction against him.[57]

[54] See *Page v. Lowther* (1983) S.T.C. 799 for a perfectly innocent scheme for deferred consideration for development which was so caught.

[55] See *Jaggard v. Sawyer*, above. As to the later assessment of damages see *Ward v. Cannock Chase D.C.* [1986] Ch. 546. The jurisdiction to grant damages in lieu of an injunction (or specific performance) which was formerly in Lord Cairn's Act 1858, is now contained in Supreme Court Act 1981, s. 50.

[56] The four rules and this paragraph are taken from the well-known judgment of A.L. Smith J. in *Shelfer v. City of London Electric Lighting Co. Ltd* [1895] 1 Ch. 287, recently applied in *Jaggard v. Sawyer* and *Gafford v. Graham*, above.

[57] The fact of oppression was the guiding factor in the decision by the Court of Appeal in *Gafford v. Graham*, above, at n. 49 in awarding damages in lieu. It is clear from that authority and from *Sefton v. Tophams* [1965] Ch. 1140 at 1169, that some special case needs to be shown by the defendant to avoid an injunction where there is jurisdiction to grant it.

Chapter 16

DISCHARGE AND MODIFICATION OF RESTRICTIVE COVENANTS UNDER LAW OF PROPERTY ACT 1925, s. 84(1) BY THE LANDS TRIBUNAL

Introduction

16–01 This Chapter considers the means by which restrictive covenants can be removed or altered in cases where they appear to serve no useful function, or are a hindrance to activity on land which is (or which appears to be) burdened by them. There may be instances where all the parties whose interests which are affected can agree on the terms by which covenants can be removed or altered. But in other cases it is necessary to consider how this can be achieved where such agreement is not possible.

In such cases the jurisdiction to discharge or modify restrictive covenants is exercised by the Lands Tribunal under Law of Property Act 1925, s. 84(1) and this chapter is devoted to an examination of that jurisdiction.

How can I get rid of or change a restrictive covenant?

16–02 The short answer to the question is: "only with difficulty".

Why?

Restrictive covenants over freehold land do not have a defined life. Unlike covenants in leases where at the end of the term the covenants will cease to have effect, there is no automatic termination of the life of restrictive covenants which affect freehold land.[1] They are not subject to any perpetuity rules—unlike certain other contractual agreements such as options—which limits their duration. The fact that they are "old" does not make them any the less effective. Covenants which have passed their centenary may be none the less effective than those which are mere striplings by comparison. The mere fact of their existence can, therefore, operate as a potential hindrance to the

[1] In the context of landlord and tenant there may well be an extension of the life of covenants in a lease by virtue of the various statutory means by which protection is given to landlords, but the point which is being made here is that ultimately covenants in leases have the prospect of termination, whereas those affecting freeholds are, like freeholds themselves, of potentially indefinite duration.

economic development of land; particularly where social or environmental change has caused covenants to be regarded as obsolete.

16–03 Unless use can be made of the planning, local government, or compulsory purchase legislation to "override" covenants standing in the way of development (and as explained in Chapter 12 above there is a limited capacity to do this and at the cost of compensating those affected) there is no means by which covenants can be discharged, or their terms modified, other than with the agreement of all entitled to the benefit of them, or crucially, by using the jurisdiction under Law of Property Act 1925 s. 84(1).

For private individuals or developers, securing the agreement of all concerned to a release, or making an application under section 84(1) which is successful may be the only way to free land from the burden of covenants, or to alter that burden as a result of a modification. The procedure for seeking a declaration under Law of Property Act 1925 s. 84(2), which may be used in suitable cases to "clear off" covenants which are no longer enforceable (see Chapter 15 above), is complex, time-consuming and costly.

There may be difficulty with a declaration of right as regards finding all those entitled to enforce, just as there is under section 84(2). Although insurance may sometimes be an option (see Chapter 18 above), it may not be available if the risk of enforcement is too great, or the premium too large. It is, therefore, in such cases that the jurisdiction of the Lands Tribunal to discharge or modify restrictive covenants can be considered and if appropriate, invoked.

Enter—the Lands Tribunal and Section 84(1)

16–04 The full text of section 84(1) and the subsections linked to it is found at Appendix 1.

In summary, the Lands Tribunal will only discharge or modify restrictive covenants where it can be shown that one of four conditions are met, *i.e.*

- there is *agreement* between all entitled to the benefit of it that there should be a discharge or modification;
- the covenant is, in effect, *obsolete*;
- the covenant restricts reasonable use of land, confers *no practical benefit of substantial value* on those entitled to enforce it (or is contrary to the public interest) and the *loss* of the covenant *can be compensated in money*;
- *no injury* will be caused to those entitled to the benefit of the covenant by reason of its discharge or modification.

WHO CAN APPLY?

16–05 Two classes of person may apply:

- "any person interested in any freehold land affected by any restriction" (section 84(1))
- a person interested in leasehold land affected by any restriction, provided the lease was granted for a term of more than 40 years, of which 25 years have already expired. (section 84(12))[2]

In each case it is the person with an interest in the burdened land who is going to be the applicant. In practical terms this will usually be the owner of the freehold to that land, or if the application is being made under section 84(12) it will be the person in whom the lease is vested.

16–06 Ignoring the freehold/leasehold distinction the class of applicants also encompasses:

- purchasers under an uncompleted contract[3];
- a mortgagee;
- option holders;
- joint applicants *e.g.* where a vendor of land is selling it for development and the purchaser under contract who is to carry it out, joins with the vendor in making the application. The latter usually has the greater financial interest in the success of the application. The contract may be conditional on its success, in which case both may be said to be equally interested in the outcome!

It is sometimes the case that a leaseholder may wish to apply to vary the covenants on the freehold reversion (with no doubt the approval of the reversioner) and there seems no reason why as a person "interested" in the freehold that lessee should not be able to apply.[4]

The problems posed by applicants who are original covenantors or where covenants have been recently imposed and are the subject of the application are dealt with at paragraph 16–114 below.

WHO CAN OBJECT?

16–07 (a) Those who appear to be entitled to the benefit of the restriction.

[2] See also in this context the jurisdiction to vary leases in Landlord & Tenant Act 1987 Pt IV.
[3] *Re Pioneer Properties* (1956) 7 P.&C.R. 264.
[4] In *Re Independent Television Authority's Application* (1961) 13 P.&C.R. 222, the applicant was that body holding under an agreement for a lease for five years, with seemingly the freeholder's consent to the application.

Since *Federated Homes*[5] more objectors will be able to show entitlement to benefit as they can show that the benefit will have passed to them under the implied annexation effected by section 78 of the Law of Property Act 1925. In this type of objector will be the *freehold* owner of the land benefited (or which claims to be benefited) by the restrictive covenant.

(b) It is also possible for a *tenant* of the land benefited by the restriction to object, for under section 78 a person with an estate derived from the freehold (a lease) can enforce a restrictive covenant taken for the benefit of that land.[6] In practice it may well often be the tenant who will be more concerned to object than the freeholder, unless the application is clearly going to diminish the value of the reversion. There may, however, be difficulties in the way of tenants who successfully object to the extent that the application is allowed only on payment of compensation, for if the tenant's interest is a short one the diminution in value may be negligible, although less difficulty will be encountered in measuring the loss of amenity, and in the solatium for the effect of building works, for example.[7] Equally, it may well be the case that the freeholder whose interest is subject to a long lease or a number of long leases will not suffer much by way of diminution by comparison with the tenant(s).[8]

16–08 (c) Those who have some right to enforce by virtue of a statute. They will be objecting as "custodians of the public interest"; for example the National Trust, or a local authority entitled to enforce under the statute by virtue of which the covenant was imposed.[9]

On what grounds can an application be made?

Each ground is considered below.

Sub-paragraph (a)

16–09 *"that by reason of changes in the character of the property or the neighbourhood or other circumstances of the case which the Lands Tribunal may deem material, the restriction ought to be deemed obsolete".*

There are generally two types of change which will lead to an application under this ground being contemplated.

First, where social changes make the restriction obsolete.

[5] [1980] 1 W.L.R. 594; see Chap. 8, para. 8–16 above for the significance of this decision.
[6] *Smith v. River Douglas Catchment Board* [1949] 2 K.B. 500 establishes the proposition that the tenant can enforce.
[7] See para. 16–95 below for the measure of compensation.
[8] See *Re Vaizey* (1974) 28 P.&C.R. 517.
[9] See *Gee v. National Trust* (1956) 17 P.&C.R. 6; *Re Martin's Application* (1988) 57 P.&C.R. 119; see Chap. 10 for statutory imposition of covenants.

Secondly, where environmental changes have occurred which make the restriction obsolete.

An example of the former type will include the changed attitude to the sale of alcohol; an example of the latter will be the presence of flats amongst houses and a greater density of houses, or a mix of residential and non-residential uses.

There are two questions which have to be asked when an application is made under sub-paragraph (a)

Question 1

16–10 Have there been material changes in:

- the character of the land which is the subject of the application; or
- in the neighbourhood of it; or
- some other material change in circumstances

since the covenant which it is sought to discharge or vary was imposed?

Question 2

16–11 If there have been such changes, ought the covenant to be deemed obsolete in the sense that it no longer fulfils its original purpose and what was that purpose?

The following material changes may lead to the original purpose of the covenant no longer being served and therefore being treated as obsolete.

- changes in the character of the property, *e.g.* use in breach for many years as a shop and not a dwelling house; a hotel used as flats; a school used as flats.[10]
- changes in the character of the neighbourhood. "Neighbourhood" has a wide definition and may mean a larger area than the immediate neighbourhood of the property within the application. The question of what is the neighbourhood is a question of fact. It is usually the applicant who will point to a wide definition of the neighbourhood, thereby trying to get in as many changes since the covenant was imposed as possible. The objector, on the other hand will try to limit the area of the neighbourhood so as to show that there are fewer changes which are not material.
- other material circumstances which have changed, *e.g.* dormant schemes of development. These words (*i.e.* material circumstances) are to be read *eiusdem generis* (together with) the earlier words which refer to the land within the application or the neighbourhood. Plannings matter alone will not amount to a material circumstance.

[10] *Re Forestmere* (1980) 41 P.&C.R. 390.

- the effect of large council estates.[11]

Practical tips for applications under sub-paragraph (a)

16–12

- identify by means of a series of Ordnance maps (or, in user cases plans showing the uses of property in the neighbourhood) the changes which will be relied upon as regards the application land. Mere neglect of that land will not be a change in character. Photographic evidence, both past and present may be of assistance. Local authorities will often have archive aerial photographs taken over a number of years (usually for planning purposes) and these can be used to show the changes in a neighbourhood. The Ordnance Survey office may also be able to supply photographs taken during mapping.

- do the same thing as regards the changes to the neighbourhood—once you have tried to define it.

- list the changes, *e.g.* conversion of large house to multiple accommodation; construction of industrial units; use of gardens for houses. Use colour coded plans. Identify planning consents within the neighbourhood.

- identify the purpose of the covenant which is the subject of the application. Was it to protect a particular house, which still warrants that protection? Was it to protect a larger area from development, which has now taken place? Was it to protect the amenity of an estate, or was it to protect purely commercial interests? In the former case the purpose may be more likely to be capable of fulfilment, than in the latter, where the commercial interests (*e.g.* competition between trades) may have changed beyond recognition.

- if the purpose has been identified (there may be more than one) ask the vital question whether that purpose can no longer be carried out. An example would be the preservation of the integrity of a building scheme where changes of use from purely residential to some hotel user has taken place. The purpose for which the original covenant was taken was to preserve the "good character" of the original estate, and it may be debatable whether further hotel development would, in view of the changes which have already occurred, really make much difference. In such a case it can be argued that the original purpose of the covenants cannot be fulfilled. This problem is one which emerges from time to time in schemes dating from the nineteenth century in seaside towns in the south west of England, such as Torbay and Torquay.

- Beware the trap that can arise where the greater the changes in the neighbourhood, the greater the importance of the preservation of the

[11] *Re Truman* [1956] 1 Q.B. 261 contains guidance on what is an obsolete covenant where the character of an estate has changed. Note that the restriction may be obsolete but the Lands tribunal may replace it with a new one; *Re Forestmere* (above).

covenant, rather than its discharge.[12] The previous example of the prolonged effect of changes in certain scheme covenants is one case where this trap can arise. It is also in this context that the "thin end of the wedge" argument may be mustered; this is dealt with at paragraph 16–73 below.

Illustrations of applications under subsection (a)

Section 84(1)(a)-

cases where applications succeeded:

"by reason of changes in the character of the property..."
Re Forestmere Properties Limited (1980) 41 P.&C.R. 390
• redundant cinema controls obsolete **16–13**
The leaseholders applied to modify or discharge covenants which obliged them to use a 1.41 acres site on Finchley Road, Northwest London on the fringe of Hampstead Garden suburbs exclusively for a cinema so that they could erect a block of flats upon it. As the cinema was defunct, the covenants in so far as they related to it were held to be obsolete and were modified so that residential flats could be built upon the site with the consent of the lessors.

Re Nichols' Application [1997] 1 E.G.L.R. 144
• changes lead to covenant no longer fulfilling its purpose **16–14**
The applicants wished to erect a bungalow at the rear of 27, Elms Road, Stoneygate, Leicester although a covenant in a conveyance of the property prevented any building. The character of the property, which had previously formed part of the grounds of a neighbouring detached house, had changed such that it presently had the appearance of a separate building plot waiting for development. Moreover, the covenant had originally been imposed to protect the amenity of the neighbouring house and to increase the price of an another estate upon a subsequent sale. As the neighbouring house had been demolished and replaced by a nursing home and a new dwelling house had been built at its rear and the estate had already been sold, the covenant was deemed to be obsolete.

"by reason of changes in the character of the neighbourhood..."
Re Briarwood Estates Limited (1979) 39 P.&C.R. 419
• grounds of neighbouring houses sold off for modern development **16–15**
A covenant contained in an underlease prevented the erection of more than three dwelling houses on the property known as Hill Top House, Grappenhall, Warrington. The applicants wished to divide the existing dwelling house into two and erect two further houses upon the property. At the date of the imposition of the restriction, the neighbourhood consisted of large houses in large grounds. However, as the grounds of neighbouring houses had recently been sold off as sites for modern dwellings the restriction was deemed to be

[12] See *Re Davies's Application* (1971) 25 P.&C.R. 115.

obsolete and therefore modified so as to prevent the erection of more than four dwelling houses on the property.

Re Bradley Clare Estates Limited (1987) 55 P.&C.R. 126

16–16 • destruction of benefit of mutual restrictions

Covenants contained in an indenture prevented the applicants from erecting more than one house on the property known as No. 14, the Street, Rustington, West Sussex and from using the property other than for residential purposes. The applicants wished to build sheltered housing units for the elderly. These restrictions were originally intended to ensure that the neighbourhood would not be developed other than for residential purposes. However, as a surgery had been built in the immediate neighbourhood, the benefit of the scheme of mutual restrictions had broken down and the restrictions were deemed to be obsolete.

"other material circumstances..."

Re Cox (1985) 51 P.&C.R. 335

16–17 • changes as to social conditions as to employment of staff

The freehold owner of Belfairs at Gun Hill, Chiddingly, East Sussex applied to discharge covenants which prohibited the use of Sunnyside, a building 19 feet from Belfairs, except by domestic staff employed in Belfairs so that an agricultural worker would be permitted to occupy Sunnyside. As there was no prospect that Sunnyside would ever be needed as a residence for Belfairs' domestic staff and persons who were unrelated to the occupiers of Belfairs occupied Sunnyside, the covenants were deemed to be obsolete. New restriction imposed limiting occupation or user to persons employed in agriculture.

Re Quaffers Limited (1988) 56 P.&C.R. 142

16–18 • motorway network and other buildings

Covenants in three conveyances forbade the use of property consisting of 0.86 acres of land in Worsley, Greater Manchester for trade or business and the sale of alcohol. The applicants wished to erect a hotel upon the property. The object of the restrictions was to protect the amenity of the land retained by the covenantee. As a network of motorways and a hotel had already been built within the immediate vicinity of the property, the amenity of the retained land could no longer be protected and the covenants were deemed to be obsolete.

Re Kennet Properties (1991) 72 P.&C.R. 353

• building had already destroyed view

16–19 Covenants imposed under a building scheme for the development of an estate to the south of a road known as Fortis Green, Hornsey, London forbade any building upon the paddock. The applicants wished to build 27 houses upon a site of 1.64 acres of land which formed part of the paddock. The original purpose of the covenants was to procure for the owners of each adjoining building plot an open view across his neighbour's land. As various housing developments, summer houses and a tennis club had already been built on the remainder of the paddock and impinged upon that view, the covenants were deemed to be obsolete.

cases where applications failed:

Re Davies (1971) 25 P.&C.R. 115

• land still capable of agricultural use **16–20**

A covenant presented any building within 100 yards of Loman House upon a site of 2.363 acres of land situated at West End, Somerton, Somerset. The applicant proposed to build 11 houses on the site. Although the surrounding land had changed in character from being agricultural to residential, the site, which had become neglected, was still capable of agricultural use and had to be retained as such in order to preserve the character of Loman House.

Re Gossip (1972) 25 P.&C.R. 215

• one house one plot still observed **16–21**

The applicant was the freehold owner of two detached houses which were purchased as 2 lots and were known as numbers 20 and 22, Avenue Road, New Milton, Hampshire. These lots were subject to a covenant presenting the building of more than one private dwelling house upon each plot. Although the original plotting had not been followed consistently, the restriction pattern of one dwelling house to one plot had been observed and the residential estate had been developed at a comparatively low density such that the covenant was not deemed to be obsolete.

Re Martin's Application (1988) 57 P.&C.R. 119

• attempt to build on public open space **16–22**

A covenant in an agreement made with the local authority prevented the property situated at 228, Harley Shute Road, St. Leonards, East Sussex from being used other than as a public open space. The applicants wished to build a dwelling house for which they had obtained planning permission in the garden of the property. The purpose of the covenant was to prevent excessive density in the vicinity of the property. As the proposed house would create a cramped appearance in the neighbourhood and the inspector who had granted planning permission for the proposed development and not indicated how this appearance could be overcome, the purpose of the restriction could still be achieved and it was not obsolete.

Re Houdret and Co. Limited (1989) 58 P.&C.R. 310

• attempt to convert residential to office user **16–23**

A covenant prevented the use of a grade II listed property known as St. Mary's House, 37, Market Place, Henley-on-Thames, Oxfordshire other than for residential purposes. The applicants wished to use the basement, ground and first floors of the property as offices. The purpose of the restriction (in a section 52 [now section 106] agreement) was to ensure that the property was used solely for residential purposes. This purpose could still be achieved as there was a demand in the market for its residential user notwithstanding the noise pollution levels and other inherent disadvantages from which the property continually suffered.

Re Towner & Goddard (1989) 58 P.&C.R. 316

16–24 • language of covenant important

An agreement under section 52 of the Town and Country Planning Act 1971 (now section 106) forbade any sort of erection on land forming part of the gardens of two properties situated in Cookham Dene Close, Chislehurst, Kent. The applicants proposed to erect two tennis courts with chain-link fencing all around their perimeter in the gardens of the properties. It was argued that the restriction should be deemed obsolete in so far as it prohibited the erection of tennis courts but that it could still apply to restrict the development of sheds, greenhouses and summer houses. This was rejected because a restriction cannot be deemed obsolete merely with regard to its effect rather than its language. However the application was still allowed under section 84(1)(c).

Re North (1997) 75 P.&C.R. 117

16–25 • infilling may not detract from the quality of a neighbourhood

A covenant contained in the conveyance of Garden Cottage, Winkfield Lane, Winkfield, Berkshire prevented any building in the garden of the cottage without the consent of the neighbouring owner. The applicants proposed to erect a dwelling house and two garages in the garden. Despite some residential development, the neighbourhood had retained its attractive semi-rural character and had not materially changed. Thus, there was no need to examine the further question whether the restriction ought to be deemed to be obsolete. It was however found that the restriction's original purpose of protecting neighbouring land could still be achieved in any event.

Sub-paragraph (aa)

16–26 "that (in a case falling within subsection (1A) below) the continued existence thereof would impede some reasonable user of the land for public or private purposes or, as the case may be, would unless modified so impede such user."

"(1A) Subsection (1)(aa) above authorises the discharge or modification of a restriction by reference to its impeding some reasonable user of land in any case in which the Lands Tribunal is satisfied that the restriction, in impeding that user, either—

(a) does not secure to persons entitled to the benefit of it any practical benefits of substantial value or advantage to them; or
(b) is contrary to the public interest

and that money will be an adequate compensation for the loss or disadvantage (if any) which any such person will suffer from the discharge or modification.

(1B) In determining whether a case is falling within subsection (1A) above, and in determining whether (in any such case or otherwise) a restriction ought to be discharged or modified, the Lands Tribunal shall take into account the development plan and any declared or ascertainable pattern for the grant or refusal of planning permissions in the relevant areas, as well as the period at which and context in which the restriction was created or imposed and any other material circumstance."

16–27 (a) When considering this ground of application the following questions are usually asked:[13]

Question (i)
is the proposed user reasonable?

Question (ii)
do the covenants impede that user?

Note: As to questions (i) and (ii) where planning consent has been obtained for a definite project, few applicants will fail to satisfy these questions. In such circumstances the first two questions posed are the easiest hurdles to overcome when applying under sub-paragraph (aa)

16–28 **Question (iii)**
does impeding the proposed user secure practical benefits to the objector?

Question (iv)
if the answer to question (iii) is "yes" are those benefits of substantial value or advantage?

Note: "practical benefits" will include—

- a view
- peace and quiet
- light[14]
- the open character of the neighbourhood[15]
- but not:—
- bargaining power and the capacity to extract a ransom.[16]

16–29 **Question (v)**
is impeding the proposed user contrary to the public interest?

13 *Re Bass Ltd's Application* (1973) 26 P.&C.R. 156 sets out the questions asked under this ground of application, which are paraphrased here.
14 *Re North's Application* (1997) 75 P.&C.R. 117; preservation of a view and light.
15 *Re Martins' Application* (1988) 57 P.&C.R. 119; preservation of a public open space for that purpose.
16 See *Gilbert v. Spoor* [1983] Ch. 27 and *Stannard v. Issa* [1987] A.C. 175 on views and other practical benefits. See *Stockport MBC v. Alwiyah Developments* (1983) 52 P.&C.R. 278 for authority that bargaining power and its value in "ransom" terms is not a practical benefit.

Note:

- only in rare cases, even where the application under subsection (aa) is by a local, or public authority, is the answer likely to be yes. Such applications are rare in view of the powers given to local authorities to override covenants set out in Chapter 12, above.
- it may well be that a proposal (*e.g.* to allow sheltered housing) is within the public interest. But the fact that this is so, does not mean that the restriction (in impeding that user) is contrary to the public interest. It may be in the public interest to preserve certain elements of a neighbourhood, *e.g.* to preserve the types of amenity referred to under question (iv) above. Only where the proposal *is so important* that it is almost an exceptional case, will such an argument succeed.[17]

16–30 In all cases the applicant will need to put before the Lands Tribunal the following evidence in order to satisfy section 1(A) and section 1(B):

- the planning matters referred to in subsection (1B). This evidence is very important and should not be overlooked, or its effect underestimated.
- the planning consent relating to the applicant's site.
- the pattern of the grant or refusal of planning consent in the "relevant areas"; this term is not defined but would appear to include the areas both benefited and burdened by the covenant which is the subject of the application.[18]

In this context it is important to note that in applications under subsection (aa), planning evidence is not going to be decisive save in rare cases, such as where there is a shortage of local housing land.[19] See the illustrations below for cases which show how this principle operates.

Question (vi)

16–31 if either (i) the benefits secured by the covenants are not of substantial value or advantage or (ii) if impeding the proposed user is contrary to the public interest will money be adequate compensation?

Note: Compensation is dealt with under paragraph 16–95 below and reference should be made there for the principles upon which it is awarded. But at this stage it is necessary to have some idea of those principles in order to answer the question posed above. There is an element of circularity here, but it is unavoidable in view of the exercise which has to be carried out in order to see if the application under subsection (aa) will succeed.

[17] *SJC Construction* (below) may be an example of an exceptional case; see also *Re Bradley Clare* (1987) 55 P.&C.R. 126.

[18] See Practice Note 5/97 as to the manner in which expert evidence is to be admitted, reproduced at App. 4 below.

[19] As occurred in *Re SJC Construction Co. Ltd's Application* (1974) 28 P.&C.R. 200.

- for ease of reference, adequate compensation is defined in section 84(1) as either:

    (i) a sum to make up for any loss or disadvantage suffered by that person in consequence of the discharge or modification; or
    (ii) a sum to make up for any effect which the restriction had, at the time when it was imposed, in reducing the consideration then received for the land affected by it.

The practical answer to question (vi) is usually as follows: **16–32**

- if the Lands Tribunal has reached a provisional conclusion that the benefits secured by the covenants are not of substantial value, the compensation is likely to be small if assessed under section 84(1)(i). Such a conclusion would support an application under subsection (aa). If, however, compensation were to be assessed on the alternative basis under section 84(1)(ii) the outcome is more speculative and there may be more room for argument on that measure that money will not be adequate compensation.[20]

- in contrast, if the compensation could be shown to be substantial (at least on a provisional basis) that would tend to show that the benefit of the covenant is of substantial value or advantage and the application is unlikely to succeed under subsection (aa).[21]

- if the Lands Tribunal has reached a provisional conclusion that impeding the proposed user is contrary to public interest the compensation may well be large, but adequate to compensate for the loss of amenity.[22]

- where the objector is a statutory or quasi-statutory body (*e.g.* local authorities or the National Trust) acting as "custodians of the public interest" it may be impossible to show that money compensation will be adequate. In which case the application will fail under this ground, but may be successful under subparagraph (c) referred to below.[23]

Practical tips for applications under subsection (aa)

- identify, at an early stage, what are the practical benefits which are of substantial value or advantage secured by the covenant which is the subject of the application. If you act for an objector this will be a crucial part of your opposition. If you act for the applicant your task will be to show either a lack of such benefits, or that the value or **16–33**

[20] *Re Vaizey* (1974) 28 P.&C.R. 517—where the interest of the objector was in reversion to long leases.
[21] See *Re Bushell* (1987) 54 P.&C.R. 386, where £30,000 was said to represent the loss in value in the property with the benefit of a covenant to protect a view, and that led the Tribunal to conclude that the benefit of that covenant was of substantial view.
[22] *Re SJC Construction Co. Ltd* above.
[23] As occurred in *Re Martins' Application* (1988) 57 P.&C.R. 119. There a money payment would not have removed the adverse effect of the proposed development on a public open space which the local authority was entitled to enforce in the public interest.

advantage is small and is capable of being the subject of adequate compensation.

- identify and place clearly before the Tribunal the matters referred to in section 1(B). This means setting out the planning evidence, and the relevant evidence relating to the covenant itself. Consider why the covenant was imposed, and what was the context of such imposition. Is this a case of a tight scheme, or an isolated covenant?

- consider what expert evidence will be required on any of the issues raised by the questions posed above, and particularly on the question of compensation and its adequacy, or otherwise.

Illustrations under sub-paragraph (aa)

Section 84(1)(aa)

(a) is the proposed user reasonable?

- yes, where planning permission and detailed plans are to hand

Re Bass Limited (1973) 26 P.&C.R. 156

16–34 A brewery based near City Road, Smethwick, Birmingham wished to use land subject to restrictions preventing its use other than for residential purposes as a loading area for lorries making deliveries to the brewery. Assuming the restrictions were not in place, the proposed user was considered to be reasonable as it had received planning permission and businesses within the Birmingham area had to be preserved. However, the proposal was not in the public interest because it was largely of the brewery's own making and the restrictions secured practical benefits for the objectors.

Re North (1997) 75 P.&C.R. 117

16–35 Proposed user of a garden for the erection of a house and two garages in Winkfield, Berkshire (a residential neighbourhood) was a definite project which had been granted planning permission and was therefore reasonable. However, the restrictions secured practical benefits of a substantial value for the owners of a neighbouring house, Foliejon Garden House. Thus, the application failed.

- no, where scheme covenants are present

Re Bromor (1995) 70 P.&C.R. 569

16–36 The applicant wished to demolish a semi-detached house in Drummond Drive, Stanmore, Middlesex so as to permit the construction of an access road for the proposed development of a triangular piece of land to the rear of the house. The house was subject to a covenant which prevented its use other than as a dwelling house. As the house was part of the Hill House estate where a building scheme existed, there was a great presumption that the covenant would be upheld and therefore a greater onus of proof upon the applicant. It was doubted whether the proposed user of the land was reasonable as in an earlier case (see *Fletcher* LP/56/1987) the construction of a roadway upon land where a house and garden already existed to serve development to the rear of the house was considered to be an unreasonable use of the subject land.

(b) the continued existence of the covenants would impede the proposed user

- it may be necessary to show that no *other* restriction will impede the proposed user. **16–37**

(c) does impeding the user secure practical benefits to the objectors?
Practical Benefits

- these must be secured by the covenant and not for example, by some indirect route, such as local authority policy.

Re O'Reilly (1993) 66 P.&C.R. 485
16–38 The applicant wished to develop houses upon land in Arnhem Drive, Chatham which was sold subject to a restriction which provided that "Not without the prior consent of the council in its capacity as vendor [was the applicant] to use the land or any part thereof otherwise than for the purpose of parking and garaging cars." As the applicant could cease to use the land for off-street parking without being in breach of the restriction, such practical benefit as there was in providing off-street parking was not a benefit secured by the restriction.

View

Gilbert v. Spoor [1983] Ch. 27
16–39 Restrictions gave residents benefit of preventing any interference, by erection of dwelling houses, with the view across the Tyne Valley from a certain part of The Centurion Way (the approach road), or from public seats situated thereon or from the vicinity of the seats. It was perfectly reasonable to say that the loss of a view just round the corner from the land may have an adverse effect on the land itself.

Stockport Metropolitan Borough Council v. Alwiyah Developments (1983) 52 P.&C.R. 278
16–40 Council claimed benefit of being able to provide 11 houses forming part of a larger estate in Romiley, Stockport, Cheshire with a view down to the Goyt Valley. Not a practical benefit secured by restrictions as no evidence that the view provided the council with an advantage in carrying out its duties as a housing authority in housing tenants or that the tenants of the relevant houses cared about the view.

Re Purnell (1987) 55 P.&C.R. 133
16–41 Planning permission had been granted for a chalet-bungalow to be built in the garden of a dwelling in the Chelsfield Park Estate in Orpington, Kent. A restriction forbade the erection of more than one dwelling house per plot of

land on the estate. The residents' association and its members would be injured if the restriction were to be modified as the neighbourhood would lose the advantage of its open development and therefore its almost unique character in the area.

Quiet

Re Wards Construction (Medway) Limited (1973) 25 P.&C.R. 223

16–42 An application to erect a block of 12 flats on land in Gillingham, Kent. Restrictions so that could only build detached or semi-detached houses. Objectors had special reasons for wanting a feeling of space and quiet and were found to value space and quiet and light. The development proposal would blot out the sky and sunlight and the application was therefore refused.

Light

Re North (1997) 75 P.&C.R. 117

16–43 The restriction was of substantial benefit to the objectors as it prevented the deterioration of the view and the obstruction of light from and to the windows in the flank wall of the rear living room of Foliejohn Garden House.

Privacy, pubic amenity, open space

Re Martins' Application (1988) 57 P.&C.R. 119

16–44 The restrictions were a practical benefit to the corporation in preventing detriment to the visual amenity of the area. The proposed house would be visually unacceptable because the width of the plot was inadequate and in the context of the relaxed density of houses in the area would constitute a cramped form of development. The cramped appearance would prejudice the amenities of the neighbourhood which the corporation had a duty to protect.

The preservation of an identity of an established estate

Re Collins and Others (1974) 30 P.&C.R. 527

16–45 Stockton House Estate, Fleet, Hampshire subject to covenants within a building scheme which were of substantial advantage because they helped to maintain the ethos of the estate. The estate was suburban but the proposed development was urban in character due to its density and the numbers and types of roads. The development would also increase traffic, noise and involve loss of privacy and the felling of a high number of trees and shrubs. Moreover, some purchasers had specifically bought the properties in reliance upon the scheme of covenants.

Re Brierfield (1976) 35 P.&C.R. 124

16–46 50, Manor Way, Onslow Village, Guildford was subject to a restriction but not more than an average of five houses to the acre were to be built and that Onslow Village Limited should determine the number of houses on each plot. Onslow Village Limited was under a moral obligation to their purchasers to safeguard the covenants and to safeguard the character of the village maintaining the standards of quality and density of housing in the area. The proposal would lead to the development of the whole frontage of Abbott's Close and Manor Way, and double the existing density of housing. The application therefore failed.

Re Kalsis (1993) 66 P.&C.R. 313

16–47 Plot on Wentworth Estate, Virginia Water, Surrey with restriction of building to one house and lodge for use of servant or occupier. The construction of a two-storey house or a bungalow in the garden of the property was a reasonable user. The roads committee argued that the restriction was of practical benefit to them as custodian of the interests of the estate in preserving the system of covenants. This was accepted but neither the scheme of covenants, nor the committee's role would be rendered ineffective by the applicant's proposals. Therefore the restriction was modified so that the applicant was permitted to build a bungalow (but not a house) on the property. (Compare *Re Henman* (1970) 23 P.&C.R. 102—below)

Re Willis (1997) 76 P.&C.R. 97

16–48 Planning permission for change of use of council house in Castle Donington, Leicestershire as bed and breakfast establishment. Restriction forbade use of the house for any trade or business. The restriction did not secure practical benefits for the council by preventing a deterioration in the amenity of the area because the bed and breakfast user did not cause such deterioration. Moreover, the proposed development would not set a precedent for applications for further bed and breakfast use on the estate. Thus, the application would not undermine the scheme of covenants which was policed by the council as the custodian of the public interest for the benefit of the residents of the estate.

Freedom from traffic and all that goes with it

Re Bass Limited (1973) 26 P.&C.R. 156

16–49 Restrictions preventing use of land as loading and unloading area for deliveries to brewery secured a substantial benefit for the owners of premises on City Road as they prevented the noises, fumes, vibration, dirt and risk of accidents which was associated with the delivery lorries.

Re Wallace and Co. (1993) 66 P.&C.R. 124

16–50 The applicant wished to build a block of 6 garages on land to the rear of numbers 29–37 Perth Road, St. Leonards-on-Sea, East Sussex and upon which it had covenanted not to build at all. The proposed development would involve increased use by vehicles of the subject land and the access way thereto. The covenant provided the council with the benefit of being able to resist the proposed development in the interests of adjoining occupiers upon this basis.

Noise and generally undesirable social activity

Re Solarfilms (Sales) Limited (1993) 67 P.&C.R. 110

16–51 Proposed user of a bungalow as a day nursery for children in Grane Park, Halingden, Lancashire. The covenants ensured that Grane Park retained its character as an exclusively residential enclave and avoided the traffic disturbance which would be caused by the user as a day nursery.

Freedom from caravans

Re Hopcraft (1993) 66 P.&C.R. 475

16–52 Covenant preventing use of land at Lucky Lite Farm, Horndean, Waterlooville, Hampshire other than for agricultural and horticultural purposes. It was proposed to use the land for the storage of touring caravans. The public at large derived substantial benefit from the maintenance of the application land in its open and undeveloped state. The enjoyment of the public footpaths which offered extensive views of the countryside across the subject land would be seriously diminished if caravans were stored on the land. The covenant therefore secured a substantial benefit to the council as the custodian of the public interest.

Nasty carports and other unaesthetic structures

Re Livingstone (1982) 47 P.&C.R. 462

16–53 The applicants wished to modify a covenant preventing any external alterations or additions to the front or side elevations of the property so that they could maintain the carport which they had erected at the side of their house in Ambroseden, near Bicester in Oxfordshire. The carport, which consisted of PVC roof sheeting on a steel frame, was an eyesore in that it could deteriorate and its roof sheeting could become discoloured. The covenant therefore secured practical benefits to Ambroseden Court Limited (the original covenantee) as it could thereby prevent any deterioration of the visual amenity of the area.

16–54 **(d) are the practical benefits of substantial value or advantage?**

- a question of fact and degree

The right to build without being in breach of covenant is *not* a practical benefit: *Re Hydeshire* (1993) 67 P.&C.R. 93.

Two questions

1. what interest does the objector have?

- freeholder in possession
- freeholder subject to a lease or licence

in the latter case whether the covenants secure benefits of *substantial* value/advantage may be open to doubt *e.g. Re Vaizey* (1974) 28 P.&C.R. 517

16–55 Mrs Vaizey had let a block of flats on long leases such that his interest was limited to the freehold reversions of the flats and a freehold interest (in possession) of the common parts of the block of flats and the undeveloped parts of the protected land. Thus, the covenants secured no practical benefit for Mrs Vaizey and she could be adequately compensated for her loss.

But a reversionary freeholder may have a moral obligation to enforce which may be a benefit of substantial value to him: where building schemes exist, for example.

2. what is substantial in terms of either value or advantage (if not both)?

Something which is of importance in money terms *or* in some other way which is of advantage to the landowner with the benefit of the covenant.

e.g. the loss of a view has a value—Re Carter (1973) 25 P.&C.R. 542
Nuisance during building operations and partial loss of sea view valued at £200; partial loss of outlook over pleasant garden valued at £100.

the prevention of "intolerable nuisances" during building operations of practical benefit
Re Tarhale Limited (1990) 60 P.&C.R. 368

16–56 *the right to vet plans*
Re Reynolds (1987) 54 P.&C.R. 121—the development of Woodside was allowed but as the garage of the property did not need to be built so close to Wharf Cottage, the objectors were awarded £500 in respect of minor changes to the development plans which could have been made for their benefit.

the preservation of the "ethos" of an estate
• a practical benefit of substantial *advantage* (even if not of value).

16–57 *Re Collins and Others* (1974) 30 P.&C.R. 527
Preservation of Stockton House Estate, Fleet, Hampshire: see above at paragraph 16–45.

Re Henman (1970) 23 P.&C.R. 102
16–58 Preservation of Wentworth Estate.
The continuance of scheme of covenants secured benefits for Wentworth Estate Company and Roads Committee as elected representatives of the owners and would discourage others from using any "in-filling" argument in attempting to develop their land.

Re Lee (1996) 72 P.&C.R. 439
16–59 Covenant preventing more than one house per plot formed part of a building scheme created in the 1960s in Hardwick Court, Pontefract, West Yorkshire. Applicant had planning permission to build another house in her garden. A building scheme establishes a system of local law applicable to the whole estate

and creates a presumption that restrictions under it will be upheld and therefore a greater burden of proof on the applicant to show that the requirements of section 84 are met. Although the construction of the extra house was a reasonable user of land, the covenant secured one general and two specific benefits which were of substantial value to the objector who lived opposite the proposed development. The general benefit was enjoyed by all members of Hardwick Court and was the right to object to the intensification of development in contravention of the restriction and maintain the status quo. The specific benefits secured to the objector were the preservation of the present outlook from her property over the applicant's garden and the prevention of the increase in traffic and parking problems in the hammerhead at the end of Hardwick Court. However, the prevention of disturbance from building works which were estimated to last for approximately six months was not considered to be a benefit of substantial value or advantage.

(e) contrary to the public interest?

16–60 This is an *alternative* to putting the application on the footing that the covenant does not secure any practical benefits of substantial value or advantage to those entitled to the benefit.

Note: factors under IB to be taken into account under this alternative head, just as before.

Only in some cases will this alternative succeed. Why?

(i) In many cases the evidence re planning policy (admitted under IB) will show that such evidence is *consistent* with the terms of the restriction.

Illustration

Re Mansfield D.C. (1976) 33 P.&C.R. 141

16–61 Restriction on land for use as cattle market consistent with planning policy on land use. Planning permission for proposed use as leisure centre. Not contrary to public interest for cattle market user to continue. It may have been contrary to the public interest to enforce the covenant if the applicants could, for example, have shown that there was no suitable alternative site for the leisure centre and that it was wholly impracticable or uneconomic to continue the cattle market at the present site or indeed any other site. No such evidence upon the facts.

(ii) The fact that planning permission has been granted for the development which is in conflict with the covenant does not mean that the covenant, in stopping the proposed development, is contrary to the public interest.

Re Davies (1971) 25 P.&C.R. 115

16–62 Planning permission means that a particular form of development is not contrary to the public interest, it does not mean that it is contrary to the public interest if the proposed development is not permitted. Planning permission sought for 11 houses on a site in Somerton. No evidence of public interest other than general evidence of a need to build houses to meet the demand from elsewhere in the county.

Re Wallace and Co. (1993) 66 P.&C.R. 124

16–63 Application to erect six garages for which planning permission had been granted on a plot of land to the rear of some terraced houses on Perth Road, St Leonards-on-Sea, East Sussex. Not contrary to the public interest to prevent the proposed development because there was no need for further off-street parking in the immediate area. On-street parking in Perth Road did not present any specific problem or danger.

Re Hopcraft (1993) 66 P.&C.R. 475

16–64 Grant of planning permission merely a factor which Lands tribunal can take into account in the exercise of its discretion. The Planning Acts and the Lands Tribunal's jurisdiction under the Law of Property Act 1925 were two separate regimes. The public interest required that the subject land be kept free from development rather than as a site for the storage of touring caravans. Although the occupants of touring caravans parked them in driveways or gardens in the district, there was no evidence that the owners left them there because of lack of storage sites.

Re O'Reilly (1993) 66 P.&C.R. 485

16–65 Restriction which impeded the proposed development of land for six houses in Chatham was contrary to the public interest. Although the development had been granted planning permission, there was no evidence of any need for housing in the area or that the removal or modification of the restriction would end or reduce vandalism in the area.

However, there may be cases where the public interest requirement *can* be made out, but those are likely to be rare.

Illustrations

- need for care homes

Re Lloyd and Lloyd (1993) 66 P.&C.R. 112

16–66 Planning permission for change of use to community care home for psychiatric patients in Worthing area. This use was contrary to the restriction which permitted use as a school or boarding house. It was government policy to discharge psychiatric patients into community care and there was a desperate need for such a home in the Worthing area. Therefore public interest requirement met.

- shortage of housing land

Re S.J.C. Construction Company Limited (1974) 28 P.&C.R. 200

16–67 Planning permission was granted for a two-storey block of flats to be built on land in Cheam. Restriction which permitted the erection of a single dwelling house upon the subject land. At the time of the application, a dwelling house which had previously been built upon the land had been demolished and the proposed flats had been constructed up to first-floor level. The restriction was contrary to the public interest because there was a scarcity of housing in the whole of the South East of England including the area of Sutton and Cheam and the building work which had already been carried out would be wasted unless the restriction was modified.

- unnecessary demolition of housing

Re Fisher & Gimson (Builders) Limited (1992) 65 P.&C.R. 312

16–68 Application for discharge or modification of restriction providing that a third of an acre of land in Solihull, West Midlands, should only be used as garden land, so as to permit the retention of a house and garage erected there. The objectors had also commenced proceedings to enforce the restriction in the High Court and claimed mandatory orders that *inter alia* the house and garage be pulled down and demolished.

These proceedings had been adjourned to await the outcome of the application. If the restriction was enforced there was a real risk that important housing accommodation would be demolished and that was contrary to the public interest. As the restriction, therefore, impeded a reasonable user of the land contrary to the public interest, it was modified so as to permit the development retrospectively. Compensation of £6,000 was awarded to reflect price of release or by reference to other releases achieved by consent.

But compare:

Re Hunt (1996) 73 P.&C.R. 126

16–69 A dwelling house had been erected in the rear garden of 251, Marlborough Road, Swindon pursuant to planning permission. This development was in breach of covenants under a building scheme whereby the erection of only one house was permitted per plot and each house had to be built within the building line. The development was obtrusive in relation to the remainder of the scheme area as it had been built well in advance of the building line and had a cramped appearance. Moreover, to allow the application would have the effect of opening the first breach in a carefully maintained scheme of development and would render it more difficult to oppose further subdivisions of lots with the consequent threat of increasing density and loss of character i the neighbourhood. Thus, the covenants secured a substantial practical benefit, namely the assurance of the continued integrity of the building scheme. To pull the dwelling house down was *not* contrary to the public interest because there was no scarcity of land available for housing development in the area and a writ claiming an injunction to enforce the covenants had not been issued.

(e) will money be adequate compensation?

16–70 The Lands Tribunal must be satisfied that:

(i) money is an adequate substitute for the loss arising from the discharge and modification; and

(ii) such money which the Lands tribunal has power to award under section 84(1)(i) or (ii) (see below) is adequate compensation.

Note:
if no loss would be caused by discharge or modification, this question does not arise: *Re Willis* (1997) 76 P.&C.R. 97; see above, at paragraph 16–48.

Sub-paragraph (b)

16–71 "that the persons of full age and capacity for the time being or from time to time entitled to the benefit of the restriction ... have agreed, either expressly or by implication, by their acts or omissions, to the same being discharged or modified".

(a) This ground is unlikely to be relied on at the time of the application in view of the obvious point that if all the persons with the benefit are agreed that the discharge or modification should go ahead, they can achieve this end by deed.

(b) But there are cases where at the date of the application it is possible that there will be a class of persons who, by the time of the hearing, have not lodged notices of objection or have withdrawn those lodged. In such cases the applicant should rely on this ground as an alternative to his main ground.[24]

(c) Even if there are no objectors the Lands Tribunal still has a discretion as to whether to discharge or modify.[25]

(d) It is important in practice, when relying on this ground, that any notice of application must make it clear to those upon whom it might be served, or to whom it might be directed, what will be the effect of any Order the Tribunal may make on the application. Thus, where an application is made seeking discharge and modification in the alternative, the consequences of each alternative must be made clear in the notice of application. If there is room for misunderstanding the effect of one or other of the consequences of an order being made for one of the alternatives claimed, the tribunal is entitled to refuse to exercise its discretion to refuse to make an Order under subsection (b) in respect of that part of the application, even though there may be no objection to it. It is, therefore, vital that the effect of alternative heads of application is made clear to potential objectors in any notice

[24] See precedent A7–09 at App. 7.
[25] *Re University of Westminster's Application* [1998] 3 All E.R. 1014, CA.

of application.[26] It may also be worth making a decision at an early stage, and certainly before the application is drawn and made, whether it is preferable to make the application for either discharge or modification and not both, even in the alternative. In many cases the application will be focussed on the need to modify, and the reality will be that discharge is not desired. This course, which requires an early decision to "nail one's colours to the mast" may be wise in order to avoid any later difficulty of the type that arose in *Re University of Westminster*.

Practical tips for applications under sub-paragraph (b)

16–72

- is it certain that all relevant consents are to hand? A failure to respond is not evidence of consent.
- has the application made it clear what the consequences of the relief sought are, particularly if there are alternatives between discharge and modification? The notice must be drawn so as to make it clear "beyond the possibility of misunderstanding".
- is this a case where modification (as opposed to discharge) is really what is sought?

Illustrations of cases under subsection (b)

Section 84(1)(b)

Re Child Brothers, Limited (1958) 10 P.&C.R. 71

16–72/1 Application for the modification of covenants affecting 14.53 acres of land which was formerly part of the Whitstable Manor Estate, Whitstable so that 100 houses could be built. If a building scheme existed, it had been more honoured in the breach than in the observance. The permitted number of houses had been exceeded upon 14 out of the 22 plots of land. No building scheme was found to exist but in any event if such a scheme had existed the evidence of the general disregard of the covenants meant that they would have been impliedly waived under paragraph (b).

Re Robinson and O'Connor (1964) 16 P.&C.R. 106

16–72/2 Restrictions imposed on the user of a shop in Timperley, Cheshire, for the benefit of two adjacent shops which forbade its use except for specified trades. Applicants wished to modify the restrictions so as to continue to use the shop as an off-licence (this use had commenced a year before the hearing). Although the objectors had indicated that they were generally willing to consider agreeing

[26] It was the failure to make the effect of a discharge, as opposed to a modification, clear in the notice ("beyond the possibility of misunderstanding") which justified the tribunal in *Re University of Westminster*, above, in refusing to make an order under subsection (b) for discharge; agreement to that part of the application could not be inferred from the absence of objection.

to such use and their solicitors had sent a letter in these terms, they had not given their irrevocable consent in writing to the user such that the application failed under paragraph (b).

Re Goodban (1970) 23 P.&C.R. 110

16–72/3 Restriction prohibited erection of more than one detached or one pair of semi-detached dwelling-houses on a site in Caversham, Reading. Application to permit the erection of four private dwelling-houses on the site. The objectors did not have the benefit of the restrictions because no building scheme with mutual covenants existed. The benefit of the restriction vested in the Caversham Park Estate Company whose rights had been assigned to Davis Contractors Limited. The assignee consented to the proposed development and the restriction was therefore modified under paragraph (b).

Re Fettishaw (No. 2) (1973) 27 P.&C.R. 292

16–72/4 The applicants sought modification of certain restrictive covenants to enable them to erect a five-storey block of flats on a site in Wimbledon Hill Road, London SW19. After certain objectors had withdrawn from the proceedings, the applicants agreed terms with the remaining objectors upon the basis that the restrictions should be modified to permit a four-storey block of flats with parking space below the level of the ground floor, the applicants should enter new restrictive covenants with the objectors and also pay them a sum towards their costs. Thus, the objectors had expressly agreed to modify the covenants under paragraph (b) whilst any other persons who may potentially object, had by implication, by their failure to come forward despite the publicity given the application, agreed to the restrictions being modified.

Re Dare and Beck (1974) 28 P.&C.R. 354

16–72/5 As all objectors entitled to the benefit of the restrictions had withdrawn their objections, the Lands Tribunal allowed the application to be amended to seek modification under paragraph (b). The restrictions were modified in accordance with the development plans annexed to the application under that paragraph.

Re Lloyds Bank Limited (1976) 35 P.&C.R. 128

16–72/6 The bank applied as the administrators of the estate of the deceased owner of the bungalow in St. Briavels, Gloucestershire, to discharge covenants which applied to the land forming part of the curtilage of the bungalow. In about 1951, in breach of covenant, the deceased's predecessor in title built the bungalow which encroached upon protected land and was used to store trade materials for business. The objectors were unaware of these breaches until the date of the application and did not object to the retrospective modification of the covenants so as to allow the encroachment by the bungalow. However, they opposed the application to discharge the covenants. Although the objectors could be deemed to have condoned the breach both for the extension of the bungalow and for its use for trade purposes, their acquiescence could be met by modification and did not warrant a total discharge of the covenants.

Re Cornick (1994) 68 P.&C.R. 372

16–72/7 0.041 acres of land in Bridport, Dorset to be used for the construction of three dwelling-houses. Land subject to restriction that to be used exclusively for a jam factory. The objector did not object to the discharge of the covenant but claimed he was entitled to compensation. Therefore the restriction was discharged under paragraph (b). The objector was awarded compensation of £5,000 upon the basis that he would have obtained a higher price for the land from the applicant if no stipulation restricting the use of the site had been agreed at the time of the purchase.

Re University of Westminster 1998 E.G.C.S. 118

16–72/8 The university applied to discharge or modify restrictions limiting the use of its buildings fronting Marylebone Road, London NW1, for specified educational uses so as to permit their use for general educational purposes. Although there were no objectors, the applicants were not entitled to an order for the discharge of the restrictions, either as of right or as the inevitable result of the exercise of the Tribunal's discretion. The Court of Appeal upheld the Tribunal in exercising its discretion as to whether or not to grant relief. Upon the facts of the case the Tribunal had correctly decided to modify the restrictions, rather than discharge them, having regard to the interests of those whom the restrictions may have been intended to protect and having regard to the fact that the application had not made it clear what the consequences of discharge (as opposed to modification) would be.

Sub-paragraph (c)

16–73 "that the proposed discharge or modification will not injure the persons entitled to the benefit of the restriction".

When will this ground be used?

- to stop vexatious or frivolous objections.[27]
- as a long stop to prevent vexatious or frivolous objections[28]
- where it can be shown that the proposed discharge or modification will not injure those entitled to the benefit. The emphasis is on the words *proposed discharge or modification*. It is not the proposed *development* which is being examined under this ground. Thus, it may be necessary to look at the scheme of the covenants. If, for example, in a development scheme the discharge or modification would cause the enforceability of the scheme to be vulnerable, that would be an injury. An application in such a case on this ground would fail. The replacement of one "eyesore" with another would be objectionable if the effect would be to injure those with the benefit.[29] Local authorities with an interest in

[27] *Ridley v. Taylor* [1965] 1 W.L.R. 611; *Stockport MBC v. Alwiyah Developments*, above.
[28] *Ridley v. Taylor*, above.
[29] *Re Forestmere* (1980) 41 P.&C.R. 390.

enforcing covenants as "custodians of the public interest" will be entitled to oppose applications made under this subsection on the footing that they have an interest in preserving covenants which secure advantages to the inhabitants, such as amenity, or residential space.[30]

- where there is evidence that the covenants that are the subject of the application are being used simply to extract money and not to control development, the Lands Tribunal may well conclude that there is no injury.
- in some cases the argument is raised that, whereas the instant application may not injure, its future effect may do so, for example in schemes of development. This is often known as the "thin end of the wedge" argument.

  It is a potentially serious argument to be dealt with on the merits of each case.[31] Whilst the Tribunal cannot bind itself to a future course of action, it will have regard to the scheme of covenants as a whole and to the maintenance of the integrity of such covenants. Thus, where an application threatens the integrity of such covenants, the preservation of such integrity is of substantial practical benefit to those with the benefit of the covenants, and if that is so, the argument that the application does not injure will fail. The Tribunal will also have regard to the fact that if the instant application succeeds, that may have an effect on future applications and the context in which they will be considered. The thin end of the wedge argument is, therefore, to be looked at with care by both applicants and objectors. Such an argument will assist those objecting by showing that there are practical benefits of value or advantage when applications are made under subsection (aa) and in showing that there is injury under subsection (c). For the applicant the argument may be difficult to rebut, unless there are few properties affected by the covenants, or where there is no real scheme.[32]

Practical tips for applications under subsection (c)

16–74

- bearing in mind the burden of proving a lack of injury, if you are for the applicant, is my expert evidence going to stand up to scrutiny?
- is this a case where the thin end of the wedge argument has any merit? It is a potentially useful weapon for objectors.

[30] See *Re Martins' Application* (1988) 57 P.&C.R. 119, (open space); *Re Houdret* (1989) 58 P.& C.R. 310 (residential as opposed to officer user in town centre).

[31] *Re Emery* (1956) 8 P.&C.R. 113; *Re Saviker (No. 2)* (1973) 26 P.&C.R. 441; *Cryer v. Scott Bros (Sunbury) Ltd* (1986) 55 P.&C.R. 183.

[32] See *McMorris v. Brown* [1999] A.C. 142, for approval by the Privy Council of the approach taken by the tribunal in *Re Snaith & Dolding's Application* (1995) 71 P.&C.R. 104, which is summarised above. For an instance where there was no scheme and adjacent properties would not be affected by proposed development, see *Re Chapman* (1980) 42 P.&C.R. 114, where the "thin end of the wedge" argument was rejected. See also *Re Hextall's Application* (1998) (LP36/1997, George Bartlett Q.C. President) where the "thin end of the wedge" argument was rejected in the context of covenants not part of a scheme.

Illustrations under subsection (c) and of the "thin end of the wedge" argument

Section 84(1)(c)

When will this ground be used?

To stop vexatious or frivolous objections

Ridley v. Taylor [1965] 1 W.L.R. 611

16–75 *The general rule*: "My own view of paragraph (c) is that it is, so to speak, a long stop against vexatious objections to extended user ... [u]nder paragraph (c) the objection must be related to his [the plaintiff's] own proprietary interest. ... [The textbooks] suggest that paragraph (c) may be designed to cover the case of the, proprietorially speaking, frivolous objection. For my part I would subscribe to that view."

Russell L.J. held that the Lands Tribunal had incorrectly modified a restriction preventing the user of a dwelling house as five self-contained flats in Mayfair.

Re Brown (1977) 35 P.&C.R. 254

16–76 The applicant wished to conduct alteration and extension works in accordance with conditional planning permission to the front of No. 32, Stag Lane. Restriction preventing any alteration to existing building at No. 32 for the benefit of the freeholder of No. 34. Restrictions modified to allow renovation work because the objector's complaints that would interfere with light and air were "trivial". In fact the renovations would enhance the value of No. 34 rather than affect it detrimentally.

Re Pearson (1978) 36 P.&C.R. 285

16–77 The applicant wished to alter the barn in grounds of his dwelling house in Cubbington, Warwick and use as a nursing home. Restrictions in favour of occupiers of adjoining land preventing the use of the subject land except as a dwelling house and preventing any alteration to the existing buildings. Objectors claimed that if the application were granted, it would be more difficult for them to get planning permission for their own land for industrial purposes. As the objectors could not reasonably be expected to get planning permission in any event, the objectors did not suffer any prejudice by the discharge or modification of the restrictions to permit the alterations to the barn.

Where it can be shown that the proposed discharge or modification will not injure those entitled to benefit

Re Beecham Group Limited (1980) 41 P.&C.R. 369

16–78 The applicant wished to erect buildings upon a 10 acre site in Sompting, West Sussex for the manufacture of desensitising vaccines. Site subject to a restriction that no buildings to be erected save for purposes incidental to its use as playing fields. The District Council did not own any land capable of being benefited by the restriction and did not object to the development on aesthetic grounds. Thus it would not be injured by any proposed modification.

Re Chapman (1980) 42 P.&C.R. 114

16–79 The applicant wished to build a dwelling house in a quarter of an acre of the garden of Mere Cottage, Old Woking Road, Woking. Restriction prevented more than two houses (which already existed) on the plot for the benefit of Nos 135 and 139, Old Woking Road. The occupiers of Nos 135 and 139 would not be injured by the development because it would be screened from their view by a line of trees and No. 137 which was interposed between the objectors' houses and Mere Cottage.

Re Farmiloe (1983) 48 P.&C.R. 317

16–80 The applicant wished to convert a coach house with 260 square yards of land on the Selly Hall Estate, Birmingham, into a dwelling house. Land subject to a restriction requiring each dwelling house to have a quarter of an acre of land. No evidence that any of the objectors would suffer any direct detriment in the enjoyment of their properties or any immediate diminution in their value. The increase in density of housing as a result of the proposal was negligible and would result in an attractive improvement to Upland Road. Restrictions modified to permit proposed development.

Re Cox (1985) 51 P.&C.R. 335

16–81 The owner of Sunnyside, Chiddingly, East Sussex wished to use an adjoining house known as Belfairs as a residence for an agricultural worker. Restrictions that Sunnyside only to be used as a residence for domestic staff of Belfairs and that not to be sold off or let separately from Belfairs. The Council would not be injured by any proposed modification of the restrictions since no new dwelling house was to be erected and therefore there was no breach of planning policies applicable to the area.

Re Towner & Goddard (1989) 58 P.&C.R. 316

16–82 Applicant proposed to build tennis courts with chain-link perimeter fencing in gardens of Nos 1 and 2, Cookham Dene Close, Chislehurst, Kent. The gardens formed part of the metropolitan green belt and were subject to a restriction preventing any building in the area. The council as custodian of the public interest claimed that the openness of the view would be lost if the tennis courts were built. As the view was not open but a view of houses and their gardens, the existence of tennis courts in the gardens would not appear out of place and the council would not suffer any injury.

Re Hydeshire Limited (1993) 67 P.&C.R. 93

16–83 Applicant proposed to build five houses on a site covering No. 180, Jersey Road, Osterley. Covenants imposed in 1922 and 1923 limited the number and type of houses to be built on land which included the site of No. 180. The 1923 covenant only permitted the erection of two houses on No. 180. The proposed development would result in a total of eight detached houses on land including No. 180, whilst a 1922 covenant permitted only six. The owner of number 188 objected, as he was also proposing to build two houses on the site of No. 188. If the proposed development were completed *before* his own proposals were executed, he would be in breach of covenant in constructing two further houses on the site of No. 188. Application succeeded under paragraph (aa) as the owner of No. 188 did not have a practical benefit in seeking to preserve the right to build on his land without being in breach of covenant. The application would have succeeded under paragraph (c) in any event for the injury claimed by the objector was not as a result of the proposed modification but as a consequence of the objector's own failure to get his building done earlier at a time when the restriction would not have prohibited him.

Where there is evidence that the covenants are used simply to extract money and not to control development

Re Bennett and Tamarlin Limited (1987) 54 P.&C.R. 378

16–84 Restriction imposed on four-storey, end-of-terrace house and a three-storey mid-terrace house in Plymouth permitting their use only as private residence. Applicant proposed to use them for five self-contained flats and a maisonette. The trustees of the St Aubyn Discretionary Trust would not suffer any loss of amenity and there would be no diminution in value of any property retained by them. The trustees had been and were using the restrictions for a purpose for which they were not intended, namely to enable them to extract money as a consideration for agreeing to modifications of the restrictions. This loss of bargaining power was not a factor to be taken into account under paragraph (c).

"Thin end of the wedge argument"

Re Emery (1956) 8 P.&C.R. 113

16–85 Applicant proposed to build second house in grounds of property in Roundwood Park, Harpenden, Hertfordshire although a restriction permitted only one house on each plot. The objectors would be injured by the proposed development to the extent that the whole scheme and lay-out of the estate would be broken if the application were granted. Moreover, in time, many houses might be built upon vacant land forming part of the wood by the severance of existing plots or the mutual rearrangement of boundaries, if the application were allowed.

Re Saviker (No. 2) (1973) 26 P.&C.R. 441

16–86 Henry Boot Estates Limited laid out the Orchard Estates, Staines, for building purposes. Out of 240 plots, 92 remained unsold and were therefore vested in Boot which let them out. All the plots were subject to a restriction permitting only one house per plot for the benefit of Boot. A purchaser applied to build a second house on his plot. To allow the application would mean the beginning of the breakdown in Boot's system of "one plot, one house" and therefore the basis upon which Boot sold houses to residents on the estate.

Re Beech (1990) 59 P.&C.R. 502

16–87 Applicant proposed to use terraced house in Harborough Road, Kingsthorpe, Northampton, as an annex for adjoining solicitors' offices. Restriction preventing use other than for residential purposes. Necessary to consider council's position as owner of adjoining property, in the capacity of housing authority, and as local planning authority. Legitimate objective to seek to preserve residential enclave in predominantly commercial setting of Harborough Road and to oppose continuing process of conversion of property to non-residential uses. Moreover, if the scheme of covenants created upon the sale of council property to sitting tenants were breached once, it would be more difficult for other modifications to be resisted and reduce the availability of housing stock at the lower end of the market. Thus the restriction secured a substantial advantage to the council under paragraph (aa).

Re Solarfilms (Sales) Limited (1993) 67 P.&C.R. 110

16–88 Applicant proposed to use bungalow in Grane Park, Haslingden, Lancashire as nursery school although restriction that must only be used as private residence. Restriction secured practical benefit and advantage to objectors under paragraph (aa) because it allowed them to preserve the character of Grane Park as an exclusively residential enclave, and without traffic problem.

Re Snaith and Dolding (1995) 71 P.&C.R. 104

16–89 Applicant proposed to build a second house in the curtilage of a house known as Westwood, Blackhall Lane, Sevenoaks and which formed part of the Wilderness Estate. The estate was subject to a building scheme of mutually binding covenants which *inter alia* permitted only one house on each plot. To allow the application would deprive the objectors of a substantial benefit secured by the covenants, namely the assurance of the integrity of the building scheme. The erection of the house would also alter the context in which further subdivisions of estate plots would be considered. Thus the objectors could preserve the integrity of the scheme and forestall further applications of a similar kind.

Re Hunt (1996) 73 P.&C.R. 126

16–90 A house had been built in advance of the building line in the garden of a plot forming part of a building scheme in Swindon. Restrictive covenants in the building scheme provided that only one house was to be built on each plot and that each house was to be within the building line. To grant the application would have the effect of opening the first breach in a carefully maintained and successful scheme of development, and would render it more difficult to resist further applications for the subdivision of plots with the consequent threats of increasing density and loss of character. The restrictions therefore secured a substantial practical benefit for the objectors, namely the assurance of the continued integrity of the building scheme.

Where argument rejected:

Re Willis (1997) 76 P.&C.R. 97

16–91 Semi-detached house in Castle Donington, Leicestershire was proposed to be used as a bed and breakfast establishment. Restrictions imposed by council upon the sale of property to the applicant prevented any use of the property for trade or business. The council claimed that if the application were allowed, it would be the thin end of the wedge and would set a precedent for the introduction of further commercial uses onto the residential estate. As there were very few properties on the estate which were capable of being so converted and each application must be considered upon its own merits, the proposed modification did not set a precedent.

Re Love and Love (1993) 67 P.&C.R. 101

16–92 Erection of garage in character with house and not detrimental to amenity of area, which was of no great architectural merit, permitted. "Thin end of the wedge" argument rejected.

WHAT ARE THE PRINCIPAL MATTERS WHICH WILL AFFECT THE LANDS TRIBUNAL'S DISCRETION UNDER ANY OF THE GROUNDS?

16–93 (a) The matters set out in paragraph (1B) of section 84.

- the development plan.
- local structure or unitary plans.
- the period and context in which the covenant was created or imposed. Where the covenant is part of a building scheme, or where it is clear that the covenants support a "cohesive" approach to the maintenance of a certain standard or style of development, the greater the burden of proof on the applicant to show that the requirements of section 84 have been met.[33]
- the age of the covenant.
- whether the applicant is a recent or original covenantor. Such an applicant may have to satisfy the Tribunal to a higher degree of proof but equally the emphasis nowadays may be more on the other matters referred to above and it is important that these are put before the Tribunal. (See paragraph 16–115, below).
- the planning consent for the proposed development on the land within the application.

16–94 (b) The Tribunal must have jurisdiction to entertain an application as one which falls within section 84(1). The covenant to be discharged or modified must be in the nature of a restriction on user.[34] Applications relating to covenants within subsections (7) and (11) of section 84 will

[33] See *Re Lee's Application* (1996) 72 P.&C.R. 439 for a recent decision emphasising this important factor.

[34] See *Re Milius* [1996] 1 E.G.L.R. 209 where the tribunal questioned whether a covenant under Housing Act 1985, s. 159, restricting the class of owner, fell within s. 84(1) as a "restriction ... as to the user [of the land]."

not be entertained. In addition certain statutes expressly exclude the Lands Tribunal's jurisdiction.[35]

(c) Where the applicant wants a temporary modification only or a personal licence to act in breach of the restriction the tribunal will decline jurisdiction.

(d) The Tribunal will not rewrite the restriction, for example by inserting additional words which are unrelated to the need to modify.[36]

What compensation will the Lands tribunal award?

Generally

16–95 The Lands Tribunal has a discretion in determining what sum by way of compensation it is just to award. That leads to the result that there is no hard and fast formula which governs the means by which compensation can be determined. Under section 84(1) there are two alternative heads and each requires the application of different principles. The text of the alternatives is as follows:

(i) a sum to make up for any loss or disadvantage suffered by that person in consequence of the discharge or modification; or

(ii) a sum to make up for any effect which the restriction had, at the time when it was imposed, in reducing the consideration then received for the land affected by it.

Principles applicable under paragraph (i) **16–96**

"a sum to make up for any loss or disadvantage suffered by that person in consequence of the discharge or modification".

This means that:

(a) Any compensation given must be as a result of loss suffered as a consequence of the discharge or modification of the restriction.

(b) The mere existence of the jurisdiction under section 84 and the fact that its existence diminishes the ability of the covenantee to extract the price of a release from the covenantor (assuming the continued existence of the covenant) does not allow the Lands Tribunal to award compensation based on the loss of such bargaining power, or the opportunity to exercise it. Such loss is attributable to the failure of the covenantee to negotiate prior to an application to the Lands

[35] See National Trust Act 1971, s. 27 and Chap. 10 above.

[36] *Re North's Application* (1997) 75 P.&C.R. 117, the Tribunal refused to add words so as to imply a condition of reasonableness as to the granting of consent.

tribunal by the covenantor. Such loss (attributable, in effect, to such failure) is not attributable to the makings of any order by the Lands Tribunal.[37]

(c) Thus, what is recoverable is often measured by reference to "loss of amenity."

There is no hard and fast formula for what governs the calculation of this sum, but, in practical terms this can include:

16–97 (i) *Diminution in value of the objector's land or his interest in it*

This may not always be substantial. It will be for the parties to adduce expert evidence from their valuers what such diminution is in terms of effect on the value of the benefited land. Again there is no hard and fast formula here, but within the scope of such diminution the following factors can be isolated and, where appropriate, can be given a value:

- loss of the benefit of certain obvious amenities such as loss of a view.[38]
- the loss of other benefits which can have an effect on value, even if no "hard and fast" value can be placed on them. For example consider the effect of the potential increase in noise or traffic which development may bring.

16–98 (ii) *What would be the price of a release?*

This means what those with the benefit of the covenant which is the subject of the application would have regarded as a fair price for a licence to carry out what is proposed, which but for the prospective exercise of the tribunal's jurisdiction, would be in breach of it. The starting point is invariably an assessment of the net development value of the land which is the subject of the application. The second stage is to ask what proportion of that should be regarded as a fair price for a release.

It is sometimes said that this requires compensation to be assessed by reference to a fixed percentage of the developer's gain. But this is not so for two reasons. First, it is important to note that the tribunal must be satisfied that in any case where this approach is being advocated, those with the benefit would have obtained the price of a release on this basis. The fair price of a release will be dictated by the degree of loss of amenity. Secondly, the percentage itself is not fixed and its size must reflect all the factors which affect the circumstances in which the price of the release is being assessed. Although one third is described the "Stokes" percentage it is mis-

[37] *Stockport MBC v. Alwiyah* (above).
[38] *Gilbert v. Spoor* (1983) Ch. 27.

leading to think that this is going to determine the award.[39]

The question may be put this way in order to try to assess the amount due:

"What would the outcome of friendly negotiations have been—assuming both sides had made a serious attempt to assess the net development value of the subject land?"

Because the Tribunal has a wide discretion, it may go as high as 50 per cent of the developer's gain, as it did in the SJC Construction, or it may go to a much lower percentage, such as 5 per cent. Equally, it may simply look at what has been agreed as the "licence fee" in other cases in the locality where others have agreed releases or variations of the same covenants without invoking the tribunal's jurisdiction.[40] Such "comparables" may, therefore, be of some importance in establishing a benchmark for compensation under paragraph (i). Where loss of amenity is slight the fair price of consent will also be slight.[41]

(ii) *A* "solatium" *for the effect of building works*

16–99 The Tribunal may decide that the effect of the discharge or modification is such as not to cause any loss to those with the benefit of the covenant in terms of diminution in the value of that land however measured, but that proposed works of building which will be sanctioned by the discharge or modification will be a nuisance to those with the benefit while the works are being carried out. In such cases the Tribunal may award a sum designed to compensate those so affected for three months, or thereabouts, by nuisance caused by noise and dust, etc.

The amount is not going to be high. In *Re Gaffney's Application* (1974) 35 P.&C.R. 440, £500 was described as generous. Allowing for inflation since then, an award of £1,000 may be a realistic ceiling.

Principles applicable under paragraph (ii)

16–100 "a sum to make up for any effect which the restriction had, at the time when it was imposed, in reducing the consideration then received for the land affected by it".

(a) Compensation has to be assessed by reference to the difference between

[39] See *Re S.J.C. Construction* (1975) 29 P.&C.R. 322, for the way in which the tribunal approaches this method of assessment. See Chap. 15, para. 15–38 above for the manner in which the courts have applied the "licence" or release fee principle in the assessment of damages. The approach of both the tribunal and the courts will often be the same.

[40] As it did in *Re Fisher & Gimson* (1992) 65 P.&C.R. 312.

[41] *Stockport MBC v. Alwiyah* (1983) 52 P.&C.R. 278.

the price paid for the burdened land subject to the restriction and the price which would have been payable for the same land free from any restriction.

(b) Unlike compensation under paragraph (i) where the person entitled to the benefit of the covenant suffers loss by reason of the discharge or modification, under paragraph (ii) compensation is based on the price or value of the applicant's land. Under paragraph (ii) the applicant should be effectively disgorging the saving he made when he bought the land subject to the restriction, as opposed to a purchase of the same land without it. But as is seen below, it is difficult to establish this "saving". The emphasis is, therefore, on the words *"a sum to make up for"*. This means that the tribunal may only be able to go part of the way (if it is able to proceed under paragraph (ii) at all) to establishing what effect the restriction had on the consideration part for the land.

16–101 (c) There are a number of problems inherent in any attempt to award compensation under paragraph (ii). They are:

- The burden lies on the objector to show that he is entitled to compensation under either paragraph (i) or (ii), but in the case of a claim under paragraph (ii) he must show that the price was reduced on account of the restriction. In many cases it may be impossible to show this. In fact in some cases, particularly in scheme covenants, the presence of the scheme and the "select" nature of the estate may have increased the price of the land. Covenants may not, therefore, always be depreciatory in their effect on value.
- No allowance is made for inflation or deflation. The measure is historic. So a price based on a purchase in 1935 or 1975 is compared with a price for the same land at that date without a restriction. Once again the stress is on the words "a sum to make up for" the reduction.
- Quite apart from problems with historic evidence of value in many cases it may be impossible to show what the difference is, if any. Many residential estates are developed where restrictions are imposed and plots are sold at a price which can hardly be dissected to discover what lower price would have been paid at that time. Accordingly, the approach can only be one which adopts "intelligent guesswork" or "roughly and ready inference". However, it may be clear that land has a difference in value where for example the covenant allows a permitted density of houses and where the application to modify is seeking a double of the original permitted density.[42] The words "a sum to make up for" are repeated to show

[42] As to rough and ready inference see *Re Bowden* (1983) 47 P.&C.R. 455 and *Re Cornick* (1994) 68 P.&C.R. 372. For an instance of a clear difference in land value under this paragraph see *Re New Ideal Home Ltd* (1978) 36 P.&C.R. 476.

that the approach to compensation under paragraph (ii) cannot be accurate, and the paragraph does not require it to be so.

Finally, it is important to remember that the Tribunal is not obliged to order compensation in every case where the covenant is discharged or modified. It is entitled to take the view that if there is no evidence of loss or disadvantage, or any difference under paragraph (ii), it may decline to make any award of compensation.[43]

WILL THE COMPENSATION AWARDED VARY ACCORDING TO THE GROUND ON WHICH DISCHARGE OR MODIFICATION IS SOUGHT?

16–102 The following general principles apply so far as they emerge from the authorities.

Applications under paragraph (a)

(Obsolete covenants)

16–103 A claim for loss or disadvantage under paragraph (i) is not likely to succeed if the covenant is obsolete. But a claim based on the difference in value of the land under paragraph (ii) above might well succeed.[44]

Applications under paragraph (aa)

(No practical benefits, etc.)

16–104 If relief is granted on the basis that the covenant does not secure any practical benefit of substantial value or advantage (section 84 (1A)(a)) an award under paragraph (i) will usually be small in view of the lack of any substantial value or advantage in the covenant. However, by way of contrast, in some cases substantial compensation has been held to be adequate. The pattern is not altogether clear here and paragraph (ii) can be relied upon where there is a marked difference in original value.

If relief is granted under section (1A)(b) (contrary to the public interest) an award can clearly be granted under either paragraph (i) for the loss or disadvantage may well be substantial, or under paragraph (ii).

Applications under paragraph (b)

(Consent cases)

If the affected parties consent there is no reason why an award cannot be made under paragraphs (i) or (ii).

[43] *Re Willis* (1997) 76 P.&C.R. 97 at 113, is an example of this.

[44] See *Re Quaffer's Application* (1988) 56 P.&C.R. 142, for an example of this, where there was on loss or disadvantage suffered by the discharge of obsolete covenants and any loss of bargaining power as a result of the jurisdiction to discharge was not allowable, following *Stockport MBC v. Alwiyah Developments* (1983) 52 P.&C.R. 278, noted at para. 16–96 above. For the facts of *Re Quaffer* see the illustrations of applications under paragraph (a) above at para. 16–18.

Applications under paragraph (c)

(No injury)
The same principles apply here as they do under applications under paragraph (a). As there is no injury no compensation is likely to be awarded under paragraph (i), there being no loss or disadvantage suffered in such a case. But as under paragraph (a) there is still the possibility of an award under paragraph (ii).

How can the application be made and what are the stages to its final determination?

16–105 The application must follow the procedure set out in the Lands Tribunal Rules 1996, principally Part V of those Rules (printed in Appendix 4). Also printed in Appendix 4 are the Practice Directions issued by the Tribunal. These should be followed at each stage where applicable.

In addition it is helpful for applicants to have sight of the explanatory leaflet which can be obtained free from the Tribunal and which is updated from time to time.

16–106 The stages are as follows, with reference in parentheses in each stage to the relevant rules and the party primarily responsible for that stage, if not the Tribunal.

Stage 1
(Applicant: rule 13)
Make the application noting the detail which is required under rule 13. No form is prescribed, but a form will be provided by the Tribunal. (See precedent in Appendix 7 at A7–09).

Stage 2
(Applicant/Lands Tribunal: rule 14)
Consider what notices/advertisements are required. The Tribunal will give directions as to service. (See precedents in Appendix 7, at A7–11 and A7–12).

Stage 3
(Objector: rule 15)
Lodge form of objection. No form is prescribed but the objector may be asked to give particulars under rule 15(2) and a specimen can be obtained from the Tribunal. (See precedent in Appendix 7 at A7–10).

Stage 4
16–107 (All parties/Lands Tribunal: rule 38 and 39)
At this stage the applicant will need to certify that all objectors have lodged their objections and their title to object by showing that they have the benefit of the covenant within the application. The applicant must also certify whether and to what extent such objections are admitted. To the extent that such title

is not admitted the objectors will have to show their title to object. Consider at this stage:

- whether any interlocutory applications are required;
- use of pre-trial review; see Practice Direction 4/1997;
- amendments required;
- whether to exclude objectors who do not have title to object under section 84(3A);
- in complex cases, whether any decision is required under section 84(2) as to construction or enforceability of the restriction before the Lands Tribunal, thereby requiring the application to be suspended for the time being.

Obtain orders and directions accordingly.

Stage 5
(All parties: rule 42)
Consider the use to be made of expert evidence. Obtain orders and directions accordingly. Consider also the use of assessors under rule 29A if special knowledge is required by the tribunal, but this is extremely rare. **16–108**

Try to agree facts. It is wrong to instruct experts not to agree them.[45] See Practice Direction 5/1997 for the duties of expert witnesses.

Stage 6
(All parties)
Consider the extent to which orders and directions are required as to:

- discovery: rule 34
- whether the default procedure under rule 46 should be used.

Note: An application under rule 43 for the hearing of a preliminary issue is not appropriate for applications under section 84(1). In such cases directions are given as to the hearing by the Tribunal or by the Court of matters which require prior determination, such as the title to object, or construction under section 84(2) or 84(3A); see stage 4 above and Practice Direction 1/1997.

Stage 7
(All parties: rules 17 and 27)
Consider whether this is a case where the Lands Tribunal can make a determination without an oral hearing. (For example, where all parties are agreed, or where there are no objections to the application).
Note: The simplified procedure under rule 28 is *not* used in applications under section 84.

[45] See the warning given in *Re Nichols' Application* (1997) 1 E.G.L.R. 144.

Stage 8
(All parties: rules 29 and 33)
Full hearing, which is invariably with a view by the Tribunal of the site. Procedure will usually follow that of a civil action. See Practice Directions 2 and 6/1997.

WHAT ORDERS CAN THE LANDS TRIBUNAL MAKE?

As to the substance of the application

(a) The Lands Tribunal may make an order in terms of the application, or may dismiss it.

(b) The Lands Tribunal may make a "provisional" order in terms that an order for modification will be made if certain new restrictions are accepted.

(c) The Lands Tribunal may make an order under section 84(1C) imposing new restrictions for old.[46]

(d) The Lands Tribunal will in suitable cases make an order for payment of compensation within a specified time (which may be paid into court) and provide that until the compensation is paid the order for discharge is not to come into effect. The Lands Tribunal may order that the compensation will carry interest at such rate and for such period and calculated in such manner as the Tribunal directs; rule 32 applying Arbitration Act 1996, s. 49.[47]

As to costs

16–109 (a) Costs are *entirely* at the discretion of the Tribunal: rule 52.

(b) Unless either party has made a sealed offer as to costs under rule 44 (as to which see below) the practice is as follows:

(i) an applicant who loses normally pays the objector's costs.
(ii) an applicant who wins and does not have to pay any compensation can expect either to recover some or all of his costs from the objector(s) or, at least, an order that each side bears their own costs.
(iii) if the applicant wins but has to pay compensation, he can expect to have to pay the objector's costs unless there are grounds for saying that there should be no order as to costs; for example where the application was substantially taken up by a claim to compensation which failed.
(iv) the scale of costs will usually be on the High Court scale.

[46] As it did in *Re Forestmere* (1980) 41 P.&C.R. 390, where it removed controls relating to use of the land as a cinema and imposed new ones relating to residential restrictions.
[47] App. 4.

(v) the practice set out above may vary to reflect the hostile nature of the application (the more hostile the more likely there will be adverse orders as to costs) and additionally orders for costs may be made to reflect the conduct of the parties; for example penalising those who charge their position "mid-stream."

(c) The use of *Calderbank letters* and *sealed offers* under rule 44 must always be considered in an application before the Lands Tribunal. In practice in applications under section 84 the use of sealed offers is rare and Calderbank letters are used and encouraged to be used. **16–110**

Certain points are worth bearing in mind as to such offers—however made.

- they must be unconditional.
- any offer should be directed at influencing the exercise of the Lands Tribunal's discretion in respect of costs. The main protection given by them is by showing that such offers, if accepted, would have shortened, if not avoided, the hearing.
- offers are important where, for example, payment of compensation will only arise if the Lands tribunal decides to modify, and the only issue is whether there should be modification, compensation being agreed.

It is important to consider Calderbank offers where the applicant can put forward an alternative restriction, or where an offer of compensation can be made.

(d) See Practice Direction 8/1997 generally on fees, costs and the position of legally aided parties in respect of costs.

Important points to remember when the order of the Lands tribunal has been obtained

Either party may need to consider an *appeal* which lies by way of case started to the Court of Appeal. The time limit is within four weeks from the date of the decision.[48] See Practice Direction 7/1997 as to the form of the case stated. Note that no appeal lies from the Tribunal on its award as to costs without leave of the tribunal or the Court of Appeal.[49] **16–111**

If there is to be no appeal: **16–112**

(a) in unregistered titles

- the order must be kept with the title deeds and, if there is modification which requires an entire vacation of the registered

[48] See Land Tribunal Act 1949, ss. 3(4) and 11(a) and CPR, Sched. 1 and RSC, O. 61 therein.
[49] See Supreme Court Act 1981, s. 18(1A) and RSC, O. 59 therein.

covenant, application should be made to the Land Charges Registry for removal of the D(ii) entry.

- If there is modification which does not require vacation the person entitled to the benefit of the covenant should re-register the covenant as modified by lodging the order at the Land Charges Registry and requesting variation of the entry of the covenant. It is important at this stage if no other to ensure that the order of the tribunal is correctly drawn up; see (c) below as to the practice as to the order.

(b) In registered titles:

- in respect of the *benefited land*, unless in the very rare instance of the benefit being entered on that title, nothing needs to be done. If, exceptionally, the benefit is entered, the order should be lodged with the land or charge certificate to that title for the appropriate entry to be made so as to reflect the order.
- In respect of the *burdened land*, application is made under section 84(8) of the Law of Property Act 1925 and section 50(3) of the Land Registration Act 1925 to have the entry modified so as to reflect the order. This usually leads to the District Land Registry noting the order on the register and sewing a copy up with the land or charge certificate and filing a copy in the Registry. Where a discharge occurs the whole entry may be cancelled. Where there is evidence that the benefit has been entered the Registry may require production of the land or charge certificate to the benefited title to make a mirror entry on that title. The need for a check on the terms of the order is repeated.

(c) It is usually the practice of the Tribunal to send a draft of the proposed order to the parties for their approval or comments before it is finally drawn up. This is the opportunity to ensure that there are no errors in it which would be incorporated in any entry on the Land Charges Register, or on the title to property registered at H.M. Land Registry. This practice will invariably apply where the application can proceed without the need for a hearing, in which case the applicant gets a draft of the proposed order for approval or comment once the application has been determined.[50]

How long does it take for an application in the Lands tribunal to be determined?

16–113 (a) Where there is no objection, applications can be disposed of within three months from inception to determination.

(b) Where there is objection, the length of time taken will depend upon

[50] Arbitration Act 1996, s. 57, subs. (3)–(7) and for enforcement see s. 66 thereof, both provisions being at App. 4.

the urgency of the application, and the manner in which the parties proceed. In broad terms, the time taken will be equivalent to that of a civil action in the High Court.

(c) The Tribunal aims to despatch its decision to all parties within two months from the close of the hearing in the vast majority of cases. There are a minority of cases where special factors apply which mean that this time is exceeded. In some cases (rare) the decision can be given *ex tempore*, either in full, or briefly with reasons to follow, usually within one week.

Miscellaneous

16–114 The Lands Tribunal has jurisdiction where granted to discharge or modify statutory covenants; see Chapter 10 and the statutes in Appendix 2.

It is considered possible to restrict the right of the covenantor to make an application under section 84.

In some cases, particularly in development agreements, an application to the Lands Tribunal (if made) may be expressed so as to trigger the payment of money. In any case where a pure restriction is imposed, there seems no reason why the covenantor or his successor should not apply under section 84 to modify or discharge that restriction.

However, if the covenant is drawn in such a way as to trigger a payment of money on any application, no application under section 84 could be made in respect of such a covenant because it would not be a restriction as to the user of land within section 84(1); see paragraph 16–94 above.

The problem of original covenantors and recent covenants

16–115 In the past there have been suggestions (almost of "moral outrage") that the tribunal should be slow to allow applications made by original covenantors, and there should be a like degree of reluctance where covenants were imposed recently.

The present position is that such an applicant will face a very heavy burden, but there is no longer any "moral indignation" in such applications. The fact that the original covenantor is the applicant (or the fact that the covenant is a recent one) is merely one of the matters (albeit an important one) which the tribunal can and must take into account.[51]

[51] For the old view see *Ridley v. Taylor* (1965) 16 P.&C.R. 113; for the modern and current view, see *Jones v. Rhys-Jones* (1974) 30 P.&C.R. 451, as applied in *Re Beech* (1990) 59 P.&C.R. 502.

CHAPTER 17

PRACTICAL DRAFTING POINTS

17–01 The preceding chapters in this book have dealt with the existence, validity and enforceability of restrictive covenants which are already in being. This chapter devotes a little attention to the creation of restrictive covenants.

PRELIMINARIES

17–02 It is always going to be the case that the context in which in which covenants are imposed and the instructions given to the draughtsman will govern the terms of the covenants. A set of covenants to control a new housing development will differ from covenants imposed on the sale of a plot of land for one house in the former grounds of a larger house. Likewise restrictions as to trading, or use of land or buildings may have to be quite specific. For example, it may be desirable to limit the use of land for agricultural purposes, but with a proviso for the release of that covenant on payment of a sum geared to the difference between agricultural and housing value. We are not concerned here with the means by which the obligation to pay may be secured, but the importance of drafting a covenant which cannot be evaded and which is clear in terms of the restriction imposed.

The starting point will, invariably be a set of instructions and some precedents. They can be used as a starting point, as with all precedents, but can never be regarded as the model, at least as to the terms of the restrictions themselves. The form of the precedents should, however, be used where they define how the benefit of the covenants is to run.

17–03 Finally a word about plain English. The Plain English Campaign deserves credit for improving the quality of many legal documents.[1] It had been an aim in writing this book to produce a set of covenant precedents which conformed to the aims of that campaign. That aim proved difficult for two reasons. First, the law of restrictive covenants, particularly that concerned with the running of the benefit, demands that certain forms of words are used, and these appear almost to have been elevated to terms of legal science.[2] This may be an

[1] The author acknowledges the assistance he has derived from the Campaign's handbook—*Language on Trial, The Plain English Guide to Legal Writing*.

[2] *e.g.* the words so that "the benefit may be annexed to".

overstatement but it was felt to be too radical (and possibly dangerous) to produce a set of forms which might satisfy the Plain English Campaign but which might fail the tests set by the rigours of the law. Secondly, many of the modern forms do use language which is clearer and more direct in terms of the obligations which are specified in Appendix 7 the precedents attempt to meet these difficulties as best they can.

POINTS TO WATCH

17–04 Where covenants are to be used never use the word "stipulation", and the verb "to covenant" must be used in the operative part.[3]

Covenants can be expressed to be entered into jointly and severally, and there is no harm in saying so, even though section 81(1) of the Law of Property Act 1925 has made it unnecessary to do so since January 1, 1926.[4]

Consider with care how the benefit is to be annexed and to what land and how that land is to be identified and who is to enforce the covenant; is the right to be given to the owners for the time being so as to allow them to enforce within section 56 of the Law of Property Act 1925?[5] The best way to achieve this is to use words of annexation and to define the benefited land by reference to a (clear) plan.[6]

Limit liability to ownership of the burdened land and possession of it—particularly if the covenants themselves could impose vicarious liability by virtue of words such as "permit" and "suffer".[7]

17–05 The covenants themselves should be directed at what is permitted or not as the case may be. Modern forms will do this. Older forms are to be avoided; references to soapboilers and fellmongers are really out of place these days. Define nuisances by reference to words such as "activity which would materially affect the use and enjoyment of the [benefited land]". Or in relation to covenants against noise define what is not allowed by reference to the latest BSI or ISO standard.

If the obligations are to be qualified with obligations not to withhold consent unreasonably, or to approve plans within a given period, say so.

If a scheme of development is to be imposed state that this is intended.[8] Consider whether a power to vary should be inserted; these can affect the existence of a scheme.[9]

Avoid putting positive covenants in the same schedule as restrictive ones.

17–06 Avoid uncertainty of drafting or of terminology so that the covenant is unenforceable.

If there are no parts of covenants which might be thought to be uncertain

[3] For the danger created in doing so see Chap. 1, para. 1.6 above.

[4] While on the subject of unnecessary words, the frequently ignored Law of Property Act 1925, s. 61 treats the singular as including the plural and the masculine the feminine etc., thereby saving some space in "definitions" clauses.

[5] See Chap. 6, para 6–08 above.

[6] See Precedents at App. 7.

[7] See Chap. 14, para. 14–18 above.

[8] See Precedents at App. 7.

[9] See Chap. 8, para. 8–31 above.

in their effect or operation, keep them in a separate paragraph in the schedule so that the Court can sever them.

Consider the restrictions required in the context carefully.

17–07 Where land use is to be restricted in respect of residential buildings consider:

- is the building (to be built) not to be used other than as a private dwelling house?
- is the same to be in the occupation of one family?
- is no trade or business to be carried on at the property?
- what about detached houses—as opposed to semi-detached ones?
- are fences to be permitted beyond a certain point, or is it to be an open plan development with no structures or erections beyond that point?
- what about aerials and satellite dishes, protection of trees, and the parking of cars, caravans, trailers and boats?
- what about preventing the growth of the dreaded *Cupressus Leylandii*, or any trees above a certain height or beyond a certain point?

Where specific uses are to be prevented, or sole uses are to be permitted, consider:

- is the use to be restricted to the traditional concepts such as the retail shop or garage, or some other business.
- do you want to prevent the use of land for access to some business, or in some other way to facilitate it?[10]
- do you want to define use by reference to the Use Classes order?
- in rural areas, where developments are taking place, often using existing farmhouses and buildings, they may want protection against intensive pig rearing, chicken houses and muck heaps—amongst other things capable of sending the temperature up between farmers and their neighbours.

17–08 Where plans are to be approved or consents or variations granted, say by whom they are to be given, providing for alternatives or substitutes, and make any provisos (such as consent not to be unreasonably withheld) express. If necessary list the factors which might be relevant.[11]

In the rare cases where covenants are to be recreated following unity of seisin, use a form of words which makes it clear that this is to occur.[12]

Finally, a short word on the Precedents in Appendix 7.

[10] See *Elliott v. Safeway Stores plc* [1995] 1 W.L.R. 1396, for an instance where the covenant was not drawn in such a way so as to prevent use of land for access to a business.

[11] See the approach to assignment of leases in the amended provisions of Landlord & Tenant Act 1927, s. 19, s. 19(1A) where the criteria for reasonableness can be set out in the lease.

[12] See Chap. 13, para. 13–09 and Precedent A7–05 at App. 7.

These are merely suggestions. Many readers will have a favoured choice of published, or "in house" forms. But as precedents are good servants but bad masters, occasional references to other sources can keep the relationship between the user and the supplier of such forms fresh. **17–09**

CHAPTER 18

INSURING RESTRICTIVE COVENANTS

18–01 Imagine the distress of your client if their development site or property was rendered valueless through restrictive covenants being enforced. Problems of this nature probably occur more often than you realise as many cases are not reported in the press. The purpose of this chapter is to explore insurance as a potential solution to the problems created by restrictive covenants affecting freehold land by looking at the availability of insurance, underwriting considerations, costs and the scope of policy cover.

Restrictive covenant indemnity insurance is underwritten by a number of insurance companies in the United Kingdom as part of their legal indemnities accounts. It can provide a quick and cost effective solution and covers the named insured and successors in title against the enforcement or attempted enforcement of restrictive covenants.

THE AVAILABILITY OF INSURANCE

18–02 As a general principal insurance is provided when the restrictive covenants are no longer appropriate. There are a number of issues which affect the availability of restrictive covenant insurance:

Cover for breach of covenants

18–03 It is available for those who are breaching covenants relating to land and not for those who are seeking to enforce their benefit of a covenant. Those seeking to enforce a right such as a restrictive covenant may find that they are covered under a legal expenses insurance policy if they have one.

Freehold covenants

Restrictive covenant indemnities are generally available to cover covenants affecting freehold titles. Where leasehold covenants have been imposed, the covenantee, being the landlord, is usually known and available to negotiate a deed of variation.

However, insurance is sometimes provided for leasehold covenants contained in older long leases where the landlord is missing.

Restrictive not positive

The insurance is available for *restrictive* covenants only. There may be an element of uncertainty. For example, the requirement to maintain an area of land not built upon, on the face of it, is a positive covenant but would be interpreted as limiting the use of the site. If it is unclear, the underwriter will consider the intention rather than the wording.

If the covenant is positive, insurance will not be offered as a solution as such covenants are enforceable between the two parties to the deed.

The use of the property

18–04 A restrictive covenant indemnity policy will usually specify the proposed use of the land or property. There are very few limitations as to the uses which may be insured. They can range from a minor change of use or development, *e.g.* one house being in a rear garden, to the development of a large industrial complex. Insurance is also available for a continuation of an existing use which is in breach of covenants. As the breach has already occurred this is regarded as a lesser risk by the underwriter.

Geographical area

The majority of policies are issued for restrictive covenants burdening land in England and Wales. Insurers will also consider other areas such as Northern Ireland, Channel Islands and occasionally Scotland where different legal considerations apply.

Unknown covenants

Insurance is also available for the potential breach of unknown restrictive covenants. This may occur where deeds have been lost or destroyed or the land has been registered with possessory title and there is an entry on the Charges Register showing that the property is subject to any restrictive covenants that exist.

Not always an alternative to negotiation

Insurance will not be offered to cover any possible situation where restrictive covenants are being breached. If the deed imposing the covenant is only a few years old, the covenantee still exists and is in a position to offer a release, insurers are unlikely to accept the risk. Similarly, in areas where attempts are often made to enforce covenants by residents (particularly where there are building schemes) cover may not be available.

Residual risks

18–05 Once negotiations with the beneficiary of the covenant have commenced it is too late to seek insurance to cover the risk of enforceability by that particular party. However, if there is a residual risk because the benefit has annexed to owners of the surrounding land, insurance may be offered once the release has been completed.

As an underwriter considers each restrictive covenant enquiry individually it is good practice to submit a proposal at an early stage in the conveyancing procedure to see whether insurance is likely to be available or whether a release is necessary.

WHY INSURE?

18–06 There are a number of reasons why people choose to insure restrictive covenants. Alternatives to insurance include: self insurance, compulsory purchase, negotiation with the covenantees and application to the Lands tribunal or court action. However, a restrictive covenant indemnity can be useful in providing a quick and permanent solution.

Insurance transfers the risk of financial loss owing to the enforcement of restrictive covenants from the property owner to the insurer. A single premium is paid and in return the policy is issued in perpetuity. Financial compensation (including legal costs and expenses) is payable to the insured in the event of the covenants being enforced and the use or development of the property not continuing.

Lenders and mortgagees often require the additional security afforded by insurance and loans may be subject to restrictive covenant indemnity insurance being in place.

18–07 A policy may unlock the development potential of site and increase the value of it. A site which is subject to restrictive covenants that potentially prevent a proposed development will be worth more if there is a restrictive covenant indemnity in force which enables the development to proceed.

A restrictive covenant indemnity is an option available to the client when consultation with the covenantee is impossible. The covenantees and/or the extent of the land with the benefit may be unknown especially if the covenants are old. Also, the benefit may have annexed to many different parties in cases where the land has been split up and sold.

Insurance is an alternative to the Lands Tribunal or the High Court. An application to the tribunal or court can be a fairly long and expensive process and there is no guarantee of success. In some cases insurance may be available even if the matter is not suitable for the tribunal or court.

18–08 Finally, by suggesting that restrictive covenants are insured the practitioner is providing the most complete advice to clients and should hopefully reduce the risk of a negligence claim if covenants are subsequently enforced.

UNDERWRITING & INFORMATION REQUIRED

18–09 The insurance company or broker will usually supply a checklist or proposal form showing the information required to consider the risk of insuring restrictive covenants. All information supplied to the insurer is treated as the proposal for insurance. Any material facts which come to light during the solicitor's usual conveyancing investigations or during the planning process must be supplied to the insurer to make certain that the practitioner is not at fault for non-disclosure which could lead to the policy being avoided at a later date.

The underwriter takes into account both legal and practical information when deciding whether to insure and the terms and premium that will apply. When looking at a proposal for insurance consideration is given to the nature of the covenants, the surrounding area and the local reaction to any plans to change the use of or develop the property.

Not all of the information shown below will have to be supplied in every case. The amount of detail required by the underwriter will depend upon the likely enforceability of the covenants and the area concerned.

The covenants

18–10 It is useful for the insurer to see a copy of the original deed which imposed the restrictive covenants as the shortened version contained in the land registry office copies do not automatically clarify the exact nature of the covenants. For example, where a building scheme exists it is not always immediately clear from the office copy entries. Also, the information in the charges register is unlikely to detail the precise position or extent of the land affected by covenants.

The key elements of the deed which the underwriter will take into account are the age, the covenantees, the enforceability of the restrictive covenants and the stipulations.

1. Age

It would normally be expected that recent covenants (*e.g.* those imposed within the last 25 to 30 years) would be less attractive to the underwriter as a risk than older covenants. However, age is not a factor which is considered alone. It is not uncommon for nineteenth century covenants to be the subject of insurance claims. Conversely, numerous sites which are potentially breaching restrictive covenants imposed in the 1970s and early 1980s have been insured and the developments completed without claims occurring.

2. The covenantees

18–11 The proposer should provide the underwriter with as much information as possible regarding the original covenantees or where relevant, the specific estate concerned as it is essential for risk assessment, particularly for more complex cases.

Local solicitors or estate agents may be aware of the existence of specific covenantees and the need to obtain releases or approval for developments. If the covenantee is a company, a search should be supplied to show whether the company still exists, has been dissolved or taken over.

Some insurance companies retain records showing whether particular covenantees or estates still exist and are problematic meaning that negotiation with them is necessary.

One of the major risks occur where covenantees or estates have in the past given their approval or those which having been dormant for some time suddenly decide that the covenants are of interest. However, many covenantees will have long since sold their estates and not have an interest in the area concerned. Records built up over the years by insurers can be invaluable in such cases.

3. The enforceability of the covenants

18–12 The covenanting clause is considered in conjunction with the use of the property and the area. The underwriter will look at the deed which imposed the covenants (if available) or the office copy entries in detail to consider whether in his opinion the covenants are likely to be enforceable and whether additional information is needed. If the benefit of the restrictive covenants appears to have annexed to land surrounding the site in question the underwriter may require office copy entries of surrounding properties to be supplied.

Building schemes are some of the most difficult cases to underwrite particularly in view of the high level of enforceability and as shown above, the fact that a building scheme exists may not be immediately evident from the information supplied.

If counsel's opinion has been sought, a copy should be supplied to the insurer as in some cases it may improve their view of the risk. The underwriter will not request counsel's opinion as a matter of course but will occasionally do so if there are other adverse features.

Proposals for restrictive covenant indemnities where covenants are likely to be enforceable are treated prudently. Obviously, there are some risks for which insurance will not be provided.

4. Stipulations

18–13 Common stipulations for which insurance is required include:

- density restrictions, *e.g.* two houses per plot,
- height restrictions,
- building lines,
- limitations as to the use of the property, *e.g.* no alcohol sales and
- approval of plans.

As with enforceability of covenants, the stipulations will be considered by the underwriter in conjunction with the proposed use of the property and the surrounding area.

The property and surrounding area

18–14 A detailed description of the property is required and often a plan is attached to the policy document to clearly identify the property being insured.

The insurer will consider the previous and proposed use of the property and any development plans to assess whether it conforms to the character of the neighbourhood. Difficulties can occur when a proposed use is new to the area and does not "fit in" with its surroundings. For example, commercial developments such as nursing homes in residential areas can prove unpopular with local residents and may consequently make the restrictive covenant risk unattractive to the underwriter.

One defence which is sometimes valid if a claim occurs is that an area has changed significantly since the covenants were imposed so that in practice, they are no longer relevant. Old O.S. plans may be requested in some cases to see how much an area has changed particularly where the covenants are relatively old. An up-to-date O.S. plan of the property and those immediately surrounding it can also prove useful in some cases.

Local reaction

18–15 When a property is being developed, the insurer will ask to see copies of any responses (including supportive letters) or objections to the planning application. This is useful as it helps to assess the reaction to the development of those who may have the benefit of the covenants. The number and nature of objections and any concerted reaction from Residents' Associations or other local groups are a good guide to the popularity or otherwise of the proposed use. Any other letters which are received by the client which are in opposition to the proposed development should also be submitted to the underwriter for consideration.

Lack of objection to planning applications may lead to a false sense of security particularly as it is not normal practice for planners to take restrictive covenants into account. Insurers have had claim in cases where there were no significant objections to the planning application but the letter of protest is received once the development works have commenced.

On the other hand, there are some cases with many strong objections where the underwriter is still able to provide insurance. In such situations, a detailed appraisal of the legal position and a favourable counsel's opinion can help to make a difference.

18–16

Summary

Availability of Insurance	*Underwriting Considerations*	*Information Required*
Cover for breach of covenants	Restrictive covenants	Deed or office copies
Freehold covenants	Age	The covenantees
Restrictive not positive	Covenantees	Are the covenants registered enforceable?
Geographical area: mainly England & Wales	Enforceability	O.S. plans of property and surrounding land
Unknown covenants	Stipulations	Use of property
Residual risks	Property and surrounding area	Development plans
Insurance is not always an alternative to negotiation	Local reaction	Objections to planning permission

The costs

18–17 It is general practice for underwriters to take into account the full value of a site once it has been developed and base the premium rate on this. Most claims tend to occur in the early stages of development. However, costs can still be substantial. Legal expenses alone can easily extend to tens of thousands of pounds. Lenders and any future purchaser of the property will usually insist that the indemnity is for the full value of the property.

Risk are considered individually by the underwriter and because each case is different, restrictive covenant indemnity insurance does not lend itself to standard rating. As a rough guide, for a restrictive covenant indemnity where you are insuring the full value of a property for £1,000,000 you could expect to pay anything from £1,000 to £5,000. In some cases, where there are unattractive features an excess may be applied *i.e.* the insured pays the first £X.

Policy cover

18–18 A number of companies provide restrictive covenant insurance as part of a portfolio of legal indemnities. Individual policy wordings vary but in practice there are a number of standard features. As an example, a copy of the Royal & Sun Alliance standard wording can be found at Appendix 5.

1) The policy covers a defined "insured use" and contains a description of the property insured.

2) Cover operates following the attempted enforcement of any insured restrictive covenants.
3) Options available in the event of a valid claim being made include the following:
   - defence of the allegation by seeking to prove that the covenants are not enforceable.
   - compensating a person who shows he has the benefit of the covenants and can enforce them thus allowing the development to proceed or the use to continue.
   - indemnity to the insured, if it proves impossible to proceed with the insured use.

The method of settling the claim will depend upon the circumstances of the individual case, the time that the claim is made and progress in any development.

4) Key features of the indemnity to the insured are as follows: **18–19**

* Loss in market value

Where it is not possible to find an acceptable solution to allow development to proceed, the insured is compensated for the difference in market value of the property with and without the covenants. In the most serious cases, the residual value may be very low.

* Cost of works/fees

By the time covenants are successfully enforced considerable costs may have been incurred. Indemnity is provided for the cost of works already undertaken prior to the enforcement action and architects' and surveyors' fees.

* Demolition costs **18–20**

Where necessary, the costs of demolishing the buildings on the site and restoring the property to its original condition are paid.

* Costs and expenses (incurred with insurer's consent)

This may include legal fees incurred in defence of the claim, compensation payable to a successful claimant and costs awarded against the insured.

5) Policy exceptions

Claims are excluded if the insured decides to approach the parties believed to have the benefit of the covenant or makes an application to the Lands tribunal. As we have already seen, these are potential solutions to restrictive covenants but insurance is an alternative. Such actions could easily provoke a claim.

18–21 6) Limits of indemnity

Most underwriters will look to insure risks based in the full value of the property once any development works are complete. Lower limits can be considered but lenders will often insist on cover for the full value.

The maximum amount payable under the policy is the limit of indemnity.

7) Unusual features compared to other insurance contracts

Unlike most insurance contracts, the policies are single premium, usually without time limit and cover automatically passes to successors in title. In addition, mortgagees and lessees can normally be included without further payment.

18–22 8) Extensions of cover

The standard policy does not include cover for loss of rent or other consequential losses such as loss of profits. Insurers will consider adding such extensions in some cases.

In conclusion, restrictive covenants are a complex legal area and can prove to be an expensive and real trap for the unwary. Problems can arise when you least expect them and it is not always the obvious cases which lead to claims.

It is certainly worth asking whether insurance is available. Initial reactions and often decisions can be given by the underwriter upon receipt of fairly basic information. Insurance provides a quick and cost effective solution to the problem and has the potential to provide financial indemnity if the worst happens.

Appendices

Appendix 1

Statutory Material (extracts)

Conveyancing and Law of Property Act 1881

58.—(1) A covenant relating to land of inheritance, or devolving on the heir as special occupant, shall be deemed to be made with the covenantee, his heirs and assigns, and shall have effect as if heirs and assigns were expressed. **A1–01**

(2) A covenant relating to land not of inheritance, or not devolving on the heir as special occupant, shall be deemed to be made with the covenantee, his executors, administrators, and assigns, and shall have effect as if executors, administrators, and assigns were expresssed.

(3) This section applies only to covenants made after the commencement of this Act. (January 1, 1882.)

Law of Property Act 1925

Persons taking who are not parties and as to indentures **A1–02**

56.—(1) A person may take an immediate or other interest in land or other property, or the benefit of any condition, right of entry, covenant or agreement over or respecting land or other property, although he may not be named as a party to the conveyance or other instrument.

(2) A deed between parties, to effect its objects, has the effect of an indenture though not indented or expressed to be an indenture.

Benefit of covenants relating to land

78.—(1) A covenant relating to any land of the covenantee shall be deemed to be made with the covenantee and his successors in title and the persons deriving title under him or them, and shall have effect as if such successors and other persons were expressed.

For the purposes of this subsection in connexion with covenants restrictive of the user of land "successors in title" shall be deemed to include the owners and occupiers for the time being of the land of the covenantee intended to be benefited.

(2) This section applies to covenants made after the commencement of this Act, but the repeal of section fifty-eight of the Conveyancing Act 1881 does not affect the operation of covenants to which that section applied.

Burden of covenants relating to land

79.—(1) A covenant relating to any land of a covenantor or capable of being bound by him, shall, unless a contrary intention is expressed, be deemed to be made by the covenantor on behalf of himself his successors in title and the persons deriving title under him or them, and, subject as aforesaid, shall have effect as if such successors and other persons were expressed.

This subsection extends to a covenant to do some act relating to the land, notwithstanding that the subject-matter may not be in existence when the covenant is made.

(2) For the purpose of this section in connexion with covenants restrictive of the user of land "successors in title" shall be deemed to include the owners and occupiers for the time being of such land.

(3) This section applies only to covenants made after the commencement of this Act.

Covenants binding land

80.—(1) A covenant and a bond and an obligation or contract under seal made after the thirty-first day of December, eighteen hundred and eighty-one, binds the real estate as well as the personal estate of the person making the same if and so far as a contrary intention is not expressed in the covenant, bond, obligation, or contract.

This subsection extends to a covenant implied by virtue of this Act.

(2) Every covenant running with the land, whether entered into before or after the commencement of this Act, shall take effect in accordance with any statutory enactment affecting the devolution of the land, and accordingly the benefit or burden of every such covenant shall vest in or bind the persons who by virtue of any such enactment or otherwise succeed to the title of the covenantee or the covenantor, as the case may be.

(3) The benefit of a covenant relating to land entered into after the commencement of this Act may be made to run with the land without the use of any technical expression if the covenant is of such a nature that the benefit could have been made to run with the land before the commencement of this Act.

(4) For the purposes of this section, a covenant runs with the land when the benefit or burden of it, whether at law or in equity, passes to the successors

in title of the covenantee or the covenantor, as the case may be.

Power to discharge or modify restrictive covenants affecting land

84.—(1) The Lands Tribunal shall (without prejudice to any concurrent jurisdiction of the court) have power from time to time, on the application of any person interested in any freehold land affected by any restriction arising under covenant or otherwise as to the user thereof or the building thereon, by order wholly or partially to discharge or modify any such restriction on being satisfied—

(a) that by reason of changes in the character of the property or the neighbourhood or other circumstances of the case which the Lands Tribunal may deem material, the restriction ought to be deemed obsolete; or

(aa) that (in a case falling within subsection (1A) below) the continued existence thereof would impede some reasonable user of the land for public or private purposes or, as the case may be, would unless modified so impede such user; or

(b) that the persons of full age and capacity for the time being or from time to time entitled to the benefit of the restriction, whether in respect of estates in fee simple or any lesser estates or interests in the property to which the benefit of the restriction is annexed, have agreed, either expressly or by implication, by their acts or omissions, to the same being discharged or modified; or

(c) that the proposed discharge or modification will not injure the persons entitled to the benefit of the restriction.

and an order discharging or modifying a restriction under this subsection may direct the applicant to pay to any person entitled to the benefit of the restriction such sum by way of consideration as the Tribunal may think it just to award under one, but not both, of the following heads, that is to say, either—

(i) a sum to make up for any loss or disadvantage suffered by that person in consequence of the discharge or modification; or

(ii) a sum to make up for any effect which the restriction had, at the time, when it was imposed, in reducing the consideration then received for the land affected by it.

(1A) Subsection (1)(aa) above authorises the discharge or modification of a restriction by reference to its impeding some reasonable user of land in any case in which the Lands Tribunal is satisfied that the restriction, in impeding that user, either—

(a) does not secure to persons entitled to the benefit of it any practical benefits of substantial value or advantage to them; or

(b) is contrary to the public interest;

and that money will be an adequate compensation for the loss or disadvantage (if any) which any such person will suffer from the discharge or modification.

(1B) In determining whether a case is one falling within subsection (1A) above, and in determining whether (in any such case or otherwise) a restriction ought to be discharged or modified, the Lands Tribunal shall take into account the development plan and any declared or ascertainable pattern for the grant or refusal of planning permissions in the relevant areas, as well as the period at which and context in which the restriction was created or imposed and any other material circumstances.

(1C) It is hereby declared that the power conferred by this section to modify a restriction includes power to add such further provisions restricting the user of or the building on the land affected as appear to the Lands Tribunal to be reasonable in view of the relaxation of the existing provisions, and as may be accepted by the applicant; and the Lands Tribunal may accordingly refuse to modify a restriction without some such addition.

(2) The court shall have power on the application of any person interested—

(a) to declare whether or not in any particular case any freehold land is, or would in any given event be, affected by a restriction imposed by any instrument; or

(b) to declare what, upon the true construction of any instrument purporting to impose a restriction, is the nature and extent of the restriction thereby imposed and whether the same is, or would in any given event be, enforceable and if so by whom.

Neither subsections (7) and (11) of this section nor, unless the contrary is expressed, any later enactment providing for this section not to apply to any restrictions shall affect the operation of this subsection or the operation for purposes of this subsection of any other provisions of this section.

(3) The Lands Tribunal shall, before making any order under this section, direct such enquiries, if any, to be made of any government department or local authority, and such notices, if any, whether by way of advertisement or otherwise, to be given to such of the persons who appear to be entitled, to the benefit of the restriction intended to be discharged, modified, or dealt with as, having regard to any enquiries, notices or other proceedings previously made, given or taken, the Lands Tribunal may think fit.

(3A) On an application to the Lands Tribunal under this section the Lands Tribunal shall give any necessary directions as to the persons who are or are not to be admitted (as appearing to be entitled to the benefit of the restriction) to oppose the application, and no appeal shall lie against any such direction; but rules under the Lands Tribunal Act 1949 shall make provision whereby, in cases in which there arises on such an application (whether or not in connection with the admission of persons to oppose) any such question as is referred to in subsection (2)(a) or (b) of this section, the proceedings on the application can and, if the rules so provide, shall be suspended to enable the decision of the court to be obtained on that question by an application under that subsection, or by rules of court.

(5) Any order made under this section shall be binding on all persons, whether ascertained or of full age or capacity or not, then entitled or thereafter capable of becoming entitled to the benefit of any restriction, which is thereby discharged, modified or dealt with, and whether such persons are parties to the proceedings or have been served with notice or not.

(6) An order may be made under this section notwithstanding that any instrument which is alleged to impose the restriction intended to be discharged, modified, or dealt with, may not have been produced to the court or the Lands Tribunal, and the court or the Lands Tribunal may act on such evidence of that instrument as it may think sufficient.

(7) This section applies to restrictions whether subsisting at the commencement of this Act or imposed thereafter, but this section does not apply where the restriction was imposed on the occasion of a disposition made gratuitously or for a nominal consideration for public purposes.

(8) This section applies whether the land affected by the restrictions is registered or not, but, in the case of registered land, the Land Register shall give effect on the register to any order under this section in accordance with the Land Registration Act 1925.

(9) Where any proceedings by action or otherwise are taken to enforce a restrictive covenant, any person against whom the proceedings are taken, may in such proceedings apply to the court for an order giving leave to apply to the Lands Tribunal under this section, and staying the proceedings in the meantime.

(11) This section does not apply to restrictions imposed by the Commissioners of Works under any statutory power for the protection of any Royal Park or Garden or to restrictions of a like character imposed upon the occasion of any enfranchisement effected before the commencement of this Act in any manner vested in His Majesty in right of the Crown or the Duchy of Lancaster, nor (subject to subsection (11A) below) to restrictions created or imposed—

(a) for naval, military or air force purposes,

(b) for civil aviation purposes under the powers of the Air Navigation Act 1920, of section 19 or 23 of the Civil Aviation Act 1949 or of section 30 or 41 of the Civil Aviation Act 1982.

(11A) Subsection (11) of this section—

(a) shall exclude the application of this section to a restriction falling within subsection (11)(a), and not created or imposed in connection with the use of any land as an aerodrome, only so long as the restriction is enforceable by or on behalf of the Crown; and

(b) shall exclude the application of this section to a restriction falling within subsection (11)(b), or created or imposed in connection with the use of any land as an aerodrome, only so long as the restriction is enforceable by or on behalf of the Crown or any public or international authority.

(12) Where a term of more than forty years is created in land (whether before or after the commencement of this Act) this section shall, after the expiration of twenty-five years of the term, apply to restrictions, affecting such leasehold land in like manner as it would have applied had the land been freehold:

Provided that this subsection shall not apply to mining leases.

Notices

Regulations respecting notices

196.—(1) Any notice required or authorised to be served or given by this Act shall be in writing.

(2) Any notice required or authorised by this Act to be served on a lessee or mortgagor shall be sufficient, although only addressed to the lessee or mortgagor by that designation, without his name, or generally to the persons interested, without any name, and notwithstanding that any person to be affected by the notice is absent, under disability, unborn, or unascertained.

(3) Any notice required or authorised by this Act to be served shall be sufficiently served if it is left at the last-known place of abode or business in the United Kingdom of the lessee, lessor, mortgagee, mortgagor, or other person to be served, or, in case of a notice required or authorised to be served on a lessee or mortgagor, is affixed or left for him on the land or any house or building comprised in the lease or mortgage, or, in case of a mining lease, is left for the lessee at the office or counting-house of the mine.

(4) Any notice required or authorised by this Act to be served shall also be sufficiently served, if it is sent by post in a registered letter addressed to the lessee, lessor, mortgagee, mortgagor, or other person to be served, by name, at the aforesaid place of abode or business, office, or counting-house, and if that letter is not returned through the post-office undelivered; and that service shall be deemed to be made at the time at which the registered letter would in the ordinary course be delivered.

(5) The provisions of this section shall extend to notices required to be served by any instrument affecting property executed or coming into operation after the commencement of this Act unless a contrary intention appears.

(6) This section does not apply to notices served in proceedings in the court.

Registration under the Land Charges Act 1925, to be notice

198.—(1) The registration of any instrument or matter [in any register kept under the Land Charges Act 1972 or any local land charges register] shall be deemed to constitute actual notice of such instrument or matter, and of the fact of such registration, to all persons and for all purposes connected with the land affected, as from the date of registration or other prescribed date and so long as the registration continues in force.

(2) This section operates without prejudice to the provisions of this Act respecting the making of further advances by a mortgagee, and applies only to instruments and matters required or authorised to be registered in any such register.

Restrictions on constructive notice

199.—(1) A purchaser shall not be prejudicially affected by notice of—

(i) any instrument or matter capable of registration under the provisions of the Land Charges Act 1925, or any enactment which it replaces, which is void or not enforceable as against him under that Act or enactment, by reason of the non-registration thereof;

(ii) any other instrument or matter or any fact or thing unless—

(a) it is within his own knowledge, or would have come to his knowledge if such inquiries and inspections had been made as ought reasonably to have been made by him; or

(b) in the same transaction with respect to which a question of notice to the purchaser arises, it has come to the knowledge of his counsel, as such, or of his solicitor or other agent, as such, or would have come to the knowledge of his solicitor or other agent, as such, if such inquiries and inspections had been made as ought reasonably to have been made by the solicitor or other agent.

(2) Paragraph (ii) of the last subsection shall not exempt a purchaser from any liability under, or any obligation to perform or observe, any covenant, condition, provision, or restriction contained in any instrument under which his title is derived, mediately or immediately; and such liability or obligation may be enforced in the same manner and to the same extent as if that paragraph had not been enacted.

(3) A purchaser shall not by reason of anything in this section be affected by notice in any case where he would not have been so affected if this section had not been enacted.

(4) This section applies to purchases made either before or after the commencement of this Act.

Land Registration Act 1925

A1–03 **Notices of restrictive covenants**

50.—(1) Any person entitled to the benefit of a restrictive covenant or agreement (not being a covenant or agreement made between a lessor and lessee) with respect to the building on or other user of registered land may apply to the registrar to enter notice thereof on the register, and where practicable the notice shall be by reference to the instrument, if any, which contains the covenant or agreement, and a copy or abstract of such instrument shall be filed at the registry; and where any such covenant or agreement appears to exist at the time of first registration, notice thereof shall be entered on the register. In the case of registered land the notice aforesaid shall take the place of registration as a land charge.

(2) When such a notice is entered the proprietor of the land and the persons deriving title under him (except incumbrancers or other persons who at the time when the notice is entered may not be bound by the covenant or agreement) shall be deemed to be affected with notice of the covenant or agreement as being an incumbrance on the land.

(3) Where the covenant or agreement is discharged [modified or dealt with] by an order under the Law of Property Act 1925, or otherwise, or the court refuses to grant an injunction for enforcing the same, the entry shall either be cancelled or reference made to the order or other instrument and a copy of the order, judgment, or instrument shall be filed at the registry.

(4) The notice shall, when practicable, refer to the land, whether registered or not, for the benefit of which the restriction was made.

Appendix 2

Statutory Material (extracts)

Town and Country Planning Act 1990

[Planning obligations **A2–01**

106.—(1) Any person interested in land in the area of a local planning authority may, by agreement or otherwise, enter into an obligation (referred to in this section and sections 106A and 106B as "a planning obligation"), enforceable to the extent mentioned in subsection (3)—

(a) restricting the development or use of the land in any specified way;

(b) requiring specified operations or activities to be carried out in, on, under or over the land;

(c) requiring the land to be used in any specified way; or

(d) requiring a sum or sums to be paid to the authority on a specified date or dates or periodically.

(2) A planning obligation may—

(a) be unconditional or subject to conditions;

(b) impose any restriction or requirement mentioned in subsection (1)(a) to (c) either indefinitely or for such period or periods as may be specified; and

(c) if it requires a sum or sums to be paid, require the payment of a specified amount or an amount determined in accordance with the instrument by which the obligation is entered into and, if it requires the payment of periodical sums, require them to be paid indefinitely or for a specified period.

(3) Subject to subsection (4) a planning obligation is enforceable by the authority identified in accordance with subsection (9)(d)—

(a) against the person entering into the obligation; and

(b) against any person deriving a title from that person.

(4) The instrument by which a planning obligation is entered into may provide that a person shall not be bound by the obligation in respect of any period during which he no longer has an interest in the land.

(5) A restriction or requirement imposed under a planning obligation is enforceable by injunction.

(6) Without prejudice to subsection (5), if there is a breach of a requirement in a planning obligation to carry out any operations in, on, under or over the land to which the obligation relates, the authority by whom the obligation is enforceable may—

(a) enter the land and carry out the operations; and

(b) recover from the person or persons against whom the obligation is enforceable any expenses reasonably incurred by them in doing so.

(7) Before an authority exercise their power under subsection (6)(a) they shall give not less than 21 days' notice of their intention to do so to any person against whom the planning obligation is enforceable.

(8) Any person who wilfully obstructs a person acting in the exercise of a power under subsection (6)(a) shall be guilty of an offence and liable on summary conviction to a fine not exceeding level 3 on the standard scale.

(9) A planning obligation may not be entered into except by an instrument executed as a deed which—

(a) states that the obligation is a planning obligation for the purposes of this section;

(b) identifies the land in which the person entering into the obligation is interested;

(c) identifies the person entering into the obligation and states what his interest in the land is; and

(d) identifies the local planning authority by whom the obligation is enforceable.

(10) A copy of any such instrument shall be given to the authority so identified.

(11) A planning obligation shall be a local land charge and for the purposes of the Local Land Charges Act 1975 the authority by whom the obligation is

enforceable shall be treated as the originating authority as respects such a charge.

(12) Regulations may provide for the charging on the land of—

(a) any sum or sums required to be paid under a planning obligation; and

(b) any expenses recoverable by a local planning authority under subsection (6)(b),

and this section and sections 106A and 106B shall have effect subject to any such regulations.

(13) In this section "specified" means specified in the instrument by which the planning obligation is entered into and in this section and section 106A "land" has the same meaning as in the Local Land Charges Act 1975.

Power to override easements and other rights

237.—(1) Subject to subsection (3), the erection, construction or carrying out, or maintenance of any building or work on land which has been acquired or appropriated by a local authority for planning purposes (whether done by the local authority or by a person deriving title under them) is authorised by virtue of this section if it is done in accordance with planning permission, notwithstanding that it involves—

(a) interference with an interest or right to which this section applies, or

(b) a breach of a restriction as to the user of land arising by virtue of a contract.

(2) Subject to subsection (3), the interests and rights to which this section applies are any easement, liberty, privilege, right or advantage annexed to land and adversely affecting other land, including any natural right to support.

(3) Nothing in this section shall authorise interference with any right of way or right of laying down, erecting, continuing or maintaining apparatus on, under or over land which is—

(a) a right vested in or belonging to statutory undertakers for the purpose of the carrying on of their undertaking, or

(b) a right conferred by or in accordance with the telecommunications code on the operator of a telecommunications code system.

(4) In respect of any interference or breach in pursuance of subsection (1), compensation—

(a) shall be payable under section 63 or 68 of the Lands Clauses Consolidation Act 1845 or under section 7 or 10 of the Compulsory Purchase Act 1965, and

(b) shall be assessed in the same manner and subject to the same rules as in the case of other compensation under those sections in respect of injurious affection where—

(i) the compensation is to be estimated in connection with a purchase under those Acts, or

(ii) the injury arises from the execution of works on land acquired under those Acts.

(5) Where a person deriving title under the local authority by whom the land in question was acquired or appropriated—

(a) is liable to pay compensation by virtue of subsection (4), and

(b) fails to discharge that liability,

the liability shall be enforceable against the local authority.

(6) Nothing in subsection (5) shall be construed as affecting any agreement between the local authority and any other person for indemnifying the local authority against any liability under that subsection.

(7) Nothing in this section shall be construed as authorising any act or omission on the part of any person which is actionable at the suit of any person on any grounds other than such an interference or breach as is mentioned in subsection (1).

National Trust Act 1937

A2–02 **Power to enter into agreements restricting use of land**

8. Where any person is willing to agree with the National Trust that any land or any part thereof shall so far as his interest in the land enables him to bind it be made subject either permanently or for a specified period to conditions restricting the planning development or use thereof in any manner the National Trust may if it thinks fit enter into an agreement with him or accept a covenant from him to that effect and shall have power to enforce such agreement or covenant against persons deriving title under him in the like manner and to the like extent as if the National Trust were possessed of or entitled to or interested in adjacent land and as if the agreement or covenant had been and had been expressed to be entered into for the benefit of that adjacent land.

National Trust Act 1971

Restrictions for protection of Trust property **A2–03**

27. Section 84 of the Law of Property Act 1925 (which contains power to discharge or modify restrictive covenants affecting land) shall not apply to restrictions imposed (whether before or after the passing of this Act) for the purpose of—

(a) preserving; or

(b) protecting or augmenting the amenities of; or

(c) securing the access to and enjoyment by the public of;

any property which is or becomes inalienable by or under section 21 (Certain property of Trust to be inalienable) of the Act of 1907 or by section 8 (Mansion and lands to be inalienable by National Trust) of the National Trust Act 1939.

National Parks and Access to the Countryside Act 1949

Agreements with Nature Conservancy for establishment of nature reserves **A2–04**

16.—(1) The Nature Conservancy Council may enter into an agreement with every owner, lessee and occupier of any land, being land as to which it appears to the Nature Conservancy Council expedient in the national interest that it should be managed as a nature reserve, for securing that it shall be so managed.

(2) Any such agreement may impose such restrictions as may be expedient for the purposes of the agreement on the exercise of rights over the land by the persons who can be bound by the agreement.

(3) Any such agreement—

(a) may provide for the management of the land in such manner, the carrying out thereon of such work and the doing thereon of such other things as may be expedient for the purposes of the agreement;

(b) may provide for any of the matters mentioned in the last foregoing paragraph being carried out, or for the cost thereof being defrayed, either by the said owner or other persons, or by the Nature Conservancy Council, or partly, in one way and partly in another;

(c) may contain such other provisions as to the making of payments by [the Nature Conservancy Council], and in particular for the payment by them of compensation for the effect of the restrictions mentioned in the last foregoing subsection, as may be specified in the agreement.

(4) Section two of the Forestry Act 1947 (which empowers tenants for life

and other limited owners to enter into forestry dedication covenants) shall apply to any such agreement; and where section seventy-nine of the Law of Property Act 1925 (which provides that unless a contrary intention is expressed the burden of a covenant runs with the land) applies, subsections (2) and (3) of section one of the said Act of 1947 (which provide for enforcement against persons other than the covenantor) shall apply to any such restrictions as are mentioned in subsection (2) of this section, but with the substitution for references to the Forestry Commissioners of references to [the Nature Conservancy Council].

A2–05 Green Belt (London and Home Counties) Act 1938

Enforcement of Covenants

22.—(1) Where the owner of Green Belt land or a parish council in whom Green Belt land is vested has either before or after the commencement of this Act entered into or by virtue of this Act become subject to any covenant with a local authority restrictive of the user of such land the local authority shall have power to enforce such covenant against persons deriving title under such owner or parish council in the like manner and to the like extent as if the local authority were possessed of adjacent land capable of being benefited by such covenant and as if such covenant had been expressed to be entered into for the benefit of such adjacent land.

(2) Section 84 (Power to discharge or modify restrictive covenants affecting land) of the Law of Property Act 1925 shall not apply to a restriction imposed by a deed or covenant made or entered into for the purposes of and after the commencement of this Act or to any deed or covenant which was made or entered into before such commencement but which is expressed to be made in contemplation of the passing of this Act and in which it is provided that the said section shall not apply.

City of London (Various Powers) Act 1960

A2–06 Undertakings and agreements binding successive owners

33.—(1) Every undertaking given by or to the Corporation to or by the owner of a legal estate in land and every agreement made between the Corporation and any such owner being an undertaking or agreement—

(a) given or made under seal either on the passing of plans or otherwise in connection with the land; and

(b) expressed to be given or made in pursuance of this section;

shall be binding not only upon the Corporation and any owner joining in the undertaking or agreement but also upon the successors in title of any owner so joining and any person claiming through or under them.

(2) Such an undertaking or agreement shall be treated as a local land charge for the purposes of the Land Charges Act 1925 as amended by the Law of Property (Amendment) Act 1926.

(3) Any person upon whom such an undertaking or agreement is binding shall be entitled to require from the Corporation a copy thereof.

Leasehold Reform Act 1967

Retention of management powers for general benefit of neighbourhood **A2–07**

19.—(1) Where, in the case of any area which is occupied directly or indirectly under tenancies held from one landlord (apart from property occupied by him or his licensees or for the time being unoccupied), the Minister on an application made within the two years beginning with the commencement of this Part of this Act grants a certificate that, in order to maintain adequate standards of appearance and amenity and regulate redevelopment in the area in the event of tenants acquiring the landlord's interest in their house and premises under this Part of this Act, it is in the Minister's opinion likely to be in the general interest that the landlord should retain powers of management in respect of the house and premises or have rights against the house and premises in respect of the benefits arising from the exercise elsewhere of his powers of management, then the High Court may, on an application made within one year of the giving of the certificate, approve a scheme giving the landlord such powers and rights as are contemplated by this subsection.

For purposes of this section "the Minister" means as regards areas within Wales and Monmouthshire the Secretary of State, and as regards other areas the Minister of Housing and Local Government.

(2) The Minister shall not give a certificate under this section unless he is satisfied that the applicant has, by advertisement or otherwise as may be required by the Minister, given adequate notice to persons interested, informing them of the application for a certificate and its purpose and inviting them to make representations to the Minister for or against the application within a time which appears to the Minister to be reasonable; and before giving a certificate the Minister shall consider any representations so made within that time, and if from those representations it appears to him that there is among the persons making them substantial opposition to the application, he shall afford to those opposing the application, and on the same occasion to the applicant and such (if any) as the Minister thinks fit of those in favour of the application, an opportunity to appear and be heard by a person appointed by the Minister for the purpose, and shall consider the report of that person.

(3) The Minister in considering whether to grant a certificate authorising a scheme for any area, and the High Court in considering whether to approve a scheme shall have regard primarily to the benefit likely to result from the scheme to the area as a whole (including houses likely to be acquired from the landlord under this Part of this Act), and the extent to which it is reasonable to impose, for the benefit of the area, obligations on tenants so acquiring their freeholds; but regard may also be had to the past development and present character of the area and to architectural or historical considerations, to neighbouring areas and to the circumstances generally.

(4) If, having regard to the matters mentioned in subsection (3) above, to the provision which it is practicable to make by a scheme, and to any change of circumstances since the giving of the certificate under subsection (1), the High Court think it proper so to do, then the High Court may by order—

(a) exclude from the scheme any part of the area certified under that subsection; or

(b) declare that no scheme can be approved for the area;

and before submitting for approval a scheme for an area so certified a person may, if he sees fit, apply to the High Court for general directions as to the matters proper to be included in the scheme and for a decision whether an order should be made under paragraph (a) or (b) above.

(5) Subject to subsections (3) and (4) above, on the submission of a scheme to the High Court, the High Court shall approve the scheme either as originally submitted or with any modifications proposed or agreed to by the applicant for the scheme, if the scheme (with those modifications, if any) appears to the court to be fair and practicable and not to give the landlord a degree of control out of proportion to that previously exercised by him or to that required for the purposes of the scheme; and the High Court shall not dismiss an application for the approval of a scheme, unless either—

(a) the Court makes an order under subsection (4)(b) above; or

(b) in the opinion of the Court the applicant is unwilling to agree to a suitable scheme or is not proceeding in the manner with due despatch.

(6) A scheme under this section may make different provision for different parts of the area, and shall include provision for terminating or varying all or any of the provisions of the scheme, or excluding part of the area, if a change of circumstances makes it appropriate, or for enabling it to be done by or with the approval of the High Court.

(7) Except as provided by the scheme, the operation of a scheme under this section shall not be affected by any disposition or devolution of the landlord's interest in the property within the area or part of that property; but the scheme—

(a) shall include provision for identifying the person who is for the purposes of the scheme to be treated as the landlord for the time being; and

(b) may include provision for transferring, or allowing the landlord for the time being to transfer, all or any of the powers and rights conferred by the scheme on the landlord for the time being to a local authority or other body, including a body constituted for the purpose.

In the following provisions of this section references to the landlord for the time being shall have effect, in relation to powers and rights transferred to a local authority or other body as contemplated by paragraph (b) above, as references to that authority or body.

(8) Without prejudice to any other provision of this section, a scheme under it may provide for all or any of the following matters:—

(a) for regulating the redevelopment, use or appearance of property of which tenants have acquired the landlord's interest under this Part of this Act; and

(b) for empowering the landlord for the time being to carry out work for the maintenance or repair of any such property or carry out work to remedy a failure in respect of any such property co comply with the scheme, or for making the operation of any provisions of the scheme conditional on his doing so or on the provision or maintenance by him of services, facilities or amenities of any description; and

(c) for imposing on persons from time to time occupying or interested in any such property obligations in respect of maintenance or repair of the property or of property used or enjoyed by them in common with others, or in respect of cost incurred by the landlord for the time being on any matter referred to in this paragraph or in paragraph (b) above;

(d) for the inspection from time to time of any such property on behalf of the landlord for the time being, and for the recovery by him of sums due to him under the scheme in respect of any such property by means of a charge on the property;

and the landlord for the time being shall have, for the enforcement of any change imposed under the scheme, the same powers and remedies under the Law of Property Act 1925 and otherwise as if he were a mortgagee by deed having powers of sale and leasing and of appointing a receiver.

(9) A scheme under this section may extend to property in which the landlord's interest is disposed of otherwise than under this Part of this Act (whether residential property or not), so as to make that property, or allow it to be made, subject to any such provision as is or might be made by the

scheme for property in which tenants acquire the landlord's interest under this Part of this Act.

(10) A certificate given or scheme approved under this section shall (notwithstanding section 2(a) or (b) of the Local Land Charges Act 1975) be a local land charge and for the purposes of that Act the landlord for the area to which it relates shall be treated as the originating authority as respects such charge; and where a scheme is registered in the appropriate local land charges register;

(a) the provisions of the scheme relating to property of any description shall, so far as they respectively affect the persons from time to time occupying or interested in that property, be enforceable by the landlord for the time being against them, as if each of them had covenanted with the landlord for the time being to be bound by the scheme; and

(b) in relation to a house and premises in the area section 10 above shall have effect subject to the provisions of the scheme, and the price payable under section 9 shall be adjusted accordingly.

(10A) Section 10 of the Local Land Charges Act 1975 shall not apply in relation to schemes which, by virtue of this section, are local land charges.

(11) Subject to subsections (12) and (13) below, a certificate shall not be given nor a scheme approved under this section for any area except on the application of the landlord.

(12) Where, on a joint application made by two or more persons as landlords of neighbouring areas, it appears to the Minister—

(a) that a certificate could in accordance with subsection (1) above be given as regards those areas, treated as a unit, if the interests of those persons were held by a single person; and

(b) that the applicants are willing to be bound by any scheme to co-operate in the management of their property in those areas and in the administration of the scheme;

the Minister may give a certificate under this section for those areas as a whole; and where a certificate is given by virtue of this subsection, this section shall apply accordingly, but so that any scheme made by virtue of the certificate shall be made subject to conditions (enforceable in such manner as may be provided by the scheme) for securing that the landlords and their successors co-operate as aforesaid.

(13) Where it appears to the Minister—

(a) that a certificate could be given under this section for any area or areas on the application of the landlord or landlords; and

(b) that any body of persons is so constituted as to be capable of representing for purposes of this section the persons occupying or interested in property in the area or areas (other than the landlord or landlords), or such of them as are or may become entitled to acquire their landlord's interest under this Part of this Act, and is otherwise suitable;

then on an application made by that body either alone or jointly with the landlord or landlords a certificate may be granted accordingly; and where a certificate is so granted, whether to a representative body alone or to a representative body jointly with the landlord or landlords—

(i) an application for a scheme in pursuance of the certificate may be made by the representative body alone or by the landlord or landlords alone or by both jointly and, by leave of the High Court, may be proceeded with by the representative body or by the landlord or landlords though not the applicant or applicants; and

(ii) without prejudice to subsection (7)(b) above, the scheme may, with the consent of the landlord or landlords or on such terms as to compensation or otherwise as appear to the High Court to be just, confer on the representative body any such rights or powers under the scheme as might be conferred on the landlord or landlords for the time being, or enable the representative body to participate in the administration of the scheme or in the management by the landlord or landlords of his or their property in the area or areas.

(14) Where a certificate under this section has been given for an area, or an application for one is pending, then subject to subsection (15) below if (before or after the making of the application or the giving of the certificate) a tenant of a house in the area gives notice of his desire to have the freehold under this Part of this Act,—

(a) no further proceedings need to be taken in relation to the notice beyond those which appear to the landlord to be reasonable in the circumstances; but

(b) the tenant may at any time withdraw the notice by a further notice in writing given to the landlord, and section 9(4) above shall not apply to require him to make any payment tot he landlord in respect of costs incurred by reason of the notice withdrawn.

(15) Subsection (14) above shall cease to have effect by virtue of an application for a certificate if the application is withdrawn or the certificate refused, and shall cease to have effect as regards the whole or part of an area to which a certificate relates—

(a) on the approval of a scheme for the area or that part of it; or

(b) on the expiration of one year from the giving of the certificate without an application having been made to the High Court for the approval of a scheme for the area or that part of it, or on the withdrawal of an application so made without a scheme being approved; or

(c) on an order made under subsection (4) above with respect to the area or that part of it, or an order dismissing an application for the approval of a scheme for the area or that part of it, becoming final.

Forestry Act 1967

A2–08 **Forestry dedication covenants and agreements**

5.—(1) The provisions of this section shall have effect with a view to allowing land to be devoted to forestry by means of agreements entered into with the Commissioners, being agreements to the effect that the land shall not, except with the previous consent in writing of the Commissioners or, in the case of dispute, under direction of the Minister, be used otherwise than for the growing of timber or other forest products in accordance with the rules or practice of good forestry or for purposes connected therewith; and in this Act—

(a) "forestry dedication covenant" means a covenant to the said effect entered into with the Commissioners in respect of land in England or Wales without an intention being expressed contrary to the application of section 79 of the Law of Property Act 1925 (under which covenants relating to land are, unless the contrary is expressed, deemed to be made on behalf of the covenantor, his successors in title and persons deriving title under him or them); and

(b) "forestry dedication agreement" means an agreement to the said effect entered into with the Commissioners in respect of land in Scotland by a person who is the proprietor thereof for his own absolute use or is empowered by this section to enter into the agreement.

(2) Where land in England or Wales is subject to a forestry dedication covenant,—

(a) the Commissioners shall, as respects the enforcement of the covenant against persons other than the covenantor, have the like rights as if they had at all material times been the absolute owners in possession of ascertained land adjacent to the land subject to the covenant and capable of being benefited by the covenant, and the covenant had been expressed to be for the benefit of that adjacent land; and

(b) section 84 of the Law of Property Act 1925 (which enables the Lands Tribunal to discharge or modify respective covenants) shall not apply to the covenant.

(3) (*Applies to Scotland only.*)

(4) Schedule 2 to this Act shall have effect to empower limited owners, trustees and others to enter into forestry dedication covenants or agreements and to provide for matters arising on their doing so.

Countryside Act 1968

Areas of special scientific interest **A2–09**

15.—(1) This section has effect as respects land ... which is or forms part of an area which in the opinion of the [Nature Conservancy Council] (in this section referred to as "the Council") is of special interest by reason of its flora, fauna, or geological or physiographical features.

(2) Where, for the purpose of conserving those flora, fauna or geological or physiographical features, it appears to the Council expedient ... to do so, the Council may enter into an agreement with the owners, lessees or occupiers of any such land [(or of any adjacent land)] which imposes restrictions on the exercise of rights over land by the persons who can be bound by the agreement.

(3) Any such agreement—

(a) may provide for the carrying out on the land of such work and the doing thereon of such other things as may be expedient for the purposes of the agreement,

(b) may provide for any of the matters mentioned in paragraph (a) above being carried out, or for the cost thereof being defrayed, either by the owners or other persons, or by the Council, or partly in one way and partly in another, and

(c) may contain such other provisions as to the making of payments by the Council as may be specified in the agreement.

(4) Where section 79 of the Law of Property Act 1925 (burden of covenant running with the land) applies to any such restrictions as are mentioned in subsection (2) of this section, the Council shall have the like rights as respects the enforcement of the restrictions as if the Council had at all material times been the absolute owner in possession of ascertained land adjacent to the land in respect of which the restriction is sought to be enforced, and capable of being benefited by the restriction, and the restriction had been expressed to be for the benefit of that adjacent land.

Section 84 of the Law of Property Act 1925 (discharge or modification of restrictive covenants) shall not apply to such a restriction.

(5) Schedule 2 to the Forestry Act 1967 (powers of tenants for life and other limited owners to enter into forestry dedication covenants or agreements) shall

apply to any agreement made in pursuance of this section as it applies to such a covenant or agreement.

(6) (*Applies to Scotland only.*)

(6A) In this section references to "the Nature Conservancy Council" or "the Council" are references to the Nature Conservancy Council for England, [Scottish National Heritage] or the Council, according as the land in question is in England, Scotland or Wales.

(7) The Act of 1949 shall have effect as if this section were included in Part III of that Act.

Greater London Council (General Powers) Act 1974

A2–10 **Undertakings and agreements binding successive owners**

16.—(1) Every undertaking given to a local authority by the owner of any legal estate in land and every agreement made between a local authority and any such owner being an undertaking or agreement—

(a) given or made under seal in connection with the land; and

(b) expressed to be given or made in pursuance of this section;

shall be enforceable not only against the owner joining in the undertaking or agreement but also against the successors in title of any owner so joining and any person claiming through or under them.

(2) Such an undertaking or agreement shall be treated as a local land charge for the purposes of the Land Charges Act 1925.

(3) Any person against whom such an undertaking or agreement is enforceable shall be entitled to require a copy thereof from the local authority without payment.

(4) Any charge on the land which by virtue of this section is enforceable in the manner described in subsection (1) of this section shall, for the purposes of subsection (1) of section 32 of the Building Societies Act 1962 (which prohibits advances by building societies on second mortgage), be deemed not to be a prior mortgage within the meaning of that subsection.

(5) (a) The enactments specified in Part III of Schedule 2 to this Act are hereby repealed.

(b) The enactments specified in Part II of Schedule 3 to this Act are hereby repealed so far as they relate to any part of Greater London.

(6) Any undertaking or agreement which by virtue of an enactment included in Part III of Schedule 2 or Part II of Schedule 3 to this Act was, immediately

before the passing of this Act, binding on any successors in title of any owner joining in such undertaking or agreement and on any person claiming through or under them shall, notwithstanding the repeal of that enactment, continue to be so binding and enforceable as if such undertaking or agreement were expressed to be given or made in pursuance of this section.

(7) In this section "local authority" means the Council or a borough council.

Ancient Monuments and Archaeological Areas Act 1979

Agreements concerning ancient monuments, etc. **A2–11**

Agreement concerning ancient monuments and land in their vicinity

17.—(1) The Secretary of State may enter into an agreement under this section with the occupier of an ancient monument or of any land adjoining or in the vicinity of an ancient monument.

(1A) the Commission may enter into an agreement under this section with the occupier of an ancient monument situated in England or of any land so situated which adjoins or is in the vicinity of an ancient monument so situated.

(2) A local authority may enter into an agreement under this section with the occupier of any ancient monument situated in or in the vicinity of their area or with the occupier of any and adjoining or in the vicinity of any such ancient monument.

(3) Any person who has an interest in an ancient monument or in any land adjoining or in the vicinity of an ancient monument may be a party to an agreement under this section in addition to the occupier.

(4) An agreement under this section may make provision for all or any of the following matters with respect to the monument or land in question, that is to say—

(a) the maintenance and preservation of the monument and its amenities;

(b) the carrying out of any such work, or the doing of any such other thing, in relation to the monument or land as may be specified in the agreement;

(c) public access to the monument or land and the provision of facilities and information or other services for the use of the public in that connection;

(d) restricting the use of the monument or land;

(e) prohibiting in relation to the monument or land the doing of any such thing as may be specified in the agreement; and

(f) the making by the Secretary of State or [the Commission or the local authority (as the case may be)] of payments in such manner, of such amounts and on such terms as may be so specified (and whether for or towards the cost of any work provided for under the agreement or in consideration of any restriction, prohibition or obligation accepted by any other party thereto);

and may contain such incidental and consequential provisions as appear to the Secretary of State or [the Commission or the local authority (as the case may be) to be necessary or expedient.

(5) Where an agreement under this section expressly provides that the agreement as a whole or any restriction, prohibition or obligation arising thereunder is to be binding on the successors of any party to the agreement (but not otherwise), then, as respects any monument or land in England or Wales, every person deriving title to the monument or land in question from, through or under that party shall be bound by the agreement, or (as the case may be) by that restriction, prohibition or obligation, unless he derives title by virtue of any disposition made by that party before the date of the agreement.

(6) (*Applies to Scotland only.*)

(7) Neither—

(a) section 84 of the Law of Property Act 1925 (power of Lands Tribunal to discharge or modify restrictive covenants); nor

(b) (*applies to Scotland only*).

shall apply to an agreement under this section.

(8) Nothing in any agreement under this section to which the Secretary of State is a party shall be construed as operating as a scheduled monument consent.

(9) References to an ancient monument in subsection (1A) above, and in subsection (3) above so far as it applies for the purposes of subsection (1A), shall be construed as if the reference in section 61(12)(b) of this Act to the Secretary of State were to the Commission.

A2–12

Highways Act 1980

Creation of walkways by agreement

35.—(1) An agreement under this section may be entered into—

(a) by a local highway authority, after consultation with the council of any non-metropolitan district in which the land concerned is situated;

(b) by a non-metropolitan district council, either alone or jointly with the local highway authority, after consultation with the local highway authority.

(2) An agreement under this section is an agreement with any person having an interest in any land on which a building is, or is proposed to be, situated, being a person who by virtue of that interest has the necessary power in that behalf,—

(a) for the provision of ways over, through or under parts of the building, or the building when constructed, as the case may be, or parts of any structure attached, or to be attached, to the building; and

(b) for the dedication by that person of those ways as footpaths subject to such limitations and conditions, if any, affecting the public right of way thereover as may be specified in the agreement and to any rights reserved by the agreement to that person and any person deriving title to the land under him.

A footpath created in pursuance of an agreement under this section is referred to below as a "walkway".

(3) An agreement under this section may make provision for—

(a) the maintenance, cleansing and drainage of any walkway to which the agreement relates;

(b) the lighting of such walkway and of that part of the building or structure which will be over or above it;

(c) the provision and maintenance of support for such walkway;

(d) entitling the authority entering into the agreement or, where the agreement is entered into jointly by a [non-metropolitan] district council and a local highway authority, either of those authorities to enter on any building or structure in which such walkway will be situated and to execute any works necessary to secure the performance of any obligation which any person is for the time being liable to perform by virtue of the agreement or of subsection (4) below;

(e) the making of payments by the authority entering into the agreement or, where the agreement is entered into jointly by a [non-metropolitan] district council and a local highway authority, either of those authorities to any person having an interest in the land or building affected by the agreement;

(f) the termination, in such manner and subject to such conditions as maybe specified in the agreement, of the right of the public to use such walkway;

(g) any incidental and consequential matters.

(4) Any covenant (whether positive or restrictive) contained in an agreement under this section and entered into by a person having an interest in any land affected by the agreement shall be binding upon persons deriving title to the land under the covenantor to the same extent as it is binding upon the covenantor notwithstanding that it would not have been binding upon those persons apart from the provisions of this subsection, and shall be enforceable against those persons by the local highways authority.

(5) A covenant contained in an agreement under this section and entered into by a person having an interest in any land affected by the agreement is a local land charge.

(6) Where an agreement has been entered into under this section the appropriate authority may make byelaws regulating—

(a) the conduct of persons using any walkway to which the agreement relates;

(b) the times at which any such walkway may be closed to the public;

(c) the placing or retention of anything (including any structure or projection) in, on or over any such walkway.

(7) For the purposes of subsection (6) above, "the appropriate authority" means—

(a) where the agreement was entered into by a local highway authority, that authority;

(b) where the agreement was entered into by a [non-metropolitan] district council alone, that council;

(c) where the agreement was entered into by a [non-metropolitan] district council jointly with the local highway authority, the local highway authority;

but in cases falling within paragraph (c) above the local highway authority shall before making any byelaw consult the district council, and in exercising his power of confirmation the Minister shall have regard to any dispute between the local highway authority and the district council.

(8) Not less than 2 months before an authority propose to make byelaws under subsection (6) above they shall display in a conspicuous position on or adjacent to the walkway in question notice of their intention to make such byelaws.

(9) A notice under subsection (8) above shall specify the place where a copy of the proposed byelaws may be inspected and the period, which shall not be less than 6 weeks from the date on which the notice was first displayed as aforesaid, within which representations may be made to the authority, and the authority shall consider any representations made to them within that period.

(10) The Minister of the Crown having power by virtue of section 236 of the Local Government Act 1972 to confirm byelaws made under subsection (6) above may confirm them with or without modifications; and if he proposes to confirm them with modifications he may, before confirming them, direct the authority by whom they were made to give notice of the proposed modifications to such persons and in such manner as may be specified in the direction.

(11) Subject to subsection (12) below, the Minister after consulting such representative organisations as he thinks fit, may make regulations—

(a) for preventing any enactment or instrument relating to highways or to things done on or in connection with highways from applying to walkways which have been, or are to be, created in pursuance of agreements under this section or to things done on or in connection with such walkways;

(b) for amending, modifying or adapting any such enactment or instrument in its application to such walkways;

(c) without prejudice to the generality of paragraphs (a) and (b) above, for excluding, restricting or regulating the rights of statutory undertakers, ... [... and the operators of telecommunications code systems to place] and maintain apparatus in, under, over, along or across such walkways;

(d) without prejudice as aforesaid, for defining the circumstances and manner in which such walkways may be closed periodically or temporarily or stopped up and for prescribing the procedure to be followed before such a walkway is stopped up.

(12) Regulations under this section shall not exclude the rights of statutory undertakers, ... or the operators of telecommunications code systems to place and maintain apparatus in, under, along or across any part of a walkway, being a part which is not supported by any structure.

(13) Without prejudice to subjection (11) above, regulations under this section may make different provisions for different classes of walkways and may include such incidental, supplemental and consequential provisions (and, in particular, provisions relating to walkways provided in pursuance of agreements made before the coming into operation of the regulations) as appear to the Minister to be expedient for the purposes of the regulations.

(14) Nothing in this section is to be taken as affecting any other provision of this Act, or any other enactment, by virtue of which highways may be created.

Wildlife and Countryside Act 1981

A2–13 Management agreements with owners and occupiers of land

39.—(1) A relevant authority may, for the purpose of conserving or enhancing the natural beauty or amenity of any land which is both in the countryside and within their area or promoting its enjoyment by the public, make an agreement (in this section referred to as a "management agreement") with any person having an interest in the land with respect to the management of the land during a specified term or without limitation of the duration of the agreement.

(2) Without prejudice to the generality of subsection (1), a management agreement—

(a) may impose on the person having an interest in the land restrictions as respects the method of cultivating the land, its use for agricultural purposes or the exercise of rights over the land and may impose obligations on that person to carry out works or agricultural or forestry operations or do other things on the land;

(b) may confer on the relevant authority power to carry out works for the purpose of performing their functions under the 1949 Act and the 1968 Act; and

(c) may contain such incidental and consequential provisions (including provisions for the making of payments by either party to the other) as appear to the relevant authority to be necessary or expedient for the purposes of the agreement.

(3) The provisions of a management agreement with any person interested in the land shall, unless the agreement otherwise provides, be binding on persons deriving title under or from that person and be enforceable by the relevant authority against those persons accordingly.

(4) Schedule 2 to the Forestry Act 1967 (power for tenant for life and others to enter into forestry dedication covenants) shall apply to management agreements as it applies to forestry dedication covenants.

(5) In this section "the relevant authority" means—

(a) *as respects land in a National Park and outside a metropolitan county, the county planning authority;*

(aa) as respects land within the Broads, the Broads Authority;

(b) . . .

(c) as respects any other land, the local planning authority.

(6) The powers conferred by this section on a relevant authority shall be in

addition to and not in derogation of any powers conferred on such an authority by or under any enactment.

Local Government (Misc. Prov.) Act 1982

Enforceability by local authorities of certain covenants relating to land **A2–14**

33.—(1) The provisions of this section shall apply if a principal council (in the exercise of their powers under section 111 of the Local Government Act 1972 or otherwise) and any other person are parties to an instrument under seal which—

(a) is executed for the purpose of securing the carrying out of works on or facilitating the development or regulating the use of land in the council's area in which the other person has an interest; or

(b) is executed for the purpose of facilitating the development or regulating the use of land outside the council's area in which the other person has an interest; or

(c) is otherwise connected with land in or outside the council's area in which the other person has an interest.

(2) If, in a case where this section applies,—

(a) the instrument contains a covenant on the part of any person having an interest in land, being a covenant to carry out any works or do any other thing on or in relation to that land, and

(b) the instrument defines the land to which the covenant relates, being land in which that person has an interest at the time the instrument is executed, and

(c) the covenant is expressed to be one to which this section or section 126 of the Housing Act 1974 (which is superseded by this section) applies,

the covenant shall be enforceable (without any limit of time) against any person deriving title from the original covenant in respect of his interest in any of the land defined as mentioned in paragraph (b) above and any person deriving title under him in respect of any lesser interest in that land as if that person had also been an original covenanting party in respect of the interest for the time being held by him.

(3) Without prejudice to any other method of enforcement of a covenant falling within subsection (2) above, if there is a breach of the covenant in relation to any of the land to which the covenant relates, then, subject to subsection (4) below, the principal council who are a party to the instrument in which the covenant is contained may—

(a) enter on the land concerned and carry out the works or do anything which the covenant requires to be carried out or done or remedy anything which has been done and which the covenant required not to be done; and

(b) recover from any person against whom the covenant is enforceable (whether by virtue of subsection (2) above or otherwise) any expenses incurred by the council in exercise of their powers under this subsection.

(4) Before a principal council exercise their powers under subsection (3)(a) above they shall give not less than 21 days notice of their intention to do so to any person—

(a) who has for the time being an interest in the land on or in relation to which the works are to be carried out or other thing is to be done; and

(b) against whom the covenant is enforceable (whether by virtue of subsection (2) above or otherwise).

(5) If a person against whom a covenant is enforceable by virtue of subsection (2) above requests the principal council to supply him with a copy of the covenant, it shall be their duty to do so free of charge.

(6) The Public Health Act 1936 shall have effect as if any reference to that Act in—

(a) section 283 of that Act (notices to be in writing; forms of notices, etc.),

(b) section 288 of that Act (penalty for obstructing execution of Act), and

(c) section 291 of that Act (certain expenses recoverable from owners to be a charge on the premises; power to order payment by instalments),

included a reference to subsections (1) to (4) above and as if any reference in those sections of that Act—

(i) to a local authority were a reference to a principal council; and

(ii) to the owner of the premises were a reference to the holder of an interest in land.

(7) Section 16 of the Local Government (Miscellaneous Provisions) Act 1976 shall have effect as if references to a local authority and to functions conferred on a local authority by any enactment included respectively references

to such a board as is mentioned in subsection (9) below and to functions of such a board under this section.

(8) In its application to a notice or other document authorised to be given or served under subsection (4) above or by virtue of any provision of the Public Health Act 1936 specified in subsection (6) above, section 233 of the Local Government Act 1972 (service of notices by local authorities) shall have effect as if any reference in that section to a local authority included a reference to the Common Council of the City of London and such a board is mentioned in the following subsection.

(9) In this section—

(a) "principal council" means the council of a county, district or London borough, a board constituted in pursuance of section 1 of the Town and Country Planning Act 1971 or reconstituted in pursuance of Schedule 17 to the Local Government Act 1972, the Common Council of the City of London . . . the Inner London Education Authority or a joint authority established by Part IV of the Local Government Act 1985; and

(b) "area" in relation to such a board means the district for which the board is constituted or reconstituted, in relation to the Inner London Education Authority means the Inner Education Area, and in relation to such a joint authority means the area for which the authority was established.

(10) Section 126 of the Housing Act 1974 (which is superseded by this section) shall cease to have effect; but in relation to a covenant falling within subsection (2) of that section, section 1(1)(d) of the Local Land Charges Act 1975 shall continue to have effect as if the reference to the commencement of that Act had been a reference to the coming into operation of the said section 126.

Allotments Act 1950

Abolition of contractual restrictions on keeping hens and rabbits **A2–15**

Abolition of contractual restrictions on keeping hens and rabbits

12.—(1) Notwithstanding any provision to the contrary in any lease or tenancy or in any covenant, contract or undertaking relating to the use to be made of any land, it shall be lawful for the occupier of any land to keep, otherwise than by way of trade or business, hens or rabbits in any place on the land and to erect or place and maintain such buildings or structures on the land as are reasonably necessary for that purpose:

Provided that nothing in this subsection shall authorise any hen or rabbits to be kept in such a place or in such a manner as to be prejudicial to health or a nuisance or affect the operation of any enactment.

A2–16

Pastoral Measure 1983

Power to impose and enforce covenants

62.—(1) Without prejudice to any restriction or requirement in a redundancy scheme or a pastoral scheme to which section 46 or section 47 applies, the Commissioners or the diocesan board of finance may, in exercising their powers under this Part to sell, give, exchange or let or, as the case may be, to let or license any building or land, include in the conveyance, lease or other instrument such covenants imposing conditions and requirements as to the use of the building or land concerned as the Commissioners or board think necessary or expedient to give effect to the provisions of the scheme or otherwise to secure the suitable use of the building or land; and, in a case where the land is sold, given or exchanged, any such covenants shall be enforceable as if the Commissioners or board were the owners of adjacent land and the covenants were expressed to be entered into for the benefit of that adjacent land, and in the case of covenants of a positive character as if they were negative.

(2) Where any such covenant is subsequently varied or released by agreement, any sum of money received by a diocesan board of finance in consideration of the variation or release of a covenant imposed by the board shall be paid to the Commissioners and section 51(5) shall apply in relation to the sum so paid, and in relation to any sum of money received by the Commissioners in consideration of the variation or release of a covenant imposed by them, as it applies in relation to the proceeds of any sale or exchange under section 51(2), (3) or (4).

Housing Act 1985

A2–17

Enforceability of covenants, etc.

Enforcement of covenants against owner for the time being

609. Where—

(a) a local housing authority have disposed of land held by them for any of the purposes of this Act and the person to whom the disposal was made has entered into a covenant with the authority concerning the and, or

(b) an owner of any land has entered into a covenant with the local housing authority concerning the land for the purposes of any of the provisions of this Act, the authority may enforce the covenant against the persons deriving title under the covenantor, notwithstanding that the authority are not in possession of or interested in any land for the benefit of which the covenant was entered into, in like manner and to the like extent as if they had been possessed of or interested in such land.

Power of court to authorise conversion of house into flats

610.—(1) The local housing authority or a person interested in any premises may apply to the county court where—

(a) owing to changes in the character of the neighbourhood in which the premises are situated, they cannot readily be let as a single dwelling-house but could readily be let for occupation if converted into two or more dwelling-houses, or

(b) planning permission has been granted under Part III of the Town and Country Planning Act 1990 (general planning control) for the use of the premises as converted into two or more separate dwelling-houses instead of as a single dwelling-house,

and the conversion is prohibited or restricted by the provisions of the lease of the premises, or by a restrictive covenant affecting the premises, or otherwise.

(2) The court may, after giving any person interested an opportunity of being heard, vary the terms of the lease or other instrument imposing the prohibition or restriction, subject to such conditions and upon such terms as the court may think just.

Appendix 3

Statutory Material

Land Charges Act 1972

A3–01

(1972, c. 61)

(RELEVANT PROVISIONS)

Preliminary

The registers and the index

1.—(1) The registrar shall continue to keep at the registry in the prescribed manner the following registers, namely—

(a) a register of land charges;

(b) ...

(c) ...

(d) ...

(e) ...

and shall also continue to keep there an index whereby all entries made in any of those registers can readily be traced.

(2) Every application to register shall be in the prescribed form and shall contain the prescribed particulars.

(3) Where any charge or other matter is registrable in more than one of the registers kept under this Act, it shall be sufficient if it is registered in one such register, and if it is so registered the person entitled to the benefit of it shall not be prejudicially affected by any provision of this Act as to the effect of non-registration in any other such register.

(3A) Where any charge or other matter is registrable in a register kept under this Act and was also, before the commencement of the Local Land Charges

Act 1975, registrable in a local land charges register, then, if before the commencement of the said Act it was registered in the appropriate local land charges register, it shall be treated for the purposes of the provisions of this Act as to the effect of non-registration as if it had been registered in the appropriate register under this Act; and any certificate setting out the result of an official search of the appropriate local land charges register shall, in relation to it, have effect as if it were a certificate setting out the result of an official search under this Act;

(4)

(5) An office copy of an entry in any register kept under this section shall be admissible in evidence in all proceedings and between all parties to the same extent as the original would be admissible.

(6) Subject to the provisions of this Act, registration may be vacated pursuant to an order of the court.

(6A) The county court has jurisdiction under subsection (6) above—

(a) ...

(b) ...

(c) in the case of a land charge of Class A, Class B, Class C(iv), Class D(ii), Class D(iii) or Class E, if the land affected does not exceed the county court limit in capital value or in net annual value for rating;

(d) ...

(e) ...

(6B) A reference to the county court limit in a paragraph of subsection (6A) above is a reference to the amount for the time being specified by an Order in Council under section 145 of the County Courts Act 1984 as the county court limit for the purpose of that paragraph (or, where no such Order in Council has been made, the corresponding limit specified by Order in Council under section 192 of the County Courts Act 1959).

(7) In this section "index" includes any device or combination of devices serving the purpose of an index.

Registration in register of land charges

The register of land charges

2.—(1) If a charge on or obligation affecting land falls into one of the classes described in this section, it may be registered in the register of land charges as a land charge of that class.

(2) ...

(3) ...

(4) A Class C land charge is any of the following [(not being a local land charge)], namely—

(i) ...

(ii) ...

(iii) a general equitable charge;

(iv) an estate contract;

and for this purpose—

(i) ...

(ii) ...

(iii) ...

(iv) an estate contract is a contract by an estate owner or by a person entitled at the date of the contract to have a legal estate conveyed to him to convey or create a legal estate, including a contract conferring either expressly or by statutory implication a valid option to purchase, a right of pre-emption or any other like right.

(5) A Class D land charge is any of the following (not being a local land charge), namely—

(i) ...

(ii) a restrictive covenant;

(iii) an equitable easement;

and for this purpose—

(i) ...

(ii) a restrictive covenant is a covenant or agreement (other than a covenant or agreement between a lessor and a lessee) restrictive of the user of land and entered into on or after January 1, 1926;

(iii) an equitable easement is an easement, right or privilege over or affecting land created or arising on or after January 1, 1926, and being merely an equitable interest.

(6) . . .

(7) . . .

(8) A charge or obligation created before January 1, 1926 can only be registered as a Class B land charge or a Class C land charge if it is acquired under a conveyance made on or after that date.

(9) . . .

Registration of land charges

3.—(1) A land charge shall be registered in the name of the estate owner whose estate is intended to be affected.

(2) A land charge registered before January 1, 1926 under any enactment replaced by the Land Charges Act 1925 in the name of a person other than the estate owner may remain so registered until it is registered in the name of the estate owner in the prescribed manner.

(3) . . .

(4) The expenses incurred by the person entitled to the charge in registering a land charge of Class A, Class B or Class C (other than an estate contract) . . . shall be deemed to form part of the land charge, and shall be recoverable accordingly on the day for payment of any part of the land charge next after such expenses are incurred.

(5) Where a land charge is not created by an instrument, short particulars of the effect of the charge shall be furnished with the application to register the charge.

(6) . . .

(7) . . .

(8) . . .

Effect of land charges and protection of purchasers

4.—(1) . . .

(2) . . .

(3) . . .

(4) . . .

(5) A land charge of Class B and a land charge of Class C (other than an estate contract) created or arising on or after January 1, 1926 shall be void as against a purchaser of the land charged with it, or of any interest in such land, unless the land charge is registered in the appropriate register before the completion of the purchase.

(6) An estate contract and a land charge of Class D created or entered into on or after January 1, 1926 shall be void as against a purchaser for money or money's worth ... of a legal estate in the land charged with it, unless the land charge is registered in the appropriate register before the completion of the purchase.

(7) After the expiration of one year from the first conveyance occurring on or after January 1, 1926 of a land charge of Class B or Class C created before that date the person entitled to the land charge shall not be able to enforce or recover the land charge or any part of it as against a purchaser of the land charged with it, or of any interest in the land, unless the land charge is registered in the appropriate register before the completion of the purchase.

(8) ...

Searches and official searches

Searches

9.—(1) Any person may search in any register kept under this Act on paying the prescribed fee.

(2) Without prejudice to subsection (1) above, the registrar may provide facilities for enabling persons entitled to search in any such register to see photographic or other images or copies of any portion of the register which they may wish to examine.

Official searches

10.—(1) Where any person requires search to be made at the registry for entries of any matters or documents, entries of which are required or allowed to be made in the registry by this Act, he may make a requisition in that behalf to the registrar, which may be either—

(a) a written requisition delivered at or sent by post to the registry; or

(b) a requisition communicated by teleprinter, telephone or other means in such manner as may be prescribed in relation to the means in question, in which case it shall be treated as made to the registrar if, but only if, he accepts it;

and the registrar shall not accept a requisition made in accordance with paragraph (b) above unless it is made by a person maintaining a credit account at the registry, and may at his discretion refuse to accept it notwithstanding that it is made by such a person.

(2) The prescribed fee shall be payable in respect of every requisition made under this section; and that fee—

(a) in the case of a requisition made in accordance with subsection (1)(a) above, shall be paid in such manner as may be prescribed for the purposes of this paragraph unless the requisition is made by a person maintaining a credit account at the registry and the fee is debited to that account;

(b) in the case of a requisition made in accordance with subsection (1)(b) above, shall be debited to the credit account of the person by whom the requisition is made.

(3) Where a requisition is made under subsection (1) above and the fee payable in respect of it is paid or debited in accordance with subsection (2) above, the registrar shall thereupon make the search required and—

(a) shall issue a certificate setting out the result of the search; and

(b) without prejudice to paragraph (a) above, may take such other steps as he considers appropriate to communicate the result to the person by whom the requisition was made.

(4) In favour of a purchaser or an intending purchaser, as against persons interested under or in respect of matters or documents entries of which are required or allowed as aforesaid, the certificate, according to its tenor, shall be conclusive, affirmatively or negatively, as the case may be.

(5) If any officer, clerk or person employed in the registry commits, or is party or privy to, any act of fraud or collusion, or is wilfully negligent, in the making of or otherwise in relation to any certificate under this section, he shall be guilty of an offence and shall be liable on conviction on indictment to imprisonment for a term not exceeding two years, or on summary conviction to imprisonment for a term not exceeding three months or to a fine not exceeding [the prescribed sum], or to both such imprisonment and fine.

(6) Without prejudice to subsection (5) above, no officer, clerk or person employed in the registry shall, in the absence of fraud on his part, be liable for any loss which may be suffered—

(a) by reason of any discrepancy between—

(i) the particulars which are shown in a certificate under this section as being the particulars in respect of which the search for entries was made, and

(ii) the particulars in respect of which a search for entries was required by the person who made the requisition; or

(b) by reason of any communication of the result of a search under this section made otherwise than by issuing a certificate under this section.

Miscellaneous and supplementary

Date of effective registration and priority notices

11.—(1) Any person intending to make an application for the registration of any contemplated charge, instrument or other matter in pursuance of this Act or any rule made under this Act may give a priority notice in the prescribed form at least the relevant number of days before the registration is to take effect.

(2) Where a notice is given under subsection (1) above, it shall be entered in the register to which the intended application when made will related.

(3) If the application is presented within the relevant number of days thereafter and refers in the prescribed manner to the notice, the registration shall take effect as if the registration had been made at the time when the charge, instrument or matter was created, entered into, made or arose, and the date at which the registration so takes effect shall be deemed to be the date of registration.

(4) Where—

(a) any two charges, instruments or matters are contemporaneous; and

(b) one of them (whether or not protected by a priority notice) is subject to or dependent on the other; and

(c) the latter is protected by a priority notice,

the subsequent or dependent charge, instrument or matter shall be deemed to have been created, entered into or made, or to have arisen, after the registration of the other.

(5) Where a purchaser has obtained a certificate under section 10 above, any entry which is made in the register after the date of the certificate and before the completion of the purchase, and is not made pursuant to a priority notice entered on the register on or before the date of the certificate, shall not affect the purchaser if the purchase is completed before the expiration of the relevant number of days after the date of the certificate.

(6) The relevant number of days is—

(a) for the purposes of subsections (1) and (5) above, fifteen;

(b) for the purposes of subsection (3) above, thirty;

or such other number as may be prescribed; but in reckoning the relevant number of days for any of the purposes of this section any days when the registry is not open to the public shall be excluded.

Protection of solicitors, trustees, etc.

12. A solicitor, or a trustee, personal representative, agent or other person in a fiduciary position, shall not be answerable—

(a) in respect of any loss occasioned by reliance on an office copy of an entry in any register kept under this Act;

(b) for any loss that may arise from error in a certificate under section 10 above obtained by him.

Saving for overreaching powers

13.—(1) The registration of any charge, annuity or other interest under this Act shall not prevent the charge, annuity or interest being overreached under any other Act, except where otherwise provided by that other Act.

(2) The registration as a land charge of a puisne mortgage or charge shall not operate to prevent that mortgage or charge being overreached in favour of a prior mortgagee or a person deriving title under him where, by reason of a sale or foreclosure, or otherwise, the right of the puisne mortgagee or subsequent chargee to redeem is barred.

Exclusion of matters affecting registered land or created by instruments necessitating registration of land

14.—(1) This Act shall not apply to instruments or matters required to be registered or re-registered on or after January 1, 1926, if and so far as they affect registered land, and can be protected under the Land Registration Act 1925 by lodging or registering a creditor's notice, restriction, caution, inhibition or other notice.

(2) Nothing in this Act imposes on the registrar any obligation to ascertain whether or not an instrument or matter affects registered land.

(3) Where an instrument executed on or after July 27, 1971 conveys, grants or assigns an estate in land and creates a land charge affecting that estate, this Act shall not apply to the land charge, so far as it affects that estate, if under section 123 of the Land Registration Act 1925 (effect of that Act in areas where registration is compulsory) the instrument will, unless the necessary application for registration under that Act is made within the time allowed by or under that section, become void so far as respects the conveyance, grant or assignment of that estate.

Application to the Crown

15.—(1) This Act binds the Crown, but nothing in this Act shall be construed as rendering land owned by or occupied for the purposes of the Crown subject to any charge to which, independently of this Act, it would not be subject.

(2) References in this Act to restrictive covenants include references to any conditions, stipulations or restrictions imposed on or after January 1, 1926, by virtue of section 137 of the Law of Property Act 1922, for the protection of the amenities of royal parks, gardens and palaces.

General rules

16.—(1) The Lord chancellor may, with the concurrence of the Treasury as to fees, make such general rules as may be required for carrying this Act into effect, and in particular—

(a) as to forms and contents of applications for registration, modes of identifying where practicable the land affected, requisitions for and certificates of official searches, and regulating the practice of the registry in connection therewith;

(b) for providing for the mode of registration of a land charge (and in the case of a puisne mortgage, general equitable charge, estate contract, restrictive covenant or equitable easement by reference to the instrument imposing or creating the charge, interest or restriction, or an extract from that instrument) and for the cancellation without an order of court of the registration of a land charge, on its cesser, or with the consent of the person entitled to it, or on sufficient evidence being furnished that the land charge has been overreached under the provisions of any Act or otherwise;

(c) for determining the date on which applications and notices shall be treated for the purposes of section 11 of this Act as having been made or given;

(d) for determining the times and order at and in which applications and priority notices are to be registered;

(e) for varying the relevant number of days for any of the purposes of section 11 of this Act;

(f) for enabling the registrar to provide credit accounting facilities in respect of fees payable by virtue of this Act;

(g) for treating the debiting of such a fee to a credit account maintained at the registry as being, for such purposes of this Act or of the rules as may be specified in the rules, payment of that fee;

(h) for the termination or general suspension of any credit accounting facilities provided under the rules or for their withdrawal of suspension in particular cases at the discretion of the registrar;

(j) for requiring the registrar to take steps in relation to any instrument or matter in respect of which compensation has been claimed under section 25 of the Law of Property Act 1969 which would be likely to bring that instrument or matter to the notice of any person who subsequently makes a search of the registers kept under section 1 of this Act or requires such a search to be made in relation to the estate or interest affected by the instrument or matter and

(k) for authorising the use of the index kept under this Act in any manner which will serve that purpose, notwithstanding that its use in that manner is not otherwise authorised by or by virtue of this Act.

(2) The power of the Lord Chancellor, with the concurrence of the Secretary of State, to make [rules under section [412 of the Insolvency Act 1986]] shall include power to make rules as respects the registration and re-registration of a petition in bankruptcy under section 5 of this Act and [a bankruptcy order] under section 6 of this Act, as if the registration and re-registration were required [by Parts [VIII to XI] of that Act].

Interpretation

17.—(1) In this Act, unless the context otherwise requires,—

"conveyance" includes a mortgage, charge, lease, assent, vesting declaration, vesting instrument, release and every other assurance of property, or of an interest in property, by any instrument except a will, and "convey" has a corresponding meaning;

"court" means the High Court, or the county court in a case where that court has jurisdiction;

"estate owner", "legal estate", "equitable interest", "trust for sale", "charge by way of legal mortgage", [and "will"] have the same meanings as in the Law of Property Act 1925;

"land" includes land of any tenure and mines and minerals, whether or not severed from the surface, buildings or parts of buildings (whether the division is horizontal, vertical or made in any other way) and other corporeal hereditaments, also a manor, an advowson and a rent and other incorporeal hereditaments, and an easement, right, privilege or benefit in, over or derived from land, but not an undivided share in land, and "hereditament" means real property which, on an intestacy occurring before January 1, 1926, might have developed on an heir;

"prescribed" means prescribed by rules made pursuant to this Act;

"purchaser" means any person (including a mortgagee or lessee) who, for valuable consideration, takes any interest in land or in a charge on land, and "purchase" has a corresponding meaning;

"registrar" means the Chief Land Registrar, "registry" means His Majesty's Land Registry, and "registered land" has the same meaning as in the Land Registration Act 1925;

"tenant for life", "statutory owner", "vesting instrument" and "settlement" have the same meanings as in the Settled Land Act 1925.

(2) For the purposes of any provision in this Act requiring or authorising anything to be done at or delivered or sent to the registry, any reference to the registry shall, if the registrar so directs, be read as a reference to such

office of the registry (whether in London or elsewhere) as may be specified in the direction.

(3) Any reference in this Act to any enactment is a reference to it as amended by or under any other enactment, including this Act.

Consequential amendments, repeals, savings, etc.

18.—(1) . . .

(2) . . .

(3) . . .

(4) . . .

(5) In so far as any entry in a register or instrument made or other thing whatsoever done under any enactment repealed by this Act could have been made or done under a corresponding provision in this Act, it shall have effect as if made or done under that corresponding provision; and for the purposes of this provision any entry in a register which under section 24 of the Land Charges Act 1925 had effect as if made under that Act shall, so far as may be necessary for the continuity of the law, be treated as made under this Act.

(6) Any enactment or other document referring to an enactment repealed by this Act or to an enactment repealed by the Land Charges Act 1925 shall, as far as may be necessary for preserving its effect, be construed as referring, or as including a reference, to the corresponding enactment in this Act.

(7) Nothing in the foregoing provisions of this section shall be taken as prejudicing the operation of section 38 of the Interpretation Act 1889 (which relates to the effect of repeals).

Short title, commencement and extent

19.—(1) This Act may be cited as the Land Charges Act 1972.

(2) This Act shall come into force on such day as the Lord Chancellor may by order made by statutory instrument appoint; and different days may be so appointed for different purposes.

(3) This Act extends to England and Wales only.

SCHEDULES

(not printed here)

Local Land Charges Act 1975

(1975, c. 76)

Definition of local land charges

Local land charges **A3–02**

1.—(1) A charge or other matter affecting land is a local land charge if it falls within any of the following descriptions and is not one of the matters set out in section 2 below:—

(a) any charge acquired either before or after the commencement of this Act by a local authority, water authority or new town development corporation under the Public Health Acts 1936 and 1937, . . . the Public Health Act 1961 or [the Highways Act 1980 (or any Act repealed by that Act)] [or the Building Act 1984], or any similar charge acquired by a local authority under any other ACt, whether passed before or after this Act, being a charge that is binding on successive owners of the land affected;

(b) any prohibition of or restriction on the use of land—

(i) imposed by a local authority on or after January 1, 1926 (including any prohibition or restriction embodied in any condition attached to a consent, approval or licence granted by a local authority on or after that date), or
(ii) enforceable by a local authority under any covenant or agreement made with them on or after that date,

being a prohibition or restriction binding on successive owners of the land affected;

(c) any prohibition of or restriction on the use of land—

(i) imposed by a Minister of the Crown or government department on or after the date of the commencement of this Act (including any prohibition or restriction embodied in any condition attached to a consent, approval or licence granted by such a Minister or department on or after that date), or
(ii) enforceable by such a Minister or department under any covenant or agreement made with him or them on or after that date, being a prohibition or restriction binding on successive owners of the land affected;

(d) any positive obligation affecting land enforceable by a Minister of the Crown, government department or local authority under any covenant or agreement made with him or them on or after the date of the commencement of this Act and binding on successive owners of the land affected;

(e) any charge or other matter which is expressly made a local land charge by any statutory provision not contained in this section.

(2) For the purposes of subsection (1)(a) above, any sum which is recoverable from successive owners or occupiers of the land in respect of which the sum is recoverable shall be treated as a charge, whether the sum is expressed to be a charge on the land or not.

Matters which are not local land charges

2. The following matters are not local land charges:—

(a) a prohibition or restriction enforceable under a covenant or agreement made between a lessor and a lessee;

(b) a positive obligation enforceable under a covenant or agreement made between a lessor and a lessee;

(c) a prohibition or restriction enforceable by a Minister of the Crown, government department or local authority under any covenant or agreement, being a prohibition or restriction binding on successive owners of the land affected by reason of the fact that the covenant or agreement is made for the benefit of land of the Minister, government department or local authority;

(d) a prohibition or restriction embodied in any bye-laws;

(e) a condition or limitation subject to which planning permission was granted at any time before the commencement of this Act or was or is (at any time) deemed to be granted under any statutory provision relating to town and country planning, whether by a Minister of the Crown, government department or local authority;

(f) prohibition or restriction embodied in a scheme under the Town and Country Planning Act 1932 or any enactment repealed by that Act;

(g) a prohibition or restriction enforceable under a forestry dedication covenant entered into pursuant to section 5 of the Forestry Act 1967;

(h) a prohibition or restriction affecting the whole of any of the following areas:—

(i) England, Wales or England and Wales;
(ii) England, or England and Wales, with the exception of, or of any part of, Greater London;
(iii) Greater London.

Local land charges registers, registration and related matters

Registering authorities, local land charges registers, and indexes

3.—(1) Each of the following local authorities—

(a) the council of any district;

(b) the council of any London borough; and

(c) the Common Council of the City of London,

shall be a registering authority for the purposes of this Act.

(2) There shall continue to be kept for the area of each registering authority—

(a) a local land charges register, and

(b) an index whereby all entries made in that register can readily be traced,

and as from the commencement of this Act the register and index kept for the area of a registering authority shall be kept by that authority.

[(3) Neither a local land charges register nor an index such as is mentioned in subsection (2)(b) above need be kept in documentary form.]

(4) For the purposes of this Act the area of the Common Council of the City of London includes the Inner Temple and the Middle Temple.

The appropriate local land charges register

4. In this Act . . ., unless the context otherwise requires, "the appropriate local land charges register", in relation to any land or to a local land charge, means the local land charges register for the area in which the land or, as the case may be, the land affected by the charge is situated or, if the land in question is situated in two or more areas for which local land charges registers are kept, each of the local land charges registers kept for those areas respectively.

Registration

5.—(1) Subject to subsection (6) below, where the originating authority as respects a local land charge are the registering authority, it shall be their duty to register it in the appropriate local land charges register.

(2) Subject to subsection (6) below, where the originating authority as respects a local land charge are not the registering authority, it shall be the duty of the originating authority to apply to the registering authority for its registration in the appropriate local land charges register and upon any such

application being made it shall be the duty of the registering authority to register the charges accordingly.

(3) The registration in a local land charges register of a local land charge, or of any matter which when registered becomes a local land charge, shall be carried out by reference to the land affected or such part of it as is situated in the area for which the register is kept.

(4) In this Act, "the originating authority", as respects a local land charge, means the Minister of the Crown, government department, local authority or other person by whom the charge is brought into existence or by whom, on its coming into existence, the charge is enforceable; and for this purpose—

(a) where a matter that is a local land charge consists of or is embodied in, or is otherwise given effect by, an order, scheme or other instrument made or confirmed by a Minister of the Crown or government department on the application of another authority the charge shall be treated as brought into existence by that other authority; and

(b) a local land charge brought into existence by a Minister of the Crown or government department on an appeal from a decision or determination of another authority or in the exercise of powers ordinarily exercisable by another authority shall be treated as brought into existence by that other authority.

(5) The registration of a local land charge may be cancelled pursuant to an order of the court.

(6) Where a charge or other matter is registrable in a local land charges register and before the commencement of this Act was also registrable in a register kept under the Land Charges Act 1972, then, if before the commencement of this Act it was registered in a register kept under that Act, there shall be no duty to register it, or to apply for its registration, under this Act and section 10 below shall not apply in relation to it.

Local authority's right to register a general charge against land in certain circumstances

6.—(1) Where a local authority have incurred any expenditure in respect of which, when any relevant work is completed and any requisite resolution is passed or order is made, there will arise in their favour a local land charge (in this section referred to as "the specific charge"), the following provisions of this section shall apply.

(2) At any time before the specific charge comes into existence, a general charge against the land, without any amount being specified, may be registered in the appropriate local land charges register by the registering authority if they are the originating authority and, if they are not, shall be registered therein by them if the originating authority make an application for that purpose.

(3) A general charge registered under this section shall be a local land charge, but section 5(1) and (2) above shall not apply in relation to such a charge.

(4) If a general charge is registered under this section pursuant to an application by the originating authority, they shall, when the specific charge comes into existence, notify the registering authority of that fact, and any such notification shall be treated as an application (subject to subsection (5) below) for the cancellation of the general charge and the registration of the specific charge.

(5) Where a general charge is registered under this section its registration shall be cancelled within such period starting with the day on which the specific charge comes into existence, and not being less than 1 year, as may be prescribed, and the specific charge shall not be registered before the general charge is cancelled.

(6) If the registration of the general charge is duly cancelled within the period specified in subsection (5) above and the specific charge is registered forthwith upon the cancellation or was discharged before the cancellation, then, for the purposes of section 10 below, the specific charge shall be treated as having come into existence at the time when the general charge was cancelled.

Effect of registering certain financial charges

7. A local land charge falling within section 1(1)(a) above shall, when registered, take effect as if it had been created by a deed of charge by way of legal mortgage within the meaning of the Law of Property Act 1925, but without prejudice to the priority of the charge.

Searches

Personal searches

8.—(1) Any person may search in any local land charges register on paying the prescribed fee.

(1A) If a local land charges register is kept otherwise than in documentary form, the entitlement of a person to search in it is satisfied if the registering authority makes the portion of it which he wishes to examine available for inspection in visible and legible form.

(2) Without prejudice to subsections (1) and (1A) above, a registering authority may provide facilities for enabling persons entitled to search in the authority's local land charges register to see photographic or other images or copies of any portion of the register which they may wish to examine.

Official searches

9.—(1) Where any person requires an official search of the appropriate land charges register to be made in respect of any land, he may make a requisition in that behalf to the registering authority.

(2) A requisition under this section must be in writing, and for the purposes of serving any such requisition on the Common Council of the City of London section 231(1) of the Local Government Act 1972 shall apply in relation to that Council as it applies in relation to a local authority within the meaning of that Act.

(3) The prescribed fee shall be payable in the prescribed manner in respect of every requisition made under this section.

(4) Where a requisition is made to a registering authority under this section and the fee payable in respect of it is paid in accordance with subsection (3) above, the registering authority shall thereupon make the search required and shall issue an official certificate setting out the result of the search.

Compensation for non-registration or defective official search certificate

Compensation for non-registration or defective official search certificate

10.—(1) Failure to register a local land charge in the appropriate local land charges register shall not affect the enforceability of the charge but where a person has purchased any land affected by a local land charge, then—

(a) in a case where a material personal search of the appropriate local land charges register was made in respect of the land in question before the relevant time, if at the time of the search the charge was in existence but not registered in that register; or

(aa) in a case where the appropriate local land charges register is kept otherwise than in documentary form and a material personal search of that register was made in respect of the land in question before the relevant time, if the entitlement to search in that register conferred by section 8 above was not satisfied as mentioned in subsection (1A) of that section; or

(b) in a case where a material official search of the appropriate local land charges register was made in respect of the land in question before the relevant time, if the charge was in existence at the time of the search but (whether registered or not) was not shown by the official search certificate as registered in that register,

the purchaser shall (subject to subsection 11(1) below) be entitled to compensation for any loss suffered by him in consequence.

(2) At any time when rules made under this Act make provision for local

land charges registers to be divided into parts then, for the purposes of subsection (1) above—

(a) a search (whether personal or official) of a part or parts only of any such register shall not constitute a search of that register in relation to any local land charge registrable in a part of the register not searched; and

(b) a charge shall not be taken to be registered in the appropriate local land charges register unless registered in the appropriate part of the register.

(3) For the purposes of this section—

(a) a person purchases land where, for valuable consideration, he acquires any interest in land or the proceeds of sale of land, and this includes cases where he acquires as lessee or mortgagee and shall be treated as including cases where an interest is conveyed or assigned at his direction to another person;

(b) the relevant time—

(i) where the acquisition of the interest in question was preceded by a contract for its acquisition, other than a qualified liability contract, is the time when that contract was made;

(ii) in any other case, is the time when the purchaser acquired the interest in question or, if he acquired it under a disposition which took effect only when registered under the Land Registration Act 1925, the time when that disposition was made; and for the purposes of sub-paragraph (i) above, a qualified liability contract is a contract containing a term the effect of which is to make the liability of the purchaser dependent upon, or avoidable by reference to, the outcome of a search for local land charges affecting the land to be purchased.

(c) a personal search is material if, but only if—

(i) it is made after the commencement of this Act, and

(ii) it is made by or on behalf of the purchaser or, before the relevant time, the purchaser or his agent has knowledge of the result of it;

(d) an official search is material if, but only if—

(i) it is made after the commencement of this Act, and

(ii) it is requisitioned by or on behalf of the purchaser or, before the relevant time, the purchaser or his agent has knowledge of the contents of the official search certificate.

(4) Any compensation for loss under this section shall be paid by the

registering authority in whose area the land affected is situated; and where the purchaser has incurred expenditure for the purpose of obtaining compensation under this section, the amount of the compensation shall include the amount of the expenditure reasonably incurred by him for that purpose (so far as that expenditure would not otherwise fall to be treated as loss for which he is entitled to compensation under this section).

(5) Where any compensation for loss under this section is paid by a registering authority in respect of a local land charge as respects which they are not the originating authority, then, unless an application for registration of the charge was made to the registering authority by the originating authority in time for it to be practicable for the registering authority to avoid incurring liability to pay that compensation, an amount equal thereto shall be recoverable from the originating authority by the registering authority.

(6) Where any compensation for loss under this section is paid by a registering authority, no part of the amount paid, or of any corresponding amount paid to that authority by the originating authority under subsection (5) above, shall be recoverable by the registering authority or the originating authority from any other person except as provided by subsection (5) above or under a policy of insurance or on grounds of fraud.

(7) In the case of an action to recover compensation under this section the cause of action shall be deemed for the purposes of the Limitation Act 1939 to accrue at the time when the local land charge comes to the notice of the purchaser; and for the purposes of this subsection the question when the charge came to his notice shall be determined without regard to the provisions of section 198 of the Law of Property Act 1925 (under which registration under certain enactments is deemed to constitute actual notice).

(8) Where the amount claimed by way of compensation under this section does not exceed the [county court limit], proceedings for the recovery of such compensation may be begun in the county court.

[(8A) In subsection (8) above "the county court limit" means the amount which for the time being is the county court limit for the purposes of section 16 of the County Courts Act 1984 (money recoverable by statute).]

(9) If in any proceedings for the recovery of compensation under this section the court dismisses a claim to compensation, it shall not order the purchaser to pay the registering authority's costs unless it considers that it was unreasonable for the purchaser to commence the proceedings.

Mortgages, trusts for sale and settled land

11.—(1) Where there appear to be grounds for a claim under section 10 above in respect of an interest that is subject to a mortgage—

(a) the claim may be made by any mortgagee of the interest as if he were the person entitled to that interest but without prejudice to the making of a claim by that person;

(b) no compensation shall be payable under that section in respect of the interest of the mortgagee (as distinct from the interest which is subject to the mortgage);

(c) any compensation payable under that section in respect of the interest that is subject to the mortgage shall be paid to the mortgagee or, if there is more than one mortgagee, to the first mortgagee and shall in either case be applied by him as if it were proceeds of sale.

(2) Where an interest is held on trust for sale any compensation payable in respect of it under section 10 above shall be dealt with as if it were proceeds of sale arising under the trust.

(3) Where an interest is settled land for the purposes of the Settled Land Act 1925 any compensation payable in respect of it under section 10 above shall be treated as capital money arising under that Act.

Miscellaneous and supplementary

Office copies as evidence

12. An office copy of an entry in any local land charges register shall be admissible in evidence in all proceedings and between all parties to the same extent as the original would be admissible.

Protection of solicitors, trustees, etc.

13. A solicitor or trustee, personal representative, agent or other person in a fiduciary position, shall not be answerable in respect of any loss occasioned by reliance on an erroneous official search certificate or an erroneous office copy of an entry in a local land charges register.

Rules

14.—(1) The Lord Chancellor may, with the concurrence of the Treasury as to fees, make rules for carrying this Act into effect and, in particular, rules—

(a) for regulating the practice of registering authorities in connection with the registration of local land charges or matters which, when registered, become local land charges;

(b) as to forms and contents of applications for registration, and the manner in which such applications are to be made;

(c) as to the manner in which the land affected or to be affected by a local land charge is, where practicable, to be identified for purposes of registration;

(d) as to the manner in which and the times at which registrable matters are to be registered;

(e) as to forms and contents of requisitions for official searches and of official search certificates;

(f) for regulating personal searches and related matters;

(g) as to the cancellation without an order of the court of the registration of a local land charge on its cesser, or with the consent of the authority or body by whom it is enforceable;

(h) for prescribing the fees, if any, to be paid for the filing of documents with a registering authority, the making of an entry on a register, the supply of copies of, or the variation or cancellation of, any such entry, and the making of any search of a register.

(2) Without prejudice to the generality of subscction (1) above, the power to make rules under that subsection shall include power to make rules (with the concurrence of the Treasury as to fees) for carrying into effect the provisions of any statutory provision by virtue of which any matter is registrable in any local land charges register.

(3) The power to make rules under this section shall be exercisable by statutory instrument which shall be subject to annulment in pursuance of a resolution of either House of Parliament.

Expenses

15. There shall be paid out of money provided by Parliament—

(a) any administrative expenses incurred by a Minister of the Crown or government department in consequence of this Act;

(b) any expenditure incurred by a Minister of the Crown or government department in the payment of any amount recoverable from him or them under this Act by a registering authority;

(c) any increase attributable to this Act in the sums so payable under any other Act.

Interpretation

16.—(1) In this Act, except where the context otherwise requires—

"the appropriate local land charges register" has the meaning provided by section 4 above;

"the court" means the High Court, or the county court in a case where the county court has jurisdiction;

"land" includes mines and minerals, whether or not severed from the surface, buildings or parts of buildings (whether the division is horizontal, vertical or made in any other way) and other corporeal hereditaments;

"official search certificate" means a certificate issued pursuant to section 9(4) above;

"the originating authority", as respects a local land charge, has the meaning provided by section 5(4) above;
"personal search" means a search pursuant to section 8 above;
"prescribed" means prescribed by rules made under section 14 above;
"the registering authority", in relation to any land or to a local land charge, means the registering authority in whose area the land or, as the case may be, the land affected by the charge is situated, or, if the land in question is situated in the areas of two or more registering authorities each of those authorities respectively;
"statutory provision" means a provision of this Act or of any other Act or Measure, whenever passed, or a provision of any rules, regulations, order or similar instruments made (whether before or after the passing of this Act) under an Act, whenever passed.

[(1A) Any reference in this Act to an office copy of an entry includes a reference to the reproduction of an entry in a register kept otherwise than in documentary form.]

(2) Except in so far as the context otherwise requires, any reference in this Act to an enactment is a reference to that enactment as amended, extended or applied by or under any other enactment, including this Act.

Amendments of other statutory provisions

17.—(1) ...

(2) Schedule 1 to this Act (which contains consequential amendments of other Acts and of a Measure) shall have effect.

Power to amend local Acts

18.—(1) Subject to the provisions of this section, the Lord Chancellor may by order made by statutory instrument repeal or amend any relevant local Act provision that appears to him to be inconsistent with, or to require modification in consequence of, any provision of this Act.

(2) For the purposes of this section, a relevant local Act provision is a provision—

(a) contained in any local Act passed before this Act, and

(b) providing for any matter to be, or to be registered as, a local land charge or otherwise requiring or authorising the registration of any matter in a local land charges register.

(3) An order under this section shall be subject to annulment in pursuance of a resolution of either House of Parliament and may be varied or revoked by a subsequent order under this section.

(4) Before making the order under this section the Lord Chancellor shall consult any local authority appearing to him to be concerned.

Repeals and transitional provisions

19.—(1) The enactments specified in Schedule 2 to this Act (which include certain spent provisions) and the instrument there specified are hereby repealed to the extent specified in the third column of that Schedule.

(2) Nothing in this Act shall operate to impose any obligation to register or apply for the registration of any local land charge within the meaning of this Act which immediately before the commencement of this Act was by virtue of subsection (7)(b)(i) of section 15 of the Land Charges Act 1925 not required by that section to be registered as a local land charge, except after the expiration of one year from the commencement of this Act; and a purchaser shall not be entitled to compensation under section 10 above by virtue of section 10(1)(a) or, where the charge was not registered at the time of the search, section 10(1)(b) in respect of a local land charge which at the time of the search was not required to be registered.

(3) Where any matter was immediately before the commencement of this Act registrable in a local land charges register, then, if the matter was, immediately before the said commencement, registered in the appropriate local level land charges register nothing in this Act shall affect the status of any rights therein as overriding interests under section 70(1)(i) of the Land Registration Act 1925, whether or not the matter is a local land charge within the meaning of this Act.

(4) In so far as any entry subsisting in a local land charges register at the commencement of this Act could have been made in that register pursuant to this Act, or to any statutory provision amended by or under this Act, it shall be treated as having been so made, but nothing in this Act shall render enforceable against any purchaser whose purchase was completed before the commencement of this Act any local land charge which immediately before the commencement of this Act was not enforceable against him.

Short title, etc.

20.—(1) This Act may be cited as the Local Land Charges Act 1975.

(2) This Act binds the Crown, but nothing in this Act shall be taken to render land owned by or occupied for the purposes of the Crown subject to any charge to which, independently of this Act, it would not be subject.

(3) This Act shall come into force on such day as the Lord Chancellor may by order made by statutory instrument appoint.

(4) This Act extends to England and Wales only.

Appendix 4

Lands Tribunal

The Lands Tribunal Rules 1996

(S.I. 1996 No. 1022)

PART I

A4–01

Preliminary

Citation and commencement

1. These Rules may be cited as the Lands Tribunal Rules 1996 and shall come into force on May 1, 1996.

Interpretation

2.—(1) In these Rules—
"the Act" means the Lands Tribunal Act 1949;
"the office" means the office for the time being of the Lands Tribunal;
"the President" means the President of the Lands Tribunal, or the member appointed under section 2(3) of the Act to act for the time being as deputy for the President;
"proceedings" means proceedings before the Land Tribunal;
"the registrar" means the registrar of the Lands Tribunal or, as respects any powers or functions of the registrar, an officer of the Lands Tribunal authorised by the Lord Chancellor to exercise those powers or functions;
"the Tribunal" means the member or members of the Lands Tribunal selected under section 3(2) of the Act to deal with a case;

PART II

Composition and hearings of the Tribunal

Selection and powers of members of the Tribunal

3.—(1) The President may at any time substitute a member of the Lands Tribunal for a member that he has previously selected to sit as the Tribunal or as a member of the Tribunal to hear a case.

(2) Where members of the Lands Tribunal have been selected for a class or group of cases under the provisions of section 3(2) of the Act, the President may from time to time vary the members selected.

(3) Where the President has appointed a member of the Lands Tribunal to be the chairman of any members selected under paragraphs (1) or (2) the chairman shall have the same power as the President to substitute or vary the members selected.

(4) A member of the Tribunal selected to hear a case shall have power to do anything, in relation to that case, which the President has power to do under these Rules.

Notice of hearings and sittings of the Tribunal

4.—(1) The registrar shall, as soon as practicable after the commencement of proceedings before the Tribunal, send to each party a notice informing him of the date, time and place of the hearing.

(2) Upon receipt of a notice of intention to respond from a person who is not already a party to the proceedings, the registrar shall send to that person a notice informing him of the date, time and place of the hearing.

Hearings to be in public: exceptions

5.—(1) All hearings by the Tribunal shall be in public except where—

(a) . . .

(b) it is satisfied that, by reason of disclosure of confidential matters or matters concerning national security, it is just and reasonable for the hearing or any part of the hearing to be in private.

(2) The following persons shall be entitled to attend a hearing whether or not it is in private—

(a) the President or any member of the Tribunal notwithstanding that they do not constitute the Tribunal for the purpose of the hearing; and

(b) a member of the Council on Tribunals.

(3) The Tribunal, with the consent of the parties, may permit any other person to attend a hearing which is held in private.

PART V

Applications under section 84 of the Law of Property Act 1925(a) (Relief from restrictive covenants affecting land)

Interpretation

12. In this Part—
"section 84" means a section 84 of the Law of Property Act 1925; and
"restriction" means a restriction, arising under a covenant or otherwise, as to the user of or building on any freehold land or any leasehold land held for a term of more than 40 years of which at least 25 years have expired.

Method of making application

13.—(1) A person interested in land affected by a registration who wishes to make an application under the section shall send to the registrar in duplicate an application which shall contain—

(a) the name and address of the person making the application and, if he is represented, the name, address and profession of the representative;

(b) the address or description of the land to which the application relates;

(c) the address or description of the land which is subject to the restriction;

(d) the address or description of the land which, and the identity of any person (if known) who, has the benefit of the restriction or any person whom the applicant believes may have such benefit and the reasons for that belief;

(e) the grounds or grounds in section 84 on which the applicant relies and the reason he considers that that ground or those grounds apply;

(f) a statement as to whether the applicant is applying to discharge the restriction wholly or for its modification, and if the latter the extent of the modification;

(g) a statement as to whether any planning permission has been applied for, granted or refused within the five years preceding the application in respect of the land the subject of the application;

(h) the signature of the person making the application or his representative and the date of the signature.

(2) The application referred to in paragraph (1) shall be accompanied by—

(a) a copy of the instrument imposing the restriction or, if this is not available, documentary evidence of the restriction; and

(b) a plan identifying the land to which the application relates and, so far as practicable, all the land which is subject to the restriction and the land which has the benefit of the restriction.

(3) An application may be made jointly by two or more persons whether the land in which they are interested is the same land or different parts of the land affected by the restriction.

Publication of notices

14.—(1) Upon receipt of an application, the registrar shall determine what notices are to be given, and whether these should be given by advertisement or otherwise, to persons who appear to be entitled to the benefit of the restriction.

(2) For the purpose of paragraph (1), the registrar may require the applicant to provide any documents or information which it is within his power to provide.

(3) The notices shall require persons claiming to be entitled to the benefit of the restriction, who object to the discharge or modification of it proposed by the application, or who claim compensation for such modification or discharge, to send to the registrar and to the applicant notice of any objections they may have and of the amount of compensation they claim (if any).

(4) The notices to be given under paragraph (1) shall be given by the applicant who shall certify in writing to the registrar that directions as to the giving of these notices have been complied with.

Notice of objection

15.—(1) A notice of objection to the application and a claim for compensation shall be in writing and shall be sent to the registrar and the applicant within 28 days from the publication of the notices referred to in rule 14.

(2) If the registrar requires, the person objecting shall submit a statement containing—

(a) his name and address and if he is represented, the name, address and profession of the representative;

(b) on the basis upon which he claims to be entitled to the benefit of the restriction;

(c) any ground of objection; and

(d) his signature or that of his representative and the date the statement was signed.

Suspension of proceedings

16. At any time after the registrar has received a notice of objection to the application the President or the Tribunal—

(a) of his or its own motion may, or

(b) on the application of the applicant or of any person who has given a notice of objection, shall,

suspend the proceedings for such time as he or it may consider appropriate to enable an application to be made to the High Court for the determination of a question arising under subsection (2) of section 84.

Order without hearing, etc.

17.—(1) If it appears to the President that, having regard to the applicant's interest in the land, the applicant is not a proper person to make the application, he may dismiss it and shall inform the applicant of his reasons for doing so.

(2) Where—

(a) the registrar receives no notice of objection within the time allowed by rule 15(1), or

(b) all objectors have withdrawn their objections before a hearing has taken place,

the President may, with the consent of the applicant, determine the application without a hearing.

(3) Where at or after a hearing—

(a) all objectors withdraw their objections, or

(b) the Tribunal directs that no objector shall be admitted to oppose the application,

the Tribunal may, with the consent of the applicant, determine the application without any further hearing.

Power to direct additional notices

18. If it appears to the Tribunal at any time before the determination of the application that any person who has not received notice of the application otherwise than by advertisement should have received specific notice, the Tribunal may require the applicant to give notice to that person and may adjourn the hearing to enable that person to make an objection or a claim for compensation.

Enquiries of local authorities

19. If before or at the hearing of an application the President or the Tribunal consider that enquiries should be made of any local authority within whose area the land affected by the restriction is situated, they may direct those enquiries to be made and may adjourn the case until the local authority has replied.

Provisions as to orders

20.—(1) Where the Tribunal orders the discharge or modification of a restriction subject to the payment of compensation, the discharge or modification shall not take effect until the registrar has endorsed on the order that the compensation has been paid.

(2) The Tribunal may direct that the compensation be paid within a specified time failing which the order shall cease to have effect.

(3) The Tribunal may determine that any compensation awarded shall be paid into the Court Funds Office of the Supreme Court.

. . .

PART VIII

General Procedure

Determination of proceedings without a hearing

27.—(1) the Tribunal may, with the consent of the parties to the proceedings, order that the proceedings be determined without an oral hearing.

(2) Where the Tribunal makes an order under paragraph (1), any party to the proceedings may submit written representations to the Tribunal.

(3) On or after making an order under paragraph (1), the Tribunal shall give such direction relating to the lodging of documents and representations as it considers appropriate.

(4) Rule 42 shall apply to proceedings to which this rule applies as if references to the calling of witnesses and the hearing of evidence in that rule were references to representations.

(5) The Tribunal may at any time, on the application of a party to the proceedings or of its own motion, order that the proceedings should be heard and in that event may give directions for the disposal of the proceedings in accordance with these Rules.

Simplified procedure

28.—(1) A member or the registrar may, with the consent of the applicant or appellant or, in relation to proceedings under Part IV, the consent of the person who is claiming compensation, direct that proceedings shall be determined in accordance with these Rules.

(2) The registrar shall send a copy of any direction made under paragraph (1) on all the parties to the proceedings and any party who objects to the direction may, within 7 days of service of the copy on him, send written notice of his objection to the registrar.

(3) Rule 38(6) to (9) and (11) shall apply as appropriate where an objection is received by the registrar under paragraph (2).

A4–02

(4) Paragraphs (5) to (12) shall apply to proceedings in respect of which the registrar has made a direction under paragraph (1).

(5) . . .

(6) The registrar shall—

(a) give directions concerning the filing and contents of a statement of claims by the applicant or appellant and a reply by the other parties to the proceedings; and

(b) give the parties not less than 21 days notice of the day fixed for the hearing of the proceedings.

(7) The following directions shall take effect—

(a) each party shall, not less than 14 days before the date fixed for the hearing, send to every other party copies of all documents in his possession on which he intends to rely at the hearing; and

(b) each party shall not less than 7 days before the date fixed for the hearing send to the registrar and to every other party a copy of any expert report on which he intends to rely at the hearing and a list of the witnesses whom he intends to call at the hearing.

(8) The registrar may from time to time, whether on application or of his own motion, amend or add to any direction issued if he thinks it necessary to do so in the circumstances of the case.

(9) The hearing shall be informal and shall take place before a single member of the Lands Tribunal who shall act as if he were an arbitrator and who shall adopt any procedure that he considers to be fair.

(10) Strict rules of evidence shall not apply to the hearing and evidence shall not be taken on oath unless the Tribunal orders otherwise.

(11) No award shall be made in relation to the costs of the proceedings except in cases to which section 4 of the 1961 Act apply, save that the Tribunal may make an award of costs

(a) in case where an offer of settlement has been made by a party and the Tribunal considers it appropriate to have regard to the fact that such an offer has been made; or

(b) in cases in which the Tribunal regards the circumstances as exceptional,

and if, exceptionally, an award of costs is made the amount shall not exceed that which would be allowed if the proceedings had been heard in a county court.

(12) The Tribunal may at any time, on the application of a party to the proceedings or of its own motion, order that this rule shall no longer apply to the proceedings and in that event may give directions for the disposal of the proceedings in accordance with these Rules.

Site inspections

29.—(1) Subject to paragraph (2), the Tribunal may enter and inspect—

(a) the land or property which is the subject of proceedings, and

(b) as far as is practicable, any comparable land or property to which the attention of the Tribunal is drawn.

(2) When the Tribunal intends to enter any premises in accordance with paragraph (1) it shall give notice to the parties who shall be entitled to be represented at the inspection; where the Tribunal deems it appropriate, such representation shall be limited to one person to represent those parties having the same interest in the proceedings.

Assessors

29A.—(1) If it appears to the President that any case coming before the Tribunal calls for special knowledge he may direct that the Tribunal shall hear the case with the aid of one or more assessors appointed by him.

(2) The remuneration to be paid to an assessor appointed under this rule shall be determined by the President until the approval of the Treasury.

Consolidation of proceedings

30.—(1) Where two or more notices of appeal, references or applications have been made which—

(a) are in respect of the same land or buildings; or

(b) relate to different interests in the same land or buildings; or

(c) raise the same issues;

the President or the Tribunal may, on his or its own motion or on the application of a party to the proceedings, order that the appeals, references or applications be consolidated or heard together.

(2) An order may be made with respect to some only of the matters to which the appeals, references or applications relate.

Power to select test case in appeals or references

31.—(1) Where the President is of the opinion that two or more appeals or references involve the same issues he may, with the written consent of all the parties to the appeals or references, select one or more appeal or reference to be heard in the first instance as a test case or test cases and the parties to each appeal or reference shall be bound by the decision of the Tribunal on that appeal or reference.

(2) Paragraph (1) is without prejudice to the right of the parties to each appeal or reference to require the Tribunal to state a case for the decision of the Court of Appeal.

Application of Arbitration Act 1996

32. The following provisions of the Arbitration Act 1996 shall apply to all proceedings as they apply to an arbitration—

(a) section 47 (awards on different issues, etc.), as if the words 'unless otherwise agreed by the parties' were omitted from subsection (1) and so that the reference to 'award' shall include a reference to any decision of the Lands Tribunal;

(b) section 49 (interest) subject to any enactment that prescribes a rate of interest;

(c) section 57(3) to (7) (correction of award or additional award);

(d) section 66 (enforcement of the award).

Evidence

33.—(1) Evidence before the Tribunal may be given orally and may be on oath or affirmation or, if the parties to the proceedings consent or the Tribunal or President so orders, by affidavit.

(2) Notwithstanding paragraph (1), the Tribunal may at any stage of the proceedings require the personal attendance of any deponent for examination or cross-examination.

(3) Paragraphs (2) to (7) of rule 38 shall apply to an application to the President for leave to give evidence by affidavit but as if for "registrar" in those paragraphs there were substituted "President".

(4) Nothing in the Civil Evidence Act 1972, or in rules of court made under it, shall prevent expert evidence from being given before the Tribunal by any party even if no application has been made to the Tribunal for a direction as to the disclosure of that evidence to any other party to the proceedings.

Power to order discovery, etc.

34.—(1) The Tribunal, or subject to any directions given by the Tribunal, the registrar may, on the application of any party to the proceedings or of its or his own motion, order any party—

(a) to deliver to the registrar any document or information which the Tribunal may require and which it is in the power of the party to deliver;

(b) to afford to every other party to the proceedings an opportunity to inspect those documents (or copies of them) and to take copies;

(c) to deliver to the registrar an affidavit or make a list stating whether any document or class of document specified or described in the order or application is, or has at any time been in his possession, custody or power and stating when he parted with it;

(d) to deliver to the registrar a statement in the form of a pleading setting out further and better particulars of the grounds on which he intends to rely and any relevant facts or contentions;

(e) to answer interrogatories on affidavit relating to any matter at issue between the applicant and the other party;

(f) to deliver to the registrar a statement of agreed facts, facts in dispute and the issue or issues to be tried by the Tribunal; or

(g) to deliver to the registrar witness statements or proofs of evidence.

(2) Where an order is made under paragraph (1) the Tribunal or registrar may give directions as to the time within which any document is to be sent to the registrar (being at least 14 days from the date of the direction) and the parties to whom copies of the document are to be sent.

(3) Rule 38 shall apply to this rule as appropriate both in relation to applications and where the registrar acts of his own motion.

Extension of time

35.—(1) The time appointed by or under these Rules for doing any act or taking any steps in connection with any proceedings may be extended on application to the registrar under rule 38.

(2) The registrar may extend the time limit on such terms as he thinks fit and may order an extension even if the application is not made until after the time limit has expired.

Appellant limited to grounds of appeal

36.—(1) On the hearing of an appeal under Part III or of an application under Part V, the appellant or applicant may rely only on the grounds stated in his notice of appeal, statement of case or application unless the Tribunal permits additional grounds to be put forward.

(2) If the Tribunal permits additional grounds to be put forward in accord-

ance with paragraph (1) it may do so on such terms as to costs, adjournment or otherwise as it thinks fit.

Right of audience

37.—(1) Subject to paragraph (2), in any proceedings a party may appear in person or be represented by counsel or solicitor or by any other person with the leave of the Tribunal, or, in the case of an interlocutory application, the leave of the President or the registrar.

(2) ...

Interlocutory applications

38.—(1) Except where these Rules make other provisions or the President otherwise orders, an application for directions of an interlocutory nature in connection with any proceedings shall be made to the registrar.

(2) The application shall be made in writing and shall state the title of the proceedings, and the grounds upon which the application is made.

(3) If the application is made with the consent of all parties, it shall be accompanied by consents signed by or on behalf of the parties.

(4) If the application is not made with the consent of every party the applicant shall serve a copy of the proposed application on every other party before it is made and the application shall state that this has been done.

(5) A party who objects to an application may, within 7 days of service of a copy on him, send written notice of his objection to the registrar.

(6) Before making an order on an application the registrar shall consider all the objections that he has received and may allow any party who wishes to appear before him the opportunity to do so.

(7) In dealing with an application the registrar shall have regard to the convenience of all the parties and the desirability of limiting so far as practicable the costs of the proceedings and shall inform the parties in writing of his decision.

(8) The registrar may refer the application to the President for a decision and he shall do so if requested by the applicant or a party objecting to the application.

(9) A party may appeal to the President from a from a decision of the registrar under this rule by giving written notice to the registrar within 7 days of service of the notice of decision or such further time as the registrar may allow.

(10) An appeal under paragraph (9) shall not act as a stay of proceedings unless the President so orders.

(11) Where an application under this rule is made—

(a) with respect to a case that has been included by the President in a class or group of cases under section 3(2) of the Act, or

(b) with respect to a case for which a member or members of the Lands Tribunal has or have been selected, the powers and duties of the President under this rule may be exercised and discharged in relation to the application by any member or members of the Lands Tribunal authorised by the President for that purpose.

Pre-trial review

39.—(1) The Tribunal and, subject to any direction given by the Tribunal, the registrar may, on the application of a party to the proceedings or of its or his own motion order a pre-trial review to be held and the registrar shall send to each party to the proceedings a notice informing him of the place and date of the pre-trial review.

(2) Unless the parties agree otherwise, the date of the pre-trial review shall be not less than 14 days from the making of the order that the pre-trial review should be held.

(3) The Tribunal or the registrar—

(a) shall at the pre-trial review give any direction that appears necessary or desirable for securing the just, expeditious and economical disposal of the proceedings; and

(b) shall at the pre-trial review endeavour to secure that the parties make all such admissions and agreements as ought reasonably to be made by them in relation to the proceedings;

(c) may record in the order made on the review any admission or agreement made under sub-paragraph (b) or any refusal to make any admission or agreement.

(4) Where a party seeks a specific direction he shall, so far as is practicable, apply for such direction at the pre-trial review and shall give the registrar and every other party notice of his intention to do so.

(5) If an application which might have been made at the pre-trial review is made subsequently the applicant shall pay the costs of an occasioned by the application unless the Tribunal consider that there was sufficient reason for the application not having been made at the review.

(6) Paragraphs (6) to (11) of rule 38 shall apply to a pre-trial review as if it were an interlocutory application.

(7) If any party does not appear at the pre-trial review the Tribunal or the registrar may, after given the parties the opportunity to be heard, make such order as may be appropriate for the purpose of expediting or disposing of the proceedings.

Administration of oaths

41. The registrar and the Tribunal shall have power to administer oaths and take affirmations for the purpose of affidavits to be used in proceedings or for the purpose of the giving of oral evidence at hearings.

Expert witnesses

42.—(1) This rule applies to any proceedings except an application for a certificate under Part VI.

(2) Subject to paragraph (3), only one expert witness on either side shall be heard unless the Tribunal orders otherwise.

(3) Where the proceedings relate to mineral valuations or business disturbance, not more than two expert witnesses on either side shall be heard unless the Tribunal orders otherwise.

(4) An application for leave to call more than the number of expert witnesses permitted by this rule may be made to the registrar in accordance with rule 38, or to the Tribunal at the hearing.

(5) A party shall, within 28 days or receiving a request from the registrar, send to him and to the other parties to the proceedings a copy of each of the following documents relating to the evidence to be given by each expert witness—

(a) the expert witness's report, including every plan and valuation of the land or property to which the proceedings relate (which shall include full particulars and computations in support of the valuation) which it is proposed to put in evidence; and

(b) either—

(i) full particulars of any comparable properties and transactions to which the party intends to refer at the hearing in support of his case and a statement of the purpose for which the comparison is made; or

(ii) a statement that no comparable properties or transactions will be referred to.

(6) If—

(a) an application for leave under paragraph (4) is made at the hearing and granted by the Tribunal; or

(b) at the hearing any party seeks to rely on documents not sent to the registrar or to the other parties in accordance with paragraph (5);

the Tribunal may adjourn the hearing on such terms as to costs or otherwise as he thinks fit.

Preliminary issues

43.—(1) The President or the Tribunal may, on the application of any party to proceedings, order any preliminary issue in the proceedings to be disposed of at a preliminary hearing.

(2) If in the opinion of the Tribunal the decision on the preliminary issue disposes of the proceedings, it may order that the preliminary hearing shall be

treated as the hearing of the case or may make such other order as it thinks fit.

(3) Paragraphs (2) to (7) of rule 38 shall apply to an application under paragraph (1) above as if for "registrar" in those paragraphs there were substituted "President".

Sealed offers

44.—(1) Where any party unconditionally offers or is ready to accept, any sum as compensation or by way of price, or to agree a rent or a rateable value, a copy of the offer or indication of the readiness to accept enclosed in a sealed cover may be sent to the registrar or delivered to the Tribunal at the hearing by the party who made the offer or indicated the readiness to accept and shall be opened by the Tribunal after it has determined the proceedings.

(2) An offer or an indication of readiness to accept which his sent to the registrar or delivered to the Tribunal in accordance with paragraph (1), shall not be disclosed to the Tribunal until it has decided the amount of such sum, rent or rateable value.

Withdrawal or dismissal of appeal, etc., before hearing

45.—(1) An appeal, reference or application may be withdrawn by sending to the registrar a written notice of withdrawal signed by all parties to the proceedings or by their representatives.

(2) A party may, at any time before the hearing of the proceedings, apply to the President for an order to dismiss the proceedings and the President may make such order as he thinks fit.

(3) Paragraphs (2) and (4) to (7) of rule 38 shall apply to an application under paragraph (2) as if for "registrar" there were substituted "President".

Failure to pursue proceedings or comply with Rules

46.—(1) If it appears to the Tribunal that any party to proceedings has failed to send a copy of any document to any other party or to the registrar as required by these Rules, it may—

(a) direct that a copy be sent;

(b) adjourn the further hearing of the proceedings; and

(c) require the party at fault to pay any additional costs occasioned as a result of the failure.

(2) Where a party has failed to pursue any proceedings with due diligence or has failed to comply with any of the provisions of these Rules, the registrar, or the Tribunal on the application of any party or of his or its own motion, after giving the parties an opportunity to be heard may make—

(a) an order that the proceedings be heard by the Tribunal; or

(b) an order that the proceedings be dismissed or that any party be debarred from taking any further part in the proceedings; or

(c) such other order as may be appropriate for expediting or disposing of the proceedings including an order for costs.

(3) Paragraphs (9) and (10) of rule 38 shall apply to any order made by the registrar under paragraph (2).

Failure to comply with the Rules not to render proceedings invalid

47. Any failure by any person to comply with these Rules shall not render the proceedings or anything done in pursuance of them invalid unless the President or the Tribunal so directs.

Procedure at hearing

48. Subject to these Rules and to any direction by the President, the procedure at the hearing of any proceedings shall be such as the Tribunal may direct.

Default of appearance at hearing

49.—(1) If on an appeal under part III or an application under Part V the appellant or applicant fails to attend or be represented at the hearing the Tribunal may dismiss the appeal or application.

(2) If any party to proceedings referred to in paragraph (1) other than the appellant or applicant, or any party to a reference under Part IV fails to attend or be represented at the hearing, the Tribunal may hear and determine the appeal, application or reference in his absence and may make such order as to costs as it thinks fit.

(3) Where proceedings have been dismissed or determined under this role, the Tribunal may, on the application of the party who has failed to attend within 7 days of the dismissal or termination, if it is satisfied that he had sufficient reason for his absence, set aside the dismissal or determination on such terms as to costs as it thinks fit.

Decision of Tribunal

50.—(1) Subject to paragraph (2), the decision of the Tribunal on an appeal, reference or application shall be given in writing, and shall state the reasons for the decision.

(2) The Tribunal may give its decision orally in cases where it is satisfied that this would not result in any injustice or inconvenience to the parties.

(3) The Tribunal may, and on the application of any party to the proceedings shall, issue an order incorporating its decision.

(4) Where an amount awarded or value determined by the Tribunal is dependent upon the decision of the Tribunal on a question of law which is in

dispute in the proceedings, the Tribunal shall ascertain, and shall state in its decision, any alternative amount or value which it would have awarded or determined if it had come to a different decision on the point of law.

(5) The registrar shall serve a copy of the decision or, where the decision is given orally an order stating its effect, on every party who has appeared before the Tribunal in the proceedings, and—

(a) in the case of an appeal against the decision of a valuation tribunal to the clerk of that tribunal and, if the appeal is a rating appeal, to the valuation officer;

(b) in the case of any other appeal under Part III< to the authority.

(6) If the Court of Appeal directs that any decision of the Tribunal, on which a case has been stated for the decision of the Court of Appeal, should be amended the registrar shall send copies of the amended decision to every person who was notified of the original decision.

Consent orders

51. Where the parties to proceedings have agreed the terms of an order to be made by the Tribunal, particulars of those terms signed by all the parties or by their representatives shall be sent to the registrar and an order may be made by the Tribunal in accordance with those terms in the absence of the parties.

Costs

52.—(1) Subject to the provisions of section 4 of the 1961 Act and of rule 28(11), the costs of an incidental to any proceedings shall be in the discretion of the Tribunal.

(2) The registrar may make an order as to costs in respect of any application or proceedings heard by him.

(3) A person dissatisfied with the order of the registrar under paragraph (2) may, within 10 days of the order, appeal to the President who may make such order as to the payment of costs, including the costs of the appeal, as he thinks fit.

(4) If the Tribunal directs that the costs of a party to the proceedings be paid by another party it may settle the amount of costs by fixing a lump sum or direct that the costs be taxed by the registrar on such basis as the Tribunal thinks fit, being a basis that would be applied on a taxation of the costs of High Court or county court proceedings.

(5) A party dissatisfied with a taxation of costs under paragraph (4) may, within 7 days of the taxation, serve on any other interested party and on the registrar written objection specifying the items objected to and applying for the taxation to be reviewed in respect of those items.

(6) Upon such application the registrar shall review the taxation of the items objected to and shall state in writing the reasons for his decision.

(7) A person dissatisfied with the decision of the registrar under paragraph (6) may, within 10 days of the decision, apply to the President to review the taxation and the President may make such order as he thinks fit including an order as to payment of the costs of the review.

(8) Paragraphs (8) and (10) of rule 38 shall apply to any application under this rule.

Solicitor to be on the record

53.—(1) Where a solicitor commences or responds to proceedings on behalf of a party to those proceedings he shall be noted on the record of the Tribunal as acting for that party.

(2) A party who has previously carried on proceedings in person may appoint a solicitor at anytime to act on his behalf and if he does so shall notify the Tribunal who shall note on the record that the solicitor is acting for that party.

(3) A party who has previously been represented by a solicitor may charge his solicitor at any time, or may decide to continue the proceedings in person but unless such change or decision is notified to the Tribunal the former solicitor shall be considered the representative of the party until the conclusion of the proceedings.

(4) The notifications referred to in paragraphs (2) and (3) may be given by the party or his solicitor and the person giving the notification shall send a copy to every other party to the proceedings.

(5) A solicitor who is on the record of the Tribunal as acting for a party shall be responsible for the payment of all fees of the Tribunal which are the responsibility of that party whilst he remains on the record.

Service of notices

54.—(1) Every party to proceedings shall notify the registrar of an address for service of documents on him.

(2) Where a party to proceedings is represented by a person other than a solicitor he shall—

(a) send to the registrar written authority for that representative to act on his behalf; and

(b) notify the registrar if the representative ceases to act on his behalf and, if replaced, shall give the registrar details of the new representative together with the written authority for the new representative to act on his behalf.

(3) Any document to be served on any person under these Rules shall be deemed to have been served if sent by pre-paid post to that person at his address for service.

(4) Any document to be sent to the registrar under these Rules shall be sent to him at the office.

(5) Any application or communication to be made to the President or to any member of the Lands Tribunal in respect of any case shall be addressed to the registrar at the office.

Change of address

55. A party to any proceedings may at any time by notice in writing to the registrar and to every other party to the proceedings change his address for service under these Rules.

Substituted service

56. If any person to whom any notice or other document is required to be sent under these Rules—

(a) cannot be found after all diligent enquiries have been made;

(b) has died and has no personal representative; or

(c) is out of the United Kingdom;

or for any other reason service upon him cannot readily be effected in accordance with these Rules, the President or the Tribunal may dispense with service upon that person or make an order for substituted service in such other form (whether by advertisement in a newspaper or otherwise) as the President or Tribunal may think fit.

PART IX

Transitional provisions

Transitional provisions, repeals etc

57.—(1) the Rules shall apply to proceedings commenced before the date on which they come into force as well as to proceedings commenced on or after that date.

(2) The Rules set out in Schedule 2 are hereby revoked.

Dated March 27, 1996 *Mackay of Clashfern, C.*

SCHEDULE 1

(Forms relating to Rights of Light Act 1959; not printed)

SCHEDULE 2

REVOCATIONS

(not printed)

Arbitration Act 1996

A4–03

. . . .

Awards on different issues, etc.

47.—(1) ... the tribunal may make more than one award [or decision] at different times on different aspects of the matters to be determined.

(2) The tribunal may, in particular, make an award [or decision] relating—

(a) to an issue affecting the whole claim, or

(b) to a part only of the claims or cross-claims submitted to it for decision.

(3) If the tribunal does so, it shall specify in its award [or decision] the issue, or the claim, or part of a claim, which is the subject matter of the award. [See Rule 32 above]

. . .

Interest

49.—(1) The parties are free to agree on the powers of the tribunal as regards the award of interest.

(2) Unless otherwise agreed by the parties the following provisions apply.

(3) The tribunal may award simple or compound interest from such dates, at such rates and with such rests as it considers meets the justice of the case—

(a) on the whole or part of any amount awarded by tribunal, in respect of any period up to the date of the award;

(b) on the whole or part of any amount claimed in the arbitration and outstanding at the commencement of the arbitral proceedings but paid before the award was made, in respect of any period up to the date of payment.

(4) The tribunal may award simple or compound interest from the date of the award (or any later date) until payment, at such rates, and with such rests as it considers meets the justice of the case, on the outstanding amount of any award (including any award of interest under subsection (3) and any award as to costs).

(5) References in this section to an amount awarded by the tribunal include

an amount payable in consequences of a declaratory award by the tribunal.

(6) The above provisions do not affect any other power of the tribunal to award interest.

Correction of award or additional award

. . .

57.—(3) The tribunal may on its own initiative or on the application of a party—

(a) correct an award so as to remove any clerical mistake or error arising from an accidental slip or omission or clarify or remove any ambiguity in the award, or

(b) make an additional award in respect of any claim (including a claim for interest or costs) which was presented to the tribunal but was not dealt with in the award.

These powers shall not be exercised without first affording the other parties a reasonable opportunity to make representations to the tribunal.

(4) Any application for the exercise of those powers must be made within 28 days of the date of the award or such longer period as the parties may agree.

(5) Any correction of an award shall be made within 28 days of the date the application was received by the tribunal or, where the correction is made by the tribunal on its own initiative, within 28 days of the date of the award or, in either case, such longer period as the parties may agree.

(6) Any additional award shall be made within 56 days of the date of the original award or such longer period as the parties may agree.

(7) Any correction of an award shall form part of the award.

Enforcement of the award

66.—(1) An award made by the tribunal pursuant to an arbitration agreement may, by leave of the court, be enforced in the same manner as a judgment or order of the court to the same effect.

(2) Where leave is so given, judgment may be entered in terms of the award.

(3) Leave to enforce an award shall not be given where, or to the extent that, the person against whom it is sought to be enforced shows that the tribunal lacked substantive jurisdiction to make the award.

The right to raise such an objection may have been lost (see section 73).

(4) Nothing in this section affects the recognition or enforcement of an award under any other enactment or rule of law, in particular under Part II of the Arbitration Act 1950 (enforcement of awards under Geneva Convention) or the provisions of Part III of this Act relating to the recognition and enforcement of awards under the New York Convention or by an action on the award.

Loss of right to object

73.—(1) If a party to arbitral proceedings takes part, or continues to take part, in the proceedings without making, either forthwith or within such time as is allowed by the arbitration agreement or the tribunal or by any provision of this Part, any objection—

(a) that the tribunal lacks substantive jurisdiction,

(b) that the proceedings have been improperly conducted,

(c) that there has been a failure to comply with the arbitration agreement or with any provision of this Part, or

(d) that there has been any other irregularity affecting the tribunal or the proceedings,

he may not rise that objection later, before the tribunal or the court, unless he shows that, at the time he took part or continued to take part in the proceedings, he did not know and could not with reasonable diligence have discovered the grounds for the objection.

(2) Where the arbitral tribunal rules that it has substantive jurisdiction and a party to arbitral proceedings who could have questioned that ruling—

(a) by any available arbitral process of appeal or review, or

(b) by challenging the award,

does not do so, or does not do so within the time allowed by the arbitration agreement or any provision of this Part, he may not object later to the tribunal's substantive jurisdiction on any ground which was the subject of that ruling.

Lands Tribunal

Practice Directions 1997

A4–04

These Practice Directions dated January 1, 1997 supersede all previous Practice Directions and Notes of the Lands Tribunal.

Practice Direction 1/97

Hearing of a Preliminary Issue

1. Attention is drawn to Rule 43 of the Lands Tribunal Rules 1996, which enables the Tribunal on application to order any preliminary issue in the proceedings to be disposed of at a preliminary hearing. The corresponding

provision in the 1975 Rules, now revoked, was limited to preliminary points of law.

2. The underlying purpose of Rule 43 is to secure where possible the expeditious disposal of a case at an interlocutory stage, where the effect would be to save the expense and delay which would arise if the parties had to proceed to a full hearing of the case, including disclosure and inspection of documents, the exchange of experts reports and valuations etc. Accordingly the rule should be invoked only in circumstances where determination of the preliminary issue will finally dispose of the whole case or will at least substantially reduce the length or the cost of a substantive hearing.

3. The procedure under Rule 43 is not appropriate for the determination of disputed matters of fact, unless it is plain that the determination of an issue of fact would effectively dispose of the whole case or substantially reduce the issues. Although the Tribunal may direct trial of a preliminary issue on the application of any party, an application under Rule 43 will in general be more favourably considered where all parties to the proceedings have agreed that trial of a preliminary issue would be appropriate and advantageous.

4. An application under Rule 43 should set out with precision the point of law or other issue or issues to be decided. All applications should be accompanied by a statement of agreed facts, and where the application relates solely to a point of law it must be accompanied by a statement of agreed facts sufficient to enable the issue of law to be determined without further findings of fact; in any event, an order for trial of a preliminary issue under the rule will normally require the parties to lodge a statement of agreed facts relevant to the issue before the matter is listed for the preliminary hearing.

5. **Restrictive Covenants**

   An application under Rule 43 is not appropriate for the determination of matters of title to the benefit of restrictive covenants for the purpose of applications to the Tribunal to discharge or modify restrictions under section 84 of the *Law of Property Act 1925*. That section makes specific provision for determination by the Court or by the Tribunal as to who may be admitted to oppose such an Tribunal to discharge or modify restrictions. The Tribunal has a separate procedure for the exercise of this statutory jurisdiction.

Lands Tribunal

Practice Directions 1997

Practice Direction 2/97

The Listing System

A4–05

1. **Introduction**

The Tribunal has completed a review of procedures for the listing of cases for hearing, and has now put in place a revised listing system. Its purpose is to utilise to the best advantage available resources of judicial, courtroom and staff time so that cases ready for hearing are heard and disposed of without unnecessary delay, and to ensure that all parties are given appointments for hearing at the earliest dates possible consistent of their needs and wishes. The new system will require the co-operation and goodwill of practitioners and litigants for its successful implementation.

2. **Initial Steps**

The Lands Tribunal Rules 1996 make provision for the initiating of proceedings which vary according to the nature of the case. Thus, in a rating appeal from a Valuation Tribunal, rules 6 to 8 prescribe the contents of the notice of appeal and respondent's notice of intention to respond, and require the exchange of statements of case and valuations. References of disputed compensation claims, and applications for discharge of restrictive covenants likewise require initial steps to be taken in accordance with the Rules. As soon as the appropriate initial steps are completed, and any earlier directions of the Registrar complied with, the case will be allocated to a Member or Members with a view to giving any necessary directions and appointing a date for hearing as soon as practicable. Where a case appears at the outset to raise important issues of law or fact of particular complexity, it may be allocated to a Member or Members before the initial steps are completed.

3. **The Simplified Procedure under Rule 28**

The 1996 Rules introduced a new simplified procedure to provide accelerated and economical disposal of cases where it appears (a) that no substantial issue of law or valuation practice, or substantial conflict of fact is likely to arise; and (b) that the originating party agrees to the use of the procedure. Thus all originating forms will now require the claimant, applicant or appellant to state whether or not he/she agrees to the use of the simplified procedure.

On consideration of the papers lodged, the Registrar will, if the claimant/applicant/appellant has indicated consent, assign an appropriate case to the "Simplified Procedure list" by direction under Rule 28(1). Provision is made for objection by the other party/parties, and for determination of the objection as an interlocutory matter under Rule 38.

Where a case remains in the Simplified Procedure list, the provisions of Rule 28(5) to (12) will apply, thus requiring in particular the filing of simplified pleadings, a fixed hearing date, and an informal hearing before a member of the Tribunal acting as if he were an arbitrator and adopting such procedure as the member considers fair. There will normally in such cases be no awards of costs, though Rule 28(11) makes provision for an award of costs in exceptional circumstances.

Rule 28(12) enables the Tribunal, where it appears necessary or appropriate to do so, to remove a case from the simplified procedure, and to give directions as to the further conduct of the proceedings.

A decision of the member in a case under the simplified procedure, is a decision of the Tribunal, to which the provisions for appeal by way of Case Stated to the Court of Appeal will apply.

4. **Allocation**

The President will allocate cases to a Member or Members, having regard in particular to the Members' availability and the nature of the case. Most cases will be allocated to a single Member, but those which are potentially particularly difficult or complex may be allocated to a two-member Tribunal. The initial allocation may in some cases be provisional. The Member to whom a case has been allocated will at once review the documentation in order to determine whether the issues are adequately defined and whether in other respects the case is ready for hearing. If it is not in his view ready, the Member may give directions under Rule 34 or may appoint a pre-trial review under Rule 39, and the case will be removed from the list until the requirements are met. The case will then be relisted and prepared for a hearing date. Any party may apply under Rule 38 for proceedings to be stayed, but *where no such application is made, the Tribunal will assume that the case once listed is ready to proceed and will list it for hearing.*

5. **Consultation**

In all cases the parties or their representatives will be consulted by letter before a hearing date is fixed. It will be made clear that the case is about to be listed for hearing, and that the view of the parties are sought as to the estimated length of the hearing, the venue, and suitable dates. At this stage, the parties will also be asked to identify the issues between them, and whether or not any procedural steps, such as discovery, or other directions are sought.

It is important that the response to this consultation should be prompt and clear, and so far as possible on a basis agreed between the parties. Thus, the time estimate must be realistic; reasons should be given as to suitability of venue; and though dates to be avoided may be given, a blanket exclusion of several months will not be acceptable without good reason. Views expressed will be taken into account in fixing a date and place for the hearing, but if no constructive response to consultation is received within a reasonable time (usually 14 days) the Tribunal may appoint a date and place for hearing without further reference to the parties.

6. **Counsel**

If informed that counsel are instructed, the Tribunal will contact counsel's clerk to discuss a hearing date, but it is the responsibility of counsel to ensure that their clerks respond promptly and constructively. Efforts will be made to accommodate the parties' choice of counsel so far as possible, but there can be not absolute right to be represented by a particular member of the Bar.

7. **Venue**
The Tribunal has its own courtroom accommodation only in London. It is often possible to arrange hearing date earlier in London than elsewhere. Accordingly, all parties will be offered the option of a hearing in London. Where for reasons of cost, convenience of the parties, requirement of a site inspection, etc. it is desirable for the case to be heard outside London, the preferences of the parties will be met so far as practicable in arranging court accommodation. This will usually be in a nearby major city. Cases due to last more than five days may be commenced in the provinces and adjourned to be resumed in London.

8. **Date of Hearing**
In all but the rarest of cases, the hearing date will be fixed with not less than 14 days notice to the parties. Usually the notice of hearing will be considerably more than 14 days, and will follow the process of consultation as set out above. If shorter notice is given, parties will be informed by fax or telephone that a hearing notification letter is on its way.

9. **Postponements**
It is emphasised that a hearing of the Lands Tribunal once notified takes priority over other engagements except hearings before superior courts or *force majeure* (such as sudden illness, etc.). Once the date of hearing has been fixed and notified, the Tribunal will not permit postponements and adjournments, with or without the consent of other parties, unless very good reason is shown upon application to the Member or to the Registrar, and a new date for hearing is agreed or fixed.

This policy is necessary both in the interest of other litigants waiting for their cases to be heard, and to ensure efficient use of the Tribunal's resources. Thus, the serious illness of an essential witness, properly supported by medical evidence, would no doubt be an acceptable reason for postponement, whereas the vague "unavailability" of advocate or witness would not be acceptable without a clear explanation of that person's other commitment and why it should have priority over the Tribunal hearing. If a postponement is to be sought, this must be done as quickly as possible after the notification; the Tribunal is even less willing to grant postponements nearer the hearing date.

10. **Negotiations and Settlements**
It is commonplace for negotiations to take place with a view to settlement of the issues between the parties. It is, of course, the Tribunal's policy to encourage such efforts, but the fact that negotiations are in progress does not in itself constitute adequate reason to remove a case from the list for hearing. *Practitioners are reminded that it is their responsibility to ensure that the Tribunal is kept informed of the possibility of settlement or of any other circumstances likely to affect the date or the length of a hearing.* It is

particularly important that this obligation be met where arrangements have been made for a hearing at a provincial venue. A settlement at the court door is probably a settlement that could have been achieved earlier, with consequent savings to the parties and the Tribunal.

Lands Tribunal

Practice Directions 1997

Practice Direction 3/97

A4–06 Direct Professional Access to Counsel in the Lands Tribunal

The following guidance note was agreed in 1993 between the President of the Lands Tribunal and the Local Government, Planning and Environmental Bar Association on behalf of the Direct Professional Access Committee of the Bar Council and, through that Committee, with the Royal Institution of Chartered Surveyors, the Royal Town Planning Institute, Royal Institute of British Architects, the Institute of Revenues, Rating and Valuation, and the Incorporated Society of Valuers and Auctioneers.

Guidance Note

1. This Note is intended to prove guidance upon the use of direct professional access (DPA) to barristers by members of the RICS, RTPI, RIBA, IRRV and ISVA in cases to be brought or pending in the Lands Tribunal.
2. The Bar's Code of Conduct permits a barrister to accept DPA instructions to appear in the Lands Tribunal when so instructed. The Code requires a barrister to refuse to accept instructions by DPA "if he considers it in the interests of the lay client that a solicitor be instructed". Similarly, having accepted instructions by DPA, he must decline to act further if "at any stage he considers it is in the interests of the lay client that a solicitor be instructed" (Annex E, paras. 1 and 2, Bar Council Code of Conduct).
3. Factors which may be relevant in deciding whether it is in the interests of the lay client that a Solicitor be instructed in relation to the preparation and hearing of cases in the Lands Tribunal include:

   (a) The extent to which the case involves the marshalling and mastering of legal documents such as deeds and leases;

   (b) The extent to which the case involves questions of legal difficulty;

   (c) The extent to which the case will involve interlocutory proceedings or other pre-trial organisational steps;

   (d) The extent to which questions of primary fact will be in dispute, the need for witnesses to prove such facts and the extent to which proofs may have to be taken from such witnesses;

(e) The need for the barrister to be instructed comprehensively during the course of the hearing and in particular if the person instructing him is expected to give evidence;

(f) The potential economic consequences of the case for the lay client;

(g) The experience and ability of the person instructing and his assistants.

4. DPA instructions will very rarely be appropriate with respect to:

(1) any originating application under section 84(1) of the Law of Property Act 1925 (restrictive covenants affecting land);

(2) any interlocutory application under that subsection;

(3) any objection in any such proceedings made on behalf of a person entitled to the benefit of the relevant restrictions;

(4) any preliminary issue ordered pursuant to Rule 43 of the Lands Tribunal Rules 1996.

5. In all cases the barrister ought to be asked specifically by the instructing member to advise whether it is in the interests of the lay client that a solicitor be instructed on delivery of instructions and at appropriate stages thereafter.

Members of professional bodies other than the Royal Institution of Chartered Surveyors, the Royal Town Planning Institute, the Royal Institute of British Architects, the Institute of Revenues Rating and Valuation and the Incorporated Society of Valuers and Auctioneers will not be permitted to have direct access to counsel in respect of proceedings in the Lands Tribunal.

The President proposes to keep under review with other Members the operation of DPA, and reserves the right to withdraw his agreement to the Guidance Note if circumstances or the manner in which the Guidance Note is operated, in his opinion, so demand.

Lands Tribunal

Practice Directions 1997

Practice Direction 4/97

A4–07

Pre-trial Review

1. Attention is drawn to Rule 39 of the Lands Tribunal Rules 1996 which came into force on May 1, 1996. Rule 39 replaces the former Rule 45A of

the 1975 Rules, and in substance reproduces those provision dealing with pre-trial review.

2. An order for pre-trial review may be made on application by a party or by the Tribunal of its own motion. Pre-trial review will generally be considered appropriate and will be ordered after any necessary pleadings have been delivered and expert reports and valuations exchanged. The case will at that stage be under review by the Member(s) to whom it has been allocated, or by the Registrar. Not less than 14 days notice will be given of the place, date and time of the pre-trial review.

3. A pre-trial review will not be required in cases which have been allocated to the simplified procedure introduced by Rule 28.

4. The purpose of a pre-trial review is to ensure so far as practicable that all appropriate directions are given for the fair, expeditious and economical conduct of the proceedings. To this end the parties will be expected to try to reach agreement so far as they can at or before the pre-trial review. In particular, the agreement of the parties will be sought so as to define the issues between them and as to any pleadings necessary for that purpose; the extent of discovery and necessary documentation for the hearing, including plans and photographs; the preparation of a statement of agreed facts; the venue and estimated length of hearing and dates to avoid.

5. In the course of pre-trial review, parties will be under a duty to provide to the Tribunal all such information and to produce all such documents as the Tribunal may require with a view to promoting the efficient conduct and disposal of the proceedings. Each party should so far as practicable apply on the pre-trial review for any specific direction required, and give notice to other parties of the intention to do so. If an application is subsequently made which might have been made on the pre-trial review, the applicant may be ordered to pay the additional costs incurred.

6. A party should so far as practicable be represented at pre-trial review by the counsel or solicitor by whom that party's case will be conducted at the substantive hearing.

Lands Tribunal

Practice Directions 1997

A4–08

Practice Direction 5/97

Expert Evidence

1. **Introduction**

Rule 42 of the Lands Tribunal Rules 1996 applies to expert witnesses and their evidence. It is inherent in the jurisdiction exercised by the Lands Tribunal that the Tribunal will be called upon to hear and evaluate the evidence of experts in most cases. Expert witnesses are defined as those qualified by training and experience in a particular subject or subjects to express an opinion. Most frequently the expert witness before the Tribunal will be a surveyor or valuer, but this practice direction applies equally to any witness whom it is proposed to call to give expert evidence.

2. **Duty of the Expert Witness**
The purpose of expert evidence of opinion is to assist the Tribunal in reaching a decision. The evidence should be accurate and complete as to relevant fact, and should represent the honest and objective opinion of the witness, uninfluenced by those on whose behalf the expert has been instructed. It is for that reason that the evidence is generally given on oath. If a professional body has adopted a code of practice and professional conduct dealing with the giving of evidence, then the Tribunal will expect a member of that body to comply with the provisions of the code in the preparation and presentation of his/her evidence. An expert witness who is not a member of an institution having such a code of practice should give careful consideration to the steps necessary for him to take in order to comply with his obligations in the Tribunal as an expert witness, and to ensure that those instructing him are aware of those obligations.

3. **Lodging Reports**
The procedures of the Tribunal are designed to ensure that all cases are disposed of speedily, efficiently and fairly. The role of the expert witness in these procedures is of fundamental importance. The directions given by the Tribunal will normally require the lodging and exchange of experts' reports and valuations at an early stage prior to the hearing. It is incumbent on the expert witness to prepare and submit such a report together with any valuation and details of comparable properties or transactions relied upon, fully and promptly for the purpose of lodging and exchange. It should be borne in mind that as a general rule, the expert evidence given at the hearing will be confined to those matters disclosed in the expert's reports. Experts' reports should not contain any reference to or details of negotiations "without prejudice" or offers of settlement.

4. **Agreement where possible**
Disclosure and exchange of experts reports will usually be only a first step. Thereafter, the Tribunal will normally require experts of like discipline to meet and to reach agreement as to facts, to agree any relevant plans, photographs etc, and to define those facts upon which they are unable to agree and the issues remaining unresolved between them. It has been known occasionally for retained experts to be instructed not to agree; such instructions are to be deprecated. The Tribunal will regard failure to cooperate in reaching agreement as to the facts and issues as incompatible with the expert's duty to the Tribunal.

5. **Representation**
There is provision in Rule 37 of the 1996 Rules for any party to be represented by leave of the Tribunal by a person other than a solicitor or counsel. In many simple cases, leave will be granted for a surveyor or valuer

to represent a party in order to avoid the additional costs of separate representation. In those cases allocated to the Simplified Procedure under Rule 28, such representation may well be the norm. Nevertheless it is the considered view of the Tribunal that in general it is difficult and undesirable for the same person to act both as advocate and expert witness. Accordingly, leave will not normally be granted for a non-lawyer to represent a party in any case where the Tribunal considers that the responsibilities of advocate and of expert witness are likely to conflict. It is principally because of this conflict between the roles of advocate and expert witness that Rule 37(2) has been introduced, requiring a valuation officer in rating appeals to obtain leave of the Tribunal to appear in person. Applications for leave under Rule 37(1) or (2) should so far as practicable be made in good time prior to the hearing. An application should be supported by a full statement of the grounds for it, including particulars of the applicant's experience as an advocate. Late application may necessitate adjournment, and the party responsible may thus be rendered liable to pay the additional costs incurred.

Lands Tribunal

Practice Directions 1997

Practice Direction 6/97

A4–09

Procedure at Hearings and Delivery of Decisions

1. The procedure at a hearing of the Tribunal is entirely within the discretion of the presiding member. That discretion will be exercised with a view to securing a full and fair hearing. However, the Tribunal is a court of law, and the procedure adopted will generally accord with the practice in the High Court and County Court. In particular, the claimant, applicant or appellant will begin and will have a right of reply; evidence will be taken on oath, and the rules of evidence will be applied. Where a site inspection is required, Rule 29 will limit the number of persons entitled to be present, and the Tribunal will not accept any oral or written evidence tendered in the course of a site inspection.
2. All cases assigned to the simplified procedure list will be heard by a single member acting as if he were an arbitrator under Rule 28. That rule and Practice Direction No. 2 of 1997 should be referred to for further guidance to procedure in these cases.
3. The effect of Rule 5 of the 1996 Rules is that hearings by the Tribunal take place in public save in certain rare cases, principally where the Tribunal is sitting as an arbitrator under a reference by consent.
4. In all cases of substance or complexity, the parties will be expected to provide, in good time prior to the hearing, and if possible by agreement, a bundle of relevant documents, properly paginated and excluding repetitious

and irrelevant documents, and a written summary or outline of submissions. Plans and photographs should be appropriately annotated and indexed and wherever possible, agreed.

5. The Tribunal's decision will in most cases be reserved and will be in writing; Rule 50(2) enables the Tribunal to give an oral decision extempore, but the occasions where this is thought appropriate are likely to be rare. The decision of the Tribunal may be delivered to the parties in writing or delivered orally at a resumed hearing, at the Tribunal's discretion. In cases where the decision is delivered to the parties in writing, the parties will normally be invited to make such representations as they are advised as to the appropriate form of order or as to the costs of the proceedings or other ancillary matters. Following such representations, the Tribunal's final order will be incorporated in an addendum to the decision. In cases where the decision is delivered orally, issues of costs and other ancillary matters will be dealt with at the resumed hearing. Any rights of appeal will accrue from the date when the Tribunal's decision is thus perfected either by an addendum or by a speaking order.

6. Section 3(4) of the Lands Tribunal Act 1949 gives a limited right of appeal from decisions of the Tribunal by way of Case Stated to the Court of Appeal. The procedure for such an appeal is prescribed by Order 61 of the Rules of the Supreme Court, and further guidance is given by the Tribunal's Practice Direction No. 7 of 1997.

Lands Tribunal

Practice Directions 1997

Practice Direction 7/97

Appeal to the Court of Appeal

A4–10

1. The provisions of section 3(4) of the Lands Tribunal Act 1949 restrict the right of appeal from a decision of the Tribunal to "any person aggrieved by the decision as being erroneous in point of law." The Tribunal's decision on matters of fact is final. The procedure in the Court of Appeal is governed by Order 61, r. 1 of the Rules of the Supreme Court.

Form of Case Stated

2. A prospective appellant who requires the Tribunal to state a case for the decision of the Court of Appeal may set out the grounds of appeal in the application to the Tribunal. If no grounds of appeal are specified in the application, the applicant will be invited to specify within 14 days the point or points of law which it is sought to raise in the Court of Appeal.

3. It is the obligation of the prospective appellant to define concisely and with

reasonable precision the question or questions of law which it is sought to raise. Unless the point at issue is already plainly identified in the Tribunal's decision, a question of law stated in general or vague terms such as "whether upon the findings of fact I came to a correct decision in law" will not be accepted.

4. Subject to the foregoing, such grounds of appeal as are specified in the application or subsequently, and which in the view of the Tribunal raise a point of law for the decision of the Court of Appeal will normally be reproduced in the case stated. The Tribunal will decline to state a case if no grounds of appeal are specified, or if in the view of the Tribunal the grounds of appeal specified disclose no point of law.

Evidence

5. The decision of the Tribunal will in all cases contain a statement of the substance of evidence considered to be material and the Tribunal's findings of fact. In accordance with R.S.C., O. 61, r. 1(4), a copy of the decision will be annexed to the case stated. It is inappropriate and unnecessary for a transcript of evidence or notes of evidence to be annexed, and any notes made by the member(s) of the Tribunal will not in the ordinary way be made available to the parties. An application to the Tribunal for disclosure of such notes will not, therefore, normally be entertained, but if, in exceptional circumstances, it is considered necessary for the notes to be made available, the Tribunal or the Registrar of Civil Appeals may give a direction to that effect. See *per* Sir Thomas Bingham M.R. in *Blue Circle Industries v. West Midlands County Council* (1994) E.G. 21/5/94 at 149.

Costs

6. No appeal will lie without leave in respect of the Tribunal's award of costs, which is wholly a matter of discretion. With effect from October 1, 1993, the provisions of section 18(1A) of the Supreme Court Act 1981 and Order 5, r. 1B(1)(b) of Rules of the Supreme Court require leave of the Tribunal or the Court of Appeal to appeal against an order relating only to costs. Where such leave is granted by the Tribunal or by the Court of Appeal, the appeal will proceed by way of case stated.

Lands Tribunal

Practice Directions 1997

A4–11

Practice Direction 8/97

Fees and Costs

1. **Fees**
   The fees to be taken in respect of proceedings in the Lands Tribunal are specified in the *Lands Tribunal (Fees) Rules 1996* (S.I. 1996 No. 1021). The Tribunal has no power to waive or vary those fees. Unless the Tribunal directs otherwise, the appropriate hearing fee is payable by the party initiating the proceedings, but without prejudice to any right to recover the fee by virtue of an order for costs.

2. **Costs**
   Under section 3(5) of the *Lands Tribunal Act 1949* the Tribunal has power to make orders for the costs of any party to proceedings to be paid by another party and to provide for the taxation of costs. Rule 52 of the *Lands Tribunal Rules 1996* prescribes the procedure for taxation of costs. In general orders for costs are made by the Tribunal in the exercise of its discretion in accordance with the principles applied in the High Court and county court. There is no provision for "payment into court", but by virtue of section 4 of the *Land Compensation Act 1961* an acquiring authority in a disputed compulsory purchase compensation claim may seek to protect itself as to costs by means of a "sealed offer". The procedure for a "sealed offer" to pay or to accept a sum in settlement is now extended to other proceedings before the Tribunal, by Rule 44 of the 1996 Rules. In exercise its discretion as to costs, the Tribunal may also have regard where appropriate to any informal offer of settlement, including an offer made "without prejudice save as to costs".

3. Where an order for costs is made, the Tribunal in its discretion may settle the amount of costs by assessing a lump sum, or may direct that the costs be taxed by the registrar on the basis of a scale applicable to county court proceedings, or on the standard basis applicable to High Court proceedings.

4. An appeal to the Court of Appeal in respect of the Tribunal's award of costs will lie only by leave of the Tribunal or of the Court of Appeal. Practice Direction 7 of 1997 should be referred to.

5. **Legal Aid**
   Legal Aid is available or proceedings in the Lands Tribunal on the same basis as for proceedings in any court, by virtue of Reg. 148 of the *Civil Legal Aid (General) Regulations 1989* (S.I. 1989 No. 339). Notice of issue of a legal aid certificate is required to be lodged forthwith with the Tribunal, and to be served on all other parties to the proceedings. Where the Tribunal makes a final decision, it is the duty of the solicitor or counsel representing any assisted person to bring the legal aid certificate to the attention of the

Tribunal and to ensure that an order is made for taxation of the assisted persons costs.

All other provisions of the 1989 Regulations apply as appropriate to proceedings in the Tribunal.

APPENDIX 5

ROYAL AND SUN ALLIANCE INSURANCE FORMS

PLEASE READ THIS POLICY (AND THE SCHEDULE WHICH FORMS AN INTEGRAL PART OF THE POLICY) TO ENSURE THAT IT MEETS YOUR REQUIREMENTS

A5–01

RESTRICTIVE COVENANT INDEMNITY

This Policy and the Schedule shall be read together and any word or expression to which a specific meaning has been attached in either shall bear such meaning wherever it may appear.

Whereas the Insured by the Proposal which shall be the basis of and incorporated in this contract intending to use or develop the Property for a purpose (hereinafter called the Insured Use) which is or may be held to be a breach of the Restrictive Covenants so far as they now affect the Property and are enforceable has applied to the Company for the indemnity contained herein and has paid or agreed to pay the Premium.

Now this Policy witnesses that in the event of any claimant seeking to establish that the Insured Use constitutes a breach of the Restrictive Covenants and that the benefit of and right to enforce the Restrictive Covenants is vested in the claimant the Company will subject to the terms contained herein or endorsed hereon indemnify the Insured in respect of

1. damages or compensation (including costs and expenses) awarded to any claimant on the grounds that the Insured Use represents a breach of the Restrictive Covenants
2. loss sustained by the Insured in respect of

    a. the difference between the market value of the Property on the assumption that the Restrictive Covenants are unenforceable and the market value subject to the Restrictive Covenants so far as the Insured has been ordered by the court to comply therewith both such market values being calculated by reference to prices current on the date of such court order

b. the cost of works (including architects' and surveyors' fees) for the purpose of the Insured Use begun or contracted for after the Effective Date and before the commencement of proceedings for the enforcement of the Restrictive Covenants to the extent that such expenditure is rendered abortive by court order

c. the cost of demolishing any building erected after the Effective Date for the purpose of the Insured Use or of restoring to its former condition any building altered for such purpose so far as such demolition or restoration is necessary to comply with any court order

d. costs and expenses incurred by the Insured with the written consent of the Company

The liability of the Company shall not exceed the Limit of Indemnity

Anthony P Latham,
Managing Director,
Royal & SunAlliance Global Risks Division
on behalf of Royal & Sun Alliance Insurance plc

Exceptions

The Company shall not be liable in respect of claims following any

1. communication made by or on behalf of the Insured to a person believed at the time by the Insured to be entitled to the benefit of and right to enforce the Restrictive Covenants

2. application made by the Insured to the court or to the Lands Tribunal in respect of the Restrictive Covenants

without the prior written consent of the Company
Provided that this Policy shall not be in force unless it has been initialled by an authorised official of the Company

Interpretation

For the purposes of this Policy Proposal shall mean any signed proposal form and declaration and any information in connection with this insurance supplied by or on behalf of the Insured in addition thereto or in substitution therefor

Conditions

1. The Insured shall give written notice to the Company as soon as possible after receiving information of any claim loss or occurrence for which there may be liability under this Policy with full particulars thereof Every letter claim writ summons and process shall be forwarded to the Company on receipt No admission offer promise payment or indemnity shall be made or given by or on behalf of the Insured without the written consent of the Company which shall be entitled to take over and conduct in the name of the Insured the defence or settlement of any claim or to prosecute in the name of the Insured for its own benefit any claim or to apply in the name of the Insured to the Lands Tribunal for the discharge or modification of the Restrictive Covenants and shall have full discretion in the conduct of any proceedings and in the settlement of any claim The Insured shall give all such assistance as the Company may require

2. In connection with any claims against the Insured the Company shall at any time be allowed the first option to purchase the Property at the highest price the Insured is able to obtain for the Property If any objection be made to the Insured Use by any person claiming to be entitled to the benefit of and right to enforce the Restrictive Covenants and a Queen's Counsel shall advise that such objection could not be contested with the probability of success then the Company shall not be liable under clause **2.** in respect of any sums expended without the

written consent of the Company by the Insured for the purpose of the Insured Use after the date of such advice

3. If at the time any claim arises under this Policy there be any other insurance covering the same liability the Company shall not pay more than its ratable proportion of such claim and costs and expenses in connection therewith

4. If any difference shall arise as to the amount to be paid under this Policy (liability being otherwise admitted) such difference shall be referred to an Arbitrator to be appointed by the parties in accordance with the statutory provisions in that behalf for the time being in force Where any difference is by this Condition to be referred to arbitration the making of an Award shall be a condition precedent to any right of action against the Company.

5. The due observance and fulfilment of the terms of this Policy so far as they relate to anything to be done or complied with by the Insured and the truth of the Proposal shall be conditions precedent to any liability of the Company to make any payment under this Policy

Schedule Policy Number DRAFT—August 24, 1998

Company Royal & Sun Alliance Insurance plc

Branch Themis House 31–35 St. Nicholas Way Sutton Surrey

Agency

Insured

and the Insured's successors in title and mortgagees all of whom shall be bound by the terms of the Policy

Effective Date To Be Agreed

Premium £0.00

The Premium shown includes a sum of £0.00 in respect of 4.0% Premium Tax

Property

Limit of Indemnity £0

Insured Use

Schedule	Policy Number	DRAFT—August 24, 1998

Restrictive Covenants

a) Manner and date of Imposition

b) Nature of restrictions

Signed or Initialled on the	**Examined**

*These forms have been reproduced by kind permission of Royal & Sun Alliance Insurance Group plc.

Plan I

A6–01

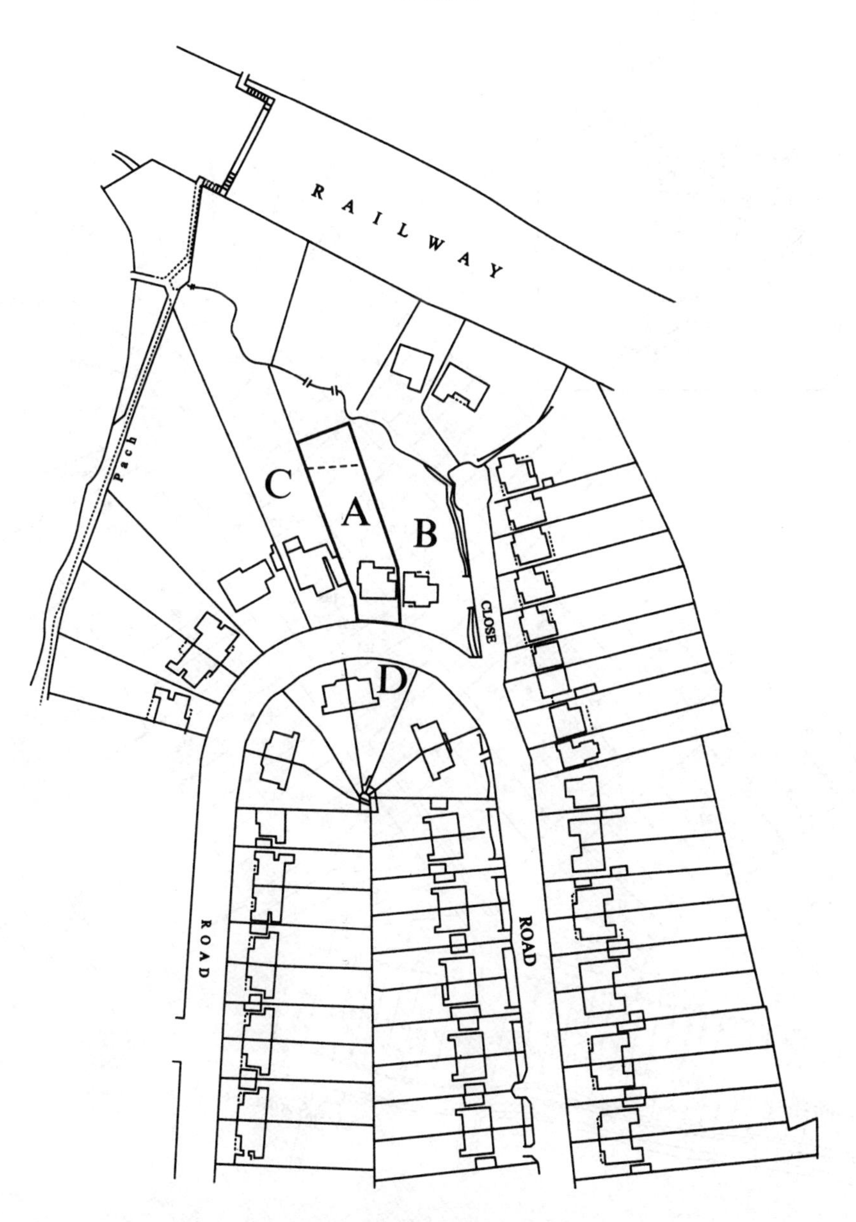

Plot A: sold off by common vendor January 1, 1990
Plot B: sold off by common vendor March 1, 1990
Plot C: sold off by common vendor November 1, 1989
Plot D: sold off by common vendor January 1, 1995. The last plot to be sold by V.

A6–02

Plan II

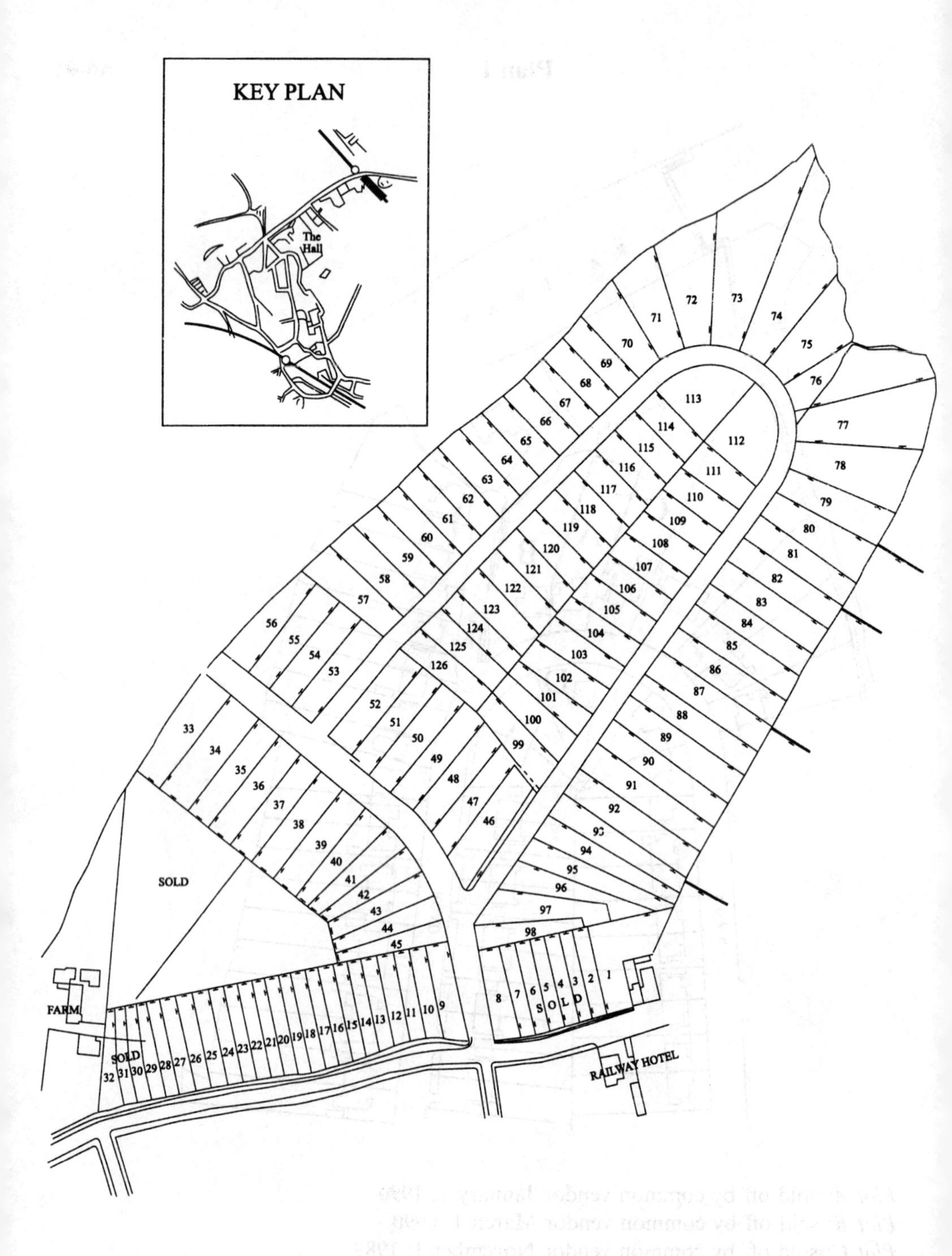

Plan II—*cont.*

	Largest width	Smallest width	Length
1	152′0″	50′0″	165′0″
2	27′0″	27′0″	148′0″
3	27′0″	27′0″	150′9″
4	27′0″	27′0″	153′9″
5	27′0″	27′0″	156′6″
6	27′0″	27′0″	157′0″
7	27′0″	27′0″	157′3″
8	48′0″	38′0″	156′6″
9	40′0″	40′0″	164′0″
10	30′0″	30′0″	152′0″
11	30′0″	30′0″	148′5″
12	30′0″	30′0″	147′10″
13	30′0″	30′0″	150′0″
14	30′0″	25′0″	152′3″
15	30′0″	25′0″	154′6″
16	30′0″	25′0″	156′4″
17	30′0″	25′0″	157′0″
18	30′0″	25′0″	156′9″
19	30′0″	25′0″	156′9″
20	30′0″	25′0″	156′7″
21	30′0″	25′0″	155′9″
22	30′0″	25′0″	153′10″
23	30′0″	25′0″	152′3″
24	30′0″	30′0″	150′6″
25	30′0″	30′0″	148′6″
26	30′0″	30′0″	147′0″
27	30′0″	30′0″	146′4″
28	23′6″	23′6″	144′6″
29	23′9″	29′9″	144′0″
30	25′0″	18′8″	143′0″
31	25′0″	18′8″	?′?″
32	40′0″	18′8″	175′0″
33	69′0″	51′0″	200′0″
34	64′0″	64′0″	198′3″
35	50′0″	50′0″	198′0″
36	50′0″	50′0″	198′0″
37	50′0″	50′0″	198′0″
38	50′0″	50′0″	198′0″
39	50′0″	50′0″	198′0″
40	50′0″	24′8″	199′0″
41	50′0″	24′8″	199′0″
42	50′0″	24′8″	197′0″
43	50′0″	32′0″	192′0″
44	41′6″	21′0″	200′0″
45	41′6″	21′0″	200′0″
46	70′0″	54′0″	220′0″
47	50′0″	50′0″	196′9″
48	50′0″	50′0″	192′3″
49	50′0″	50′0″	193′0″
50	50′0″	50′0″	196′6″
51	50′0″	50′0″	197′3″
52	65′6″	65′6″	198′0″
53	55′0″	50′0″	200′0″
54	50′0″	50′0″	201′3″
55	50′6″	50′0″	202′6″
56	50′0″	30′0″	205′0″
57	53′3″	50′0″	180′0″
58	53′3″	50′0″	179′8″
59	60′0″	50′0″	180′6″
60	50′0″	50′0″	175′0″
61	50′0″	50′0″	174′0″
62	50′0″	50′0″	174′0″
63	50′0″	50′0″	170′0″

	Largest width	Smallest width	Length
64	50′0″	50′0″	165′0″
65	50′0″	50′0″	157′0″
66	50′0″	50′0″	151′0″
67	50′0″	50′0″	148′0″
68	50′0″	50′0″	146′8″
69	50′0″	50′0″	150′0″
70	80′0″	50′0″	152′0″
71	100′0″	50′0″	166′0″
72	120′0″	50′0″	185′4″
73	204′0″	50′0″	233′0″
74	224′0″	50′0″	367′5″
75	127′0″	50′0″	136′0″
76	188′0″	50′0″	254′0″
77	144′0″	50′0″	216′0″
78	120′0″	48′6″	189′6″
79	62′0″	48′6″	194′0″
80	50′0″	82′0″	198′9″
81	50′0″	50′0″	204′0″
82	50′0″	50′0″	209′0″
83	50′0″	50′0″	211′0″
84	50′0″	50′0″	216′0″
85	50′0″	50′0″	222′6″
86	50′0″	50′0″	228′0″
87	50′0″	50′0″	235′6″
88	50′0″	50′0″	239′6″
89	50′0″	50′0″	245′0″
90	50′0″	50′0″	252′0″
91	50′0″	50′0″	258′0″
92	50′0″	50′0″	264′6″
93	50′0″	30′0″	270′0″
94	50′0″	24′0″	273′3″
95	50′0″	36′0″	262′6″
96	76′0″	60′0″	198′6″
97	80′0″	48′0″	200′0″
98	30′0″	16′0″	200′0″
99	63′0″	47′6″	189′0″
100	63′0″	47′6″	183′4″
101	53′0″	35′0″	173′0″
102	50′0″	50′0″	173′0″
103	50′0″	50′0″	168′0″
104	50′0″	50′0″	163′3″
105	50′0″	50′0″	158′6″
106	50′0″	50′0″	153′8″
107	50′0″	50′0″	149′0″
108	50′0″	50′0″	144′0″
109	50′0″	50′0″	140′0″
110	50′0″	50′0″	134′0″
111	60′0″	50′0″	129′0″
112	195′0″	30′0″	123′0″
113	190′0″	135′0″	123′6″
114	50′0″	50′0″	127′6″
115	50′0″	50′0″	131′9″
116	50′0″	50′0″	136′0″
117	50′0″	50′0″	140′3″
118	50′0″	50′0″	144′0″
119	50′0″	50′0″	148′6″
120	50′0″	50′0″	152′3″
121	50′0″	50′0″	156′9″
122	50′0″	50′0″	161′0″
123	50′0″	50′0″	165′3″
124	50′0″	50′0″	170′9″
125	50′0″	47′6″	175′0″
126	50′0″	47′6″	180′0″

APPENDIX 7

PRECEDENTS

INTRODUCTION

House style: Ancient or modern?

A7–01 An attempt has been made to follow the advice regarding clarity of language given in Chapter 17 above, and accordingly the style of the precedents which follow is designed to be more fit for the 21st than the 19th century. This may come as a shock to some readers and potential users, but in view of the need to make forms understood, ultimately, by the parties themselves, and as the precedents are being published on the eve of a new millennium, there is no reason why any lawyer should stick to the archaic and verbose style used by his ancestors. To the extent that these precedents fall short of complete modernity, this shows how hard it is to produce legal forms which are easy on the mind and which also work in a technical area of the law.

As modern conveyancing is now dominated by the system of registration of title, the forms reflect the fact that the instruments in which the covenants invariably appear will be transfers. To the extent that there are other events which cause covenants to be imposed, where no transfer of registered land is being made, it is easy to transpose transfer for deed.

Modern style has also been adopted in certain other specific instances such as the use of the words "buyer" and "seller" rather than the more archaic versions of "purchaser" and "vendor". Where the imposition of the covenants occurs on an event which is not apt to lead to such a neutral description of the parties, there is no reason why their names should not be used, *e.g.* "Mr Brown covenants with Mr Smith". As with the various types of instrument which may be used to impose covenants, the transposition from the forms should be straightforward.

One final remark by way of introduction

As the subject of the book is restrictive covenants, the emphasis of the precedents will be on such covenants. Consequently, there will be little by way of positive covenant material, save where necessary to make sense of the scheme of covenants, such as where the provision of services is to be safeguarded. To have extended the precedent material further into the field of positive covenants would have required another book dealing with the problems which such covenants pose as a matter of enforceability and how such problems can so far as possible be overcome. As a reminder, Chapter 1 above contains a brief summary of the difference between restrictive covenants and positive covenants.

Caveat user

As with any form of precedent, they should be seen as a means to an end and not as an end in themselves. In common with fire they are good servants and bad masters, so they should be treated carefully. What has been attempted is not an encyclopedia (of which there are already a number published) but a set of forms which can be used as a starting point and around which, using the forms supplied as a framework, there can be built the final structure of the restrictions and obligations to be entered into between the parties.

PART 1

Basic Nuts and Bolts

A7–02

In Part 1 there are set out the basic elements of any covenant over freehold land, of a restrictive nature, designed to bind successors in title of the covenantor and to benefit the land of the covenantee by annexation.

Element 1
The parties between whom the covenants are to be made.

(i) Where the covenants are being given by *the buyer*

The buyer covenants with the seller

(ii) Where the covenants are being given by *the seller*

The seller covenants with the buyer

Commentary

There is no need to introduce words which extend the meaning of the parties to heirs and assigns, etc. Law of Property Act 1925, ss. 78 and 79 supply these words.[1]

Element 2
The words which make it clear that the covenants are not personal:

so as to bind the property and each and every part of it whoever may be the owner of it

[1] See Chaps 5, 7 and 8 above.

Commentary
As the introduction says, these words remove any doubt as to whether the covenants are intended to be personal. They show that the covenants are to relate to the land defined as the property. The property will either be the land being sold (where the covenants are being given by the buyer) or the land being retained (where the covenants are being given by the seller).

Element 3
The words which annex the benefit of the covenant to the land for which the covenant has been taken.

> *so that the benefit is annexed to each and every part of the land which* either
> *the seller has retained* (*i.e.* where the covenants are being imposed on the buyer)
> or
> *has been conveyed to the buyer* (*i.e.* where the covenants are being imposed on the seller).

Commentary
In view of the decision in *Federated Homes Ltd v. Mill Lodge Properties Ltd* [1980] 1 W.L.R. 594, unless there are words to the contrary, Law of Property Act 1925, s. 78 will apply so as to annex the benefit of the covenant to the land intended to be benefited, and to each and every part thereof (see Chapter 8 above). It is, however, still wise to put the matter of annexation beyond doubt by these words.

It is also necessary, in practice, to define the land which is to be benefited. If this is not done there may be difficulty with the identity of such land at a later date, in the context of enforcement and title to enforce, or in the context of a release and the right to be joined in any release (see Chapter 8 above).

In practical terms, certainty of definition can be achieved by defining the land to be benefited by reference to:

- a plan
- a Land Registry Title no.—although there is no danger in this method if the estate on subsequent sales off is given a new Title no.

It is only if there is real difficulty in determining the land to be benefited should that land be defined as land "adjoining" or "near" or "neighbouring" the burdened land and even then some attempt should be made to use a plan to identify it.

See Part 2 below for annexation of the benefit in building schemes.

Element 4
Words defining what is covenanted:

> *to observe the covenants set out in the schedule below; "the covenants"*

Commentary
The effect of these words is obvious in itself; although note the use of the word "covenants" as opposed to "stipulations". Unless you are intending to create stipulations only, which may not have quite the same effect (see Chapter 1, para. 1–02 above) you should avoid the word "stipulations".

Element 5
Words limiting liability of the covenantor to the period of his ownership of the property subject of the covenants or any other interest in it.

> *and it is declared that the [buyer][[seller] will not be liable for any breach of the covenants after he has parted with all interest in or possession of the property*

Commentary
These words are present to avoid any liability once the covenantor (or his successor) has sold the burdened land, or given up possession of it (or any interest in it); see Chapter 14, para. 14–07 above.

Note: for registered titles: It is no longer necessary to apply to the Registrar to enter notice of the covenants on the register of the title of the burdened land. The old Form 43 and Rule 135 was revoked in 1997 (S.I. 1997 No. 3037), and with effect from April 1, 1998 the only obligation which arises when a transfer imposes fresh restrictive covenants is lodged, is that a certified copy of that transfer is lodged with it; see LRR, r. 135 (as substituted by S.I. 1997 No. 3037, r. 2).

Note: for both registered and unregistered titles: Chapter 4 above deals with the manner of protection of restrictive covenants by registration to ensure that they bind successors in title of the original covenantor.

Putting all Five Elements Together

Specimen Clause in Part 1 set out in its entirety

The buyer covenants with the seller
(reverse order if the covenants are being given by the seller)
so as to bind
the property and each and every part of it whoever may be the owner of it and so that the benefit is annexed to each and every part of the land which the vendor/seller has retained
(*Or*—in the case where the seller is giving the covenants)
"each and every part of the land which has been conveyed to the buyer"
(*and shown on the plan annexed shaded/edged [colour]*)
to observe the covenants set out in the schedule below ("the covenants")
and it is declared that the [buyer][seller]
(*i.e.* whoever is giving the covenants)
will not be liable for any breach of the Covenants after he has parted with all interest in or possession of the property.

Element 6 (Optional)

Are there to be covenants given by both parties in favour of each other?

If there are to be such *mutual* covenants use each set of covenants being given by first, the buyer and secondly, the seller and put the covenants themselves in a separate schedule.

For example:
The buyer covenants with the seller
so as to bind the property and each and every part of it whoever may be the owner of it and so that the benefit is annexed to each and every part of the land which the seller has retained (and shown on the plan annexed shaded/edged [colour])
to observe the covenants set out in the First Schedule below ("the buyer's covenants")
and it is declared that the buyer will not be liable for any breach of the buyer's covenants after he has parted with all interest in or possession of the Property
And further
The seller covenants with the buyer
so as to bind the property and each and every part of it whoever may be the owner of it and so that the benefit is annexed to each and every part of the land which has been conveyed to the buyer
(and shown on the plan annexed shaded/edged [colour])
to observe the covenants set out in the Second Schedule below ("the seller's covenants")
and it is declared that the seller will not be liable for any breach of the seller's covenants after he has parted with all interest in or possession of the property

PART 2

Additional elements; Building Schemes

Element 1

A7–03 **The Declaration that a scheme exists**

The seller declares as follows:
(a) he has laid out the [] Estate {shown on the plan edged blue annexed to this transfer} in plots
(b) he intends the [] Estate to be developed as a building scheme
(c) each transfer of each plot will be substantially the same as this transfer (subject to the rights reserved to the Seller referred to at (e) below)
(d) the owner of each plot is to have the right to enforce the covenants set out in Schedule [] below and imposed on the other plots on the [] Estate irrespective of the date of transfer of each plot
(e) the Seller may in [his][its] absolute discretion make alterations in the lotting of those parts of the [] Estate which have not been sold at any time and in addition [he][it] may vary or release or waive any of the covenants set out in Schedule [] below whether or not any such variation release or

waiver relates (i) to a plot already sold at the date of this transfer or (ii) to any part of the [] Estate which has not been sold or (iii) to the property

Commentary
See Chapter 8 for the reasons why it is desirable for a declaration of intention to create a scheme to be expressed. As to the optional power to vary, etc. see paragraph 8–37 of Chapter 8 as to the effect which such a power may have on the scheme. It is important to note that where a new scheme is being set up it is prudent to liaise with the local District Land Registry in advance so that the Registry is satisfied that the proposed form of transfer and plans (which should be lodged) can lead to the Registry treating the area of development as a scheme. (See Practice Leaflet No. 7 which HMLR supply free on request).

Note: if a scheme is not wanted you can declare such intention expressly:

For example:
The parties to this transfer declare that the covenants which are contained in it do not create a building scheme and the seller is free to vary or release any of the covenants into which he may enter in respect of his land and to deal with it in any way he thinks fit.

Element 2

The mutual enforcement clause.
The seller and the buyer [vendor and purchaser] (and all other parties to this transfer) declare that the covenants set out in Schedule [] below are to be mutually enforceable between each and every Buyer of plots on the [] Estate whenever they were transferred

Commentary
This reinforces the declaration of the Scheme under Element 1 above. It is not strictly necessary, but for those who prefer a "belt-and-braces" approach, it can be added to the form above.

Element 3

The covenant clause
The [buyer] covenants with the [seller] and as a separate covenant with every owner for the time being of any part of the [] Estate
so as to bind the property and each and every part of it whoever may be the owner of it
and
so that the benefit is annexed to each and every part of the [] Estate
to observe the covenants set out in Schedule [] below
and it is declared that the [buyer] will not be liable for any breach of the covenants after he has parted with all interest in or possession of the property

Commentary
This form should be used when the buyer is giving the covenants in the seller's favour and in favour of the owners of the estate within the scheme.

There are variations where:

(a) the covenant is being taken for the benefit of plots already sold, and

(b) covenants are also being given by the seller.

(c) where the buyer covenants to enforce covenants against other buyers, either directly, or in the name of the seller.

Variation (a)
The [buyer] covenants with the [seller] and as a separate covenant with every owner for the time being of any part of the [] Estate *and with every owner of any plot sold by the seller before the date of this transfer*
so as to bind the property and each and every part of it whoever may be the owner of it
and
so that the benefit is annexed to each and every part of the [] Estate *including the plots sold before the date of this transfer*
to observe the covenants set out in Schedule [] below
and it is declared that the [buyer] will not be liable for any breach of the covenants after he has parted with all interest in or possession of the property

Variation (b)
The [*seller*] covenants with the [buyer]
so as to bind {the [] Estate or the land retained by the *seller*} and each and every part of it whoever may be the owner of it
and
so that the benefit is annexed to each and every part of the Property and each and every part of it
to observe the covenants set out in Schedule [] below
and it is declared that the [seller] will not be liable for any breach of the covenants after he has parted with all interest in or possession of the [] Estate

Variation (c)
Add to any of the preceding forms—
Whenever any buyer of any part of the [] Estate breaks any of the covenants which he has entered into the buyer may be requested by the seller to enforce any covenant which any such buyer has broken, and the cost of doing this (which may include the cost of court proceedings) will be borne by the seller. If the buyer is requested to take such steps, the buyer must perform the seller's request and if the buyer does not, the seller is entitled to take action to enforce the covenant in the name of the buyer. If the seller takes action in the name of the buyer the buyer is entitled to an indemnity from the seller for the cost and expense of such action.

Commentary
This clause allows the seller to keep control of the scheme even when he has disposed of all the land which otherwise would allow him to enforce. Because this covenant is not truly restrictive, there are problems of enforcement of the obligation to take action when the land (over which the covenant is imposed) is sold. The burden of a positive covenant will not be enforceable against a successor in title; see Chapter 1, para. 1–05 above. There are various means of ensuring that this obligation runs with the land, the chief of which is a covenant that there will be a direct covenant to observe this (and other covenants) with the seller by the new buyer prior to any transfer and a restriction on the register that until there is a certificate of compliance (by entry into the deed) no dealing is to be registered. See Forms A7–05 at Part 4, below.

PART 3

The covenants

A7–04 In this part the forms of restriction themselves are set out. It is hard to generalise in view of the fact that the ultimate aim of any restriction is to control a particular use of land, and to that extent each situation may require different forms of words to be used. However, there will always be circumstances in which a "common" form of restriction will be suitable, and the restrictions which follow are designed to cater for the draughtsman who requires such a common form. Beyond these forms lie many situations where only "tailor made" forms will do, and it will be for the draughtsman to use these forms simply as a framework upon which to clothe the finished article.

In order to assist the user the following broad headings have been used by way of classification so that individual types or classes of restriction can be identified.

Classification

(i) Covenants which regulate the use of buildings.

(ii) Covenants which regulate the use of buildings and their surroundings and land use generally.

(iii) Covenants which control changes to buildings.

(iv) Covenants which deal with more specific requirements as to the control of land use including the commercial user.

(i) Covenants which regulate the use of buildings

(a) Basic user covenants: residential
The buyer covenants with the seller not to use the property:

- other than as a house
- other than as a bungalow
- other than as a dwelling house
- other than as a private dwelling house
- other than as a single private dwelling house

Optional additions to any of the above:

(1) and no more than one such house is to be built upon each plot and if one such house is built so that it occupies more than one such plot no additional private dwelling house may be built upon any other part of the plot which is so occupied,

(2) other than for the occupation of one family *or* a single household.

Commentary
See Chapter 14, para. 14–13 for the difference between each covenant. The optional words at (1) are designed to avoid the problem referred to at paragraph 14–14 where one house is built across two plots and where it is desired to build a house on part of one of the plots. The optional words at (2) prevent sub-division of occupation.

(b) Basic user covenants: business and other uses
The buyer covenants with the seller not to use the property:

- for any trade profession or business;
- for any trade profession or business other than as a doctor, dentist or solicitor and if such use is made of the property no business plate is to be placed on the outside of the property.

Commentary
These self-explanatory restrictions are often used to preserve "high class" estate developments. However, the first form is probably too broad in scope, particularly in an age when many businesses and professions can be run from home. The latter form is more specific and designed to avoid the vice of any activity which might lower the tone of the estate, which preserving a selective measure of control.

(c) Basic user covenants: more specific controls
The buyer covenants with the seller not to:

- divide the property into self-contained flats;
- use any part of the property for holiday lettings (or as an office) (or for accommodating paying guests);
- use any part of the property marked on the plan [and edged green as the case may be] other than as a garage (car space) for the parking of a private motor vehicle;

- park or keep a boat or caravan on the property;
- do anything on the property which is a nuisance or annoyance to the seller or the adjoining or neighbouring property and "nuisance or annoyance" includes anything which materially affects the use or enjoyment of the property;
- construct more than [] (private single dwelling houses) on the property.

Commentary
These specific controls are designed to protect the amenity of residential development and should be used where suitable control is required. Some of the restrictions are specific, *e.g.* as to parking of boats or caravans, and reflects recent concern over the lack of control which the planning system may be able to impose in this instance.

(ii) Covenants which regulate the use of buildings and their surroundings
The buyer covenants with the seller not to:

- keep any animals or birds on the property other than as domestic pets;
- keep any animals or birds on the property which if kept for domestic or commercial purposes cause an nuisance or annoyance to the seller or the adjoining or neighbouring property and "nuisance or annoyance" includes anything which materially affects the use or enjoyment of the property;
- store vehicles on the property;
- erect any aerial or satellite dish on the external part of any building on the property (which is visible from any road);
- allow any gardens on the property to become overgrown;
- allow drying washing on the property to be visible from any road;
- allow the area shown coloured [] on the plan to be used other than as a garden [or] other than as open visibility splay;
- plant any tree, shrub or hedge or erect any fence (beyond the line marked on the plan) *or* (on the area shown coloured [] on the plan);
- plant any tree of the variety [*Cupressus Lawsoniae* or *Cupressus Leylandii*] on the property or on any part thereof;
- allow any tree shrub or hedge to exceed [] metres in height;
- allow any tree, shrub, hedge, fence structure or erection to be placed on the area [defined by reference to a plan] and not to use that area other than a (grassed lawn) (space kept unbuilt upon and open to the sky);
- obstruct any of the accessways or parking areas [defined by reference to a Plan] build over or within a lateral distance of [] metres from the

centre line of any pipes and sewers which may be under the property;

- use any part of the property for access to or from any neighbouring or adjoining land.

Commentary
See the note under the previous set of restrictions. Here even greater specific control is being imposed, and in the context of a well-managed estate most of these controls will be needed.

(iii) Covenants controlling the changes to buildings
The buyer covenants with the seller that he will not:

- change the external appearance of any building erected on the property;
- paint the external parts of any buildings on the property other than in a colour which has previously been approved by the seller in writing (approval not to be unreasonably withheld) *or* as below;
- make any (structural) alteration to the dwelling house and garage erected on the property unless plans and elevations have been submitted for the seller's approval which may be given in writing (such approval not to be unreasonably withheld) *or* (such approval to be determined in the absolute discretion of the seller) on payment of a fee of [£];
- Erect or make any alterations to any buildings on the property which may interfere with the access of light and air to the windows (and other apertures) of the buildings on the (seller's property).

Provisos to any clause requiring consent
For the purposes of this clause:

(i) the seller in the exercise of his discretion is entitled to have regard to the following matters (but not to the exclusion of anything else which the seller may think material) when granting or refusing his consent:

- the nature of the proposed (alteration) (colour scheme);
- the effect which the proposed alteration may have upon the neighbouring or adjoining land [being the [] Estate] and its amenity;
- the effect of the proposed alteration on the [] Estate and its amenity.

(ii) the term "the seller" includes his successors in title and owners for the time being of the [] Estate or any part thereof.

(iii) To the extent that at any time written consent is required under this clause and the seller is the owner of (the [] Estate) *or* (the seller's unsold land) the written consent of that person shall be sufficient (provided that if by reason of sales off of the [] Estate (or the seller's unsold land) there is more than one owner thereof and it is not reasonably possible for the buyer to identify all the persons whose consent would (but for this proviso) be required under this clause the buyer may obtain written consent from the person or persons who appear to the buyer to be the person or persons whose consent should be obtained).

(iv) if at any time any person whose consent is required cannot be reasonably identified or if the seller (or its successor) is a Limited Company and has been dissolved or struck off the Register of Companies at or prior to the time when consent would (but for this proviso) be required the terms of this clause shall not apply so as to require consent to be obtained and in particular no consent shall be required to have been obtained from the Crown or any other person in whom the rights or assets of the said Company may have become vested).

Commentary
See Chapter 14, para. 14–09 for the problems which consent provisions bring. The optional provisos are attempts to overcome some of the problems which arise, which include potentially numerous persons with the right to grant or withhold consent, and dissolved or struck off companies, where the complexities of requiring consent from the Crown can be avoided by the form given under (iv) above.

(iv) Covenants which deal with specific requirements as to the control of the use of land and buildings

Specific uses
The buyer covenants with the seller that he will not:
Use the Property (previously defined) other than as a [defined purpose]
For example:

- landscaped area for a visibility splay;
- ornamental garden;
- woodland area (with the added obligation not to cut any trees without the consent of the seller) (see (iii) above for consent clauses);
- golf course;
- lake[s] for fish farming.

Commentary
In any individual case it is open to the draughtsman to consider precisely what use is to be permitted and to define the permitted use accordingly. This is particularly important where specific uses are contemplated over parts of land; visibility splay areas being a case in point.

Services
(Where the seller is retaining land through which services run for the benefit

of the land being sold off and where the seller may have meters or other installations on his land which control the supply):

The seller covenants with the buyer that he will not:

- interfere with the services (to be defined) which serve the property;
- do anything which would affect the quality of the services (to be defined) which serve the property;
- do anything which would have the effect of preventing the supply of services to the property; which shall include the obligation to pay for the supply of any of the services so far as it may be necessary to do so for the continuation of the supply.

And the buyer covenants with the seller that he will:

- Pay to the seller (or to the provider of any of the services as the seller may direct) for the cost of the supply of the services.

Commentary

Covenants relating to the supply of services raise a number of problems, not all of which can be cured by drafting.

There are two points which arise where services are being provided for the benefit of land being sold off—or retained.

First, there is the (negative) right to non-interference and secondly, there is the (positive) right to the supply.

The first right may be coupled with an easement for the supply and the right to non-interference can be expressed also by means of a restrictive covenant. The second right (namely the positive right to have the supply maintained) is a different matter. The right may be protected, as is suggested in the third obligation, by a restrictive covenant. But the only sure way of doing it is to impose a positive obligation to provide the supply of the service and as a condition therefor, to pay for such supply.

There are two points to be noted as regards such a means of protecting the (positive) right to a supply. First, the nature of a positive covenant is such that it may not be enforceable against successors in title of the covenantor, unless the covenant is protected by an estate rent charge or some right to re-enter—neither of which may be attractive or acceptable other than in certain types of developed estates.[2] Secondly, it is often the case that the service will be provided by a third party, being the water, gas, electricity, or telecommunications providers, and if any positive obligation is to be imposed, such an obligation may not bind such a third party. For example the gas provider may refuse to supply to unsafe appliances.[3]

The covenants above are designed to deal with the two aspects of the problem and in so far as the negative right to non-interference is concerned

[2] See Chap. 1 above.

[3] For the problems posed by the distinctions between the positive and negative obligations as regards the supply of services see *Rance v. Elvin* (1985) 50 P.&C.R. 9, applied in *Duffy v. Lamb* (1997) 75 P.&C.R. 364.

the restrictive covenants should be adequate. As regards the positive right to supply and the corresponding obligation to pay, only the simplest terms are offered.[4] To offer more would extend the scope of this part of the book too deeply into the field of positive covenants as opposed to restrictive ones.

Commercial purposes
The buyer covenants with the seller that he will not use the property other than for:

- the following classes in the Town & Country Planning Use Classes Order 1987:

[A1, A2, A3
B1–8
C1, C2, C3
D1, D2][5]

- the retail sale of goods other than hot [or cold] food or intoxicating liquor;
- food retailing.

The buyer covenants with the seller that he will use the property only for:

- a storage facility;
- a wholesale warehouse;
- a restaurant [but with no take-away facility] with a justices' licence permitting the consumption of alcohol with meals;
- the purposes of an open space;
- an amusement park;
- an hotel;
- a seller of wines beers and spirits for consumption off the premises;
- a public house;
- a private nursing home or hospital;
- a general practitioner's surgery [and pharmacy].

Commentary
Specific commercial uses raise at least two problems for the draughtsman.

[4] For more detailed forms of positive obligations as to services see Aldridge, *Practical Conveyancing Precedents*.
[5] The danger with a definition based on a reference to the Order is that it does not allow for any change in the Order. It may, therefore be preferable to define the permitted use specifically by reference to that use, as the alternatives show, and for that purpose the Use Classes Order can be a useful tool in defining such a use.

First, there is the problem of defining precisely what use is or is not to be permitted. That requires a clear understanding of what the burdened land is to be used for and what the owner of the benefited land is seeking to permit or prevent. That in turn requires care to be taken to ensure that the covenant is not one against competition *per se*, for such covenants may be held to be purely personal; "tie" covenants not to sell a certain brand of goods may be an example of this.[6]

Provided the definition of the permitted or prohibited is clear the next hurdle to overcome is how far is the defined use to be applied over the whole of the property to be burdened. An example of this problem arises in the modern "superstore" development which may extend over a number of acres. Part comprises the retail food hall (which itself may need further definition in view of the sale in some supermarkets of clothes, videos, magazines, etc.) (currently an A1(a) use within the Use Classes Order) (see above), part comprises a petrol filling-station and the remainder is used for access, parking, bus stops and amenity areas such as a picnic area, children's playground, landscaped areas and facilities for recycling. To define the permitted use over all these areas requires care. One method would be to define the various uses by reference to a detailed plan. What is not recommended is the definition of the permitted use over the whole site by reference to a single use (*e.g.* "food retailing"), for that begs the question as to the other areas within the development which are not being used for that purpose.[7]

PART 4

Other forms

Restrictions

A7–05 See Part 2, form [] above for the use of restrictions in the context of protecting positive obligations in Building Schemes.

They can be used whenever it is desired to have control over any dealing with the property over which the covenant is a burden, and as the obligation is positive, the burden will not run.

(i) Standard form

Except under an Order of the Registrar no disposition (or other dealing) by the proprietor of the land is to be registered without the consent of [identify person who has the benefit of the covenant].

(ii) Variation to cover entry into covenants

Except under an Order of the Registrar no disposition (or other dealing) by the proprietor of the land is to be registered without the consent of [identify

[6] See Chap. 8, para 8–12 under r. 1.

[7] See *Co-Operative Retail Stores Services Ltd v. Tesco Stores Ltd* (1998) 76 P.&C.R. 328 for a case where the permitted use was for "food retailing" and it was held that the use of the burdened and as an amenity area and as part and parcel of the superstore site was not a breach of that covenant, but only after an appeal to the Court of Appeal.

person who has the benefit of the covenant] unless the transferee (or other person in whose favour a disposition is made) enters into the covenants dated [] referred to at entry No. [] in the Charges register (copy filed).

(iii) Further variation to cater for "disappearance" of person with benefit of the covenants

Except under an Order of the Registrar no disposition (or other dealing) by the proprietor of the land is to be registered without the consent of [identify person who has the benefit of the covenant] unless the transferee (or other person in whose favour a disposition is made) enters into the covenants dated [] referred to at entry No. [] in the Charges register (copy filed) provided that if the transferee (or other person in whose favour a disposition is made) produces evidence that the [person who has the benefit of the covenant] cannot reasonably be found or being a limited company has been dissolved or struck off the Register of Companies no such evidence of consent shall be required.

Recreation of covenants after unity of ownership

An express affirmation or confirmation of the covenants should ideally be used to ensure revival. In the conveyance or transfer reference should be made to the original covenants, the fact of unity of seisin and the fact that it is intended that the covenants (formerly extinguished) are intended by the parties to be revived.

A suggested form of words in the operative part of any conveyance or transfer to avoid any doubt is:

> "The parties intend that the covenants referred to at clause [] are hereby expressly confirmed to be binding between the parties as if they had never been extinguished and to the intent that the benefit and burden thereof shall run with and bind the land so expressed to be benefited and burdened in accordance with the terms of [the instrument originally imposing the covenants]."

DRAFT "CIRCULAR" PRIOR TO PROCEEDINGS FOR A DECLARATION UNDER LAW OF PROPERTY ACT 1925, S. 84(2) A7–06

(See Chap. 15, Pt I for the background).

To the owner of [*address of property*]

We are the solicitors acting for [*owners and address of property; which will be that of the applicant*]. The location of that property is shown on the plan which is enclosed with this letter.

We are writing to you because our client (*Mr [] or X Ltd*) has obtained planning consent for [*describe development*].

You may already be aware of this proposal as you may have been told about it by the [*local planning authority*]. The planning consent reference is *[]* and, if you have not already done so, you may wish to inspect the application and the plans lodged at [Town Hall, etc.]. For ease of reference we enclose the decision letter giving that consent.

Our client's development means that [*houses will be erected on the land shaded green*] [*i.e. describe the effect of the proposal in clear terms*].

Over the land affected by the proposed development are some covenants imposed in [*date*] by a deed dated [] and made between [] and []. We attach a copy of the [*material parts*] of the deed. The covenants which are of particular relevance are [] and [].

It might be thought that the covenants would prevent our client from proceeding with the development, but we [*have been advised by counsel*][*have advised our client*] that the covenants are [*no longer enforceable*][*have a certain meaning*] which leads us to believe that the development would not be a breach of the covenants. [*It may be wise to say briefly why this belief is held, e.g. no annexation (pre-1925 covenants), or extinguished by past unity of seisin and never revived, nor anyone identifiable who can give consent*].

Because of the nature of the proposed development and the advice which our client has been given, we feel it would be prudent to seek the guidance of the Court as to the [*enforceability*][meaning] of the covenants.

This means that our client will issue proceedings under Law of Property Act 1925, s. 84(2) for a declaration that [*the covenants are no longer enforceable*][*have a certain meaning, etc.*]. A draft of the proposed application is attached, and for ease of reference we enclose a copy of that section of the Act.

The request we are making of you is that you consider whether you are able to consent to our client's application in terms of the order sought at the end of it.

It is our belief that you should (on consideration of the matter) consent, in view of the fact that [*you do not have the benefit of the covenant as it was never annexed to your land, etc.*] or [*it is clear that your consent is not required to the proposed development*][*i.e. explain simply why the consent ought to be forthcoming*]. If you wish to oppose you must be prepared to give legal reasons in due course why you think you are entitled to do so.

If you decide that you are unable to consent you will be able to intervene in the proceedings under section 84(2) once they are started; you will be informed of how to do this in due course. [*If you do so you may be at risk as to costs if the Court decides that the advice we have given our client is right.*][*Note: it is felt that this sentence can be omitted according to taste. Some may feel that it is rather heavy-handed at this stage*].

We have attached a form on which you can express your consent, or objection, with a spare copy for you to retain and a s.a.e. for you to return to us.

We appreciate that you will need time to consider our request. We invite you to contact your solicitor if you are in any doubt as to the meaning of this letter and the enclosures. If you are not the owner, or the sole owner of the property at [] please would you tell us who is, or forward this letter and enclosures to that person so they may contact us. We would also ask you to tell us on the form enclosed whether there is a tenant at your property and if there is a building society or bank or other lender who has a mortgage over it, and if so give us its identity and if you are able, the branch you deal with for the mortgage. You do not need to tell us anything else.

We would like to hear form you within [] days of this letter. If for any reason you think that is going to be difficult please let us know.

We thank you in advance for your assistance.

FORM FOR RETURN

A7–07

Address of property and name of owner (*i.e. addressee of the letter*)

I have read the letter dated [] from A&B solicitors and having duly considered the matter:

*CONSENT to the proposed order sought in the application by [*plaintiff*]
*OBJECT to the proposed order sought in the application by [*plaintiff*] for the following reasons:

[**delete that which is not applicable*]
The following persons are also owners with me/us of [*the property*]:

The following person(s) own [*the property*] so far as I am aware and I have no interest in it.

The following person(s) has a tenancy of [*the property*]:

The following has a mortgage over [*the property*]:

at [] branch.

Signed and dated

Lands Tribunal Forms

A7–08 *NOTE:* There are no prescribed forms, but the Lands Tribunal Rules 1996 state what has to be included in certain types of application.

What follows is a guide. In many cases there will have to be adaptation to suit individual claims. The rules numbers cited at the head of each form are not part of the form; merely a reminder of the requirements laid down by the rule in question.

For litigation forms once the application is under way (*e.g.* interim applications) see *Atkin*, Vol. 24(2).

A7–09 Form 1

Form of Application

IN THE LANDS TRIBUNAL

Application under Law of Property Act 1925, s. 84(1)
(Lands Tribunal Rules 1996, r. 13)

1. The Applicant

The applicant is [] of [] (or *the applicants are [a] or [b] of [ ]*).
His representative is [] [*solicitor*][*surveyor*][*etc.*] of [] (*or they are represented by*).
All communication should be to [*representative*].
The reference to give to him when communicating with him is [].

2. The Property in Respect of which the Application is Made

This is known as [] "the Property".
It is shown edged red on the plan attached.
Its title is [*freehold*][*leasehold for a term of* [] *years from* [].
The applicant owns the Property (*or*) owns that part coloured blue and as to that part coloured yellow the second applicant is the owner.

3. The Property which is Subject to the Restriction

This is shown edged red on the plan attached and affects the whole of the property (or affects that part of the property shaded green).

The restriction was imposed by a deed dated [*etc.*] (*describe the instrument imposing it*).

4. The Terms of the Restriction

This is in the following terms:
[]
(*If consideration was paid for the giving of the restriction say so, as this may affect compensation for a release, etc.*)

5. The Property which may have the Benefit of the Restriction and the Persons Interested in it

This is shown edged green on the plan attached.

The applicant believes that the following persons are owners of or have an interest in that land:
[]
(*Add if there is doubt as to the benefit being in those persons or those defined as doubtful, where a blanket denial of any person having the benefit would be inappropriate*).

It is not possible on the information held by the applicant at this time to say whether those people whose names appear below [*or [a] and [b], etc.*] have the benefit of the restrictions.

In due course, either after further information has been obtained, or after replies to advertisements have been considered, the applicant will state whether and to what extent he admits that the benefit of the restrictions is vested in any such persons and will define them accordingly. If necessary the applicant will ask the tribunal to make such directions as may be necessary under Law of Property Act 1925, s. 84(3A) as to who should be admitted to oppose this application. He may ask the tribunal to adjourn the application so that he may apply under section 84(2) thereof for such relief as may be appropriate.

6. The Application

The applicant applies for:

(*A discharge of the restriction in its entirety*)

—The effect of this will be to [*remove all the restrictions over the Property*]

(*A discharge of the restrictions as to the following parts* [])

—The effect of this will be []

(*alternatively for modification in the following terms*)

—The effect of this will be [] as opposed to the relief above.

(*for modification in the following terms*)

—The effect of this will be []

NOTE: you must say precisely what you want and what the effect will be. (See *Re University of Westminster* [1998] 3 All E.R. 1014 for the effect of a

failure to do so). Thus, if alternatives are used, *e.g.* discharge *or* modification say what will be the effect of each.
[*The applicant does not oppose the tribunal adding the following restrictions [ ]*]

7. The Grounds on which the Application is Made

(*Here set out the statutory ground on which the application is made and brief details of why the ground is relied upon*)
Thus under:
Para (a): give details of changes which lead to the restriction being obsolete.
Para (aa): state why the proposed user is reasonable and why the restriction does not secure any practical benefits of substantial value or advantage to those with the benefit of it.
Para (b): state that the applicant will rely for this paragraph upon those who have consented, or will consent, those who are not objecting and those who will withdraw objection before during or after the hearing.
Para (c): state why no injury will be caused to those entitled to the benefit of the restriction.

8. Relevant Planning Permissions

Within the past five years the following planning permissions have been granted in respect of the property:
[]

9. What is Enclosed with this Application

(i) The application plan. (*i.e., a modern surveyor's or O.S. plan so that all relevant properties can be identified*)

(ii) A copy of the instrument imposing the restriction [*or an abstract if no copy is available*]

(iii) Planning evidence:

- the applicant's permission;
- the relevant parts of the local planning authority's development, etc. plans;
- evidence of the pattern of permissions in the area; a plan may have to be used here

with coded references to each property affected.

(iv) a duplicate of this application. (*N.B. this requirement can be overlooked!*)

Signed

(*by the solicitors for the applicant*)

Dated

FORM 2

Objection or claim for compensation

A7–10

Notice of Objection
in the Lands Tribunal
Re: []'s Application

Application No. []

Notice of Objection (*and claim for compensation*)

(Lands Tribunal Rules 1996, r. 15)
(*Note:* this must be sent within 28 days from the publication of the notices to potential objectors under rule 14)

1. The Objector[s]

(*Define them and state who their representatives are as under Part 1 of the form of application*)

2. The Claim to the Benefit

(*State the basis upon which a claim to the benefit of the restriction is made*)
(*Annex plans and deeds and other evidence of devolution to show the title to the benefit*)

3. The Grounds Upon Which a Claim to Object is Made

(*State the grounds against the heads of claim; this may require a surveyor's input, e.g. on the importance of preserving amenity*)

(4. The Claim to Compensation)

(*State the manner in which this is claimed. Thought should be given in appropriate cases to claiming compensation rather than pure opposition where it is obvious that a claim to modify will be made*).

4/5. What is Enclosed With This Application

(i) The plan referred to above.

(ii) The evidence on which the claim to the benefit is made.

((iii) The report of [] showing the basis on which the claim to compensation is made)

Signed, etc.

Dated, etc.

FORM 3

A7–11

Form to be used where registrar directs advertisement notices to be given

Notice by Advertisement

(Rule 14)

Note: this may be used not only in newspapers, etc., but also on public display in Parish Notice Boards, etc., as directed by the Registrar under Rule 14(1).

In The Lands Tribunal **Application No. []**

In the Matter of an Application Concerning []

(*i.e. give a clear description of the land which is the subject of the application*)

TAKE NOTICE that an application has been made under Law of Property Act 1925, s. 84(1) by *[ ]* for an order of the Lands Tribunal [*state what order is sought*] a restriction on the property described above by the following instrument []

[]

The restriction is [*in the following terms*][*summarised as follows*]

[]

AND TAKE NOTICE that the [*discharge*][*modification*][*partial modification*][*with additional new restrictions*] is to the following effect:
[*copy the application here so far as possible*]

[]

AND TAKE NOTICE that the application is made on the following grounds:
[*Set out what is said in the application*]

AND TAKE NOTICE that the application and all documents lodged with it and the above mentioned [*deed*] may be inspected at [*place and times, etc.*]

AND TAKE NOTICE that any person who claims to be legally entitled to the benefit of the restriction and who wishes to object to the application or who wishes to claim compensation in respect of the effect of the order sought under application (if made) must send a Notice of Objection with, if claimed a statement of claim for compensation, to The Registrar of the Lands Tribunal at 48/9 Chancery Lane, London WC2R 1JR and to the applicant's solicitors Messrs. [] of [] quoting this application number given above and this must be done *within 28 days of the date of this notice.*

Dated, etc.

Issued by [] of [] solicitors to the applicant.

FORM 4

Certificate that notices directed by registrar have been given A7–12

(Rule 14(4))

In The Lands Tribunal **Application No. []**

In the Matter of Law of Property Act 1925, s. 84
Re: The Application made by []

In accordance with Lands Tribunal Rules 1996, r. 14(4) we certify that:

1. A copy of the application was sent by ordinary prepaid post on [*date*] to the following persons [*listed in the Schedule*].

(2. A notice was published on [*date*] in the [*Chesney Wold Bi-Weekly Mercury*] in the form of the advertisement a copy of which is attached).

(3. The said notice was exhibited for not less than [*21*] days at the following locations [*i.e. as directed by the Registrar*].

Dated, etc.

Signed, etc.

(*Solicitors for the applicant*)

To the Registrar of the Lands Tribunal

INDEX

THE COMPANION DISKETTE

Instructions for Use (continued)

In Windows 95:

1. Insert the Disk in to the A drive of your computer
2. From Start button choose Run
3. Type A:\SETUP as appropriate and click on the OK button
4. Follow the on screen instructions as prompted.

Using the Precedents with WordPerfect 5.1

WP1. Although there are variations, you would normally open a file and make a copy of it:

Press <F5>

At the prompt type in the name of the data file and press <Enter>, for example:

C:\Rescov\Prec1.wp5<Enter>

To open the file, highlight and press 1 to retrieve.

WP2. At this point it is advisable to save the document before making any other changes. MAKE SURE NOT TO OVERWRITE THE ORIGINAL DOCUMENT.

To do this press <F10>

WP3. In answer to the prompt "**Document to be saved:**", type in your *working* directory path and a name for the new document, then press <Enter>, for example:

C:\WORK\NEWDOC<Enter>

WP4. Any other amendments can now be dealt with.

Using the precedents with Microsoft Word for Windows 6

N.B. For other versions of Word, and other Windows word processors in general, the instructions will be similar, but if you are not sure refer to the documentation that came with your word processor.

W1. To open a Restrictive Covenants document in Word, select "**File, Open**" from the menu. Highlight the Negotiating Business Acquisitions directory in the "**Directories**" list box. Change "**Files of Type**" to "**All Files**". Select the desired document from the "**File Name**" list box and press **OK**.

W2. The precedents have been supplied as read-only files. At this point it would be advisable to save the document before making any other changes.

Select "**File, Save As**" from the menu. In the "**Directories**" list box, highlight your working directory such as "**work**". In the "**File Name**" list box, type a suitable document name such as "**newdoc**". Press **OK**.

W3. Any other amendments can now be dealt with.

THE COMPANION DISKETTE

Instructions for Use

Introduction

These notes are provided for guidance only. They should be read and interpreted in the context of your own computer system and operational procedures. It is assumed that you have a basic knowledge of either MS-DOS or Windows. However, if there is any problem please contact our help line on 0171 393 7266 who will be happy to help you.

Diskette Format and Contents

The diskette which accompanies this book is suitable for MS-DOS or Windows 95 computers that can read *high-density* (1.44 Mbytes) 3.5 inch diskettes. You will need approximately 300 Kbytes of free hard disk space to store the data files.

The diskette contains data files covering the *precedents* section of the book. It does not contain software, or other text or commentary.

There are copies of the data files in WordPerfect 5.1 for DOS. These are directly compatible with all later versions of WordPerfect, both for DOS and Windows, that are currently available (6.0 for DOS; 5.2, 6.0 and 6.1 for Windows and 7.0 for Windows 95) and may be imported into Word for Windows versions 2.0 and later. Most other recent word processing systems are able to import WordPerfect documents easily. Again if you have any problems please contact our help desk on the number above who will be happy to help.

Installation

We strongly recommend that you make a backup copy of the distribution diskette. If you are not familiar with the PC/MS-DOS DISKCOPY command, details will be found in your Operating Systems manual.

The following instructions make the assumption that you will copy the data files to a single directory on your hard disk (e.g. C:\Rescov), and that your diskette drive is called A:\.

In DOS:

1. Insert the Disk into the A drive of your computer
2. Change to the A drive by typing A:\
3. Type SETUP and press the <ENTER> key
4. Follow the on screen instructions as prompted.

In Windows 3.1:

1. Insert the Disk into the A drive of your computer
2. From Program Manager chose File and Run
3. Type A:\SETUP as appropriate and click on the OK button
4. Follow the on screen instructions as prompted.

Product to third parties only in connection with the provision of professional advice provided that no additional fee is directly or indirectly charged for each transmission.

7.3 All extracts must clearly reproduce the copyright notice(s).

7.4 The Licensee shall not use the Product nor authorise the Product to be used for the purpose of operating a bureau or similar service or any online service whatsoever. For the avoidance of doubt nothing in this Agreement shall prevent bona fide use of the Product on a standalone machine in the course of operating a Library.

7.5 In no circumstances without the express consent of the Licensor in writing may the Product or any part thereof be used in connection with any system of remote access, other than for purposes of e-mail or fax transmission as set out in this Clause.

7.6 The Licensee shall not do or omit to do or authorise any other person to do or omit to do any act which:

(a) would or might invalidate or be inconsistent with any Intellectual Property of the Licensor and/or Software owner in the Product and/or Software

(b) would be in breach of or otherwise inconsistent with the moral rights of the authors of the items comprising the Product.

7.7 The Licensee shall not erase remove deface or cover any trademark, trade names, numbers, copyright or other proprietary notices, guarantee, designation of origin, means of identification, disclaimer or other statement used on any media containing the Product or used in relation to it, nor shall the Licensee authorise another person to do so.

7.8 The Licensee shall promptly inform the Licensor if the Licensee becomes aware of:

(a) any unauthorised use of the Product

(b) any actual, threatened, or suspected infringement of any intellectual property of the Licensor in the Product which comes to the Licensee's notice, and

(c) any claim by any third party coming to its notice that the Product infringes the intellectual property or other rights of any other Person.

7.9 The Licensee shall at the request and expense of the Licensor do all such things as may be reasonably required to assist the Licensor in taking or resisting proceedings in relation to any infringement or claim referred to in this Clause and in maintaining the validity and enforceability of the intellectual property of the Licensor in the Product.

7.10 Except insofar as it is permitted by law, the Licensee shall not modify, reverse assemble, decompile or reverse engineer the Product or any part thereof, or permit any third party to do so.

7.11 The Licensee shall not, except to the extent necessary to exercise the Rights granted under this Agreement without the prior written consent of the Licensor:

(a) make any alterations, additions or amendments to the Product;

(b) combine the whole or any part of the Product with any other software, data or material

(c) create derivative works from the whole or any part of the Product

7.12 In no circumstances may the Software be used separately from the Product.

8. SUPPLY

8.1 The Licensor will supply to the Licensee the Product.

8.2 The Licensor reserves the right at any time to make modifications or improvements to the Product.

8.3 The Licensor reserves the right at any time to withdraw from the Product any material included in it:

(a) if the Licensor ceases, for whatever reason, to publish the publication from which such material is taken or otherwise no longer retains the right to publish such material;

(b) if in the Licensor's sole discretion the Licensor on reasonable grounds believes that such material contains any material which infringes copyright or is defamatory, obscene, unlawful, or otherwise objectionable.

9. UPDATES

9.1 During the period of the Agreement, the Licensor will use all reasonable endeavours to supply Updates to the Product.

9.2 The Licensor reserves the right to employ hardware or software methods including timelocks to render superseded versions of the Product inoperable.

9.3 On receipt of the Updates delivered by the Licensor, the Licensee undertakes to install and use the said Updates.

9.4 Within 14 days of receipt of an Update the Licensee undertakes to destroy such disk or disks as may no longer be required as a result of the Update, according to instructions supplied with the Update.

10. ONLINE UPDATES

10.1 Where Online Updates are supplied, the Licensor:

(a) shall use all reasonable endeavours to provide the Licensee with an uninterrupted service;

(b) reserves the right to suspend temporarily and without notice for reasons beyond its control any Online Service provided; and

(c) shall use all reasonable endeavours to restore access to the Online Service as soon as possible in the event of an interruption or suspension of the Service.

10.2 The Licensee shall pay all third party telecommunications charges incurred by the Licensee in order to access any Online Service.

11. LICENSOR WARRANTIES

11.1 The Licensor warrants that it has obtained all necessary rights to grant this licence.

11.2 The Licensor warrants that the physical medium on which the Product is carried will be free from defects for a period of 90 days from delivery.

11.3 In the event of any material inherent defects in the delivery media on which the Product is supplied, other than caused by accident abuse or misuse by the Licensee, the Licensor 's sole liability to the Licensee is to replace defective delivery media free of charge provided it is returned to the Licensor within 90 days of the purchase date.

11.4 Whilst reasonable care is taken to ensure the accuracy and completeness of the Product supplied, the Licensor makes no representations or warranties whatsoever, express or implied, that the Product is free from errors or omissions.

11.5 Whilst reasonable care has been taken to exclude computer viruses, no warranty is made that the Product is virus free. The Licensee shall be responsible to ensure that no virus is introduced to any computer or network and shall not hold the Licensor responsible.

11.6 The Product is supplied to the Licensee on an "as is" basis without any warranty that it will meet the Licensee's individual requirements, it being the sole responsibility of the Licensee to satisfy itself prior to entering this Licence Agreement that the Product will meet those requirements and be compatible with the Licensee's hardware/software configuration and no failure of any part or the whole of the Product to be suitable for those requirements will give rise to any right or claim against the Licensor.

11.7 The warranties set out in this clause are exclusive of and in lieu of all other warranties, conditions, terms, undertakings, and obligations implied by statute, common law, custom, trade usage, course of dealing, or otherwise, which relate to the condition and fitness for any purpose of the Product.

11.8 The Licensor shall not be liable in contract, tort, delict or otherwise for any loss of whatsoever kind including without limitation any loss of revenue business, anticipated savings or profits, loss of goodwill or data or for any indirect or consequential loss whatsoever, howsoever arising suffered in connection with the Product (whether or not caused by the negligence of the Licensor).

11.9 The aggregate maximum liability of the Licensor in respect of any direct loss or any other loss (to the extent that such loss is not excluded by this Agreement or otherwise) whether such a claim arises in contract, tort or delict shall not exceed a sum equal to that paid as the Licence Fee or Network Licence Fee for the Product.

11.10 The Licensor will have no liability whatsoever for any liability of the Licensee to any third party which might arise.

11.11 None of the terms of this licence shall operate to:

(a) exclude or restrict liability for death or personal injury resulting from the negligence of the Licensor or the Licensor's appointed agents or employees whilst acting in the course of their employment; or

(b) affect statutory rights where this Agreement is entered into as a consumer transaction (as defined by the Consumer Transaction (Restriction on Statements) Order 1976 as amended).

11.12 The Licensee shall accept sole responsibility for and the Licensor shall not be liable for the use of the Product by the Licensee, its agents and employees and the Licensee shall hold the Licensor harmless and fully indemnified against any claims, costs, damages, loss and liabilities arising out of any such use.

12. CONFIDENTIAL INFORMATION

12.1 Each party undertakes to keep confidential and not to disclose to any third party any information supplied under this Agreement designated by the disclosing party as confidential information without the prior written approval of the other party.

12.2 The parties' obligations under this Clause shall not extend to information which is publicly available or can be shown by the receiving party to have been known by it prior to disclosure or is received by the receiving party from a third party without breach of a duty to the disclosing party.

12.3 The parties' obligations under this Clause shall survive the termination of this Agreement for a period of one year from that date.

13. MISCELLANEOUS

13.1 Where two or more legal entities constitute the Licensor and/or the Licensee their liability shall be joint and several.

13.2 Where the Licensee is a body other than an individual the person signing or otherwise concluding this Agreement represents that s/he is authorised by the Licensee to sign it for and on behalf of the Licensee and to bind the Licensee thereby.

13.3 Nothing in this Agreement shall create or be deemed to create a partnership or the relationship of principal and agent between the parties and the Licensee shall have no authority to bind or to make any representation or warranty on the Licensor's behalf.

13.4 This written agreement together with the Order Form where appropriate constitutes the entire Agreement between the parties hereto.

13.5 If any provision of this Agreement or Order Form or part thereof shall be void for whatever reason it shall be deemed deleted and the remaining provisions shall continue in full force and effect.

13.6 This Agreement may only be varied in writing signed by both parties.

13.7 Neither this Agreement nor any of the rights and obligations of the Licensee hereunder may be assigned, transferred, charged, delegated, sublicensed, or otherwise disposed of in whole or in part on a temporary or permanent basis unless the Licensee has obtained the prior written consent of the Licensor.

13.8 No delay or forbearance by the Licensor in enforcing any provisions of this Agreement shall be construed as a waiver of such provision or an agreement thereafter not to enforce the said provision on that or any other occasion or another provision on another occasion.

13.9 This Agreement, including where applicable the Order Form, shall be governed by the laws of England and Wales. If any difference shall arise between the Parties touching the meaning of this Agreement or the rights and liabilities of the parties thereto, the same shall be referred to arbitration in accordance with the provisions of the Arbitration Acts 1950 to 1979, or any amending or substituting statute for the time being in force.

13.10 Any notice given by one party pursuant to this Agreement may be served at the address of the other and such notice shall be deemed to have been duly received by the addressee three days posting by correctly addressed and pre-paid first class post or immediately if delivered personally.

13.11 Neither party shall be liable for any loss suffered by the other or be deemed to be in default for any delays or failures in performance (other than failure to make payments) hereunder resulting from acts or causes beyond its reasonable control.

13.12 Headings used in this Agreement are for ease of reference only and shall not affect its interpretation.

DIGITAL PRODUCT LICENCE AGREEMENT BETWEEN

The Licensee and *The Licensor, SWEET & MAXWELL LIMITED of 100 Avenue Road, London NW3 3PF* (hereinafter called the Licensor, which expression shall, where the context admits, include the Licensor's assigns or successors in business as the case may be) wherein it is hereby agreed as follows:

1. DEFINITIONS

Product Definitions

1.1 The **Licensed Material** means any content provided by the Licensor to the Licensee pursuant to this Agreement contained on compact disc read only memory disks ("CD-ROM disks") or floppy disks or any other electronic or magnetic media ("the delivery media") together with any enhancements by way of tagging, coding or conversion, including but not limited to:

(a) any ancillary, Help or documentation files provided;

(b) any updated versions ("Updates") and;

(c) any Online Material, meaning any updating or ancillary material held online which relates to the Product and to which access may be provided by the Licensor to the Licensee pursuant to this Agreement.

1.2 The **Software** means the programs and ancillary files provided by the Licensor for the purpose of accessing, searching, displaying, printing or otherwise manipulating the Licensed Material, including software licensed from third parties.

1.3 The **Product** means the Licensed Material and the Software.

Networking Definitions

1.4 The **Network** means any system that allows access to the Product or any part thereof via any form of communications link except by remote access as defined within this Agreement.

1.5 The **Local Area Network** means a Network within a single site.

1.6 The **Wide Area Network** means a Network over more than one site.

1.7 The **Site** means the physical location(s) or address(es) at which the Product will be used as agreed between the Parties, or in default of such agreement shall be the Licensee's principal place of business.

1.8 **Remote access** means any system that allows access to the Product or any part thereof or a Network on which the Product is installed via any form of remote telephone access via modem or similar device.

Licensing Definitions

1.9 Where applicable the **Order Form** means the Licensor's standard order form as supplied by the Licensor on which any order for the Product or any part thereof is made by the Licensee including details of the Start Date, the Licence Fee, the Network Licence Fee, the Site and any other relevant information in relation to the licensing of the Product and which is incorporated into this Agreement.

1.10 The **Start Date** means the date on which this Agreement takes effect.

1.11 The **Renewal Date** means an anniversary of the Start Date

1.12 The **Licence Fee** means the fee payable by the Licensee for non-networked use of the Licensed Material.

1.13 The **Network Licence Fee** means the fee payable by the Licensee for using the Product on a Network.

1.14 The **Renewal Fee** means the fee to be paid annually prior to the Renewal Date, as notified by the Licensor to the Licensee.

2. GRANT OF LICENCE

2.1 From the Start Date the Licensor hereby grants to the Licensee, a non-exclusive, non-transferable licence to use the Product at the Site in accordance with the terms and conditions of this Agreement.

2.2 Where the Product is supplied for evaluation purposes, the Licensee may install the Product for evaluation during the period agreed and may use the material in accordance with the terms and conditions of this Agreement.

2.3 At the end of the evaluation/trial period the Licensee will remove the Product from each computer on which it has been installed unless otherwise agreed in writing by the Licensor or the appropriate Licence fee is paid.

2.4 The Product may be installed and used on a computer at the Licensee's home provided that the home computer may not be used to access the Product simultaneously with the Licensee's computer at the Site.

3. PERIOD OF LICENCE

3.1 This Agreement shall remain in force for 12 months from the Start Date and expire automatically thereafter, unless the Licensor has paid the Renewal Fee and the Network Licensee Fee if applicable to the Licensee within 30 days of the renewal invoice which shall have been sent to the Licensee not less than 30 days before the Renewal Date.

3.2 In the event of expiry of this Agreement under this Clause:

(a) the Licensee shall cease to have access to or any rights or licence in respect of the Online Service where applicable but may retain and use any the last complete delivered version of the Product in its possession at the time of expiry provided that such use shall be in accordance with such provisions of this Agreement which are stated to survive its expiry; and

(b) the Licensor shall ensure that any timelocks or other methods of rendering superseded versions of the Product inoperable shall not apply to such usage

3.3 Clauses 6, 7, 11 to 13, shall survive the termination for whatsoever reason of this Agreement.

4. PAYMENT OBLIGATIONS

4.1 The Licensee undertakes to pay the Licensor the Licence Fee and the Renewal Fee prior to each Renewal Date together with the Network Licence Fee if applicable.

4.2 Prices quoted by the Licensor are unless otherwise stated, exclusive of VAT.

4.3 The Licensor reserves the right to withhold delivery of the Product and any Updates thereof and to bar access to any Online Service until all outstanding fees are paid.

5. TERMINATION ON BREACH

5.1 The Licensor may terminate this Licence at any time immediately by written notice to the Licensee if:

(a) the Licensee has committed an irredeemable breach of this Agreement; or

(b) after the Licensee, in the Licensor's reasonable opinion, has failed to remedy a remediable breach of these terms and conditions within 14 days of being given notice to do so,

such termination being without notice and without prejudice to any claim which the Licensor may have either for moneys due and/or damages and/or otherwise.

5.2 In the event of termination of this Agreement under clause 5.1 the Licensee will

(a) cease to use the Product and remove it from any computers on which it has been installed; and

(b) within 14 days return to the Licensor (postage paid) the Product together with any copies of the whole or part thereof.

5.3 The Licensor shall have the right to appoint an independent auditor to verify such actions and the Licensee shall co-operate with such auditor.

6. OWNERSHIP AND PERMITTED COPYING

6.1 The Product is not sold to the Licensee who shall not acquire any right, title or interest (including without limitation copyright or other right in the nature of copyright or any other intellectual property right whatsoever) in:

(a) the Product or any part thereof or any update to the Product or part thereof;

(b) the delivery media upon which the Product is supplied;

(c) any documentation or material printed or otherwise transmitted under this Agreement

which shall remain the property of the Licensor or Software owner as may be the case.

6.2 All rights in the Product whether existing or which may come into existence which are not specifically granted to the Licensee by this Agreement are expressly reserved to the Licensor.

6.3 Crown Copyright material is reproduced with the permission of the Controller of Her Majesty's Stationery Office.

6.4 The Licensee shall not sublicense the Product to others and the Licensee warrants that access will not be given to the Product to any person not being an employee or partner of the Licensee, firm, company, organisation, or other entity.

6.5 The Licensee shall use its best endeavours to ensure that the Product does not fall into the hands of third parties whether as a result of theft or otherwise.

6.6 Except as permitted by law, by installation instructions supplied by the Licensor to the Licensee and by this Agreement, the Licensee shall not itself nor allow any third party to duplicate or otherwise reproduce the Product or any part thereof.

6.7 The Licensee may make one copy of the Product only for back-up purposes, which copy must be kept in the Licensee's control and possession.

6.8 The Licensee may copy the Product from the delivery media onto a hard disk controlled by a standalone computer under the installation procedure provided by the Licensor and described in the Documentation. Any other transfer to disk is not permitted.

6.9 Where a Network Licence Fee has been paid, the Licensee may copy the Product onto a Network server under the installation procedure provided by the Licensor and described in the Documentation, any other transfer to disk not being permitted.

6.10 The Licensee shall be responsible for:

(a) installing the Product and for the effectiveness of such installation; and

(b) making backup copies of the contents of the hard disk on the standalone computer or of the Network server prior to the installation of the Product or the transfer of the Licensed Material from the delivery media to hard disk or Network server under this Clause.

7. PERMITTED AND PROHIBITED USE

7.1 The Licensee shall use the Product and shall take all reasonable steps to ensure that its employees and partners use the Product:

(a) only for its own business purposes;

(b) on the system and at the Site(s) for which the appropriate Licence Fee and Network Licence Fee (if appropriate) is paid by the Licensee;

(c) only for the permitted purposes set out in this Agreement.

7.2 The Licensee, its employees or partners on its behalf, for the purposes of research during the normal course of the Licensee's business, may:

(a) view the Product on screen;

(b) print extracts from the Product;

(c) transmit by print, fax, e-mail, or other method, extracts from the Product between employees, partners or agents of the Licensee;

(d) transmit by print, fax, e-mail, or other method, extracts from the